An Educational Psychology of
Classroom Management

Educational
PSYCHOLOGY

Critical Pedagogical Perspectives

Greg S. Goodman, *General Editor*

Vol. 17

The Educational Psychology series is part of the Peter Lang Education list.
Every volume is peer reviewed and meets
the highest quality standards for content and production.

PETER LANG
New York • Washington, D.C./Baltimore • Bern
Frankfurt • Berlin • Brussels • Vienna • Oxford

CHRISTOPHER THAO VANG

An Educational Psychology of Classroom Management

Best Professional Practices in the Multicultural Classroom

PETER LANG
New York • Washington, D.C./Baltimore • Bern
Frankfurt • Berlin • Brussels • Vienna • Oxford

Library of Congress Cataloging-in-Publication Data

Vang, Christopher Thao.
An educational psychology of classroom management:
best professional practices in the multicultural classroom / Christopher Thao Vang.
p. cm. — (Educational psychology: critical pedagogical perspectives; v. 17)
Includes bibliographical references and index.
1. Classroom management—United States.
2. Educational psychology—United States.
3. Multicultural education—United States. I. Title.
LB3013.V28   371.102′4—dc23   2012010096
ISBN 978-1-4331-1572-1 (hardcover)
ISBN 978-1-4331-1571-4 (paperback)
ISBN 978-1-4539-0564-7 (e-book)
ISSN 1943-8109

Bibliographic information published by **Die Deutsche Nationalbibliothek**.
Die Deutsche Nationalbibliothek lists this publication in the "Deutsche
Nationalbibliografie"; detailed bibliographic data is available
on the Internet at http://dnb.d-nb.de/.

© 2013 Peter Lang Publishing, Inc., New York
29 Broadway, 18th floor, New York, NY 10006
www.peterlang.com

CONTENTS

List of Tables vii

List of Illustrations xi

List of Abbreviations xiii

Foreword xv

Preface xvii

Acknowledgments xxiii

PART I. THE TEACHING PROFESSION DOMAIN 1

Chapter One. Contemporary Challenges to Becoming a Teacher 3

Chapter Two. Student Teachers' Fieldwork Experience 21

Chapter Three. Building on Educational Foundations 41

PART II. THE CLASSROOM MANAGEMENT AND DISCIPLINE DOMAIN 61

Chapter Four. Approaches to Classroom Management 63

Chapter Five. Approaches to Classroom Discipline 81

Chapter Six. Managing a Positive Psychosocial Environment 99

PART III. THE MULTICULTURAL STRATEGIES MANAGEMENT DOMAIN 121

Chapter Seven. Understanding the Daily Classroom Structure 123

Chapter Eight. The Inclusive Multicultural Classroom 145

Chapter Nine. Establishing Classroom Management Strategies 169

PART IV. THE BEST PROFESSIONAL PRACTICES DOMAIN 193

Chapter Ten. Best Professional Practices 195

Chapter Eleven. Developing Strategic Management Action Plans 217

Chapter Twelve. Helpful Tips for the First Few Years 241

References 271

Index 275

LIST OF TABLES

1.1. Interests Motivating Students to Enter Teaching 4
1.2. Issues that Concern Prospective Teachers 5
1.3. Prospective Teachers' Perceptions of Reasons Teachers Quit Teaching 7
1.4. Annual Cost of Teacher Turnover in Selected Districts 8
1.5. Percent of Teachers Willing to Teach Again 9
1.6. Foci and Content of Praxis Series 10
1.7. Salaries for Public School Teachers in Selected States 13
1.8. Households with Computer, by Income and Race/Ethnicity 14
1.9. Households with internet access by income and race/ethnicity 14
1.10. Ethnic Distribution of Teachers in California 15
1.11. Ethnic Distribution of Teachers in US Public Schools 15
1.12. Student Characteristics, California and Nation 16
1.13. Comparison of Coaching and Mentoring 17
2.1. Six Phases of Placement Timeline 25
2.2. Comparison of Two Lesson Plan Formats 28
2.3. Comparison of Five-Step, ELD, and SDAIE Lesson Plan Formats 28
2.4. Examples of Applications of Pedagogical Strategies 30
2.5. Common Difficulties During Placement and Tips for Overcoming 32
2.6. Cooperating Teachers' Roles and Responsibilities 34
2.7. University Supervisors' Roles and Responsibilities 35
2.8. Teaching Apprenticeship Objectives 36
2.9. Standards for the Domains of the TPE 36
2.10. Expectations for Tasks of TPA 37
2.11. Content of Professional Portfolio 38
3.1. Chronology of American Public Education 42
3.2. Branches of Philosophy 43
3.3. Traditional Schools of Philosophy Related to Education 44
3.4. Educational Theories 45
3.5. Principles of Selected Educational Theorists 45
3.6. Various Organizations of American Schools by Grade Levels 46
3.7. Genders and Ethnicities of School Leaders 47
3.8. Suggestions for Becoming Marketable 50
3.9. Typical Interview Questions 51
3.10. Due Process Guideline for Tenured Teachers 52
3.11. Violent Behaviors Among 9th-12th Graders, 2009 52
3.12. Procedural Guidelines for Handling Suspensions and Expulsions 54
3.13. Possible Evidences of Child Abuse Under WIC 300 54
3.14. Bilingual Education Program Models 56
3.15. Comparison of New and Existing Teachers 58
3.16. Race/Ethnicity of K-12 Teachers (Percent) 58

4.1. Selected Teaching Objectives and Goals 65
4.2. Selected Basic Procedures for Classroom Management 66
4.3. Engagement Level by Activity Type 68
4.4. Ideas for Instructional Preparations 69
4.5. Selected Models of Classroom Management 70
4.6. Steps for Handling Student Misbehaviors 74
4.7. Tasks Requiring Procedural Guidelines 76
4.8 Characteristics of Inappropriate and Appropriate Teacher-Student Relationships 77
5.1. Common Causes of Misbehavior 83
5.2. Categories of Common Misbehaviors 83
5.3. Characteristics of Achieving and Underachieving Learners 84
5.4. Common Classroom Disruptions and Interruptions 85
5.5. Causes of Some Student Misconduct 86
5.6. Examples of Classroom Rules, by Grade Level 88
5.7. Examples of Logical Consequences, by Grade 88
5.8. Logical Consequences for Selected Infractions 88
5.9. Appropriate Responses for Selected Misbehaviors 90
5.10. Techniques for Dealing with Surface Behaviors 91
5.11. Disciplinary Practices Teachers Should Avoid 93
5.12 Examples of Contingent and Non-contingent Rewards 94
5.13. Selected Student Privileges and Responsibilities 94
5.14. Selected Expectations for Teachers 97
6.1. Teachers' Code of Ethics 100
6.2. INTASC Standards and Expectations for Beginning Teachers 102
6.3. Positive and Negative Psychosocial Environments 104
6.4. Selected Human Relation Skills 107
6.5. Selected Class Building Characteristics 109
6.6. Selected Student Responsibilities 110
6.7. Multiple Intelligences 111
6.8. Five Domains of Student Learning 112
6.9. Typical Daily Schedule 113
6.10. Typical K-6 Schedules 114
6.11. Examples of Classroom Rules, by Grade 114
6.12. Examples of Logical Consequences, by Grade 115
6.13. Logical Consequences for Selected Infractions 115
6.14. Basic Procedures for Classroom Management 115
6.15. Teachers' Instructional Behaviors 117
7.1. Selected Student Demographics 126
7.2. Samples of Daily Schedules 129
7.3. Five-step and Three-step Lesson Plan Formats 135
7.4. Homework Time Allocations for All Grade Levels 138
7.5. Guidelines on Religious Expression in Public Schools 139
7.6. National Statistics on Bullying in Schools 142
8.1. Major Racial Groups in America 147
8.2. Ethnicity/Race of Students 148
8.3. Ethnicity/Race of Teachers, by Type of School 148
8.4. How Teachers Sometimes Treat Low Achievers 150
8.5. Five Domains of Learning 154
8.6. Multiple Intelligences 155

8.7. Contrast of Right- and Left-brain Learners 157
8.8. Behaviors of Students with Learning Disabilities 159
8.9. The LEP Process 161
9.1. Three Philosophies of Education 170
9.2. Five Management Approaches 171
9.3. Stages of Personality Development 171
9.4. Hierarchy of Human Needs 172
9.5. Common Classroom Behaviors 173
9.6. Classroom Design Checklist 178
9.7. Selected Classroom Rules, by Grade 179
9.8. Examples of Logical Consequences, by Grade 179
9.9. Logical Consequences for Selected Infractions 180
9.10. Selected Procedures for Room Use 180
9.11. Areas Needing Procedures 181
9.12. Monitoring Strategies that Enhance Learning 182
9.13. Factors to Consider in Establishing a Positive Environment 183
9.14. Advantages and Disadvantages of Common Instructional Formats 185
9.15. Selected Forms of Communication 188
9.16. Interventions for Classroom Problems 189
9.17. Selected Special Groups of Students 190
9.18. Selected Co-teaching Models 190
10.1. Selected Best Tested Classroom Activities 197
10.2. Procedures for Basic Academic Activities 199
10.3. Checklist for Building Teacher Confidence 200
10.4. Comparison of School Curricula 202
10.5. Selected Pedagogical Approaches for ELLs and SNs 203
10.6. TPE Standards 204
10.7. Tasks of TPA 205
10.8. Comparison of Traditional and Modern Instructional Approaches 205
10.9. Selected Teaching Strategies 207
10.10. Selected Activity and Task Strategies 208
10.11: Modeling Techniques to Enhance Guided Practices 209
10.12. Three Types of Instructional Strategies 209
10.13. Engagement Level by Activity Type 210
10.14. Examples of Assessment Instruments by Type 212
10.15. Uses of Selected Types of Assessment 213
10.16. Teaching Inventory Checklist 215
11.1. Reasons Punishment Does Not Work 218
11.2. Reasons Problem Solving Works 218
11.3. Components of a Personal Classroom Management Plan 219
11.4. Do's and Don'ts for Working with Parents 238
12.1. Five-Step Lesson Plan Format Activities for Basic Teaching Practices 245
12.2. Instructional Models with Academic Plans 245
12.3. Selected Modeling Techniques 247
12.4. Phases of First-Year Teaching 248
12.5. Meanings of the Word *Diversity* 258
12.6. Steps for Developing Classroom Norms 259
12.7. Correlation Between Active Learning Role and Retention 263
12.8. Bloom's Taxonomy Cognitive Domain Levels 263

12.9. CST Proficiency Level Scores 266
12.10. CELDT Listening and Speaking Proficiency Level Scores, Grades K-12 266
12.11. CELDT Reading Proficiency Levels, Grades 2-12 266
12.12. CELDT Writing Proficiency Levels, Grades 2-12 266
12.13. Selected Multicultural Issues 267

LIST OF ILLUSTRATIONS

1.1. Typical progression of a credential program 4

1.2. Dimensions of student diversity 6

1.3. Dimensions of teacher professionalism 12

1.4. Where interns work in California 16

2.1. The four essential components of a placement 23

2.2. Basic 16-week timeline 24

2.3. Basic standards of conduct areas for student teachers 27

2.4. Triangular relationship of placement 31

3.1. Funding for public schools 47

3.2. The three domains of teacher conduct 48

4.1. Scope of classroom management 64

4.2. Four basic teaching styles 67

4.3. Samples of classroom design 73

5.1. Foci of classroom discipline 82

5.2 Standards of conduct domains for teachers 92

6.1. Essentials of the classroom environment 100

6.2. The domains of teacher conduct 103

6.3. Components of student retention of information learned 104

6.4. Components of classroom psychosocial environment 105

6.5. Selected basic seating arrangements 106

6.6. Four teaching styles 109

6.7. Three tiers of instructional strategies 116

6.8. Cycle of planning instruction 118

7.1. Components of classroom structure 124

7.2. The instructional process 125

7.3. Academic groups in every classroom 127

7.4. The teacher as the "big screen" 127

7.5. Classroom social relationships 128

7.6. Classroom health and safety issues 131

7.7. Management objectives 132

7.8. Classroom discipline 133

7.9. Types of curricular standards 134

7.10. Domains of teacher conduct 141

8.1. Psychosocial environments of students 146

8.2. Spheres of cultural diversity 148

9.1. Selected samples of classroom designs 177

9.2. Relationships among students, teachers, and learning climate 184

9.3. Process of instructional practice 184

9.4. Teacher's roles in cooperative group 186

9.5. Effects of use of incentives for reinforcement 187

10.1. Factors influencing student learning 201
10.2. Forces influencing school curriculum 203
12.1. Instructional process 244
12.2. Phases of first-year teaching 248
12.3. Pressures on teachers 251
12.4. Areas for establishing professional goals 253
12.5. The cultural iceberg 256
12.6. The six pillars of character education 261

LIST OF ABBREVIATIONS

ADD:	Attention Deficit Disorder
ADHD:	Attention Deficit Hyperactivity Disorder
API:	Academic Performance Index
ASD:	Autism spectrum disorder
BAC:	Bilingual Advisory Committee
BCLAD:	Bilingual Cross-cultural Language Academic Development
BICS:	Basic Interpersonal Communication Skills
BTSA:	Beginning Teaching Support Assessment
CALP:	Cognitive Academic Language Proficiency
CAPA:	California Alternate Performance Assessment
CBEST:	California Basic Educational Skills test
CCTC:	California Commission on Teaching Credentialing
CD:	Conduct Disorder
CELDT:	California English Language Development Test
CLAD:	Cross-cultural Language Academic Development
CMA:	California Modified Assessment
CSET:	Comprehensive Subject Examination Test
CST:	California Standards Test
ED:	Emotional disorder
ELA:	English Language Arts
ELAC:	English Learner Advisory Committee
ELD:	English Language Development
ELL:	English language learner
FEP:	Fluent English Proficient
IEP:	Individualized Education Plan
INTASC:	Interstate New Teacher Assessment and Support Consortium
KWL:	What I Know, Want to know, What is Learned
LEP:	Limited English Proficient
NCLB:	No Child Left Behind Act
NEA:	National Education Association
PDD:	Pervasive Developmental Disorder
PL:	Public Law
RICA:	Reading Instruction Comprehension Assessment
RSVP:	Responsible, Supportive (Simple), Valuable, Purposeful
RTI:	Response to Intervention
SDAIE:	Specifically Designed Academic Instruction in English
SED:	Severe Emotional Disorder
SES:	Socio-Economic Status
SIOP:	sheltered instruction observation protocol
SN:	Special Needs

STAR: Standardized Testing and Reporting
STS: Standards-based Tests in Spanish
TBE: transitional bilingual education
TPA: Teacher Performance Assessment
TPE: Teacher Performance Expectations
WIC: Welfare Institute Code

FOREWORD

In the field of teacher education, thousands of experts have written textbooks about classroom management to help prepare new teachers for what they will face in the classroom. But very few of those textbooks on classroom management have been about best professional practices in the multicultural classroom. Many scholars have, no doubt, invested a huge amount of time, energy, research, and creative thinking in exploring classroom management techniques that enhance teaching and learning in the classroom. Most of them would agree that effective classroom management is the single most important ingredient in preparing new teachers for today's schools.

This book, *An Educational Psychology of Classroom Management: Best Professional Practices in the Multicultural Classroom*, is a brilliant academic compendium that contains practical approaches, logical applications, useful techniques, tactical skills, and teaching tools needed to address the complexities of classroom management and provide best professional practices. What makes this book so appealing to prospective educators and current student teachers in the field is the way Christopher Vang carefully crafted its content to help new classroom teachers understand the nature of becoming teachers through a broad array of perspectives that foster both teaching and learning in a positive manner.

Vang knows deeply and professionally how prospective educators and new classroom teachers feel about classroom management with best professional practices since it is an intricate matter that requires applying appropriate logical disciplines in a multicultural setting. Today's classroom is culturally and linguistically diverse, and lack of effective classroom management poses a wide range of concerns for new teachers who may not be familiar with minority students who do not possess middle-class values. Moreover, some children enter the classroom with minimal understanding of their teacher's behavioral expectations and pedagogical objectives for student learning outcomes. Teachers cannot overcome these academic deficiencies without knowledge and skills of classroom management that will bridge the gap between teaching expectations and student learning outcomes; they need this information and these skills in order to develop best professional practices for all students.

In this book, the broad emphasis upon both the psychosocial and the educational psychology dimensions of learning opens prospective educators' and new classroom teachers' hearts and minds through a process of clinical training to better understand the feeling tone of teaching and managing diverse students' behaviors during instruction. This book offers comprehensive approaches, culturally responsive applications, and practical tools for everyday needs in the multicultural classroom setting. For instance, teachers know that one form of classroom management does not fit all students' behaviors, and best professional practices encompass all aspects of teaching and learning.

Vang, as a Hmong scholar, professor, and educator, brings a unique voice to the psychology of classroom management and offers a new, vibrant, sensible, and articulated voice in support of the educational challenges and demands of diverse prospective educators in teacher preparation programs. Most importantly, as a university professor, Vang is a renowned expert in the field of multicultural education, classroom management, health and science methodology, and critical multiculturalism pedagogy.

What is admirable about Vang's talent, writing, and creativity is his firsthand experience in teaching college credential courses; that is what makes this book academically relevant to the preparation and training of new teachers for today's multicultural classroom teaching. Vang's insights have a wide applicability for best professional practices. Furthermore, in this book, Vang contributes his sensitive approach to classroom management that accepts and engages all of the diverse educators in today's pluralistic and multicultural settings.

Therefore, as a long-time friend of education, I am honored to recommend his well-researched book to all prospective educators and current student teachers who are teaching students of diverse backgrounds in the public school system and are looking for new directions to better understand the practical applications of classroom management and best professional practices. To all teachers of teachers I say that the practical information in Vang's book will benefit both teachers and students in the learning circle. For that reason, *An Educational Psychology of Classroom Management: Best Professional Practices in the Multicultural Classroom* is a must-own, must- read, and must-have book.

Dr. Gregory S. Goodman
Associate Professor
Clarion University of Pennsylvania

PREFACE

Quite often when student teachers and prospective educators are asked about the most difficult challenges they face each and every day in the classroom, most say classroom management is their Number 1 concern and ongoing classroom discipline is Number 2. As most teachers would agree, without effective classroom management techniques and logical consequences for student misbehavior, it is extremely hard to deliver effective instruction that engages students in meaningful academic learning. This book, *An Educational Psychology of Classroom Management: Best Professional Practices in the Multicultural Classroom,* was written to help prospective educators and new teachers address recurring problems in the multicultural classroom setting. The content of this book was selected specifically for the everyday issues new teachers encounter involving classroom management and best professional practices. The educational psychology approach is based on up-to-date research that indicates that it is relevant to all prospective educators and new teachers.

This book gives comprehensive approaches to teacher preparation and discusses the nature of classroom management in a way that equips prospective educators with a broad array of practical tools to prepare them for unexpected challenges in instruction, management, discipline, assessment, transition, and daily routine and structure. The information will lead prospective educators and new teachers to explore their own philosophy of classroom management, philosophy of discipline, philosophy of teaching; and they learn to implement best professional practices that will help them grow and develop professionally and ethically to become the next generation of great teachers.

Keep in mind that today's classrooms are filled with students from diverse backgrounds as well as schoolteachers who are culturally diverse. There is no such a thing as "best" classroom management techniques or "best" logical consequences for discipline. No one-model-fits-all technique will work for all kinds of misbehavior that occurs in the classroom. In everyday teaching, there is no "one teaching model serves all." In this book, prospective educators and new teachers will learn how to adjust and adapt their philosophy of management and discipline to accommodate their professional practices in the multicultural classroom setting.

How Educational Psychology Is Applied in This Book

Many experts in the field of teacher education would agree wholeheartedly that psychology plays a unique role in classroom management and student discipline. Theorists Erikson, Skinner, Freud, Jung, Rogers, Redl, Wattenberg, Dreikurs, and Ginott had psychology backgrounds, and they were associated with various therapeutic psychologies in their studies and research. This means that approaches to classroom management and student discipline rely heavily on psychological premises of behavior modification, stimulation, management, and manipulation.

In this book, educational psychology is the basis for helping classroom teachers and prospective educators understand the psycho-social environment, or feeling tone, of classroom management. This is important if they are to deal with the complexities of teaching and learning in a multicultural setting where cultural diversity plays a pivotal role in how teachers manage and discipline student behaviors and, at the same time, in how students respond to teachers' actions and modify their behaviors to adjust to teachers' demands. Most importantly, psychology has become an integral part of education, involved in teaching, learning, and assessing. Psychology helps explain the different behaviors of children and adults in instructional settings and is thus critical to classroom management, instructional practices, and student learning outcomes. Therefore, in this book, educational psychology provides the foundation upon which new teachers and prospective educators can build best professional practices for all their students.

What This Book Provides for Educators

An Educational Psychology of Classroom Management: Best Professional Practices in the Multicultural Classroom is designed for everyone in the teacher education field, especially for prospective educators and new student teachers in teacher preparation programs. This is why: Classroom management and student discipline are the most difficult challenges for new teachers today. In fact, poor classroom management skills and ineffective student discipline techniques can make best professional practices ineffective, and at the same time, can cause fear and consternation. Newly hired teachers constantly battle with fear, consternation, dissatisfaction, and in some cases, personal disappointment. Moreover, the inability to manage has caused teachers more job-related stresses than anything else. The purpose of this book is to give new teachers the best foundation possible for effective classroom management and implementation of best professional practices.

In recent years, national data have indicated that high levels of frustration, feelings of inadequacy, and ineffective classroom management have led to high teacher turnover rates during the first three years of teaching. In most cases, beginning teachers find out about classroom management and student discipline problems the hard way. Many report that management issues are their most daunting concern. Some do not feel comfortable disciplining students, making referrals to the office, and contacting parents regarding student behavior.

Today's classrooms are filled with students of diverse backgrounds, and teachers are ethnically diverse as well. Each student brings his or her unique challenges, needs, and expectations to the classroom, and teachers are also unique, setting different expectations for their students. These challenges are real, and there is no question that teachers need help in meeting the many demands of today's classroom. However, classroom management and student discipline are at the top of their list. Without sensible classroom management, teaching and learning are likely to be disconnected, fragmented, capricious, and dysfunctional.

This book takes prospective educators and new student teachers on a complete tour of their career, from the beginning of their credential program to the end of their student teaching practicum. They will learn how to prepare to become teachers, proceed through the process, and go beyond the fieldwork experience into the classroom environment. This book is a complete guide for new teachers who need reassurance and an overview of classroom management and best professional practices.

Today's Teachers Face Difficult Challenges

Besides having to deal with classroom management and student discipline, prospective educators and new student teachers face a mountain of challenges today. Without doubt, their plates are full of responsibilities. Budget problems have put nearly unbearable pressure on teachers and teaching. Many teachers are threatened by district layoff and furlough policies. Class sizes are being increased exponentially as budget crises remain unresolved. Teachers are leaving the profession, creating vacancies in many schools. Observers project that teachers who teach in early grades will have 30-plus students as teacher shortages continue to loom. This will be unmanageable, and perhaps untenable.

Each academic year, the average teacher spends nearly 2 months doing informative or diagnostic assessments on student learning outcomes as mandated by district and government policies. Formal and informal assessments, such as benchmark tests and state standardized testing, place a serious time constraint on teachers; however, assessments are necessary to provide accountability in public education. New teachers usually find assessments to be a frightening experience because most do not know how to perform them as they lack experience in the assessment of student learning. Few new teachers are familiar with the instruments used to assess student learning, and when they are required to use the instruments, they often do so without proper training.

Today's teachers are commonly taught to use direct instruction modalities or scripted instructions; many are not equipped with any other teaching methodologies, strategies, or approaches. Although some school districts are now considering replacing direct instruction with the Sheltered Instruction Observation Protocol (SIOP) and/or Response to Instruction (RTI) models, nearly 75% of schools use direct instruction as the main instructional approach. This despite the fact that nearly half of all teachers believe that direct instruction cannot be a one-model-fits-all instructional methodology. Direct instruction leaves many students behind and, more importantly, teachers cannot use it to teach all subject matters creatively. There are a number of other strategies and instructional methodologies that are effective. Sometimes teaching itself is a very complicated matter. As Andrew and Jelmberg (2010) found, not everyone can be a good teacher because teaching is not designed for everyone. And not everyone learns the same way.

Furthermore, in some states such as California, new teachers are required to meet teacher performance expectations (TPE) standards and demonstrate proficiency in teacher performance assessment (TPA) tasks in order to receive their preliminary teaching credentials. To do this, new teachers have to demonstrate their knowledge and skills in making instructional adaptations of academic content for English language learners (ELLs) and students with special needs. Most student teachers find TPE and TPA requirements to be tedious. However, if teachers are deficient in these areas, how can they address the needs of all their students?

American schools are now multilingual and multicultural. The number of limited English proficient (LEP) students is rising all across the nation. Nearly 425 dialects are spoken in American schools; California alone has over 120 dialects in its schools. Nearly 40% of US students come from bilingual and/or minority backgrounds. Of the 54 million students in K-12 education, approximately 3.2 million are LEP students and 5.2 million are students with some kind of learning disabilities. Moreover, nearly 10 million students in K-12 system speak a primary language at home other than English.

The process of educating LEP students is obscure and capricious; it provides dismal academic services to LEP students. Most new teachers do not understand how schools identify LEP students, and once they are identified, teachers have no idea who is obligated to serve them. LEP students are tracked throughout the system to make sure the academic label remains intact, but so little is done to help these students excel academically. The ongoing practices of surface assessment, cosmetic education, and lip service will continue to harm the academic needs of LEP students.

Teacher shortage is a serious problem, and the shortage of special education teachers is a pressing issue nationally and, in some school districts, a crisis. Students with disabilities need teachers who understand their internal struggles to learn. Most teachers are not clinically trained or otherwise prepared to deal with students with disabilities. These students' individualized educational plans (IEP) are legally binding, but more often than not, academic services are not delivered as mandated by the Individuals with Disabilities Education Act (IDEA), Public Law 94-142, and section 504 requirements of Public Law 93-112, known as the Rehabilitation Act of 1973. The debate on full inclusion will continue while the system leaves students with disabilities in academic limbo.

Teaching is a huge responsibility that demands tremendous dedication, passion, patience, and commitment. However, the difficult challenges become insurmountable when school districts, cities, counties, states, and the federal government add layer upon layer of mandates for the new teachers in the classroom. Perhaps it is time to let teachers teach.

My Motivation for Writing This Book

As a university professor of teacher education, I have had a strong desire to write *An Educational Psychology of Classroom Management: Best Professional Practices in the Multicultural Classroom* for prospective educators and student teachers in credential programs and liberal studies programs. I have been teaching Classroom Management and Professional Practices for several years and, over the years, I have learned that prospective educators and student teachers need a book with practical ideas they can apply to everyday teaching in the classroom. This book; however, is not the only answer to all the questions and problems new teachers will have. It will serve as a guide to help new teachers find the answers they are looking for. Most importantly, they will be able to use the practical information in this book from the beginning of their pursuit of their teaching credential to the end and beyond.

How This Book Is Organized

This book contains four main parts with rich and comprehensive content organized into 12 chapters. Each chapter presents a variety of topical issues in a single domain of educational objectives. In each chapter, headings and subheadings guide the reader to the various topical issues. Part I has three chapters on broad topics related to the teaching profession domain. Part II has three chapters that present the complexities of the classroom management and student discipline domain. The three chapters of Part III give an overview of the multicultural classroom management strategies domain. Finally, Part IV has three chapters of information on the best professional practices domain.

ACKNOWLEDGMENTS

This book would not have been attempted or written without the expertise of Dr. Gregory S. Goodman. I am indebted to Dr. Goodman for his scholarship, contributions, and invaluable guidance; he is the instrumental editor for this book. Also, Dr. Goodman's kindness, friendship, mentoring, and support made this book a reality.

As always, my special appreciation goes to Mr. Christopher Myers, the Managing Director for Peter Lang Publishing. His genuine encouragement and support have made this book possible and given me the momentum to complete it.

A Personal Note

I am passionate about the content of this book based on my experiences teaching in the multiple subject credential program at California State University, Stanislaus. *An Educational Psychology of Classroom Management: Best Professional Practices in the Multicultural Classroom* truly reflects my passion for teaching classroom management and best professional practices. Over the years, my own professional development and personal growth have guided me in organizing the content of this book and in creating the conceptual framework applicable to the needs of prospective educators and new student teachers.

My observations, firsthand experience teaching both children and adults, and personal multicultural and multilingual background inspired me to organize my thoughts into a book that will help prospective educators and new teachers gain insights into classroom management and student discipline and best professional practices. I am using this book to reach out to other teachers. It is my voice, communicating quietly about the importance of becoming a great teacher for all children, giving them the best professional practices in the multicultural classroom setting.

PART I.

THE TEACHING PROFESSION DOMAIN

CHAPTER ONE

CONTEMPORARY CHALLENGES TO BECOMING A TEACHER

I touch the future, I teach.
Christa McAuliffe

Introduction

Education experts predict the staggering teacher turnover rate will cost the public school system billions of dollars each year. New teachers must be recruited to replace the outgoing teachers. Teacher retention is a national crisis. National data show that we will need hundreds of thousands of new schoolteachers over the next 20 years. California alone will need at least 30,000 new teachers to teach its population of students in K–12 classrooms that is currently 6 million and continually growing. In California and elsewhere, more teachers are needed to prepare for the increasing number of diverse students entering the education system. Teaching has become a popular major for college students even if a somewhat less popular career choice. However, the difficulties teachers face when they get in the classroom cause many to drop out of the profession. This chapter examines major challenges facing prospective educators and new student teachers in preparing to become teachers. It also discusses some of the issues that may affect their professional orientation in the pursuit of a teaching credential.

The Credential Program

Getting into the teaching zone is a big step and, for many, a very important decision. Each year teacher education preparation programs in California and elsewhere accept new applications, interview candidates, and admit teacher candidates into credential programs to begin coursework in pursuit of their preliminary teaching credentials. Most credential programs in California are 1 year in length—two semesters including winter and summer terms if necessary, as shown in Figure 1.1.

The majority of college students who chose teaching as a profession major in liberal studies, and this is quite true for most prospective educators who wish to earn a multiple-subject teaching credential to teach in the K–6 grades. The minority of college students coming from different academic disciplines are more likely to choose a single-subject teaching credential to teach in the 7–12 grades. An even smaller number of candidates chose the multiple-subject teaching credential and come from academic disciplines such as math, sociology, business, history, science, and psychology. The effort and passion put into pursuing a teaching career are unique for each prospective teacher.

At the entry interview, prospective student teachers are screened. They are asked many questions about their interest in teaching children and why they want to become classroom teachers. The purpose of the entry interview is to make sure that student teacher candidates are ready to enter the program since graduate coursework is intensive, and managing a personal life while attending day and evening classes could be challenging. In fact, a small number of prospective student teachers take more than 1 year to finish their credential programs because of financial and personal difficulties.

Figure 1.1. Typical progression of a credential program.

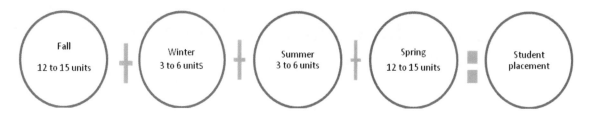

One of the most frequently asked questions in the entry interview is: "Tell us why you want to be a teacher?" The responses to this question are no surprise and somewhat consistent. Most candidates answer, "I want to be a teacher because…

1. I have been around children all my life.
2. I have worked as a volunteer in the classroom.
3. I have substituted numerous times in the classroom.
4. I have taught children before.
5. I have participated in community-based organizations.
6. I have been a bilingual aide or assistant in the classroom.
7. My parents are teachers.
8. My friends are teachers.
9. My sisters or brothers are teachers.
10. I love to work with children.

These are typical answers given by student teacher candidates. However, interviewers also hear some less typical responses. Some honestly say that teaching is what they want to do in life, that teaching is their focus and love. Students who respond this way might also express their feelings and interest in terms of having strong motivation. Some say they are inspired by past teachers, peers, or personal experiences. In an attempt to examine prospective student teachers' thinking and feelings about going into teaching and find out how they decided to pursue a career in teaching, Kauchak and Eggen (2005) administered the Interest in Teaching inventory. Their findings are shown in Table 1.1.

Table 1.1. Interests Motivating Students to Enter Teaching

Student Interest	Average Response	Ranking
Work with youth	6.4	1
Value to society	6.3	2
Self-growth	5.5	3
Content interest	5.4	4
Influence of teachers	5.0	5
Job security	4.3	6
Summer vacations	4.0	7
Family influence	3.9	8
Other careers not considered	2.6	9

Note. Information from Introduction to Teaching: Becoming a Professional (2nd ed.), by D. Kauchak and P. Eggen, 2005, Upper Saddle River, NJ: Pearson Education).

Without a doubt, going into the teaching profession is a difficult decision and commitment since today's schools are much different from those of decades ago. Federal and state mandates are strict, and scores on the academic performance index (API) that measures school improvement and quality are a constant concern. Some may think teaching is a profession rather than a career or vice versa. In reality, teaching is both. It is good to have student teacher candidates who demonstrate a passion for teaching. Teaching is more complex than simply seeing, feeling, liking, and thinking; today's teaching is not designed for someone who just wants a job. As Andrew and Jelmberg (2010) pointed out, not everyone can be a good teacher. Of course, it is also true that teaching is not designed for everyone because it requires passion, patience, dedication, commitment, and perseverance.

Passion in Teaching

Teaching is the passion of the heart. As Table 1.1 shows, people are motivated to become teachers for a variety of reasons. Most have heard both positive and negative things about teaching in a pluralistic society, and they ask some very revealing questions in class. One asked, "Do teachers have to raise children in the classroom?" Many have heard people say that teachers are babysitters. Prospective teachers feel that parents should be responsible for training their children for school and teachers should be responsible for teaching. Most realize that being a schoolteacher is overwhelmingly challenging; still, they are highly motivated to become one. Students in one of my classes identified the issues that concerned them as they prepare to enter the teaching profession (Table 1.2).

Table 1.2. Issues that Concern Prospective Teachers

Issue	Percentage of Students Expressing Concern
Budget crisis	20
Salaries	15
Classroom management	10
Discipline problems	10
TPE and TPA requirements	10
Long working hours	5
Federal, state, county, and district mandates	5
Testing, assessment, and benchmark evaluations	5
Lack of resources	5
Class size	5
Stresses, demands, politics, and requirements	10

Despite their concerns, many believe the teaching profession is a desirable career and a favorable professional choice because they want to make a difference in children's lives; they want to see the light go on in children. However, most fear that today's teaching is based on a measurement-driven curriculum approach, and most schools use a one-model-fits-all instructional methodology that leaves many children who need extra assistance behind. The main emphasis in teaching is direct instruction, the so-called teacher-centered approach or scripted instructional modalities. However, most aspiring teachers feel that teaching should be creative, and teachers should use differentiating instruction to benefit all learners since learners bring different sets of challenges to the classroom.

Figure 1.2. Dimensions of student diversity.

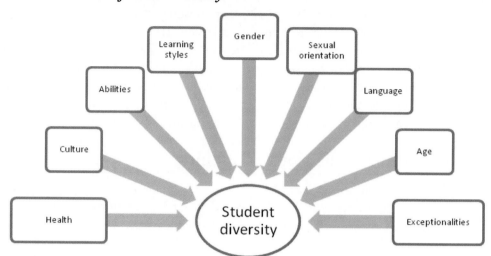

As Table 1.2 illustrates, most prospective teachers agree that classroom management is the most challenging and perhaps the most difficult academic issue facing teachers in the classroom. Many do not know how to handle or discipline students with attention deficit disorder (ADD), attention deficit hyperactivity disorder (ADHD), conduct disorder (CD), or severe emotional disorder (SED). They do not know how to work with students with physical disabilities, students with language barriers, students with learning disabilities, or students with special needs. They worry about students with medical conditions such as asthma, diabetes type I, epilepsy, convulsions, or hearing or vision impairment. Figure 1.2 illustrates the various forms of student diversity that teachers may have to consider in a multicultural setting.

In July 2011, California's governor signed a new law that required California's public schools to include the contributions of gays and lesbians in its social science curriculum. This new twist will make public education even more complex. Moreover, of the 54 million students in public schools, 5.2 million have some kind of learning disability, and 3.2 million are English language learners (ELLs).

On the one hand, the college students who are preparing to become teachers feel disheartened by the mountains of demands awaiting them each and every day in the classroom. On the other hand, many have faith in themselves that they will perform their professional duties in accordance with the law, educating all students in their classes regardless of what that requires. Deep down in their hearts, they know that teachers cannot solve all the behavioral problems in the classroom. However, they also know they have a professional responsibility and commitment to make sure that all children entrusted to them have the same opportunity to learn in an environment that is healthy and safe, and they are determined to carry out that responsibility even if their plates are full and their frustration level might be high. Most believe they can improve their professional practices through clinical training; professional development; continuing education; experience; and on-the-job opportunities such as mentoring, coaching, co-teaching, and ongoing practice.

Teacher Turnover

To elicit information and provoke discussion among teacher candidates regarding how they feel about their career choice, professional commitment, and commitment to life-long learning, I asked some of my students why they thought teachers would leave the profession. Their perceptions of the reasons for teacher turnover are given in Table 1.3.

Recent national data indicate that approximately 46% of schoolteachers leave their job within the first 5 years. One third of those leave in the first 3 years, and one half leave toward the end of the 5th year. According to the National Commission on Teaching and America's Future (NCTAF, 2003–2004), the national attrition rate for teachers climbed to 50% over a 15-year period and cost the nation's educational system nearly $7.3 billion annually. Table 1.4 illustrates the financial impact of teacher turnover on the largest school districts. The national teacher turnover rate was 16.8%; however, it was higher in some rural and metropolitan areas in different states. For instance, in California, 13% of newly hired teachers left the job in their first 2 years; 22% left by the end of the 4th year; 27% of newly hired teachers in Grades 7–12 left by the end of their 4th year; and 25% of new teachers are replacements for teachers who are leaving the public school system.

These staggering numbers validate my students' perceptions that teaching can be as difficult as any other professional job. The data surprised the students because they entered the credential programs with misconceptions about the teaching profession. Some had not heard about teacher turnover in any of their college courses, and they had thought that teaching was a stable profession.

Table 1.3. *Prospective Teachers' Perceptions of Reasons Teachers Quit Teaching*

Reason	Percentage of Students Identifying Reason
Discipline and management problems	10
Lack of administrative support	10
Lack of preparation and clinical training	10
Low salaries	10
Stresses	10
Budget shortfall	5
Burn out	5
Family issues	5
Find out the hard way	5
Health factors	5
Lack of subject matter competence	5
Testing or assessment	5
Too many demands	5
Lack of parental involvement	3
Work conditions	2

As the NCTAF (2003–2004) reported, there are many reasons teachers leave teaching. However, the commission identified the top four reasons as (1) low salaries, (2) poor working conditions, (3) inadequate preparation, and (4) insufficient mentoring support in the early years of teaching. Regardless of these data, most teacher candidates strongly believe that a lot of teacher turnover has to do with poor classroom management and ineffective student discipline because they see these as the sources of the greatest stress. Perhaps they are right.

Table 1.4. Annual Cost of Teacher Turnover in Selected Districts

School Districts	Cost
11. New York City, New York	$115,200,000
12. Los Angeles, California	$ 94,200,000
13. Miami, Florida	$ 47,700,000
14. Houston, Texas	$ 35,000,000
15. Philadelphia, Pennsylvania	$ 29,600,000
16. Dallas, Texas	$ 28,800,000
17. Fairfax, Virginia	$ 28,300,000
18. Detroit, Michigan	$ 26,500,000
19. Prince Georges County, Maryland	$ 23,200,000
20. Memphis, Tennessee	$ 21,800,000

Note. Information from *Policy Brief: The High Cost of Teacher Turnover* by National Commission on Teaching and America's Future, 2003–2004 (Washington, DC: Author). Numbers are rounded.

Improving Teacher Retention

The high cost of teacher turnover is now a national crisis for public education. A strategic action plan is required to deal with teacher shortages and teacher turnover. The NCTAF (2003–2004, p. 9) warned, "Given the high cost of teacher turnover, it is imperative that education leaders recognize the importance of teacher retention as a major policy objective in maintaining a high caliber teaching corps in every school."

Since the passage of the No Child Left Behind Act in 2001, the implementation of federal policy on public education has stalled because of a number of tough challenges: (a) insufficient funding for academic programs in public schools; (b) inconsistent strategic action planning to improve public education; (c) focus on measurement-driven curriculum; (d) use of a one-model-fits-all approach; and (e) and inability to train, retain, and recruit highly qualified teachers into at-risk schools. Moreover, the current economic recession has exacerbated these problems. As education experts foresaw, if the retention of quality teachers fails, the American educational system itself will continue to fill a leaky bucket.

Teacher shortages leave many needy students in academic limbo, and these students, who deserve the best teachers, are left to fend for themselves in the presence of inexperienced, under-qualified, underprepared, non-credentialed, and unskilled teachers. Part of the problem is the failure to equitably distribute financial resources and teaching quality across the nation's educational system. Federal and state approaches have not worked so far. Teachers have not been distributed well, well-trained and well-prepared beginning teachers have not been recruited into at-risk schools, veteran teachers have not been retained in at-risk and underperforming schools, quality teachers have not been rotated from high performing schools into underperforming schools, and no national database system has been established to track teacher turnover in order to systematically monitor teacher turnover to minimize the financial impact on local school districts.

Besides these policy issues, national effort is needed to retain teachers in the classroom. Otherwise, the nation's fragile educational system will be in imminent danger. The National Education Association (NEA, 2010) assessed schoolteachers' willingness to teach again from 1961 to 2006. As Table 1.5 shows, desire to teach has fluctuated.

Table 1.5. Percent of Teachers Willing to Teach Again

Willingness	1961	1966	1971	1976	1981	1986	1991	1996	2001	2006
Certainly	49.9	52.6	44.9	37.5	21.8	22.7	28.6	32.1	31.7	38.2
Probably	26.9	25.4	29.5	26.1	24.6	26.3	30.5	30.5	28.7	27.3
Chances about even	12.5	12.9	13.0	17.5	17.6	19.8	18.5	17.3	18.4	16.1
Probably not	7.9	7.1	8.9	13.4	24.0	22.0	17.0	15.8	15.7	12.7
Certainly not	2.8	2.0	3.7	5.6	12.0	9.3	5.4	4.3	5.6	5.8

In order to improve teaching quality and retain highly quality teachers, the system needs to put a strong emphasis on providing adequate resources to teacher preparation programs for recruitment, training, and mentoring of new teachers. Without the up-front investment in good teacher induction and intern programs such as California's Beginning Teacher Support and Assessment (BTSA) program, more teachers will enter the classroom with limited pedagogical skills and knowledge. In California and elsewhere, some districts offer the integrated program to help train new teachers. In this program, new teachers are placed in the classroom to practice teaching for at least one year while taking college courses in the credential program. Some educational institutions are now designing teacher residency programs to help train new teachers. This new concept should be further explored for its value in improving teacher recruitment and retention.

Preparation of Teachers

Over the last 30 years, teacher readiness, or preparing quality teachers, has been a topic of ongoing political debate, sparking education reform and new policies for improving public education. Nonetheless, so little has been done to improve the equitable distribution of highly quality teachers across the nation's educational system. For instance, in California, Senate Bill 2042 was enacted several years ago to revamp the state's credentialing process to improve teacher quality and instructional practices. Under this bill, new teachers have to meet the 13 teacher performance expectations (TPE) standards and perform the 4 academic tasks of the teacher performance assessment (TPA). Moreover, prior to entering a credential program, new teachers must pass the California Basic Educational Skills test (CBEST), the Comprehensive Subject Examination Test (CSET), and the Reading Instruction Comprehension Assessment (RICA). Some teacher preparation programs require new candidates to take Early Assessment Program (EAP), English Placement Test (EPT), or Entry Level Math (ELM) to fulfill the basic skills requirements. Keep in mind that the requirements for the multiple subject credential program are not the same as what is required for the single subject credential program.

Nationally, thirty-five states require new teachers to pass comprehensive teacher tests, called Praxis series, summarized in Table 1.6. However, California appears to be one of the only few states that requires so many examinations for new teachers. For example, under SB 2042, California Commission on Teacher Credentialing (CCTC) requires TPEs and TPA tasks on top of these exams for California's new teachers.

Table 1.6. Foci and Content of Praxis Series

Test	Focus	Content
Praxis I	Academic skills	Basic skills in reading, writing, and math
Praxis II	Subject	Specific subject content knowledge and professional knowledge
Praxis III	Classroom performance	Observations, work samples, lesson design, instructions, management, and sensitivity toward diverse learners

Note. Information from *Introduction to Teaching: Becoming a Professional* (2nd ed.), by D. Kauchak, and P. Eggen, 2005, Upper Saddle River, NJ: Pearson Education.

No doubt, the bar has been raised for new teachers acquiring general principles of learning and teaching. According to Blair (2000), Kauchak and Eggen (2005), Olson (2000), and Wayne and Youngs (2003), 34 states require prospective student teachers to pass a basic skills test, 30 states require secondary school teachers to pass a test demonstrating competency in the subject matter they plan to teach, and 24 states require school principals to evaluate new teachers' teaching effectiveness.

As the result of teacher shortages and turnover, this nation has not been able to recruit, prepare, and train enough new teachers in a timely manner for the thousands of schools that need quality teachers and for the millions of children in Grades K–12 who need them. The American educational system is one of the richest and most expensive systems in the world, spending billions of dollars on public education each year. Yet the output of the American educational system is not yet the best, although perhaps among the best, in the world. This nation's educational system is one of the most complex, but logical and comprehensive, educational systems.

College coursework alone is not a sufficient condition for preparing new teachers for classroom teaching. In 2001, student teachers who were finishing up the credential programs in California were asked how confident they felt about their ability to teach the content area for which they were preparing. The responses were astounding. Twenty-seven percent of the student teachers surveyed felt they were underprepared to teach language arts, especially reading; 30% felt underprepared to teach mathematics; 42% felt underprepared to teach science, history, or social studies; but 60% of all respondents felt confident in teaching all four subjects—math, history, language arts, and science. These data may explain the staggering teacher turnover figures.

There is no doubt that hiring well prepared teachers will reduce teacher attrition and its cost. But the lingering question is where to find well prepared teachers. Again, this nation has to grow its own well-trained and well-equipped teachers. Teacher preparation programs need to provide new teachers with the following:

- in-depth training in content area knowledge
- broad-based knowledge of learning styles and teaching theories
- knowledge of pedagogical skills and instructional approaches
- internship or on-the-job training adequate to gain clinical experience
- comprehensive understanding of academic standards and curriculum
- effective classroom management techniques and skills
- knowledge of assessment instruments and skill in administering them
- mentoring support from administrative staff through the use of induction programs
- guidance for developing a repertoire of teaching skills that enable them to create an effective teaching and learning environment for students

- opportunities to practice quality teaching to enhance their grasp of best professional practices

Today the process of training new teachers is similar to the one used by the fast food industry—fast, easy, convenient, and cheap. Most new teachers rush in and out of the training program through the drive-through window. To produce well-trained and well-prepared teachers, the status quo has got to be changed. The NCTAF (2003–2004, p. 10) explained the problem with the status quo: "The reality is that, in many districts, teachers are mismanaged. This mismanagement diminishes the ability of teachers to improve student learning and it dampens the desire of teachers to remain in the classroom" (p. 10).

Keep in mind that well-trained and well-prepared teachers are not created overnight. Whether one believes teachers are born or made, developing excellence in any teacher takes time, persistent effort, and hard work. Teacher preparation programs need to find new ways of making the teaching profession more attractive and more lucrative.

Benefits of Being a Teacher

For many prospective educators, going into teaching requires that they place hope over fear because they are skeptical about the job market. Most do not know for sure if they will like the job until they are actually in it. For the highly motivated, teaching is their art and their passion. For the unsure, teaching could be a great challenge they want to dare to try. For others, teaching is a matter of honor. Whatever their feelings, most go into teaching because they believe they have something they can give to others, and there are benefits they will receive from others, especially from students and parents. Teaching is the profession that offers more benefits to society than any other, followed by the professions of physician, nurse, business person, lawyer, journalist, politician, and accountant.

Teaching offers both intrinsic and extrinsic rewards. Most teachers experience intrinsic rewards in the form of internal feelings that come from deep within their hearts: understanding, appreciation, love, caring, energy, enthusiasm, and nurturing. The internal growth and development that come from teaching bring professional satisfaction that supports their emotional and intellectual well-being. The emotional rewards could be simple things, like thank-you notes, appreciative messages, gifts, awards, and commendations. Teachers receive intellectual rewards as the ongoing learning process inspires and rejuvenates their minds and souls. Teachers often say, "We teach and learn at the same time," or "We teach as we learn." Moreover, intellectual stimulation helps teachers improve their knowledge and skill, and, at the same time, their teaching facilitates student learning.

A number of extrinsic rewards come to the teacher from the outside: a good salary, vacation, job security, professional affiliations, friendships, flexible work schedules, autonomy, social status, recognition, promotion, merit pay, and popularity. However, teachers do not usually consider these extrinsic rewards among their biggest motivations for pursuing or staying in teaching. These extrinsic rewards are usually not sufficient to keep teachers in such a highly demanding job that requires tremendous energy, diligence, planning, effort, and flexibility.

In addition to or in spite of the many benefits of teaching, prospective teachers need to think about the difficulties they will encounter in teaching. As mentioned earlier, budget problems, teacher shortages, teacher turnover, large class sizes, and policy mandates sometimes make it difficult for teachers to perform their daily assignments. Responsibilities such as student discipline, management, assessments, accountability for student learning outcome, and instructional challenges could affect individual teachers' psycho-social well-being. Ingersoll (1997), Kauchak and Eggen (2005), and Labaree (1992) identified some of these responsibilities that are part of teacher professionalism; they are shown in Figure 1.3.

Whether other people see teachers as professionals or not, the fact is that without teachers there would be no other professionals. Teachers are the first professionals everyone encounters; they are the ones who teach others how to read, write, do math, and learn science. At one time, any shortage of teachers limited the learning potential of a society. However, in the late 1990s and early 2000s the number of teachers increased, and so did the learning potential for many American children. In other words, the more teachers available, the better opportunities this nation is going to provide for its citizens. Having an adequate number of teachers available to teach children is a societal necessity.

Figure 1.3. Dimensions of teacher professionalism.

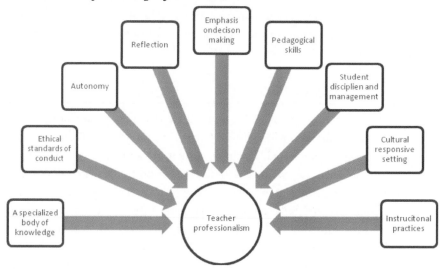

Trends in the Teaching Profession

For the 2010–2011 school year, the U.S. spent approximately $540 billion for the nation's K-12 education. Current economic trends in the teaching profession were spiraling down as this nation began a tough economic downturn in late 2007. National news media reported that nearly 45 states have serious state budget crises, and each of these states would need at least $3 billion to keep its economy moving forward. Therefore, a grand total of $125 billion is needed to rescue these states in imminent peril; otherwise, public education will suffer deep budget cuts for a number of years. Perhaps more cuts are inevitable, and school finances will worsen as the federal government continues to trim its budget to deal with the national deficit. Take one state and one city in that state as an example: California state officials face a deficit of approximately $27 billion; Fresno County faces a shortfall of at least $50 million, and the figure for the City of Fresno is $31 million.

In California, for the current education budget crisis, the California State University System of 23 campuses lost approximately $750 million as compared to the $475 million of the State Community College System of 112 campuses. These budget cuts have caused both systems to raise college tuitions ranging from 10 to 25 percent across the board. Sadly, the near future is uncertain if tax revenues continue to dwindle.

The largest school districts in California are struggling to make ends meet. For instance, the Fresno Unified School District is the fourth largest district in California and has to trim $56 million from an originally proposed $71 million in its 2011–2012 budget. The second largest district in California, Los Angeles Unified, lost nearly $250 million. In recent months, thousands of California's public schoolteachers received notices from their school districts warning them of the possibility that no job would be available next year if the budget crisis continues and no solution is found. Currently, nearly 143 of 9,500 public schools in California are in financial jeopardy. Other states face similar situations.

However, experts, policy makers, and politicians are optimistic about the current financial condition; most are used to this kind of roller coaster ride when dealing with budget issues and economic downturns. They hope the budget outlook will improve in the next few years. If not, funding for public education could be in grave jeopardy as budgets unravel at all levels of government.

The number of public school teachers in America has risen approximately 12% since 1999 (Snyder & Dillow, 2010). In 2009, there were 3.7 million full-time equivalent teachers in elementary and secondary schools. Of that number, 3.2 million were public school teachers and 0.5 million taught in private schools. Females made up 76% of public school teachers and 24% percent of teachers were males. Of the female teachers, 44% were under the age 40 and 52% possessed a master's or higher degree.

Similarly, 74% of private school teachers were females and 26% were males. In private schools, 39% of female teachers were under the age of 40 and 38% had master's degrees or higher. In recent years, the student-teacher ratio for private schools has been 13:1 as compared to 20:1 for public elementary schools and 23:1 for public secondary schools.

Of the 3.2 million public school teachers in 2009, 85% remained at the same school; 8% moved to a different school, and 8% percent left the profession. Of the 0.5 million private school teachers, 80% stayed with the same school; 5% moved to a different school, and 16% left the profession. Interestingly, nearly 26% of the public school teachers who changed schools did so because of personal factors as compared to 16% of the private school teachers. On other hand, 13% of private school teachers lost their contracts as compared to 5% of public school teachers.

The national average salary for public school teachers was $53,000, which was an increase from $44,000 5 years earlier. Kauchak and Eggen (2005) compared average and beginning salaries for public school teachers in some states; their comparisons are presented in Table 1.7.

One cautionary note is in order: If the beginning salary for new teachers does not rise in subsequent years, teachers will consider leaving teaching for other professional jobs after a few years because of dissatisfaction associated with the rising cost of living and inflation. As Ingersoll and Smith (2003) found, nearly 75% of teachers who left teaching cited low salaries as a major factor. However, prospective student teachers should not focus only on pay scales when considering becoming teachers. As Wadsworth (2001) found out in a public agenda poll, 86% of new teachers thought of teaching as a true calling; 75% considered teaching a lifelong choice; 68% reported they felt a lot of satisfaction from teaching, and 96% of beginning teachers chose teaching because that was work they love to do. This suggests that most people entering the teaching profession have high intrinsic motivation. America *can* grow its own teachers to fill the need for the next 50 years. And the time to do that is now. Otherwise, teacher shortages and turnover will put American public education at risk.

Table 1.7. Salaries for Public School Teachers in Selected States

State	Average salary	Beginning salary
California	$54,300	$34,100
Michigan	$52,400	$32,600
Connecticut	$52,300	$34,500
Rhode Island	$51,600	$30,200
District of Columbia	$51,000	$31,900

New York	$51,100	$34,500
New Jersey	$50,000	$35,300
Illinois	$49,600	$31,700
Alaska	$49,000	$36,000
Massachusetts	$48,700	$32,700
Maryland	$48,200	$31,800
Oregon	$46,000	$31,000
U.S. average	$44,300	$30,700

Note. Information from *Introduction to Teaching: Becoming a Professional* (2nd ed.), by D. Kauchak, and P. Eggen, 2005, Upper Saddle River, NJ: Pearson Education. Numbers are rounded.

Lastly, technology has changed and enhanced teaching in so many ways over the last two decades. No doubt technology will continue to be a major influence on teaching and learning. IPADs, IPODs, Smart Boards, wireless internet services, online resources, cell phones, and Skype can be used with the touch of a fingertip. Also, children as well as their teachers are more familiar with technology today than they were 20 years ago. Millions of people have access to the Internet super highway, and thousands log onto the World Wide Web (www) every minute of every hour, using Twitter, Facebook, America Online, Bing, Yahoo!, YouTube, Zynga, MSN, Google, and probably others that have been invented since I wrote this. Schoolteachers incorporate technology as part of the daily curriculum; they use video clips to enhance math and science lessons. Tables 1.8 and 1.9 reveal show the numbers of households with computer and internet access by family income and race/ethnicity. Unquestionably, technology is a great source of teaching enhancement, but it cannot take the place of real teachers.

Table 1.8. Households with Computer, by Income and Race/Ethnicity

Race/Ethnicity	Under $15,000	$15,000– $35,000	$36,000– $75,000	$76,000 and up
White	27.0%	46.0%	73.0%	90.0%
Black	13.0%	32.0%	62.0%	83.0%
Asian/Pacific Islander	53.0%	57.0%	82.0%	91.0%
Hispanic	18.0%	35.0%	61.0%	82.0%

Note. Information from NTIA and ESA, U.S. Department of Commerce, U.S. Bureau of the Census Current Population Survey supplements (as reported in Kauchak & Eggen, 2005). Numbers are rounded.

Table 1.9. Households with Internet Access by Income and Race/Ethnicity

Race/ethnicity	Under $15,000	$15,000– $35,000	$36,000– $75,000	$76,000 and up
White	21.0%	39.0%	67.0%	86.0%
Black	9.0%	23.0%	55.0%	77.0%
Asian/Pacific Islander	45.0%	52.0%	76.0%	90.0%
Hispanic	13.0%	23.0%	51.0%	76.0%

Note. Information from NTIA and ESA, U.S. Department of Commerce, U.S. Bureau of the Census Current Population Survey supplements (as reported in Kauchak and Eggen, 2005). Numbers are rounded.

Need for More Teachers

So, the question is: Why become a teacher?

The answer is because the quest for new well-trained and well-prepared teachers is so important, and new teachers who are of high quality are a societal necessity to save the American public schools. Otherwise, a large number of American children and youth will not receive the caliber of education they really deserve. Most importantly, the system needs more teachers who have minority backgrounds. African American and Hispanic males are underrepresented as teachers in the system. In other words, the system faces a serious shortage of African American and Hispanic male teachers while the number of male teachers from other ethnic groups is rising slightly. Moreover, nearly 35% of US students are African American children; the lack of male role models in the classroom for these children is appalling. Table 1.10 depicts the ethnicity of teachers in California, and Table 1.11 illustrates the ethnicity of teachers in the U.S.

As Tables 1.10 and 1.11 show, the ethnicities of public school teachers do not reflect the cultural diversity of the student population in California or in the nation. More needs to be done to recruit teachers of diverse cultural backgrounds; otherwise, the disproportionate distribution of American teachers poses a serious concern in educating multicultural and multilingual students in a pluralistic society.

Table 1.10. Ethnic Distribution of Teachers in California

Ethnicity	Number	Percent
American Indian/Alaskan Native	1,865	0.6
Asian	14,230	4.6
Pacific Islander	684	0.2
Filipino	3,677	1.2
Hispanic	44,388	14.5
Black not Hispanic	13,851	4.5
White not Hispanic	221,051	72.1
Multiple or no response	6,902	2.3
Total	306,548	100.0

Note. Information from *Status of the American Public School Teacher, 2005–2006,* by the National Education Association (2010).

Table 1.11. Ethnic Distribution of Teachers in U.S. Public Schools

Ethnicity	Type of School			
	All Schools	Elem.	Secondary	Combined
White non-Hispanic	83.7%	82.1%	84.3%	88.6%
Black non-Hispanic	7.4%	8.4%	7.3%	5.3%
American Indian/Alaska Native	0.6%	0.4%	0.6%	1.3%
Asian	1.4%	1.3%	1.4%	0.7%
Hawaiian/other Pacific Islander	0.2%	0.2%	0.2%	0.2%
Hispanic	6.0%	6.8%	5.5%	3.3%
Multiple race, non-Hispanic	0.7%	0.8%	0.7%	0.6%
Total	100.0%	100.0%	100.0%	100.0%

Note. Information from *Status of the American Public School Teacher, 2005–2006* by the National Education Association (2010).

In 2005, the *Sacramento Bee* newspaper reported that interns who are learning to become teachers overwhelmingly work without the supervision of an experienced teacher in schools that largely serve students of color as shown in Figure 1.4 ("Poor Students," 2005). The article furthered stated that 85% of the interns work in schools where at least 60% of the students are non-White. California's lowest-performing students attend schools with the least prepared and least trained teachers, and educators are concerned about the rapid route into the profession. The fact that interns are overwhelmingly in charge of minority students has raised alarm across the state and perhaps nationwide. The ethnic distributions of public school students in California and the U.S., as well as some of their other characteristics, are compared in Table 1.12.

Table 1.12. Student Characteristics, California and Nation

Characteristic	California	Nation
White	31.9%	58.0%
Black	8.0%	16.9%
Asian/Pacific Islander	11.0%	4.4%
Hispanic	45.2%	19.5%
American Indian/Alaska Native	0.8%	1.2%
Economically disadvantaged	47.9%	36.7%
English language learner	24.9%	7.8%
With disabilities	10.6%	12.8%
Migrant	2.5%	0.6%
LEP students	1.5 million	3.2 million

Note. Data from the National Educational Association (2010) and the California Department of Education (2005–2006). Some numbers are rounded.

Figure 1.4. Where interns work in California.

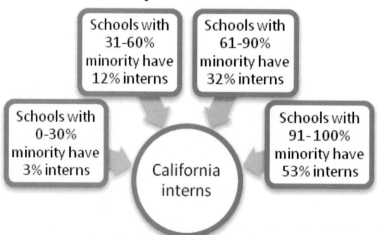

Despite the fact that the current economic downturn has exacerbated the nation's educational system's fiscal difficulties, without a diverse body of schoolteachers the school system is in peril. If thousands of teachers face the possibility of losing their jobs and millions of children are crowded together in classrooms where good academic teaching is nearly impossible, the fact of the matter is: America needs to prepare its children for the future. And that preparation requires teachers more than anything else. Worse than the prospect that in the next several years, when the student-teacher ratio reaches 30:1, classrooms may become unmanageable; student discipline may be chaotic, and instructional practices may be improvised and impoverished, is the concern that the supply of teachers will be scarce if America does not start recruiting, preparing, training, hiring, and retaining highly qualified teachers today. The tough question is: Who will be there for the children and the children's children if fewer and fewer people choose to become teachers today? Perhaps, now is the best time ever to become a teacher.

Coaching and Mentoring

Today, not all student teachers and new teachers receive consistent professional coaching and mentoring. However, not all coaching and mentoring happen the same way. Some coaches and mentors are better than the others, and some coaching and mentoring experiences are better than some others. Moreover, new teachers and student teachers, as protégés, respond to coaching and mentoring differently. Nevertheless, these experiences play a big role in new teachers' professional development and growth.

Coaching and mentoring are different. As Lawson (2007) explained, coaching was designed to help teachers for specific purposes and short-term goals whereas mentoring was developed to help them with long-term goals and broad purposes as shown in Table 1.13. Coaching takes place during the student teaching practicum or the fieldwork experience; mentoring happens during the first 2 years of teaching.

Table 1.13. Comparison of Coaching and Mentoring

Coaching	Mentoring
1. Focus is primarily on how to improve issues at work or specific aspects of the job, like teaching, assessing, disciplining, planning, managing, etc.	2. Emphasis is on long-term career, and any discussion of the current job is put into a wide context of future ambitions, etc.
3. Time frame is typically a fixed period, and once the problem has been resolved or the skills passed on, the contract or training comes to an end.	4. Time frame is the duration of the relationship because targets are more long-term; and there is no specific end to the relationship.
5. Coaching scheduling is based on meetings that are normally and carefully structured at regular intervals.	6. Mentoring scheduling is based on flexibility of goals; issues at stake and meetings are scheduled informally with great scope.
7. Coach's age and experience are not factors. The coach does not have to be an expert or more senior in either age or overall experience.	8. Mentor's age and experience are factors. Mentors are chosen for their expertise and knowledge in a specific field or area, and the mentor is far more experienced than the protégé.
9. Coaching agenda is based on the need to achieve immediate and specific goals; learning objectives are often set by management or the program.	10. The mentoring agenda is loose; the mentee sets the agenda based on needs regarding long-term goals.
11. In practice, coaching is forced upon person to improve performance.	12. In practice, mentoring is voluntary; mentee seeks mentor for guidance, etc.

13. In practice, coaches are paid a stipend, fee, or other compensation.	14. In practice, mentors require no compensation. They act out of goodwill, duty, and gratitude.

There are several types of coaching for student teachers: team coaching, performance coaching, skills coaching, career coaching, management and discipline coaching, professionalism coaching, planning or one-on-one coaching, curriculum development coaching, assessment coaching, and communication of student learning coaching. The coaching process may include emulation, imitation, guided solo, and formal observation. There are also several approaches to mentoring. The Beginning Teaching Support Assessment program, designed to mentor newly hired teachers, is an example of a mentoring program.

Student teachers should take advantage of whatever coaching and mentoring are offered because both provide life-saving information they will need for survival later on. Both coaching and mentoring are essentially for new teachers to help curb duress, distress, pressure, burnout, and teacher turnover during the first few years of teaching. Keep in mind that clinical training for new teachers cannot be effective without proper coaching and mentoring. Many student teachers have been placed in classrooms with little or no coaching or mentoring; most have left their placements with confusion and uncertain practices.

One gray area often lacking direct coaching and mentoring is internship. Thousands of interns are now teaching in the classrooms with little or no prior teaching experience. In most cases, these interns are left to fend for themselves, and many of them learn what they can about teaching the hard way.

To stimulate prospective teachers to think about contemporary challenges to becoming teachers, here are some helpful questions to ponder:

- What really motivates you to become a teacher?
- What inspires you to become a teacher?
- Why do you want to become a teacher?
- What is it like to be a teacher in a multicultural classroom?
- What roles will and should I perform?
- How will my teaching expectations affect my life as a teacher?
- How do I know I am ready to take up all the challenges?
- What grade would I enjoy teaching?

Last, but not least, this nation needs more teachers who specialize in special education. As Table 1.12 illustrates, nearly 13% of students in K–12 grades have some kind of learning disabilities. The number of special education teachers has shrunk substantially over the last 2 decades. Many students with learning disabilities lack quality teachers who can provide them with a meaningful education.

Summing Up

This chapter described the many issues that may affect today's new teachers and their interest in teaching. The number of American teachers in K–12 grades has risen substantially over the last 30 years. However, the number of K–12 students is increasing exponentially, especially the student population of ELLs and students with special needs, and the teacher shortage and teacher turnover have put the nation's educational system at risk. New teacher attrition is costly and is a big factor impacting the current financial health of public schools. Each year approximately $7.3 billion is lost as the result of teacher turnover. On top of that, nearly 46% of public school teachers leave teaching in their first 5 years. This staggering number is now considered a national crisis.

Education experts and policy makers predict that this nation will need hundreds of thousands of new teachers in the next 50 years; otherwise, the distribution of highly qualified teachers across the educational system will remain inequitable. If the current trends continue, students who deserve the best teachers would continue to be taught by underprepared, unskilled, non-credentialed, and un-qualified teachers.

Lastly, to minimize the impact of the negative trends, America needs to grow its own teachers to prepare for the educational firestorm that is coming. At the same time, resources need to be distribut-ed across the educational system to enable teacher preparation programs to recruit prospective stu-dents, train new teachers, and create more teacher induction programs to allow new teachers opportunities to gain clinical experience. The bottom line is: more teachers are needed—high-quality teachers of every ethnic background.

CHAPTER TWO

STUDENT TEACHERS' FIELDWORK EXPERIENCE

Education must bring the practice as nearly as possible to the theory.
Horace Mann

Introduction

In the 1980s salaries in the teaching profession were low; however, teachers were well respected and aspirations to the profession were high. At the same time, many new teachers had difficulty finding jobs in the public school system. As a result, many college graduates who intended to become teachers ended up accepting employment in other professional fields, such as business, sales, government, and civic employment. Then, in the 1990s, the demand for teachers increased as the student population in the nation's educational system increased steadily. Today, despite all the financial problems, there are barely enough teachers in the classrooms, and this nation is facing a serious teacher shortage as teacher turnover rates continue to climb. In California alone, approximately 50,000 substitute teachers enter classrooms every day to take the places of regular teachers who are out for professional and personal reasons. This chapter discusses how today's student teacher practicum prepares and trains new teachers to get ready for teaching in the multicultural classroom setting.

The Fieldwork Experience

In California and elsewhere, teacher preparation programs review eligibility criteria and academic records of potential student teachers for field placements in K–12 classrooms. The real purpose of field placement is to clinically train new teachers by placing them with experienced teachers in real classroom situations.

Placement criteria include, but are not limited to, successful completion of academic coursework, passing of one or more state tests (such as the California Subject Examination Test, the California Basic Education Skills test, and the Reading Instruction Comprehension Assessment), completion of a certain number of K–12 observation hours, teaching experience, passing Task 1 of the Teacher Performance Assessment, and overall academic standing. Student teachers do not have to pass all examinations required for their preliminary credential prior to placement. Each teacher preparation program has its own set of written regulations and policies that help student teachers meet these placement criteria.

In California, under Senate Bill 2042 requirements, teacher preparation programs are required to produce written policies regarding field placement or create a student teaching handbook that contains program information for student teachers, cooperating teachers, and university supervisors. The handbook must include specific, detailed information about student teaching placement, and it generally has basic questions and answers that help student teachers understand placement expectations. For instance, it may describe weekly teaching activities, dress codes, professional ethics, attendance and punctuality policies, formative evaluations, and formal observation.

Getting ready for student teaching placement is a big step with huge responsibilities for all credentialed student teachers because it is a clinical test of their teaching abilities, skills, and knowledge of academic subject matter based on the state's academic standards and mandates. It tests the student teacher in areas such as pedagogical skills, instructional planning, lesson plan design, delivery of instruction, assessing student learning outcomes, making adaptations, classroom management, disciplinary actions, and employment of professional best practices. Planning ahead of time gives the edge of readiness. Great preparation is needed to be ready for student teaching placement. However, the design of most credential programs puts some students at a disadvantage since not all students are finished with their coursework prior to student placement. Quite often, some student teachers are overloaded with concurrent assignments; they may be taking one or two courses along with the student teaching practicum. This heavy workload can overwhelm students with pressure, frustration, anxiety, stress, and health-related issues. Keep in mind that student teaching placement requires 7 to 8 hours of work each day, 5 days a week. In other words, it is a full-time job without pay. On top of that, student teachers may have to participate in some school functions during or after school hours; they may have to attend IEP, English Language Advisory Committee (ELAC), Bilingual Advisory Committee (BAC), student study team (SST), and staff development meetings; participate in parent/teacher conferences; come to back-to-school night and open house; and take part in other curricular activities.

On the other hand, many student teachers are ready and eager for their fieldwork. Usually, ready students plan ahead, finish up all coursework prior to student placement, pass all required examinations on time, attend student teacher orientation, deal with any academic discrepancy, and organize a plan of action. Especially ready students also have a back-up plan in case they encounter unexpected problems or unanticipated situations during student placement. For instance, they make arrangements for babysitting, take care of transportation issues, save enough money for expenses during fieldwork, plan vacation before or after student teaching, and get a support system in place.

In reality, despite how well student teachers prepare, something will always come up during student placement. However, planning ahead enables them to avoid or eliminate some situations. Often, family matters get in the way of student teaching placement halfway through, and familial issues sometimes are difficult to deal with. Therefore, it is imperative for student teachers to organize their personal lives as well as their professional lives in order to alleviate unexpected stress, reduce pressure, and remove obstacles that might come up during fieldwork. Known health conditions should not be considered barriers to the completion of student teacher placement; however, new health issues may arise since student teachers are vulnerable to contracting illnesses from students and colleagues. Each year, a very small number of student teachers do not finish their fieldwork due to medical needs and family issues. Delay is not uncommon. Some students might fail their student teacher placements because of clinical and placement-related factors. Others may prolong their fieldwork with extensions due to financial hardship, employment issues, and personal needs.

In addition, a small number of student teachers who have had teaching experience in the classroom may apply for fieldwork experience credit to substitute for the first half of their placement (Practicum I). If their requests are granted by the program, they are required to do only 7 weeks of student teaching placement, which is the second practicum.

During this clinical trial, the student teacher is under lots of pressure from all directions. The placement process can have many variations; however, the four components illustrated in Figure 2.1 are essential to every placement. Student teachers have to be able to show their willingness and ability to work well and professionally with the three other components. The goal of the process is to help student teachers get trained clinically and professionally. But because teachers are held to high standards in society, it is desirable that student teachers demonstrate their abilities and commitment to the profession and the students as clearly as possible. Otherwise, they and their supervisors are left with the question: "How will they handle a real teaching job if they are struggling with student teacher placement?" All student teachers would do well to keep this question in mind while pondering their student teaching practica.

Figure 2.1. The four essential components of a placement.

As Figure 2.1 shows, if one element is missing, the student teaching placement is incomplete. All four parts are equally important, and each part plays a vital role in placement. Keep in mind that if student teachers should fail their fieldwork for any reason, they can always petition the program for a second or perhaps a third chance to redo it.

The Student Teaching Placement Practica

In California, the student teaching placement is referred to as student teaching Practica I and II. These terms are used interchangeably with the term *fieldwork experience*. Not all student teaching practica are without cost in California or elsewhere. Cooperating teachers receive a very small financial stipend to compensate them for their time and their mentoring. University supervisors receive mileage reimbursement for traveling to visit classrooms. All things considered, student teaching practica are costly but worth the cost.

As mentioned previously, in some programs the first half is Practicum I and the second half is Practicum II. The duration of placement varies, typically ranging from 7 to 16 weeks. Usually it is a semester placement, except for students in integrated programs and school districts' internship programs.

The way the practicum works is that student teachers are assigned to a school site, and they are expected to start the placement 2 weeks prior to the beginning of the academic semester. However, the official schedule is not in effect until the first day of the semester. In other words, some students may be in the field longer than what the program is designed for. In most cases, the placement calendar can be modified or adjusted to fit the total number of weeks required for the program. For instance, some students may finish their placements a little bit earlier or later than the end of the semester, depending on the type of classroom or school in which they are placed—traditional or year-round schedule, private or public school, traditional or charter school. Typically, normal placement might last a total of 18 weeks from the beginning to the end of student teaching. Self-placement is not allowed in most programs, and student teacher candidates cannot solicit schools in their neighborhood in order to have their student teaching placements with classroom teachers they know well. In rare situations, teacher assistants or bilingual instructional aides may be placed with teachers with whom they have been working for a number of years. However, those teachers have to agree to supervise the student teachers as required by program policies and regulations.

Placement also depends on the program's design. Some programs require student teachers to complete two placements at two different grade levels. Today, most programs require a single placement with two different practica with the same cooperating teacher in the same classroom. In other words, student teachers are doing Practicum I and Practicum II together. Each practicum involves coursework with the equivalency of three or five units. As mentioned previously, some students do only 7 weeks placement if their request to have credit for prior fieldwork experience is approved by the program.

Typically, the student teaching practica are based on a predesigned schedule that guides all involved parties throughout the placement process. Under Senate Bill 2042, a basic 16-week placement timeline may have four equal blocks of 4 weeks each as depicted in Figure 2.2. The timeline can be further divided into six distinct phases as outlined in Table 2.1. Each phase has specific activities that help the student teachers perform the tasks that meet placement expectations. The timelines facilitate the process through smooth transitions.

Figure 2.2. Basic 16-week timeline.

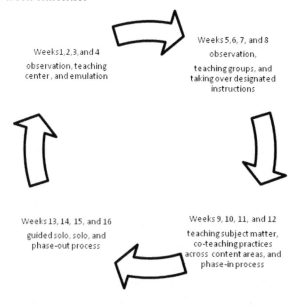

To explain the process a little more thoroughly, detailed information for the first two phases, weeks 1–6, is given below.

- During weeks 1 and 2, the orientation, observation, and beginning of teaching practices are initiated formally. The student teacher, cooperating teacher, and university supervisor meet to go over all paperwork, questions, the placement objectives, and goals. After discussing pre-conference, formal observation, and post conference expectations, the student teacher and the cooperating teacher set a tentative schedule for conducting formal observation at least once per week for the next 14 weeks. During this time, the student teacher needs to take time to observe teaching at different grade levels with different teachers to gain insight into different styles and methods of teaching prior to assuming teaching responsibilities in the placement classroom. It is also crucial for the student teacher and cooperating teacher to spend time together to review the placement expectations and develop an action plan together.

- During weeks 3, 4, 5, and 6, the formal observation begins. The university supervisor observes formal lesson teaching. A formal observation lasts about 20 to 45 minutes, depending on the type of lesson plan used. The main goal during these weeks is to allow the student teacher some teaching responsibilities. For instance, the cooperating teacher might assign the student teacher to teach math or reading to small groups at first and later to a large group or the whole class. The purpose of this practice is to help the student teacher make the transition into teaching. As student teachers assume a regular teaching load, they start to feel the overall pressure of maintaining order in the classroom, but they have the assistance of the cooperating teacher. The student teacher should receive constructive feedback from both the cooperating teacher and the university supervisor.

Table 2.1. Six Phases of Placement Timeline

Timeline	Focus	Typical activities
Weeks 1 and 2	Orientation, observation, beginning of placement, and assuming limited teaching load	Meet with supervisor, set observation schedules, plan a course of action, visit different grade levels, and design five-step lesson plan for formal observations
Weeks 3, 4, 5, and 6	All in weeks 1 and 2, assume regular teaching load, manage students, give group instruction, formal observation, and become responsible for specific content areas	Deliver instruction, design instruction, manage, discipline, direct, use detailed lessons, and do planning. Note: first formal evaluation due
Weeks 7, 8, 9, 10, and 11	All in weeks 1-6, teaching load increases, teach two or three subjects, observation continues, take more control of instruction and class, and teach whole class	Move from one content area to two or three content areas of teaching, increase responsibilities, maintain order in the class, and plan daily instructions Note: second formal evaluation due
Weeks 12 and 13	All in weeks 1–11, start guided solo, teach all subjects, practice classroom management,	Do planning for all subjects, take over class as guided, learn how to implement daily routine

	do lesson planning, assess student learning, monitor progress, and take full control of teaching	and schedule, and focus on taking over full responsibility for all teaching
Weeks 14 and 15	All in weeks 1–13, solo weeks, take over class, provide full instruction, maintain order, manage class at all times, and take charge of class	Take over all instruction and the class—being the classroom teacher. Note: summative assessment due (early)
Week 16	All in weeks 1–15, phase out process, relinquish teaching responsibilities, and plan for termination	End of placement, plan to exit, do observation hours, portfolio, and final check out. Note: summative assessment due

One cautionary note is in order: Most placement problems occur in the earlier part of the term rather than toward the end of student teaching. If difficulties arise, they generally appear in the first several weeks, when the student teachers start assuming a greater portion of the teaching load. In a normal situation, student teachers who are able to pass the first part of student teaching are generally able to complete the second part.

Furthermore, each placement has its own ups and downs, and not all placements at the same grade level at the same school are the same. All student teachers are unique in so many ways, as are all cooperating teachers and university supervisors. Student teachers' personal expectations cannot always be met because what they want to see in the placement may be different from what they learned in college coursework or what they have experienced in life. Their training in student teaching practica could be a real eye opener; they could even experience the opposite of what they had hoped. In addition, their students are likely to be culturally and linguistically diverse. Therefore, student teachers must realize that many factors go into student teaching practica in a multicultural classroom setting; student teaching placement, so-called on-the-job training, could be one of the best or perhaps one of the worst experiences ever.

Ethical Standards of Professional Conduct

As with any other profession, teaching has its own ethical and professional standards of conduct. New teachers are expected to develop themselves professionally prior to entering the classroom. The National Education Association has developed a national Code of Ethics for all teachers, and each teacher preparation program uses its own ethical standards of conduct. For instance, the ethical and professional standards used during student teaching practica require all student teachers to adhere to accepted standards in the areas depicted in Figure 2.3. These fundamental standards of conduct are crucial for professional development and growth in placement. Formative and summative evaluations reflect the teacher's adherence to these standards as well as other pedagogical standards, such as those required for TPE and TPA. For the most part, upholding these standards of conduct in the practica helps prepare new teachers, who will become the next generation of teachers, for the professional career to which they aspire.

Figure 2.3. Basic standards of conduct areas for student teachers.

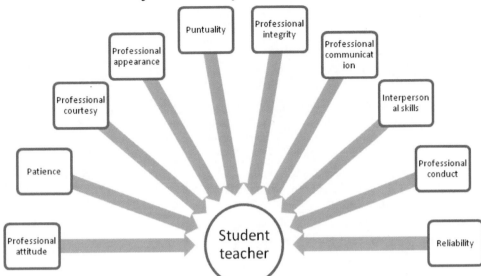

Today's teachers perform multiple roles. Without standards of conduct, teachers may not recognize how important all their roles are and how their actions can influence people's perceptions positively or negatively. As Vang (2010) and Kauchak and Eggen (2005) explained, some of the most important roles teachers play in society are those of caring professional, creator of productive learning environments, ambassador to the public, collaborative colleague, learner and reflective practitioner, role model, facilitator, mentor, educator, protector, guide, and strong advocate for children and their education. So many responsibilities require teachers to be trustworthy, and in order to gain and maintain public trust, teachers need to hold themselves to high standards of conduct.

Lesson Plan Design Formats

Before they are far into their programs, student teachers learn that the main instructional strategy they will be taught throughout the placement is the direct instruction model. However, most teacher preparation programs give student teachers the option to use two lesson plan design formats such as the Five-Step plan and the inductive plan compared in Table 2.2. In practice, there are advantages and disadvantages to each of these formats, depending on the learning objective, content area standards, and pedagogical applications. Student teachers should explore these and other formats for the fitness of their styles and design for each specific learning objective. Keep in mind that learning styles should be considered as well when designing a lesson for diverse learners. Most student teachers understand that direct instruction is not a one-model-fits-all approach to teaching. Teachers' creativity in shaping instruction to the needs of their students, such as utilizing hands-on and minds-on activities, is what makes learning happen.

Student teachers should develop a detailed lesson plan for each lesson taught during fieldwork. The lesson plans can be reviewed by the cooperating teacher or the university supervisor for accuracy and professional quality. For each formal observation, student teachers are required to use a well-designed lesson plan with detailed information that includes state-adopted standards and learning objectives.

Table 2.2. Comparison of Two Lesson Plan Formats

Five-Step Lesson Plan	Basic Activities	Inductive Lesson Plan	Basic Activities
Step one: Anticipatory set, or introduction	Prepare, engage, review, preview, purpose, tapping, learning objective	Step 1: Introduction or anticipatory set	Give directions, procedures, demo, review, preview, engagement
Step two: instruction or gather input	Model, explain, demo, illustrate, examples, samples, questions, answers, directions, guided practice	Step 2: Activity, lesson development, or procedure	Detailed information, monitor, question, answer, feedback, discussion
Step three: Guided practice	Practice, demo, monitor, guide, check for understanding, do exercise, drill, give feedback	Step 3: Wrap-up or debrief	Close, evaluate, assess, question, answer, review, recite, reflect
Step four: Assessment, closure, or evaluation	Recap, review, give more practice, check for understanding, independent practice, worksheet, group work		
Step five: Independent practice	Give more practice, review, apply, assess, test, timing, homework		

Since the two formats illustrated in Table 2.2 lack accommodations, modifications, adaptations, and interventions for students who require special instructions, student teachers should also consider using English Language Development (ELD) and Specifically Designed Academic Instruction in English (SDAIE) lesson plan formats as backup plans. These are compared with the Five-Step direct instruction model in Table 2.3. Keep in mind that English language learners and students with special needs will not benefit from the two lesson plan formats unless other instructional strategies are incorporated and/or integrated with the direct instruction model. Failing to use multiple strategies can leave many students behind.

Table 2.3. Comparison of Five-Step, ELD, and SDAIE Lesson Plan Formats

Component/ structure	Five-Step Lesson Plan	ELD Lesson Plan	SDAIE Lesson Plan
Format	Five steps: 1. Anticipatory set or introduction 2. Instruction, modeling, or presentation 3. Guided practice 4. Closure, evaluation, or assessment 5. Independent practice	Eight steps: 1. Catalyst (introduction or anticipatory set) 2. Written expression 3. Skill development 4. Guided practice 5. Practice reading 6. Extended practice (indep. practice) 7. Independent practice 8. Evaluation	Seven scaffolds: 1. Modeling 2. Bridging 3. Contextualization 4. Schema building (guided practice) 5. Representation of text 6. Metacognitive development 7. Evaluation

Content focus	1. English language arts content- area grade- level standards 2. little variance or modification for diverse language learners 3. English-only instruction	1. ELA/ELD grade- level content-area standards 2. Focus on ELLs' language development—listening, speaking, reading, and writing skills 3. Partial bilingual instruction	1. ELD grade-level content-area standards 2. ELL mastering of grade-level content standards 3. Primary language instruction or partial bilingual instruction
Presentation/ instructional model	1. Basic elements of instruction 2. Orderly progression and presentation 3. Teacher-centered 4. Teacher-directed 5. Scripted instruction 6. One-way instruction	1. Sheltered instruction approach 2. Slow pace 3. Extra practice 4. Allow language development 5. Orderly progression and presentation 6. Teacher- and student-centered instruction 7. Promote vocabulary development and new skills	1. Whole-language approach 2. Concept approach 3. Scaffolding strategies 4. Student-centered activities 5. Sheltered instruction approach 6. Slow pace 7. Primary language support 8. Allow language development

Furthermore, none of these lesson plan formats clearly explains how use of pedagogical strategies such as accommodations, modifications, adaptations, and interventions are implied academically in lesson design. As required for TPE standards and TPA tasks, student teachers must design lessons that include these pedagogical applications to target specific students who may need to have individualized instruction. Prescribing special or individualized instructions is critical. Using multiple instructional strategies imposes a difficult challenge for student teachers because extra time and effort are required and, most importantly, it is impossible to design special instruction for each individual student's needs. To help student teachers understand these pedagogical challenges, Table 2.4 gives examples and clarifications for further consideration when designing lesson plans that include students with special needs or students with difficulties in English.

One cautionary note for student teachers: There does not appear to be much difference between adaptations and interventions; however, in practice, the two can be quite different. An intervention is the use of intensive applications and approaches in individualized instruction. On the other hand, an adaptation is used to provide inclusive instruction to all students simultaneously as well as spontaneously in the classroom setting. In some cases, accommodations and modifications are sufficient approaches; however, they are not exactly the same as adaptations.

Table 2.4. Examples of Applications of Pedagogical Strategies

Lesson plan objective	Accommodations	Modifications	Adaptations	Interventions
Life cycle	Use technology, video clips, animation, picture books, transparencies, overhead projector, etc....	Simplify life cycle, give short directions, step-by-step instruction, modeling, samples, visual aids, regalia, pictures, etc....	Parts-to-whole approach, label each stage, connect pictures to life cycle, hands-on activity, bridging, key terms, chart, organizer, etc....	Think pair/share, small-group activity, extra practice, more time on task, review, reflection, KWL, scaffolding, etc....
Basic math	Assign specific homework, review, problems, overhead projector, independent practice, etc....	Limit number of problems, limit correct answers, model, use examples, practice incorrect problems, etc....	Use study guide, more practice, focus on specific skills or problems, guided practice, use manipulatives, extra time, skill development, etc....	Review, more practice, pair up, use differentiating instruction, process vs. product approach, comprehension, etc....
Reading	Ask questions, use clear and concise directions, put questions on the board, limit problems, peer tutor, partnership, etc....	Slow pace, clear enunciation, adjust the level of difficulty, choice of book, extra time, pair up, use graphic organizer, pictures, etc....	Study guide, focus on specific skills, vocabulary words, realia, transparency, overhead projector, comprehension, reciprocal teaching, details—action, plot, scene, character, etc....	Pair up, word bank, review key concepts, extra time, KWL, organizer, short questions, short answers, etc....
Personal timeline	Pair up, give examples, model, cooperative learning, bilingual books, etc....	Sentence frames, specific details, use outline, bilingual resources, practice, extra time, etc....	Appropriate resources, focus on ability, monitor progress, feedback, extra time, use guide or outline, pair up, etc....	Monitor progress, pair up, sentence frames, focus on specific details, outline, chart, etc....

Some Survival Tips for Student Teachers

Student teaching placement can be a real gamble, and there are win-win situations. For some, the whole thing is a sink-or-swim situation because the student teachers do not know what kind of classroom they are going into. They have no idea who the cooperating teachers will be and who will be assigned as their university supervisors until the day comes. Nonetheless, most placements are very beneficial. Sometimes a placement may seem negative at the beginning but may turn out to be not as bad as it was first thought to be. On some occasions, however, the placement could be very difficult. Personality and attitude conflicts are generally the most serious problems in student teaching placement. If there is no personality click between the student teacher and cooperating teacher, the placement could be just a matter of survival. However, if the two get along well, the placement will be meaningful. In addition to personality conflicts, differences in professional philosophy and teaching styles play a big role in student teaching; however, these differences can be addressed positively. For instance, slight disagreements on disciplinary methods used in the classroom or classroom management skills could be discussed formally and informally.

Any failure in open communication is a huge negative for student teaching placement. Sharing ideas, resources, and the teacher's manual is difficult if there is little or no open communication between the student teacher and the cooperating teacher. Some cooperating teachers may not openly share feedback with the student teacher, and some give little or no mentoring. In such cases, the student teachers are left to fend for themselves while struggling to meet demands from the cooperating teacher and the university supervisor. This is mental torment for those student teachers who are quiet, culturally reserved, and timid or sensitive to criticism. This placement situation is referred to as "don't ask, don't tell." To survive and succeed in their fieldwork, student teachers must understand the triangular relationship of placement, as shown in Figure 2.4, and the great power of a cooperating and communicating team.

Figure 2.4. Triangular relationship of placement.

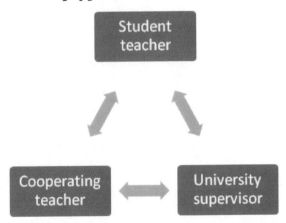

One potential problem area has to with the structures, routines, and procedures in the classroom. In some cases, the placement becomes unproductive as it progresses because the cooperating teacher lacks these fundamental elements needed for a well-functioning classroom. An unproductive classroom makes placement of no benefit to the student teacher, and in practice, that is totally unfair.

Problems could also arise with formative and summative evaluations if any of the three parties—student teacher, cooperating teacher, or university supervisor—is sensitive to discussing evaluation details. Student teachers may be ranked low on some skills because their cooperating teachers have neither demonstrated nor taught them the skills. Sometimes, university supervisors' scoring on formal observation is inconsistent, or detailed information does not support the scoring. Such difficulties should be discussed openly in the preconference and postconference meetings to make sure that future evaluations accurately reflect teaching performance.

Sometimes, things are just plain difficult because of any small animosities or hidden feelings the parties have toward one another. For instance, student teachers are sometimes advised by their cooperating teachers and university supervisors to amend their lesson plan design in different ways, and satisfying both is extremely difficult to do so. In other words, the student teachers are pulled in different directions by two people at the same time. A worst case scenario occurs when the cooperating teacher and the university supervisor join together as a team and criticize the student teacher's teaching skills or performance. When this happens, the placement process is traumatic and the student teacher becomes a victim.

Whether conditions are mostly positive or mostly negative, no placement is perfect. Therefore, student teachers should learn some survival tips for their placements, and, at the same time, they need to anticipate situations that may arise unexpectedly. For example, student teachers will face tremendous pressure if they delay TPA tasks until the last minute. Some common difficulties encountered during student teaching placement are listed in Table 2.5 together with tips for dealing with them.

Table 2.5. Common Difficulties During Placement and Tips for Overcoming

Possible Problems	Tips for Dealing with Problems
Exhaustion, fatigue, tiredness, feeling burned out, lack of energy, unmotivated	Plenty of rest and sleep, multivitamins, exercise, eat healthy food, take time off, plan, organize resources, focus on big things, seek professional assistance
Stress, anxiety, frustration, feeling overwhelmed, pressure, worry	Plan ahead, manage time, be organized, focus on positive, have pride, have self-esteem, find support system, be flexible
Personal needs (clothes, dressing, grooming, appearance)	Be organized, plan, be appropriate, be aware of weather conditions, be aware of classroom environment, situational consideration, choose wisely
Medical conditions, medications, seasonal illnesses, flu, migraine, work-related symptoms	See medical professionals, take medications as directed, take preventive measures, take time off, plenty of rest and sleep, reduce stress
Losing or gaining weight, losing appetite, overeating, listless	Reduce stress, eat well, exercise, take time off, rest, be organized, plan, see professionals, plenty of sleep
Family matters, childcare, death, hospitalization, sickness, accident, finances, separation, divorce	Arrangements, support system, take time off, save, plan, find resources, manage stress, make good decisions, see professionals
Transportation problems, car breaking down, gas money	Public transportation, find reliable car, preventive services, support system, save, bike, plan, ask for accommodations, carpool
Personal injuries, car accident, fall, slip	See professionals, treatment, report, be cautious, use preventive measures, time off, rest, get doctor's note, request help or delay

Pregnancy, parenthood, maternity	See professionals, reduce stress, be cautious, eat well, plenty of rest, plenty of sleep, take medications as directed, appropriate outfits, limit physical activity, take vitamins as directed
Concurrent coursework	Plan ahead, ask for accommodations, be organized, reduce stress, rest, manage time, task oriented, study with friend, share notes
Criticism, feedback, evaluations, low scores, improvement plan	Think constructively, learn to accept criticism positively, ball in whose court, learning is growing, focus on positive things, ask for help, reflect, improve, creativity, differentiating instruction
Unproductive placement, incompatibility, personality issues, attitude problems, cannot get along	Ask for help early, consider changing placement, try not to gamble, be considerate, be adaptable, be flexible, be cordial, be professional, do not react with flight or fight, delay
BCLAD students (Hmong, Spanish, etc....)	Teaching in two-way or dual language instruction, need to identify SN only for TPA tasks 2, 3, and 4.
Observation hours	Do early planning, organize schedules, use prior experiences or fieldwork hours, do during phaseout, strategize a block of time
Portfolio	Plan early, collect all documents needed, organize resources, follow directions and outline, prepare, see samples
TPA Tasks (1, 2, 3, 4)	Plan, organize, strategize, take Task 1 early along with methods courses, take 2 and 3 early, get permission slips early, identify ELs and SN early, starting Task 4 before solo weeks

Keep in mind that student teaching placement is a clinical trial and error process rather than a measure of perfect teaching. There is no such thing as perfect classroom management techniques and skills. There is no perfect one-model-fits-all methodology; no perfect teaching style; no perfect learning style; and no perfect teacher, cooperating teacher, or university supervisor. Also, student teaching placement is not a one-size-fits all situation. There is no best way to clinically train teachers. The process is designed to equip new teachers with up-to-date teaching practices as much as possible in order to get them ready for real classroom teaching. Hopefully, these survival tips will enable student teachers to deal effectively with their cooperating teachers, their university supervisors, and all the students in their classes.

The Cooperative Teacher's Roles

In the student teaching practica, the cooperating teachers play multiple and integral roles, mentoring the student teachers throughout the whole placement, from the beginning all the way to the end of student teaching. In most cases, cooperating teachers are the single most important individuals on the student teaching placement team. Without them, clinically training and preparing new teachers are nearly impossible. Their roles, without doubt, are the most crucial ones. However, not all their responsibilities are written down in the student teaching handbook. Also, their roles vary from program to program. Table 2.6 illustrates the major roles and responsibilities the cooperating teachers assume in order to facilitate the process of student teaching.

Table 2.6. Cooperating Teachers' Roles and Responsibilities

Role	Responsibilities
Mentoring/coaching	Guiding, modeling, meeting, planning, transferring, co-teaching, soloing, phasing in and out, evaluating, supporting, practicing, giving feedback, supervising, assisting, etc....
Evaluation	Completing formative assessments and summative assessment, criticism, feedback, discussion, debriefing, reviewing, editing lesson plan, etc....
Instructional practices	Planning, implementing, evaluating, feedback, designing lesson plan, applying grade-level content area standards, teaching all subjects, assessing student learning, parent/teaching conference, etc....
Classroom management	Modeling, guiding, disciplining, making referrals, contacting parents, modifying, conferencing, etc....
Formative assessments	Ranking, scoring, conferencing, sharing, discussing, giving suggestions, passing TPE standards, etc....
Summative assessment	Checking off TPE standards, passing and meeting standards, discussing, conferencing, recommending, etc....
Co-teaching	Prescribing teaching assignments, observing, taking over instruction, infusing, instilling, guiding, modeling, apprenticing, supervising, etc....
Guided solo	Phasing in process, increasing workload, taking over instruction, managing whole class, teaching all subjects, co-teaching, modeling, etc....
Solo	Giving full teaching workload, planning, instruction, managing, disciplining, following routines and procedures, teaching all subjects, taking over the class, etc....
Phasing out	Assuming full teaching, guiding, transferring workload, working on weak competencies, conferencing, debriefing, terminating, etc....

Keep in mind that these additional roles and responsibilities are added on top of the obligatory workload of the cooperating teachers in their primary teaching positions, and it may be impossible for them to perform every single role and meet every responsibility as required. Cooperating teachers are different in so many ways, such as in regard to classroom design, teaching methods, management skills, instructional practices, and classroom structure and routine. Moreover, student teachers quickly learn that emulation is the key to making their placements smooth since a majority of the time in clinical trial is spend on learning on the cooperating teachers' teaching techniques, skills, styles, management skills, disciplinary philosophies, and professional attributes. In some cases, formative evaluations may not truly and entirely reflect the performance of the student teachers. In other words, the student teaching practicum is 80% teaching emulation and 20% creation.

The University Supervisor's Roles

Similar to cooperating teachers, university supervisors play multiple roles and have critical responsibilities. However, their roles and responsibilities are far less demanding than those of the cooperating teachers. One very important responsibility for fieldwork supervisors is to make sure the student teachers receive appropriate, professional, adequate, and beneficial clinical training in the placement. Table 2.7 presents the major roles and responsibilities for university supervisors. In most cases, the university supervisor acts as the middleman between the student teacher and the cooperating teacher.

Table 2.7. University Supervisors' Roles and Responsibilities

Role	Responsibilities
Initial conference	Arranging initial conference or orientation with both cooperating teacher and student teacher to go over the placement, documents, forms, and formal observation scheduling, etc.…
Formal observation	Setting weekly observation schedule, holding preconference and post-conference for each formal observation, evaluating, debriefing, sharing feedback, discussing, suggesting, etc.…
Intermittent conference	Having formal and informal meetings with both parties to share progress, improvement, changes, or adjustments; answering questions; mediating minor issues, etc.…
Forms and documents	Making sure all forms and documents are completed on time, accurate, turned in, and signed off; explaining; discussing; evaluating; verifying, etc.…
Formative assessments	Collecting two formative assessments, reviewing TPE standards, evaluating, signing off, discussing, debriefing, explaining, etc.…
Summative assessment	Collecting summative forms, reviewing TPE standards, passing, evaluating, signing off, discussing, debriefing, correcting, explaining, etc.…
Preconference	Arranging preconference to review, evaluate, and edit lesson plans, teaching issues, management problems, supporting, assisting, planning, etc.…
Postconference	Arranging postconference to review, debrief, and discuss formal observations, giving feedback, suggesting, explaining, sharing strengths/weaknesses, etc.…
Final conference	Collecting all forms and documents, signing off, reviewing, evaluating, finalizing, terminating, submitting, etc.…

Supervisors are different in style, degree of supervision they provide, and experience. Some supervisors tend to score student teachers lower, and others may score higher; some may prearrange formal observations ahead of time, and others schedule them as needed; some hold pre-conferences prior to the beginning of teaching, and others hold them just before the delivery of instruction; some are detailed evaluators and others are task-oriented evaluators; some require lesson plan design a day or two ahead of time, and others ask for a copy at the time of the observation. These distinctions make a big difference in student teaching.

Regardless of the characteristics of the supervisor, student teachers should always focus on teaching, managing, and disciplining the class. At the same time, they should learn as much as possible from their cooperating teachers and university supervisors. Keep in mind that the input of university supervisors accounts for only a small part of the total placement. Consider, for example, that they observe student teachers once per week for 14 weeks. The total requirement is eight formal observations plus one initial and one final conference. For each formal observation, supervisors are required to hold a preconference and a postconference. All required meetings add up to a total of more than 30. However, university supervisors can fail student teachers.

Ultimate Goal of Student Teaching Placement

The ultimate goal of student teaching placement is for student teachers to earn their preliminary teaching credentials as mandated by state laws. To achieve this goal, student teachers have to successfully pass all apprenticeship objectives required by teaching credential regulations, meet all the requirements of their teacher preparation program, and pass their clinical training. The fieldwork component is usually the last step in achieving the goal of becoming a teacher. Table 2.8 lists the major objectives all student teachers must reach in order to be recommended for a preliminary teaching credential in California.

Table 2.8. Teaching Apprenticeship Objectives

Objective	Performance Measure
Undergraduate coursework	Bachelor's degree (BA or BS)
Credential program coursework	30 plus units, California frameworks and content standards
CBEST	Passing
CSET	Passing
RICA	Passing
Fieldwork experience	Passing clinical training
Teacher performance expectations	Passing all 13 TPE standards
Teacher performance assessment	Passing all four TPA tasks

The fieldwork experience component consists of clinical training in the classroom and the evaluation of performance in meeting teacher performance expectation (TPE) standards and completing teacher performance assessment (TPA) tasks. Table 2.9 shows the standards for each domain of the TPE, and Table 2.10 lists the expectations for the four major task assignments of the TPA.

Table 2.9. Standards for the Domains of the TPE

Domain	Standards
Domain A: Making subject matter comprehensible to students	TPE 1: Specific pedagogical skills for subject matter instruction
Domain B: Assessing student learning	TPE 2: Monitoring student learning during instruction TPE3: Interpretation and use of assessment
Domain C: Engaging and supporting students in learning	TPE 4: Making content accessible TPE 5: Student engagement TPE 6: Developmentally appropriate teaching practices TPE 7: Teaching English learners

Domain D: Planning instruction and designing learning experience for all students	TPE 8: Learning about students TPE 9: Instructional planning
Domain E: Creating and maintaining effective environments for student learning	TPE 10: Instructional time TPE 11: Social environment
Domain F: Developing as a professional educator	TPE 12: Professional, legal, and ethical obligations TPE 13: Professional growth

Table 2.10. Expectations for Tasks of TPA

Task Description	Expectations
Task 1: Subject-specific pedagogy	Using subject-specific pedagogical skills (TPE 1), planning for instruction (TPE 4, 5, 6, 9), planning for assessment (TPE 3), and making adaptations (TPE 4, 6, 7)
Task 2: Designing instruction	Establishing goals and standards (TPE 8, 9), learning about students (TPE 8, 9), planning for instruction (TPE 8, 9), making adaptations (TPE 4, 6, 7), using subject-specific pedagogical skills (TPE 1), and reflection (TPE 13)
Task 3: Assessing learning	Establishing goals and standards (TPE 8, 9), planning for assessment (TPE 3), learning about students (TPE 8, 9), making adaptations (TPE 4, 6, 7), analyzing student learning evidence (TPE 3), and reflection (TPE 13)
Task 4: Culminating teaching experience	Establishing goals and standards (TPE 8, 9), learning about students (TPE 8, 9), describing classroom environment (TPE 10, 11), planning for instruction (TPE 4, 5, 6), making adaptations (TPE 1, 4, 5, 6, 7), using subject-specific pedagogical skills (TPE 1, 4, 5, 6, 7), analyzing evidence of student learning (TPE 2, 3, 13), reflection (TPE 13)

TPE and TPA reinforce each other throughout the clinical training in the classroom. Cooperating teachers and university supervisors use TPE standards to evaluate student teachers' teaching performance in both formative assessments and the summative assessment. TPA tasks are designed to measure student teachers' application of TPE standards by demonstrating their teaching skills and knowledge in written form. One cautionary note: TPA tasks are hectic and time consuming, and student teachers should make plans to complete these tasks at their earliest convenience in a timely manner.

Task 1 is not terribly difficult, but Tasks 2, 3, and 4 require creative thinking and logical planning. For instance, they may require getting permission slips, identifying ELLs and SNs, or planning an especially good lesson for videotaping for Task 4. Student teachers should pay special attention to the following areas while completing Tasks 2, 3, and 4: (a) planning for instruction or instructional activities, (b) adaptations for ELs and SNs, (c) assessment design, (d) learning about students or descriptions of students, and (e) reflection. A large number of the students who fail TPA do so because they are weak or have insufficient information in one of these areas.

Keep in mind that not all student teachers are required to complete TPA tasks. Some students are required only to turn in a professional portfolio binder with a professional vita and a collection of documents detailing their coursework and professional development and trainings. The purpose of a portfolio is to help student teachers get ready for the future, especially for employment.

Planning for the Future

Toward the end of student teaching placement, it is time for student teachers to really think about the next move in their professional careers beyond the clinical experience. Finishing up the student teaching practica is a dream come true and a real hope for better opportunities in life. Education has provided the new teacher with an opportunity for change and growth. However, new teachers must be prepared to compete for a position doing what they have been trained to do. How do they apply for their preliminary credentials? Are they ready to compete for real teaching jobs? How long will it take them to find a job? What steps do they need to take to find a job? To whom should they talk? Where do they find job opportunities? And what jobs can they apply for other than teaching? These are basic questions lingering in their minds as they ponder the limited number of job opportunities available in times of economic distress.

To help student teachers plan for short-term needs, Table 2.11 lists some practical ideas of items to be included in their professional portfolio. The content of the professional portfolio is similar to that of the credential portfolio except that the professional portfolio is a cumulative binder of all documentation, and the credential portfolio is a compilation of employment-related documents in a package ready for submission when applying for a job.

Table 2.11. Content of Professional Portfolio

Item	Purpose/Format
1. Formal letter of introduction	Introduce self, sell self
2. A cover letter	Professional appearance, courtesy, politeness
3. Current resume or curriculum vita	One page or two pages max
4. Letters of recommendation	At least three, but more are better
5. Reference list with emails and telephones	At least three professionals, but more are better
6. Copies of teaching credential and degrees	Use copies first, keep original for later
7. Copies of all academic transcripts	Use copies first, keep original for later
8. Copy of Certificate of Clearance	Use copies
9. Copies of awards, honors, trainings, etc…	Supporting candidacy, make impression
10. Philosophy of education	Your belief about teaching and education, specific, etc.…
11. Professional referrals	Connecting with people through referrals
12. Who you know vs. what you know	Who you know is better, but who knows you is the best.
13. Interview questions	Have a set of interview questions handy; practice!
14. Substitution, clinician, tutorial, etc…	To get one foot in the door, be patient, keep trying, etc.…

15. Online resources, mobility, flexibility	EDJOIN website, surf the web for job openings, keep eyes open, etc....

Despite all the difficult challenges that lie ahead, the next generation of teachers has to aim high, dream big, and be optimistic about the future. To maintain an optimistic realism, consider the following questions:

- What kind of teacher do I want to become?
- What are some of the difficulties in teaching and student learning?
- What are some of the rewards in teaching I should expect?
- What would help me enjoy my profession?
- How will mandates and reform affect my life as a teacher?
- Am I confident in my education foundations?
- Am I ready for the challenges?

Summing Up

This chapter gave student teachers an overview of student teaching placement, also called fieldwork experience or student teaching practica I and II. The particulars of student teaching practica vary across all teacher preparation programs in California and elsewhere. In California, under SB 2042, student teachers have to deal with TPE and TPA requirements in addition to their clinical training in the classroom. These requirements are difficult challenges because of time constraints. Most credential programs are designed to take 1 year or two semesters, and the way classes are scheduled makes it impossible for student teachers to finish all coursework prior to student teaching placement. Many take more than one course concurrently with student teaching. When all things are considered, student teachers are under extreme pressure as they try to fulfill the fieldwork requirements.

For the most part, TPA tasks impose the most difficult challenges because Tasks 2, 3, and 4 require a minimum number of hours for the writing portion for each task, and on top of that, student teachers have to identify ELLs and SNs for each of these tasks. Moreover, they have to have permission slips from every single student in the class in order to produce a 20-minute videotape of a lesson for evaluation. Yet, making adaptations for ELLs and SNs appears to be the weakest competency of new teachers. Most importantly, the clinical training allows student teachers to experience real teaching with real classroom teachers in a multicultural setting. Whether the training is a real eye opener or a somewhat traumatic experience, student teachers appreciate having the opportunity to be trained by real people.

CHAPTER THREE

BUILDING ON EDUCATIONAL FOUNDATIONS

A teacher affects eternity; he can never tell where his influence stops.
Henry Adams

Introduction

Schoolteachers are very special people who provide great benefits to society. Teaching requires innermost altruism, commitment, dedication, passion, patience, and professional conviction. The lives of teachers are complex, as are their responsibilities and duties. Each and every day, teachers plan, deliver instruction, make decisions, and perform multiple roles inside and outside the classroom. Teaching can be a stressful and demanding job; it is not for everyone. However, great teachers find teaching satisfying in so many ways. Great teaching not only lifts students, but it also inspires and guides learners by giving them knowledge and ideals. This chapter describes the many aspects of the teaching profession in order to help new teachers understand the complexities of the foundations of public education and, at the same time, encourage teachers to build on those strong foundations so they become the next generation of great teachers for today's schools.

The Foundations of Education

Most new teachers have limited background knowledge about the foundations of public education. A brief historical overview of the evolution of American public education should be helpful to new teachers. New teachers may wonder how schools are governed, financed, and influenced by government.

This nation's educational system started in the 1600s and continues to evolve even in the present day. Kauchak and Eggen (2005), Ornstein and Levine (2006), and Ryan and Cooper (2001) provide good outlines of the major events in the evolution of education in the United States. Table 3.1 lists some of those events for the first three centuries, showing the European and colonial influence on American education.

The timeline of American education can be divided into four major historical segments: the colonial period (1600s–1775), the early national period (1776–1820), the Common School movement (1821–1865), and the evolution of the American high school (1866–1900s).

In the early 1900s, known in history as the Progressive Era, this nation put strong emphasis on new ideas for reforming public education. As a result, the teacher-centered approach was replaced by approaches that were more student centered. However, this methodology was short lived.

In the mid-1950s, sometimes called the period of the education of cultural minorities, the nation's public education system was transformed by desegregation to allow equal opportunities in public education to all citizens. At the same time, bilingual education came to the forefront, and people demanded academic services for language minority students.

Table 3.1. Chronology of American Education

Year of Influence	Major Events and Reformations
1636	Harvard College established
1642	Massachusetts Compulsory School Law enacted
1688	William and Mary College established
1689	English Act of Toleration enacted
1690	*New England Primer* published
1751	Franklin's Academy established
1762	Rousseau's *Emile* published in France
1780	Sunday Schools established
1789	U.S. Constitution became law with no mention of education
1791	Philadelphia Sunday School Society established
1798	Monitorial School established in England
1802	West Point established
1812	New York Monitorial schools established
1817	New York State superintendent appointed
1818	School for the Deaf established in Boston
1819	Owen's Infant School established
1821	University of Virginia established
1821	First American high school established in Boston
1825	Emma Willard's School for Girls established
1827	*Education of Man* published by Friedrich Froebel
1832	High schools required in Massachusetts
1837	School for the Blind established in New York
1837	Report of Prussian School by Calvin Stowe
1839	Horace Mann became secretary of school board in Massachusetts
1840	First American normal school established in Massachusetts
1846	Compulsory education enacted in Rhode Island
1848	Laboratory science established in college; taught at Harvard and Yale
1849	Education for the retarded established in Boston
1852	General tax law for schools enacted in New York
1855	Attendance law enacted in Massachusetts
1860	German-speaking kindergarten school established in Boston
1861	English kindergarten established in Boston
1862	M.I.T. established
1874	28 American cities require school superintendents
1890	Court found tax support legal for high schools
1893	Negro colleges established in the South
	Special education begun in Rhode Island
1909	Junior high school established in Berkeley, California
1910	Junior college established in Fresno, California
1910	Many high schools established in the U.S.
1913	*Educational Psychology* published by Thorndike
1914	Smith-Lever Act enacted to encourage agriculture
1916	Dewey's *Democracy and Education* published
1917	Smith-Hughes Act enacted to encourage vocational schools

In the early 1900s, known in history as the Progressive Era, this nation put strong emphasis on new ideas for reforming public education. As a result, the teacher-centered approach was replaced by approaches that were more student centered. However, this methodology was short lived.

In the mid-1950s, sometimes called the period of the education of cultural minorities, the nation's public education system was transformed by desegregation to allow equal opportunities in public education to all citizens. At the same time, bilingual education came to the forefront, and people demanded academic services for language minority students.

Since then, in the modern era, this nation's education system has focused on teaching and learning that serve as the principal instruments for national purposes and social change. Leaders at all levels of government became more concerned about public education, and they have been taken a more active role in education policy and reform. For example, government has mandated national academic standards, set national goals, required academic testing programs, and offered financial incentives to boost public education.

During the periods of tribulation, teacher education was not as high quality as it is today. Colonial teachers were often college graduates, but they had little or no professional or clinical training in education. Mastery of elementary subjects and completion of limited coursework were considered adequate for high school teachers because teaching was based on sound knowledge alone. Teachers were not prepared through clinical training in psychology or pedagogical methods of teaching. Early public and private normal schools (teacher training institutes) were low-level academic institutions and provided limited practice in teaching and little coursework in learning philosophies. As a whole, these academies cannot be considered of professional quality according to the modern view.

Educational Philosophies and Theories

American education is deeply rooted in the emphasis on philosophical principles and fundamental theories of past educators and theorists who were mostly from Europe. Their educational philosophies have shaped public education in so many ways, and sometimes it is difficult to decipher what from these philosophies is beneficial and what is not so beneficial to both teachers and students. To help new teachers understand these philosophical roots, Table 3.2 gives an overview of the branches of philosophy, and Table 3.3 shows the traditional schools of philosophy. Without a doubt, these views undergird most educational decisions, policies, and teaching methods in the present day.

Table 3.2. Branches of Philosophy

Branch	Emphases	Main Question	Applications in Education
Axiology	Morality, rightness, ethics, value, beauty, quality, aesthetics	How we react, behave, respond, express, understand, think	Behavior, emotion, character, civility, appreciation, understanding, expression, empathy, feeling
Epistemology	Knowledge, skills, implications, rationale,s application, manipulation, inference, methodology	How we teach, learn, think, use, apply, plan, approach	Teaching styles, learning styles, how to teach, how to learn, approach, strategy, activity, design, modality, schema
Logic	Reasoning, understand-	How we organize,	Order, organization, priority,

	ing, making decisions, retention, analysis, comprehension, application, relating, differentiating, emulation, reconstruction, invention, renovation	analyze, order, structure, develop sequence of events, chart	structure, planning, guiding, showing, modeling, classification, sequence, scaffolding, instillation, infusion, introduction, direction, instruction, presentation
Metaphysics or Ontology	Realness, genuineness, quality, beauty, existence, authenticity, originality, attribute, innateness, unique, difference, core values, honesty, loyalty	How we gain knowledge, perceive, conceptualize, comprehend, understand, imply, interpret	Knowledge, skills, worthiness, values, understanding, difference, realness, originality, authenticity, innate quality, perception, genuineness

Table 3.3. Traditional Schools of Philosophy Related to Education

Traditional Philosophy	Emphases	Focus in Education
Idealism	Ideas, concepts, perceptions, existence, realness, construction, retention, etc....	Teaching and learning focus on ideas, ideological approach, perception, conception, contextualization, bridging, interpretation, analysis
Realism	Realness, existence, creation, originality, authenticity, extrapolation, minds-on, innateness, genuineness, purity	Experimentation, observation, interpretation, inference, prediction, projection, reasoning, criticism, analysis, feeling, touching, tasting
Pragmatism	Practice, experience, trial, hands-on, minds-on, construction	Hands-on, minds-on, practice, rehearsal, trial, exercise, coaching, apprenticeship, supervision, guiding, modeling
Existentialism	Creation, unique, originality, empathy, existence, choice, freedom, formation, nature	Compassion, empathy, feeling, caring, regard, support, unique, respect, learning circle, teamwork, pairing

As Tables 3.2 and 3.3 illustrate, the traditional schools of philosophy and the various branches of philosophy are similar in some ways but distinct in many ways as well. It is hard to say which one is more prominent in today's practices. All still have influence in educational curricula and teaching methods in general. Therefore, new teachers should be familiar with the philosophies of education. Keep in mind that even though this discussion is about philosophies of education, these philosophies are not exclusive to education; they are rooted in larger philosophies of how the world works and what is important. As these philosophies are applied to education, they become educational theories. Theories are focused on specific approaches whereas philosophies describe generally broad approaches. Table 3.4 presents some of the common theories of education.

As Table 3.4 illustrates, the different theories of education share some approaches and have some significant features in common. No one philosophy provides a model that fits all circumstances. The diversity of theories presents challenges in teaching and learning. Table 3.5 presents a brief historical overview of the beliefs expressed by some pioneers in the field who influenced education and whose principles remain significant in today's educational practices.

Table 3.4. Educational Theories

Theory	Emphases	Approaches
Perenialism	Perpetuality, long-lasting, continuity, constancy, enduring, infinity, future orientation	Process, life-long learning, sequence, timing, growth, development, maturity, experience, practice, trial, analysis, discussion, experimentation, hands-on, minds-on, inference
Essentialism	Importance, knowledge, skills, tactics, applications, formula, theory, principle, rule, reasoning, application, implication, core value, originality	Mastery, core values, content knowledge and skills, reading, writing, mathematics, speaking, speech, codes, rules, information, direction, instruction, process, procedure, routine, schedule
Progressivism	Construction, realness, existence, development, process, existence, understanding, comprehension, retention, observation, inference, communication, practice, trial	Study, understanding, application, retention, construction, performance, testing, practice, trial, experience, process, product, critical thinking, technicality
Postmodernism	Control, power, governance, ruling, marginalization, imperialism, oppression, discrimination, segregation, limited opportunity, hegemony, hidden curriculum	Equal opportunity, equality, SES, collaboration, watered-down curriculum, desegregation, improvised, impoverished, at-risk, disabilities, prejudice, racism, discrimination, socio-academics

Table 3.5. Principles of Selected Educational Theorists

Theorist	Year of Impact	Theory	Theoretical Principles
Arnold Gesell	1925	Maturational theory	Personal development has biological basis; bad and good experiences; body types of endomorph, ectomorph, and mesomorph
B.F. Skinner	1974	Behaviorist theory	Environment has role in individual development or behavior modification and programmed learning
Sigmund Freud	1935	Psychoanalytical theory	Behavior disorders, behavioral problems, and psychodynamic models designed for children with special needs
Jean Piaget	1952	Constructivist theory	Based on logico-mathematical knowledge, individualism, or autonomy in learning
Lev Vygotsky	1978	Socio-historical theory	Emphasis on socio-historical context, language and literacy learning, and child's Zone of Proximal Development

Urie Bronfenbrenner	1979	Ecological System theory	Emphasis on the influence of microsystem, mesosystem, exosystem, and macrosystem
Howard Gardner	1983	Multiple Intelligences	Eight types of intelligence: linguistic, logical/mathematical, visual/spatial, musical, bodily/kinesthetic, interpersonal, intrapersonal, and naturalist
John Dewey	1956	Learner's experience or prior knowledge approach	Learner's experience is the starting point of instruction, instead of using rigid and programmed curricula
Jerome Bruner	1966	Knowledge theory	Enactive, iconic, and symbolic modes; also, the spiral curriculum approach
Lawrence Kohlberg	1969	Constructivist theory	Preconventional stage, conventional stage, and postconventional or principled stage

Education Finance and Organization

The intricacy of philosophies and educational theories helped organize and reform the nation's educational system as it forced re-examination of the core values of public education, educational goals, and methods of teaching. From the 1600s to the early 1900s, the organization of American schools was pretty much based on socio-academics. In other words, the poor got poorer schools and the rich got richer schools. This theoretical approach is still in practice today and plays a major role in the funding of public schools through local property taxes, state revenues, and federal funds (Ryan & Cooper, 2001), as shown in Figure 3.1. In the early 1900s, there were over 100,000 school districts; however, consolidation, competition, legal mandates, and financial difficulties have reduced the number of districts substantially.

As of today, there are approximately 14,000 school districts and nearly 100,000 K–12 schools in the U.S. (National Center for Education Statistics, 2010). Table 3.6 shows different ways American schools are organized by grade level. In the modern era, the nation's educational system is critically political when it comes to governance and finance. Undoubtedly education and politics are inseparable. However, the struggle between school leaders and politicians or policy makers to control public education has resulted in a myriad of mandates, requirements, policy changes, and measurement-driven curricula over the last three decades

Table 3.6. Various Organizations of American Schools by Grade Levels

Type of school	Grade levels
Preschool or nursery school	Prekindergarten
Elementary	K, K–1, K–2, K–3, K–4, K–5, K–6, K–8
Middle	5–8, 6–8, 7–8
Junior high	7–8, 7–9, 8–9, 6–8
High school	7–12, 9–12, 10–12,

Note. Information from National Center for Education Statistics (2010).

One way of looking at school governance is to examine a school's leadership. School leaders play a big role in the organization of American schools. Over the last two decades, school leadership has changed dramatically as more female educators have become more involved in public school leadership, assuming greater leadership roles as administrators, principals, and superintendents. Table 3.7 illustrates the gender and ethnic characteristics of today's school leaders.

Figure 3.1. Funding for public schools. (Ryan & Cooper, 2001).

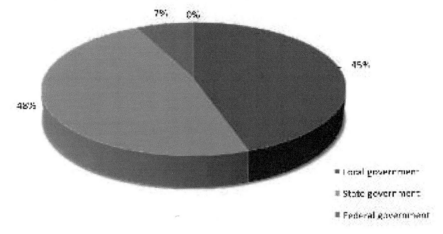

Table 3.7. Genders and Ethnicities of School Leaders

Gender / Ethnicity	Super-intendents	High School Principals	Junior/middle School Principals	Elementary School Principals
Gender:				
Male	89.0%	79.0%	67.0%	45.0%
Female	11.0%	21.0%	33.0%	55.0%
Ethnicity:				
White	96.0%	86.0%	83.0%	81.0%
African American	2.0%	8.0%	10.5%	12.0%
Hispanic	1.0%	3.4%	5.0%	5.0%
Asian	0.0%	0.9%	0.7%	0.7%
Native American	0.7%	1.0%	0.8%	0.7%
Other	0.3%	0.7%	0.0%	0.6%

Note. Information from *Digest of Education Statistics, 2009* (NCES publication 2010–2013) by T. D. Snyder and S. A. Dillow, 2010, Washington, DC: U.S. Department of Education. Numbers are rounded.

Legal and Ethical Standards for the Teaching Profession

Ethical and legal influences on the teaching profession have been important in the evolution of the foundations of public education; these standards have helped bring changes and reforms as leaders have sought to meet public demands for equal protection and fair treatment. Federal laws have been enacted that ensure that all children receive fair and equal opportunities to access schooling regardless of citizenship status.

Education experts believe laws serve two main purposes in education: (a) regulating teachers' responsibilities while protecting their constitutional rights and civil liberties, and (b) responding to past problems in ways that ensure the same problems will not occur again. For instance, the law requires teachers to be licensed by the state, and licensure regulations regulate their teaching rights, privileges, and responsibilities. However, the law cannot clearly instruct teachers how to make their decisions regarding professional practices and academic freedoms. Moreover, the law limits teachers' freedoms in some areas, such as copyrights, political campaigning, use of corporal punishment, and religious indoctrination in the classroom. Just as in other professions, teaching has sensitive issues that require professional decision making and ethical standards of conduct. Figure 3.2 illustrates the three domains of teacher conduct: ethical, legal, and professional. Teachers are held to high standards of conduct because they are influential individuals who can affect children positively or negatively, even changing the lives of learners in so many ways.

Figure 3.2. The three domains of teacher conduct.

Both teachers and students have the basic rights enumerated in the founding documents of this nation: the right to life, liberty, and the pursuit of happiness. These imply other specific rights, such as the individual's right to privacy. However, a teacher's life is subject to controversial interpretations when applying these principles because the law cannot restrict teachers' lives in their free time outside the classroom. For instance, teachers with AIDS or HIV should not be subject to termination of employment or removal from the classroom due to concerns about spreading these diseases to children in their classes. The same is also true in the case of students with AIDS or HIV. Schools cannot exclude these students because of their medical condition or health issues. For teachers, moral standards may apply in the case of notoriety if teachers' private lives and/or activities damage their credibility as role models for the children they teach. When all things are considered, all three domains of teacher conduct are incredibly important.

Federal and state laws provide basic professional guidelines for teachers to help them make professional decisions, and at the same time the laws specify what teachers must and can do legally on the job. Similarly, professional codes of ethics monitor teachers' professional conduct and provide basic guidelines for what teachers should do ethically to become knowledgeable role models, conscientious practitioners, nurturing mentors, and caring professionals. In the United States, the federal government has a powerful influence on public education; however, most of the direct legal mandates, requirements, and responsibilities for training, recruiting, and hiring teachers, and running public schools are the purview of the state and the local school district.

The Teaching Contract

Legally, teachers are protected by collective bargaining laws or unionized labor contractual laws. A teaching contract is a legal document of employment agreement between a licensed teacher and a governing local school board. As required, the contract is signed by both parties and is legally binding; however, the possibility of revocation exists in some districts that allow teachers to breach the contract. Generally, however, it is advisable for new teachers to carefully read the contract's fine print before signing.

Today, the teaching contract is usually offered on a yearly basis. It is a common practice to allow school districts to evaluate teaching performance. The current hiring practice is good for screening purposes but is ineffective in promoting quality teaching because more than a single year is needed to train quality teachers. Generally, teachers need at least 3 years to become proficient in teaching and at least 5 years to master the art of teaching.

Unfortunately, the current method of hiring puts students' learning at risk. Frequent subbing and changing of teachers definitely disrupt student learning and academic progress. However, if the current rate of teacher turnover continues and the teacher shortage grows, more students will wind up with different teachers each day.

The Teacher Interview Process

Even though collective bargaining laws are in place, the practices for hiring new teachers have changed over the last decade because of new federal and state mandates for teachers. For instance, the NCLB Act of 2001 requires all public school teachers to be well trained and well prepared or to be highly qualified teachers. This legislation sent many unqualified teachers back to school for further clinical and academic training at the same time that school districts were battling with tenured teachers who met the requirements only minimally. To make sure new teachers are highly qualified to teach, school districts have changed their hiring practices. Some districts require new teacher candidates to teach an actual lesson to students in class as part of the interview process. Others offer yearly teaching assignments, internship opportunities, and long-term substitution positions. The purpose of these practices is to get to know the person before offering a teaching contract. Without these cautionary practices, hiring and firing are common during teachers' probationary periods.

In this technological age, most information is posted online. This makes hunting for teaching jobs easy, but getting an interview is very difficult because of budget problems and the current economic downturn. Most districts advertise employment opportunities online at sites such as EDJOIN. Application forms and documents can be downloaded and submitted via e-mail. Applicants are selected from a large pool online and screened electronically. Sometimes districts have difficulty finding viable candidates.

However, new teacher candidates must bear in mind some basic guidelines that will enhance their chances of getting a job interview and perhaps make them more marketable when applying for job. Table 3.8 lists several practical ideas besides having a professional portfolio and/or a credential file to help new teachers apply for jobs and prepare for job interviews.

Table 3.8. Suggestions for Becoming Marketable

Filling out Job Application	Preparing for Interview
▪ Answer all questions	▪ Rehearse and practice
▪ Be neat and professional	▪ Come prepared and ready
▪ Be honest	▪ Arrive on time
▪ Be organized	▪ Groom appropriately
▪ Be legible and error free	▪ Dress appropriately and comfortably
▪ Give specific and concrete details	▪ Speak clearly and professionally
▪ Do not give inaccurate information	▪ Use standard English
▪ List reference(s) clearly	▪ Sit calmly, comfortably, and ready
▪ Include electronic portfolio (if required)	▪ Express passion, empathy, desire, caring, and love toward working with children
▪ Include credential file (if required):	▪ Be specific and concrete
☐ Cover letter	▪ Manage your time
☐ Letter of introduction	▪ Be sincere and honest
☐ Resume or vita	▪ Be flexible
☐ Letter of recommendation	▪ Be adaptable
☐ References	▪ Be reliable
☐ Degree(s)	▪ Be a team player
☐ Contact information	▪ Anticipate unexpected questions
☐ Work experience(s):	▪ Be open-minded
✓ List paid and unpaid teaching experience	▪ Be cordial and professional
✓ Be organized and clear	▪ Be assertive but respectful
✓ Include specific duties/responsibilities	▪ Avoid slang, but have sense of humor
Submit on time	▪ Be competitive
	▪ Bring questions
	▪ Be informative/knowledgeable of school data
	▪ Maintain eye contact and shake hands
	▪ Be polite and courteous—say thank you

Keep in mind that a professional portfolio, a complete credential file, an impressive job application, and good references can get an interviewee to the door, but to get the job, the interviewee must demonstrate his or her teaching skills and competencies to the interviewers. Being marketable does not mean employable. Employability is not based solely on clinical training, coursework, resume, references, and academic standing. In today's world, most often time employment is offered because of who you know, not what you know. In other cases, people look for what you know rather than who you know. However, making connections with people through referrals is one of the best ways to land a job. Table 3.9 illustrates how to respond to some commonly asked interview questions to help new teachers prepare for the interview process.

Teacher candidates should be prepared to answer questions asked directly or indirectly. Some questions are straightforward and require firm and straight answers: Please tell us why you want this particular job? Why do you believe you would be the best choice for the job? Other questions are more difficult and are often based on hypothetical situations requiring action under pressure. If the content of the question is unclear, it is appropriate to ask the interviewer to repeat, paraphrase, and/or clarify the question; this will give you a few seconds to prepare your answer mentally. As many experts suggest, effective interviewing depends on four basic principles: practice, preparation, personality, and professionalism.

Table 3.9. Typical Interview Questions

Question	Samples of response
Please tell us a little bit about yourself.	Keep your answer brief. The focus is on your experiences, interests, communication skills, personality, attitudes, and social skills.
What are your strengths and/or weaknesses in teaching, education, management, discipline, student assessment, or planning instruction?	Strengths: Your attributes, personal qualities, strong areas, specialty, creativity, philosophy, traits. Weaknesses: Areas you can improve, make gains, lack experience. Include new requirements, mandates, changes, new challenges, etc.
What do you know about our school? What do you like about this particular job? Why do you want to work here?	Your opportunity to express interest in the job; your experience, skills, expertise, knowledge; your reasons to apply for this job at this place.
Why should we hire you? How would you convince us to hire you? Tell me why I should hire you now?	Your chance to sell yourself quickly. Give your highlights of experience, personal qualities, attributes, interests, availability, vision, goals, philosophy. Tell what you would bring to the job.
What would you do in this situation (cheating, stealing, disciplining, managing, fighting, parents' concerns, complaining, bullying, failing, grading, etc....)	Hypothetical situations are common; there are no right or wrong answers. Be frank and honest, be open to ideas, ask for assistance, take precautions in dealing with new challenges, take appropriate approaches, seek advice, be considerate.

Understanding Teacher Tenure

One area of which new teachers should be aware is tenure. Legally, tenure provides protections for teachers who pass the 2-year probationary period; they cannot be dismissed without cause. Tenure gives teachers job security, safeguarding them from being abused for political and personal reasons. However, even tenured teachers can be dismissed during a reduction in workforce. In other words, school districts can eliminate teaching positions as a result of declining student enrollment, budget cuts, program cancellations, and consolidation of programs or schools. However, getting rid of a tenured teacher is not easy. Even so, some tenured teachers have lost their jobs for reasons such as allegations of child abuse, sexual harassment, child pornography, negligence, causing injuries, leaving students unsupervised, incompetence, insubordination, criminal convictions, unethical behavior, and mishandling school funds. Any of these actions would put teachers on a school's blacklist for years. Blacklists are compiled for issues related to ethical and professional misconduct beyond normal standards. Table 3.10 lists basic due process guidelines for tenured teachers. Newly hired teachers should consult with their union representatives to learn more about teacher tenure and due process.

Table 3.10. Due Process Guidelines for Tenured Teachers

Procedural Protocol	Yes	No
Written notification of charges	✓	
Adequate time for review of all charges	✓	
Adequate time for rebuttal	✓	
Access to evidence, records, and witnesses	✓	
Right to hold hearing with impartial party	✓	
Right to be represented by legal counsel	✓	
Opportunities to refute the charges	✓	
Opportunities to cross-examine witnesses	✓	
Assurance that school board decision is based on hearing and evidence of the charges	✓	
Right to review school board meeting minutes	✓	
Review of transcript and record of meetings	✓	
Right to appeal decision	✓	
14th Amendment protection	✓	
Administrative leave with or without pay	✓	
Termination without conviction of felony charges		✓
Only union members have rights		✓

Professional Liability and Protection

Normally, school is a safe place to work; however, violence sometimes occurs in schools. Teachers are threatened; students are bullied and teased, and drug- and gang-related activities are present inside and outside the classrooms. Bullying has become a national crisis affecting thousands of school children. The school environment is not free of social, behavioral, psychological, emotional, and psychiatric problems. For example, teen pregnancy, suicide, substance abuse, health issues, diseases, poverty, delinquency, and dropout are parts of everyday life. Table 3.11 analyzes the types and incidence of violence and school violence in the U.S. among students in Grades 9–12 reported in 2009.

Table 3.11. Violent Behaviors Among 9th–12th Graders, 2009

Violent Behaviors	Violent Behaviors at School
32% involved in physical fight anywhere ☐ 39% of males ☐ 23% of females ☐ 4% were cyber-bullied	11% involved in physical fight at school ✓ 15% of males ✓ 7% of females
18% carried a weapon anywhere ☐ 27% of males ☐ 7% of females	6% carried weapon to school 8% were threatened or injured with weapon at school
5% did not go to school because felt unsafe	20% bullied on school property ✓ 21% of females ✓ 19% of males
Juvenile arrests ☐ 1,280 for murder ☐ 3,340 for forcible rape	23% offered, sold, or given illegal drugs by someone on school grounds

☐   56,000 for aggravated assault

Fewer than 1% of homicides and suicides occurred on school grounds
- 109 separate incidents
- 116 students killed
- 65% gunshot wounds
- 27% stabbing and cutting
- 12% beating

10% of city teachers threatened
6% of suburban teachers threatened
5% of rural teachers threatened

Note. Information from Centers for Disease Control and Prevention, 2008, 2010a, 2010b.

Teachers are legally liable and responsible for the social welfare of all students at all times during school hours. They act *in loco parentis*, in the place of parents. Teachers are responsible for supervising and safeguarding children from harm while they are under their supervision. Although parents trust teachers and school personnel to provide protection for their children, injuries still occur. The failure of teachers or school staff to protect children from harm or injury is considered negligence. Over the years, parents have brought lawsuits against teachers and school districts for alleged abuse, negligence, injury, and unequal access to quality schooling.

Students' Privacy Rights

One area regarding rights of which new teachers should be aware is religion. Everyone has a right to his or her religious beliefs. Today, teaching about different religions is controversial, and advocating for a particular religion is prohibited by federal statutes. Prayer is not allowed in school.

Students' freedom of speech is a gray area; one person's expression may inhibit the rights of another, and freedom of speech is therefore limited by law. However, schools recognize that students have freedom of speech in a process in which their individual freedoms do not impinge on the rights of others. Expressing oneself, exchanging thoughts, and debating are time-honored ideals in our democracy.

Similarly, what constitutes permissible search and seizure based on probable cause remains obscure and, in most cases, controversial. Nevertheless, the courts have upheld the legality of metal detectors at school entrances as a nonintrusive form of permissible search and seizure.

The bottom line is that the right to privacy is not crystal clear and well defined in all cases. Each situation is unique; therefore, new teachers have to think carefully when dealing with the confidentiality of students' academic records and medical needs. These are super-sensitive areas, and private information is sometimes shared without proper authorization. New teachers also need to consider using a democratic process in order to respect the rights of all students. For instance, the practice of exchanging papers and having students grade one another's assignments may be considered an invasion of privacy.

Students also have rights in disciplinary actions. A suspension of more than 10 days and any expulsion require due process to keep from violating the rights of students and their parents. Schools have to implement basic procedural guidelines such as those listed in Table 3.12.

Keep in mind that minor suspensions, often handled as internal affairs, may not require these procedures and that schools have full authority to discipline students and all parties involved seems fitting. For any suspensions or expulsions, parents must be informed and notified properly and in a timely manner.

Table 3.12. Procedural Guidelines for Handling Suspensions and Expulsions

Procedures
✓ Written notice to student and parents
✓ List of specific charges or alleged incidents
✓ Place, date, and time of hearing
✓ Hearing held by impartial party
✓ Procedural protocol and process
✓ Access to records and witnesses
✓ Right to legal counsel
✓ Cross-examining witnesses
✓ Submit evidence to counter charges
✓ Access to written documents, transcripts, or tape recordings of all proceedings
✓ Access to findings and recommendations
✓ Right to appeal

Child Abuse Laws

According to state licensure regulations, schoolteachers are mandatory reporters when they have a reasonable suspicion of child abuse. The terms *child abuse* and *child endangerment* are used interchangeably. If teachers fail to report, the state can revoke the teacher's credentials, and the school district may have reasonable cause to terminate employment. Hundreds of thousands of children are abused each year. Some suffer lifelong injuries and physical trauma. Each state has its own set of laws to deal with child abuse. In California, Welfare Institute Code (WIC) 300 covers criminal charges against child abusers. Table 3.13 lists the possible evidences associated with typical child abuse allegations that would arouse reasonable suspicion. Keep in mind that injuries such as bruises, welts, lacerations, broken bones, internal injuries, and shaken baby syndrome are not always visible to the naked eye. However, teachers should not examine the child's body for injuries at any time. Such an examination would be considered intrusive and perhaps constitute a violation of the child's right to privacy. Only medical professionals are allowed to unclothe children to examine them for any injuries under the clothes.

Table 3.13. Possible Evidences of Child Abuse Under WIC 300

Type of Abuse	Evidences Constituting Reasonable Suspicion
Sexual abuse	Depression, withdrawn, act strange, genital pain or swelling, venereal disease, painful urination, hysteria, display unusual sexual behaviors, teen pregnancy, bleeding, discharge, secretion,
Physical abuse	Bruises, welts, swellings, bald spots, bite marks, fractures, pinch marks, hand print impression, broken bones, internal injuries, black eye, torn clothes, burn marks, lacerations, abrasions, gash marks
General neglect	Hungry, unkempt clothing, body odors, chronic head lice, filthy house,

	animal feces, lacking clothes or school supplies, no heat, no air conditioning
Severe neglect	Malnutrition, child abandonment, infection, diseases, sickness, burning, unsanitized home, infested environment, poison, overdose, chaining, seclusion, isolation
Medical neglect	Refuse surgery, refuse treatments, refuse to monitor medicine, refuse to take child to the doctor for checkup, refuse to deal with health issues
Emotional abuse	Withdrawn, speech disorder, substance abuse, conduct disorder, sleep disorder, antisocial, destructive, delinquent, sad, distraught, lonely, low-self esteem, poor appetite
Psychological abuse	Nightmare, paranoia, delusion, psychosis, sleeping problems, depression, despondence, antisocial, destructive, delinquent, nervous habit, rocking, biting, sucking, substance abuse, health issues

With any child abuse report or referral, the teacher has to fill out an abuse history form. Teachers can remain anonymous; however, because teachers are mandatory reporters, it is professionally appropriate for them to provide their name and contact information. If a teacher makes a false report or falsifies allegations, liability issues may emerge. Barring such falsehoods, mandatory reporters are protected by state laws and are legally immune from liability. Because custody battles are common, teachers need to be aware of family court orders. In most cases, schools require that copies of court orders be kept in the main office. As required by law, teachers must act in good faith and without malice to protect all children in their care.

Keep in mind that teachers can be abusers themselves; some have been caught abusing children on the job, especially sexually. Many teachers also have been wrongfully accused; however, some teachers have been convicted of sexual molestation for having sexual relationships with their students. Therefore education experts recommend that teachers do not touch their students, and that is the bottom line. Any physical contact, such as hugging, tapping, touching, and patting, should be limited and professionally appropriate; otherwise, teachers walk a very thin line. Talks or conferences with students during recess, during prep time, after school, and at lunch time should be engaged in only with extreme care. Perhaps the door could be left open or a third person could be present nearby. If teachers need to deal with individual students regarding confidential issues, they should do so in a formalized process, such as a conference with other teachers, parents, administrators, or school staff. If teachers are accused of child abuse, they have the right to seek legal counsel through their local union. Accused teachers may also retain private legal counsel if they have the desire and financial means to do so.

Children's protective social workers have full responsibility to investigate any child abuse allegations. They can talk to the child alone without teachers, administrators, parents, police, or legal guardians. The law allows children to have complete privacy while talking with social workers about any alleged abuse. If allegations appear founded, the children who have been abused will be removed from their parents temporarily. A protective hold (WIC 300) will be placed on the children by a law enforcement officer. The officer will notify the legal guardian of the child. School administrators and teachers may have to explain the situation to the legal guardian following the removal of the child.

Mandatory reporters can follow up on reported cases to find out more about the status of the case; however, disclosure of information is illegal and only limited information will be given to the reporters. Keep in mind that it is not the teacher's job to determine if abuse really happened; that is the responsibility of the children's social workers and law enforcement officers. Some cautionary notes for teachers:

1. Any child under the age of 5 is considered at high risk for abuse.
2. Homelessness alone is not an abuse issue.
3. Failure to meet minimum standards of living is not an abuse issue.
4. Custody issues are not abuse issues.
5. Teen girlfriend/boyfriend conflicts are not abuse issues.

Bilingual Education Programs

In California today, new teachers are licensed by the state with Cross-cultural Language Academic Development (CLAD) or Bilingual Cross-cultural Language Academic Development (BCLAD) credentials. Other states may have similar licensure requirements for new teachers. In the past, California issued three main types of preliminary teaching credentials: regular credential, CLAD credential, and BCLAD credential. The regular credential is designated for monolingual teachers whose practice is English-only instruction. The CLAD credential is given to monolingual and bilingual teachers who have been trained in bilingual and/or dual language instruction across the content area standards. The BCLAD credential is designated for teachers who are bilingual in a primary language such as Hmong, Lao, Vietnamese, Portuguese, Russian, German, Spanish, etc. A BCLAD credential is appropriate at K-6 grade levels for teaching that uses primary language support in instruction, such as ELD, SDAIE, dual language instruction, and two-way immersion programs.

Bilingual education programs are still popular in practice, but very few schools offer two-way immersion and dual language instruction with strong emphasis in primary language to LEP and ELL students. To help new teachers familiarize themselves with different bilingual program models, Table 3.14 presents the characteristics of various approaches to providing academic services to LEP students.

Table 3.14. Bilingual Education Program Models

Model	Goal	Possible Outcome	Target	Socialization Process
Transitional	Achieve English proficiency (L2)	Subtractive bilingualism—losing L1	Language-minority students of diverse backgrounds	Assimilationist approach
Maintenance	Achieve bilingualism and biliteracy (L2 and L1)	Additive bilingualism—L2 and L1	Language-minority students of diverse backgrounds and mainstream students	Pluralist approach
Enrichment, or two-way immersion	Achieve bilingualism and biliteracy (L2 and L1)	Additive bilingualism—L2 and L1	Language-minority students of diverse backgrounds and mainstream students	Pluralistic approach, but L1 may not be available

Enrichment immersion	Achieve bilingualism and biliteracy (L2 and L1)	Additive bilingualism—L2 and L1	Language-minority students of diverse backgrounds and mainstream students	Pluralistic approach, but L1 may not be available
Two-way immersion	Achieve bilingualism and biliteracy (L2 and L1)	Additive bilingualism— L2 and L1	Language-minority students of diverse backgrounds and mainstream students	Pluralistic approach, but L1 may not be available
English immersion, or saturation	Achieve English proficiency (L2)	Subtractive bilingualism—losing L1	Language-minority students of diverse backgrounds	Assimilationist approach

Note. Information from *The Foundations of Dual Language Instruction* (3rd ed.), by Lessow-Hurley, 2000, New York: Addison Wesley Longman.

New teachers should bear in mind that the academic goal of these programs is to help ELLs become proficient in English, not to become fluent in their primary language (L1). Each model has advantages and disadvantages, and careful consideration must always be given when implementing these program models. Consider, for example, that the additive or subtractive bilingualism of these models may have direct impact on the academics of LEP students. So far, transitional bilingual education (TBE) appears to be the only model that promotes proficiency in English.

A New Wave of Teachers

Building on education foundations helps new teachers grow and glow at the same time. Keep in mind that politics and education are inseparable. All levels of government take an active role in controlling, influencing, and reforming public education. The status quo is not perfect, but it is far better today than 60 years ago when public education was separate but unequal. Today, public schools provide equal opportunities to all children based on the assumption of desegregation; however, in practice, a hegemonic ideology is well established, and *de facto* segregation takes place each and every day in the classroom. In other words, all children have equal access to schooling, but not all children have equal access to a quality education. This nation needs more teachers and, most importantly, must recruit and hire teachers of all cultural backgrounds. The socioeconomic characteristics of teachers do not reflect the diversity of the student population.

New teachers should define themselves as professionals who are becoming the next generation of great teachers. They may ask themselves this question: What kind of teacher do I want to become? Teaching is a complex endeavor and new teachers must be willing to face all the possible challenges and overcome obstacles along the way in order to achieve successes. New teachers need to be knowledgeable, skillful, well trained, well prepared, and aware of laws because Americans are litigious people. They must build on America's education foundations and utilize current best professional practices. They need to think about how people convey U.S. ideals and values through the employment of hidden curricular activities to the children of different cultures and traditions.

The new wave of teachers will be slightly different from the existing teaching force. As Kauchak and Eggen (2005) reported, the majority of US public schoolteachers are White (87%) and a much smaller percentage of teachers are African American (8%) and Hispanic (4%). The number of teachers of other ethnic minorities is declining. Interestingly, the ethnic distribution of the student population is doing exactly the opposite. Darling-Hammond (1996) pointed out that the percentage of students of non-European backgrounds is reaching 90% in many large urban areas. To illustrate to importance of recruiting teachers of diverse cultural backgrounds to proportionately reflect the cultural diversity of the student population, Table 3.15 gives the characteristics of new and existing teachers in the workforce (Kauchak and Eggen, 2005; Darling-Hammond and Sclan, 1996). Table 3.16 shows the race and ethnicity of teachers in Grades K–12.

Table 3.15. Comparison of New and Existing Teachers

New Teachers	Teachers Currently in the Force
79% female	74% female
91% White	87% White
Average age: 28 years	Average age: 43 years

Table 3.16. Race/Ethnicity of K–12 Teachers (Percent)

Type of School	White	Black	Amer. Indian	Asian	Pacific Island	Hispanic	Multiple race	Minority
Elem.	82.1	8.4	0.4	1.3	0.2	6.8	0.8	17.9
Second.	84.3	7.3	0.6	1.4	0.2	5.5	0.7	15.7
Combined	88.6	5.3	1.3	0.7	0.2	3.3	0.6	11.4

Note. Information from *Digest of Education Statistics, 2009* (NCES publication 2010–2013) by T. D. Snyder and S. A. Dillow, 2010, Washington, DC: U.S. Department of Education.

In California, the TPE standards and TPA tasks should give newly trained teachers the tools they need to become teaching professionals. Making adaptations for ELL and SN students is challenging; however, without adaptations many students of diverse backgrounds would be left to fend for themselves in the classroom. As Ovando, Combs, and Collier (2006) warned, English instruction could be the silent killer of minority students in the English classroom. For new teachers, the bottom line is: The language of instruction does not matter, but the quality of instruction does.

The new wave of teachers should be prepared to enter the classroom ready to carry out what they believe teaching and learning are all about. To provoke their thoughts about their readiness, here are some questions for new teachers:

- How do the law, ethics, and professionalism influence my teaching?
- Am I clear about my rights, responsibilities, and roles?
- Do students have rights and responsibilities?
- How do I hold students academically accountable for their learning?

- Am I comfortable with teaching all students?
- How will I manage student behaviors?

Summing Up

This chapter presented a comprehensive overview of educational foundations to provide new teachers with a broad base of knowledge so they can understand the history of public education. The rich content of this chapter also helps new teachers understand how schools are governed, financed, and influenced by state and federal government. The teaching profession is like a scaffold or stepping stones. The triangular power domains of ethics, professionalism, and legality play pivotal roles in guiding teachers to become conscientious, responsible, ethical, and caring role models and professionals. Their role as professional educators is to teach children to become productive and responsible citizens.

The laws specify teachers' rights and responsibilities. State licenses give teachers the right and privilege to educate children. The teaching contract authorizes teachers to teach academic subjects and specifies the legal requirements school districts lay down for employment. Academic freedom is protected by the U.S. Constitution. As in any profession, teachers are not immune from liability. Acting *in loco parentis*, teachers are held accountable for their actions and behaviors. Laws pose difficult challenges for teachers, but they are necessary to protect the welfare of the students under their charge.

The teaching profession is a complex endeavor and requires professional tenacity. Students have a number of rights that are protected by the U.S. Constitution; these may pose instructional challenges to teachers. Mention of religion in the public school system is still controversial. Teachers' private lives are subject to public scrutiny. That is why building on educational foundations is so important.

PART II.

THE CLASSROOM MANAGEMENT
AND DISCIPLINE DOMAIN

CHAPTER FOUR

APPROACHES TO CLASSROOM MANAGEMENT

It's not what the teacher does that's important; it's what the teacher gets the children to do.
Phil Schlecty

Introduction

The beauty of teaching is in the creative art of teachers. The more teachers learn about using teaching tools, the more competent they become. Classroom management works in a similar way. The more teachers practice applying managerial skills, the more effective they become. Classroom management is a great challenge for new teachers for many reasons. Teachers cannot do what parents can do at home to gain and maintain control of a group of children. When it comes to management and discipline, children at home are really quite different from students in the classroom. Teachers must learn to develop the right approaches in applying academic management and discipline techniques in order to modify student behaviors. This chapter presents the basic principles of classroom management to provide new teachers with a broad overview of some of the managerial challenges they will encounter each and every day in the classroom.

What Is Classroom Management?

It all depends on one's philosophy of management and discipline. Each teacher defines classroom management differently and uniquely. Also, one's life experience, educational background, cultural awareness, and teaching experience predetermine how one approaches classroom management and student discipline in general.

Successful teachers are effective managers. Well-organized teachers are better managers. The scope of classroom management is broad because management is necessary in many different areas, all mixed together: teaching, learning, instruction, activities, assessment, planning, resources, and lesson plan design. Various education experts define classroom management differently; however, most agree on one fact: without good classroom management, teaching is practically impossible. So, instead of trying to define what classroom management is, let's find out what elements are part of the management of the teaching and learning processes.

Classroom management is an ongoing process that involves ongoing curricular activities established by the teacher to facilitate effective and efficient teaching and learning in a formalized setting that requires quality instruction, positive social interactions, active engagement, academic learning stimulation, construction of knowledge and skills, and dissemination of information through formal transference. As Kauchak and Eggen (2005) explained, classroom management is the process of creating and maintaining orderly classrooms. Similarly, Ryan and Cooper (2001) defined classroom management as a set of teacher behaviors that creates and maintains conditions in the classroom that permit instruction to take place efficiently and effectively. Figure 4.1 displays the many components of classroom management.

Figure 4.1. Scope of classroom management.

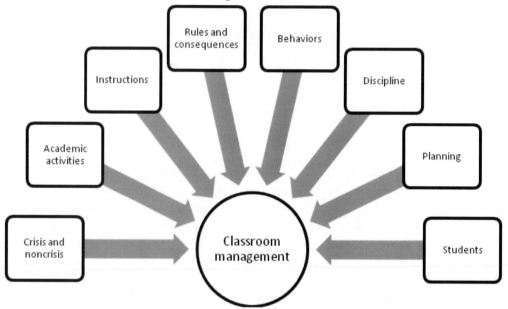

In practice, classroom management is complex in nature and could mean different things to different teachers. Basically, however, it is simply maintaining order so that effective and efficient teaching and learning takes place in the classroom. Sufficient order must be present for students to follow the teacher's directions to engage in learning what is presented to them in class. Maintaining order means eliciting compliance, respect, and subordination from students. Maintaining order in the classroom means establishing rules and discipline.

What teachers do in class is not as important as what the teachers train their students to do. Good classroom management occurs when teachers have trained the students to act properly in the learning circle. Classroom management is less about what the teachers do and more about how the teachers get the children to perform academically.

Purposes of Classroom Management

Classroom management is necessary for a number of reasons. Manning and Bucher (2007) observed that various forms of classroom management practices serve a variety of purposes. They include:

> …strategies to assure physical and psychological safety in the classroom…techniques for changing student misbehaviors and for teaching self-discipline…methods to assure an orderly progression of events during the school day…and instructional techniques that contribute to students' positive behaviors. (p. 282)

To help teachers understand the purposes of classroom management strategies and techniques, Table 4.1 lists some of the broad objectives and specific goals of teaching tht require order in the classroom. Without rules, order, and discipline, students are not effective in performing expected academic tasks, and teachers therefore cannot achieve their teaching objectives and goals.

Table 4.1. Selected Teaching Objectives and Goals

Teaching Objective	Teaching Goals
Delivery of instruction	Rules, procedures, managing, directing, reinforcing, behaving, reacting, sharing, understanding, comprehension, retention
Instructional activities	Student involvement, grouping, cooperative learning, learning tasks, managing, engagement
Group cooperation	Responsibilities, order, rules, benefits, community, sharing, willingness, exchanging
Learning expectations	Concepts, skills, ideas, retention, comprehension, application, construction
Testing, assessment, or evaluation	Learning, retention, construction, application

Furthermore, Burden (2003) and Burden and Byrd (2003) listed eight steps teachers can take to achieve effective classroom management:

1. Select a philosophical model.
2. Organize the physical environment.
3. Manage student behaviors.
4. Create respectful collaboration and interaction.
5. Establish a supportive learning environment.
6. Manage and facilitate instruction.
7. Promote health and safety.
8. Interact with people to achieve classroom management objectives.

Both Burden (2003) and Burden and Byrd (2003) suggested that theoretical models work better and are more useful than philosophical models because theoretical frames have narrow applications for analyzing, managing, and understanding student and teacher behaviors.

The goal of classroom management is to achieve effective teaching and learning in the classroom. To reach this goal, teachers have to establish a positive learning environment in which students feel accepted, safe, loved, supported, respected, included, protected, cared for, and valued. Such an environment cannot be created overnight. Teachers need to plan and prepare well.

Classroom Management Preparations

To prepare a classroom conducive to learning, teachers need to carefully craft a plan of action to deal with a variety of management issues; otherwise, attempts at teaching could be disorderly. Classroom management requires a systematic approach and strategies that are flexible and adaptable. Consider, for example, creating a check list of items you may need to consider as basic procedures for your specific grade level. Table 4.2 list, some basic procedures teachers may find handy and practical in preparing for classroom management. Keep in mind that each grade level requires its own procedures, and the procedural activities need to be rehearsed with students until they are thoroughly familiar with them.

Bear in mind that children need to be trained on these procedures in order for them to comply with your classroom management expectations. Making management preparations takes diligent leadership and persistent effort. Burden and Byrd (2003) suggested that teachers pay special attention to these areas: (a) the school environment; (b) gathering support materials; (c) organizing materials; (d) classroom procedures; (e) classroom helpers; (f) class lists and rosters; (g) home/school communication; (h) birthdays and other celebrations; (i) distributing textbooks; (j) room identification; (k) room arrangement; (l) seat selection and arrangement; (m) room decoration; (n) size of room; and (o) display of animals, plants, and other fossils. The goal of these preparations is to make sure the environment is conducive to all learning activities.

Table 4.2. Selected Basic Procedures for Classroom Management

Procedure	Possible Procedural Activities
Beginning of class/opening procedures	Roll call, absentees, tardy students, academic warm-up routines, behaviors, distributing materials, adjustment
Line up	Going out, coming in, outside the door, on the playground, going to assembly, dismissal
Room/school areas	Shared areas, teacher's desk, water fountain, bathroom, student desks, learning center stations, playground, lunchroom/cafeteria
Setting up independent work areas	Defining work alone, identifying problems, resources, solutions, scheduling, checkpoints
Instructional activities	Contact between teacher and students, student movement, signals for attention, signals for teacher, initiatives, participation, group rotation, passing materials, behavior in group, behavior outside group, academic engaged time
Ending class	Putting things away, clean up, backpacks, homework, clothes, personal items, dismissing class
Interruptions	Rules, orders, conduct, delays, talk among students, out-of-seat policies, pencil sharpening
Work requirements	Heading papers, pencil or pen, neatness, legibility, incomplete work, late work, missed work, due dates, make-up work, supplies, coloring, drawing, cursive, manuscript
Communicating assignments	Posting, orally giving, turning, returning, homework, provision for absentees, incomplete work, collecting
Monitoring student work	Independent work, group work, presentation, completion in class, completion of homework, progress, challenges, difficulties
Checking assignments in class	Exchange papers, go over answers, grading papers, turning work, collecting work, correction, practicing
Grading procedures	Assigning report grades, recording grades, extra credit work, grading criteria, grade contracts, record keeping
Academic feedback	Reward system, incentives, reinforcers, posting work, informing parents, record keeping, feedback on papers, progress, improvement
In case of an emergency	Fire drills, health and safety, lockdown, poison, injury, choking, fire, flood, tornado, rain

Philosophical Approaches to Instructional Preparations

Believe it or not, ineffective classroom management contributes to poor academic performance. Management problems are a major cause of job-related stress, fear, consternation, and dissatisfaction for new teachers. Generally, teacher behavior is the single most important factor in determining the psycho-social environment of the classroom. And teacher behavior is inextricably associated with the teacher's teaching style and philosophical approach to designing instructional practices. Each teacher is unique when it comes to dealing with management and discipline problems. Figure 4.2 illustrates the basic teaching styles teachers use in today's classrooms (Cummins, 1981; Vang, 2010).

Figure 4.2. Four basic teaching styles.

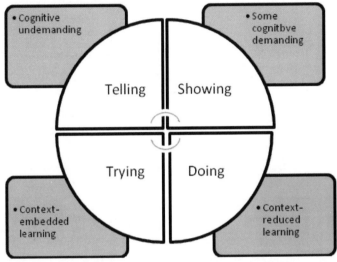

Note. Information from *An Educational Psychology of Methods in Multicultural Education* by C. T. Vang, 2010, New York: Peter Lang.

The appropriateness of teaching style depends on the grade level, and no teaching style is perfect for all or any grade. As Figure 4.2 suggests, a combination of teaching styles gives teachers the best flexibility. Teaching style plays a major role in how teachers handle management and discipline problems. Sometimes the teaching style itself contributes to student misbehaviors in the classroom. For instance, teaching that is too boring, too difficult, too easy, too fragmented, or that does not engage students academically may encourage students to respond inappropriately (Kounin, 1970). Moreover, today's teaching styles are usually more teacher centered than student centered. This style often triggers disruptions and misbehaviors. In practice, a sensible approach is needed. Education experts suggest that teachers use a collaborative approach to be certain that teaching results in learning. Otherwise, teaching is a one-way street.

The philosophical approaches to tackling classroom management and discipline problems are based on the teacher's life experience, educational background, psycho-social integrity or feeling, professional readiness and preparation, and tolerance or intolerance toward student misbehaviors. These factors affect the way individual teachers approach discipline and maintain order in the classroom. For example, a teacher who uses an inflexible form of management to discipline students in Grades K–2 is likely to have a chaotic classroom because young children need a more flexible management style that allows them to adjust their behaviors as they learn. Also, an inflexible, rigid teaching style requires the teacher to spend a lot of time disciplining and managing students, and the teacher therefore has less time for teaching and academic engagement. The majority of students, especially young students, do not learn by listening but by doing. Table 4.3 shows that different types of activity have different levels of student engagement.

Table 4.3. Engagement Level by Activity Type

Activity Type	Engagement Level	Examples of Tasks
Minds-on activities with concrete materials	High	Writing or jotting down thoughts and reflections in journal after conducting an experiment
Hands-on activities with concrete materials	High	Doing firsthand experience, observing an experiment, or conducting an investigation in a group
Visiting school garden	High	Observing different plants or vegetables, picking some leaves for experiment, or harvesting some fruits
Computer lab activities	Medium to high	Logging onto websites to find out more about a specific topic or finding answers from computer
Guided discussions	Medium to high	Students participate in learning activities, ask questions, listen to peers, take a role in the learning process, and work responsibly. Teacher is a guide or facilitator, not the leader and controller.
Reading activities	Low to medium	Reading aloud, silent reading, or teacher reads and students listen
Listening and watching the teacher	Low	These types of activities barely engage students or hold their interest
Listening only	Very low	These types of activities are considered disengaging
Lecturing or preaching	Very low	These types of activities are not academically appropriate for Grades K-12

Note. Information from *An Educational Psychology of Methods in Multicultural Education* by C. T. Vang, 2010, New York: Peter Lang.

To achieve a high engagement level, teachers must carefully consider all possible challenges to instructional practices ahead of time. It is also wise to anticipate situations that may arise. A Plan B should be in place in case Plan A does not work, and extra activities should be planned for minimum days. To help teachers make effective instructional preparations, Table 4.4 illustrates some of the instructional challenges that are worth considering when pulling all things together to organize a plan.

Keep in mind that instructional preparation may require teachers to be in a mental-image mode when considering and organizing instruction. In other words, teachers should have mental images in their minds when making preparations. Being in a good mental state helps teachers prepare efficiently and effectively. Teachers need to be mentally organized as well as physically organized. Mental organization refers to the way teachers rehearse, practice, and encode planned information. Physical organization refers to how teachers understand all the environmental factors of the classroom settings.

Table 4.4. Ideas for Instructional Preparations

Preparation	Proposed Actions
Daily lesson plan	Daily lessons, activities, materials, and actions; teaching scheme; subject areas; academic tasks; group work; organize into weekly plan
Weekly plan	Weekly schedules, lesson plans, activities, materials, organize instructions, resource binders, copies of materials
Skeleton plan	Weekly and monthly organizer of lessons, activities, materials, resources, instructions; unit planning; layout ideas for weekly, detailed actions
Short-range plan	Create a list of things that need to be done in a short time, curricular activities, curriculum guide, pace calendar, weekly planner
Long-range plan	Create a rough list of things that need to be done in the near future, curriculum guide, pace calendar, weekly planner, monthly planner, goals
Instructional planning, student activity, or pedagogical approaches	Resources, supplemental books, copies, hands-on, minds-on, video clips, websites, papers, pencils, task activities, group work, independent practice, instruction, modeling, guided practices, assessment, adaptations
Adaptations	Scaffolds, bridges, contextualization, schema building, graphic organizer, KWL, reciprocal teaching, ELD, SDAIE, regalia, visual aids, Pictionary
Student assessment	Testing, evaluation, check for understanding, review, practices, drills, exercises
Re-teaching plans	Reflection, re-teach, additive, subtractive, deductive, inductive, changes

According to Burden and Byrd (2003), teachers may need to include skeleton plans as well as tentative schedules in their instructional preparations. They may need to plan for tentative student assessment, for homework, for backup materials and resources, for the opening class routine, for folders for substitute teachers, and for policy sheets. All these items should be clearly stated in the course syllabus. Depending on the grade level, students should receive a copy of the course syllabus that outlines the introductory information related to the content of the class such as classroom policies and procedures, course objectives, course requirements, and instructional methods.

Theories of Classroom Management

As mentioned previously, philosophical approaches to teaching practices are broader than theoretical principles of classroom management. Each teacher brings his or her own set of theories to the classroom based on the teacher's personal and cultural experiences, psycho-social immediacy, clinical training experiences, emotional and psychological tolerance, and coherency or incoherency of stimulus response in class. For example, some teachers deliver instruction quickly, clearly, and loudly; some speak slowly and quietly; and others are somewhere in between. The teachers' theories about how best to deliver instruction have direct impact on classroom management because they are received differently by different students.

There are three types of students in any class. One type can adjust to just about any teaching management style. A second type fluctuates in ability to adjust to the teacher's style according to their interest in the subject matter. The third type often lags behind, confused, lost, and adrift in an inability to follow the teacher's instruction. Teachers should carefully consider why some students are on-task while others are off-task. They should ask themselves if their theories about teaching practices hinder some of their students.

In best professional practices, teachers operate according to flexible theories. To help teachers build their repertoire of management skills, Table 4.5 presents a variety of theoretical models from theorists who have greatly influenced teaching and classroom management. The theorists offer a variety of approaches to alleviate discipline problems; however, keep in mind that there is no best model that fits all. New teachers have to learn what works best for them and their situation because each class and each student are different. Each model has distinct advantages and disadvantages, and perhaps some may feel uncomfortable at first. However, without trying them out, how will you know what will work?

Table 4.5. Selected Models of Classroom Management

Theorist	Background	Model	Basic Approaches
Alfie Kohn	Human behavior and social therapy	Beyond discipline	Perspective approaches, positive, correction, change, rewards, punishments, consequences
B. F. Skinner	Psychology	Behavior modification	Stimulus approaches, positive and negative reinforcements, reward system, logical consequences, modify behavior
Barbara Colorosa	Sociology, teacher, philosophy, and theology	Inner discipline	Time and effort approaches, responsible behaviors, natural consequences, conflict resolution, little praise and punishment
Carolyn Evertson & Alene Harris	Project coordinators, trainers, and authors	Managing learner-centered classrooms	Learner-centered approaches, clear rules, clear expectations, yearly approaches, instructional management
Forrest Gathercoal	Law instructor, principal, coach, and teacher	Judicious discipline	Behavioral guideline approaches, damage, loss, threats, health, safety, ethics, discipline
Frederic Jones	Psychology	Positive classroom management	Positive procedural approaches, limitations, affirmative, cooperation, simple rules, practical applications
Fritz Redl & William Wattenberg	Child analysis & group therapy	Group life and classroom discipline	Self-control approaches, responsible for own behaviors and actions, provide supports, different students with different behaviors, apply pleasant and unpleasant, manipulate to modify actions
Haim Ginott	Psychology	Congruent commu-	Feeling approaches, self-discipline,

		nication	alternative discipline, harmony
Jacob Kounin	Psychology	Instructional management	Effective teaching approaches, use quality instruction to influence student behaviors, teaching strategies, management
Jane Nelsen, Lynn Lotte, & Stephen Glenn	Education specialists, family therapists, & psychology	Positive discipline	Altruism approaches, caring, supporting, encouragement, respect, order, social skills, meetings
Jerome Freiberg	Professor of education	Consistency management and cooperative discipline	School-wide approaches, self-discipline, climate, caring, cooperation, academic achievement
Lee Canter and Marlene Canter	Educators, clinical social workers, and special education teachers	Assertive discipline	Right approaches, rules, hierarchy of consequences, responsible behaviors
Linda Albert	Professor of education, teacher, and columnist	Cooperative discipline	Influence approaches, connection, contribution, less controlling, code of conduct, climate, self-discipline
Patricia Kyle, Spencer Kagan, and Sally Scott	Researchers, writers, educators	Win-Win Discipline	"We" approaches, responsible behaviors, self-discipline, instructional practices, long-term approaches, self-management
Richard Curwin & Allen Mendler	School teachers & psychology	Discipline with dignity	Dignity approaches, flexibility, fairness, rules, modeling, understanding
Rudolph Dreikurs	Medical doctor, psychiatrist, and psychotherapy	Democratic teaching and management	Cause approaches, mistaken goals, democratic teaching, encouragement, and logical consequences
Thomas Gordon	Psychology	Self-control, discipline, and teacher effectiveness training	Self-discipline approaches; "I" message, not "you" messages; conflict resolution approaches
William Glasser	Psychiatry	Choice theory and quality schools	Psychological needs approaches; healthy and safe environment; support qualities of life; provide nurturing, caring, and understanding setting

Note. Information from *Elementary Classroom Management* (3rd ed.) by C. M. Charles and G. W. Senter, 2002, Boston, MA: Allyn & Bacon.

Choosing the best theoretical approach to classroom management depends on the situational applicability of the model in modifying problem student behavior. Using one specific model may not benefit all students; however, applying a combination of practices from different models is a sensible approach to the needs of everyday management and discipline.

Whatever model is used, the basic principle of classroom management is that the teacher's verbal and nonverbal behaviors influence student behaviors either intentionally or unintentionally. In other words, teachers should model good behaviors in class at all times. Teachers are like the big screen in a theater, and classroom management is like pictures on the screen that students are watching. Teachers should develop a clear and systematic repertoire of management skills with careful consideration of the connection between teaching and learning, the relationship between teaching and discipline, the motivations of both on-task and off-task students, and the different learning expectations of teachers and students. They need a systematic approach to managing and disciplining students during instruction and academic engagement time, and they need both prevention and intervention strategies that help maintain appropriate student behaviors.

Classroom management problems directly affect teaching and learning in a number of ways. For instance, teachers who have low tolerance will spend more time correcting misbehaviors than teachers who can ignore small disruptions. On the other hand, students who are disciplined by teachers several times a day may lose interest in instruction and other curricular activities. Teachers need to define discipline problems clearly, differentiating between major and minor misbehaviors, in order to utilize hierarchical approaches in a timely and wise manner. Otherwise, students may comply with teachers' demands but be unable to learn because they are fearful of or intimidated by harsh discipline.

The Physical Classroom Environment

One prominent contributor to management problems is the classroom setting. Most teachers design their classrooms to meet their needs rather than the needs of the students. Many teachers keep their classrooms neatly organized and clean, but some classrooms are dirty, messy, cluttered, and in disarray. Classroom design has a direct impact on student learning despite the quality of the teacher. The physical arrangement of the items in the classroom—seats, bulletin boards, bookshelves, rules and logical consequences posters, student work, centers, supplies, and mat area—should be conducive to the multiple learning activities that take place in the room. The layout must be conducive to teaching and learning. Additionally, certain arrangements are required for health and safety procedures, such as fire drills and precautions in case of earthquake, fire, or other emergency. Most importantly, the classroom must be hazard free to prevent accidental injuries.

Designing a classroom that meets all requirements and expectations is challenging; however, if the room does not lend itself to teaching and learning, how can teachers expect students to behave well in the class? A classroom must look like a place where formalized teaching and learning can take place. As Doyle (1986) observed, the modern classroom must be a multidimensional setting (for multipurpose use), a simultaneous setting (because many things happen at the same time), an immediate location (where teaching, learning, and activities happen rapidly and unexpectedly), an unpredictable environment (where unexpected twists and turns are the norm), and a public location (a place everyone can share, use, clean, and own). Figure 4.3 below illustrates several models of classroom design.

Normally, the seating charts of today's classrooms are organized in a variety of shapes and forms such as an L shape, a horseshoe, cemetery plots, rows, a half square, a half rectangle, an F shape, square groups, rectangle groups, a straight line, and an E shape. There is no best seating chart for all students; the different grade levels may require different seating charts. Teachers must arrange seating to meet the needs of their students. They should consider changing the seating periodically to accommodate changing teaching and learning circumstances.

Moreover, teachers need to take the following factors into consideration when designing the layout of the class: mobility, visibility, accessibility, auditory focus, class participation, social contact, learning climate, transitions, health and safety, handicap access, resources, storage, bookshelves, computer desk, and student work display. The four walls of the classroom are usually limited to two useful ones because one wall contains windows and a door and the other wall has a blackboard or whiteboard. So the two remaining walls can be used for a bulletin board, posters, student work, pictures, and more.

Figure 4.3. Samples of classroom design.

Possible arrangements for independent work/tests/beginning of the year/lectures

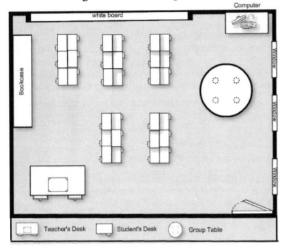 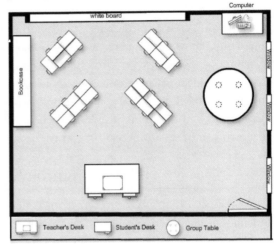

Possible arrangements for group work/stations

 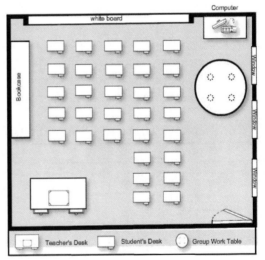

Possible arrangements for demonstration/discussion

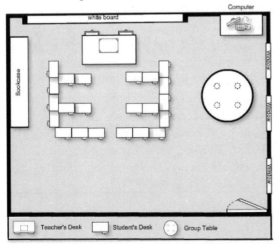 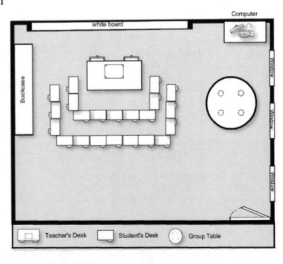

Teachers should orchestrate the classroom elements to make the room like an auditorium in which all attendees in the audience can see, hear, and watch the show. If students cannot access the instruction from a corner or the back, the teacher cannot expect them to learn what is covered in class. If the teacher cannot see all students, it is hard to manage the class. Teachers have only two eyes, but some classroom designs would work only if teachers had four eyes. Therefore, the classroom design needs careful consideration to maintain a positive psycho-social environment. A positive setting means the learning environment is warm, caring, cooperative, and supportive and contributes to positive student learning outcomes. A negative learning environment is inhibiting, cold, uncaring, distractive, disruptive, punitive, harsh, and depriving. Such negative elements may exacerbate other management and discipline problems such as off-task behavior, side talking, dawdling, looking out the window, moving out of seat, inattentiveness, and apathetic attitudes.

Plan to Handle Student Misbehaviors

Teachers must anticipate classroom management and discipline problems. Establishing procedural guidelines to handle student misbehaviors early is a wise way to start a school year because discipline can fall apart if there is no plan in place. Moreover, minor issues can be eliminated if there is a plan that anticipates them; however, without a plan, little misbehaviors can turn into big hassles. Table 4.6 lists several practical steps that can help teachers prepare for dealing with student misbehaviors in class (Burden & Byrd, 2003). These procedures are merely guidelines; they can be modified according to the needs of students and teachers. As with any rules, policies, and procedures, teachers need to make sure they are enforceable in a manner that does not harm students academically. For example, if students keep breaking the same rules because of the nature of the classroom environment and these infractions are unintentional, teachers need to revisit the rules and make necessary adjustments.

Table 4.6. Steps for Handling Student Misbehaviors

Step	Possible Actions
Establish rules and procedures	Praise, modifications, rewards, reinforcements, consequences, guidance, process
Provide support in class	Give support, cue, reinforce, praise, recognize, monitor, maintain
Give situational assistance	Direct, redirect, get back on task, inattentive, work avoidance, reinforce, refocus
Apply mild responses	Non-punitive approach, use "I" messages, verbal, nonverbal, eye contact, ignore, signal, proximity control, touch control, call on, issue warning
Apply moderate responses	Punitive approach, lose privileges, remove objects, logical consequences, correct, modify
Apply strong responses	Punitive approach, aversive stimuli, give reprimands, refer to an officer, contact parents, send notes home, conference
Make a referral	Send to an officer; see administrators, school psychologist, counselor, learning director, etc....
Conference or meet with students	At recess, after school, before school, during prep time, special arrangements

Teachers can take all the steps listed in Table 4.6 if they have the time to help students modify their misbehaviors. In most cases, however, teachers run out of time because too many things are going on at the same time. That is why having a plan in place is always a good way to save time and energy. For example, holding conferences or meeting with students to discuss misbehaviors is virtually impossible because of time constraints. However, teachers are required to hold meetings with students and parents to discuss chronic misbehaviors and deal with severe student actions in order to decrease the unwanted behaviors.

Creating Classroom Rules

Teachers must have clear consciences when creating classroom rules; otherwise, rules will be broken by the teachers as well as the students. For instance, some teachers apply inconsistent discipline and logical consequences for the same and/or similar behaviors, and in some cases, teachers use favoritism while disciplining students for the same and/or similar rule infractions. Classroom rules are intended to serve the best academic interests of all students rather than restrict students' learning abilities. In some cases, rules are created to control student behaviors; however, in most cases, rules are established to foster teaching and learning in the classroom. Whether the classroom rules serve the learning needs of the students depends on how teachers apply them to maintain order in the classroom. Some use negative terms and others use only positive terms. Consider, for example, the CRSVP approach in helping creating rules: C=clear language, R=reasonable expectations, S=simple to understand, V=valuable logical consequences, and P=purposeful management and discipline to motivate learning.

Rules would be unnecessary if all students were well behaved all the time. If all students followed all of the teacher's directions, spoke politely, and respected others, classroom rules would not be required. However, misbehaviors and misconducts occur in every classroom, and rules are needed so students know what proper conduct is. Classroom rules are general codes of conduct established to enforce general behavioral standards that all participants are expected to follow in the formalized setting where teaching and learning are taking place. Teachers need to carefully craft classroom rules for their particular setting and grade level. Burden and Byrd (2003) suggested that teachers examine the need for rules, select appropriate rules, select rewards and consequences for following or not following the rules, teach and review the rules, and obtain commitment from the students to adhere to the rules. Complex rules should be avoided.

Creating Classroom Procedures

In practice, classroom rules will not work without classroom procedures. Creating classroom procedures requires well-planned actions and thorough consideration because teachers and students cannot function without procedural protocols. Ordinary classroom tasks require specific procedural guidelines: taking a test, lining up, going out to lunch, coming back to class, questioning and answering during class, and conducting experiments. Procedural guidelines for responding to a possible earthquake are different from procedural guidelines for handling chemicals during scientific experiments. Go back and look at Table 4.2 for a list of some of the areas for which teachers need to establish procedures. Whether the procedures are explained to students in written or verbal form, students need to know them. Teachers have the responsibility to train students to learn how to follow these procedures correctly. Otherwise, the classroom could quickly become chaotic and dysfunctional.

Teachers need to recognize the situations that will need specified classroom procedures and then determine how they would like to guide students through these situations on a daily basis. Table 4.7

illustrates some of the situations teachers may consider important for establishing procedural guidelines. Keep in mind that, as with rules, procedures need to be easily understood and enforceable. They should be posted where they are visible to all students. They must be stated in terms that are familiar to students.

Table 4.7. Tasks Requiring Procedural Guidelines

Situation	Task or Area
Room use	Desks, storage, pencil sharpener, sink, drinking fountain, bathroom, learning stations, computer areas, centers, display areas, coat racks,
Out of room	Cafeteria, playground, office, library, bathroom, drinking fountain, fire drills
Transitions	In, out, beginning, leaving, returning, ending, free time, down time
Class activities and participation	Signals, think-pair-share, assistance, group work, discussion, out of seat, distributing work, makeup work, handing back work
Group work activity	Sharing, responsibility, doing task, discussion, moving in and out, distributing materials
Daily routines and schedules	Attendance, tardiness, absence, instructions, activities, group work, process, supplies, movement, transitions, pullout rotation, behaviors

As Tables 4.7 and 4.2 suggest, establishing procedural guidelines for all areas in the entire classroom minimizes the likelihood of chaos and makes management and discipline easier. Most importantly, teachers have to teach and review all procedural guidelines prior to doing any academic task, and they must make sure students understand the procedures. Teachers should re-teach, review, and revisit the procedures whenever necessary to protect the health and safety of all participants in the classroom.

Organizing Proactive Approaches

Once a system of classroom management has been established, teachers usually organize their thoughts, plans, preparations, and materials for developing instructional approaches in the first few days or weeks of school. Starting a teaching job is challenging for new teachers because it requires a large amount of work. Experts suggest that new teachers who are starting a new job consider doing the following to create an active learning environment (Burden, 2003; Burden & Byrd, 2003; Good & Brophy, 2000):

1. Greet students at the door. Welcome students to class with a handshake or high five.
2. Have an introduction activity, an icebreaker that introduces you to your students.
3. Present learning course objectives to your students.
4. Clearly state your rules, procedures, and academic expectations. Take time to go over them with students and practice with them.
5. Use successful lesson plans. Plan simple, uncomplicated, and student-centered lessons to promote student success.

6. Focus on the whole class. Prescribe activities for the whole class, monitor behaviors, and reinforce with appropriate responses.
7. Be mobile, visible, and vigilant. Supervise students at all times, move around, and monitor students' on-task behaviors.
8. Anticipate problems. Have plans in place to handle any potential problems.
9. Monitor student behaviors. Make sure students comply with all rules, procedures, and expectations.
10. Implement intervention strategies. Stop any inappropriate behaviors right away.
11. Use an ability-level approach. Base lesson plans on student abilities.
12. Hold students accountable. Make sure students complete work in class, do assignments, and turn work in.
13. Recognize students' needs. Be aware of their attention or inattention, confusion, work avoidance, boredom, and reactions.
14. Be clear, concise, and explicit when giving directions, instructions, and procedural guidelines.
15. Keep the lesson flow. Maintain student interest, answer questions, provide feedback, and focus on student behaviors.
16. End the class period with basic procedures that manage student activities.

Organizing instructional approaches is a plan of action teachers like to take when they first start teaching a class. There are other ways to approach instructional organization; the approach depends on the teacher's level of comfort, confidence, readiness, preparation, and energy. The beginning mode of some teachers is fairly simple and mundane. Other teachers overwhelm students by bombarding them with assignments.

Maintaining Good Rapport with Students

Managing and disciplining are big tasks for teachers, and students who must be disciplined are affected by the teacher's demeanor, attitudes, personality, and actions. Maintaining good rapport with students is essential to the emotional, psychological, and academic development and growth of the learners. Teachers must forge positive relationships with all their students in a manner that fosters teaching, learning, and social interactions; otherwise, the teacher-student relationship could be strained by negative feelings and profound animosities. Table 4.8 lists the characteristics of appropriate and inappropriate teacher-student relationships. Students often expect teachers to be their best friends; however, all friendship should be cordial and professional. At no time should teachers take advantage of any student for personal gain or gratification.

Table 4.8 Characteristics of Inappropriate and Appropriate Teacher-Student Relationships

Inappropriate relationship	Appropriate relationship
▪ Mean to students	▪ Advocating for students' needs
▪ Emotional	▪ Real teachers for all students
▪ Intimidating	▪ Inclusive and welcoming
▪ Impatient	▪ Serving students' academic interests
▪ Scornful	▪ Providing guidance
▪ Scolding approaches	▪ Helping make choices

- Too rigid
- Too stern
- Acting like a parent
- Assuming parental role
- Sharing too much personal information
- Too intimate
- Violent toward students
- Hostile toward students
- Spending time alone with students
- Socializing with students
- Treating students as own children
- Allowing student to invade personal space
- Too friendly with students
- Favoritism
- Taking advantage of students for personal interests
- Abusive, Yelling, Screaming, taking advantage of students, having bad attitudes, and displaying unpleasant personality.

- Protecting from harm
- Aware of students' social, emotional, academic, and psychological circumstances
- Enabling students to grow academically
- Providing opportunities
- Empowering
- Promoting success and achievement
- Showing affection and acceptance prfessionally
- Encouraging students to overcome problems
- Firm
- Pleasant
- Courteous
- Respectful
- Professional

Multicultural Approach

Teachers must realize that not all students are raised with middle-class American values, and students come from diverse socioeconomic backgrounds. At the very least, teachers must leave their cultural baggage at home when teaching in the multicultural classroom. Some teachers appear to be negative toward students who lack middle-class American values. For example, teachers may demand that students look them in the eye when misbehaviors occur in the classroom, but they may have students who for cultural reasons refuse to look them in the eye while being disciplined. Such cross-cultural issues maybe seem insignificant on the surface, but they could affect children deeply.

Today's classroom is like a rainbow. Students come from diverse socioeconomic backgrounds, as do their teachers. Not all minority students possess the middle-class values and behaviors assumed in most classrooms. However, most minority students are well behaved because of the expectations of their culture and their parents. Teaching ELL and SN students could be extremely difficult for teachers who do not speak the languages of these students, such as Spanish, Hmong, Chinese, Punjabi, Farsi, and Filipino. On the other hand, acquiring the language skills needed for academic tasks in class is a difficult challenge for language-minority students. A multicultural approach is crucial in helping all students learn. As Jones and Jones (2001) pointed out, academic achievement and student behavior are greatly influenced by the quality of the teacher-student relationship.

Moreover, Vang (2010) wrote that the goal of multicultural education for all can be promoted and reached through the following measures:

1. Develop integrated content instruction and curricula. Students should be guided to make learning connections through the units or themes the teacher has developed to teach all stu-

dents. At the same time, the teacher should integrate language instruction and content instruction so as to keep all students on the same page with the same objectives and goals.

2. Create social empowerment that promotes learning. Do this by engaging students in meaningful and relevant communication during teaching to stimulate learning opportunities that allow students to use language as a medium of interaction to improve learning skills and social confidence. One useful strategy is to employ cooperative learning or small groups to help students interact with one another while exchanging ideas.

3. Prescribe more hands-on and minds-on activities. For instance, instead of using rote memorization to encode and decode facts and information, design a hands-on activity that engages students in firsthand experience and allows them to digest what they have just learned through the activity before asking them to share how they understand what has happened in oral or written form.

4. Set up clear, concise, and specific expectations for learning. For instance, for students with the family value of filial piety or with strict parental rules, enforce their good and responsible behaviors in class by having clear classroom rules, routine procedures, assignment guidelines, and learning outcomes that keep students motivated. Consistency saves teachers time, time they can use to help students who need extra assistance. Classroom expectations should be reviewed on a regular basis as a disciplinary tool to hold students academically accountable.

5. Deal with issues of cultural diversity. Teachers who take the time to learn about their students' cultural identities have a greater chance of helping their students improve their self-concept, self-image, self-worth, and self-esteem because they build cultural connections with their students.

6. Combat prejudice in the learning environment. The teacher plays a vital role in reducing prejudice by modeling behaviors and attitudes and refusing to tolerate prejudicial or discriminatory remarks in the learning environment, demonstrating that all students are socially and culturally equal. Teachers can reduce or eradicate cultural misconceptions by introducing resources as well as instructional practices that help students learn from one another about their cultures and traditions.

7. Create equal opportunities for learning. Strategize teaching schemes that enable you to assist students who are having difficulties in understanding assignments. This may mean devoting extra time in or out of class to certain students. Also, reflective teaching allows teachers to assess themselves based on student learning outcomes.

8. Provide equity of instruction. Some students may need individualized instruction regardless of how many times the teacher has covered or repeated a lesson. Individualized instruction is one of the most effective teaching modalities for helping language-minority students learn.

9. Use differentiated instruction modalities. For instance, to accommodate the different learning styles of all students, incorporate integrated content instruction as part of the instructional process and use a variety of instructional approaches to enable all students to tap into the learning objective. One approach is to engage students' prior knowledge as much as possible in order to make the learning inspirational and relevant to real-life situations.

10. Maintain good rapport with all students. Quite often students perform poorly in class because of personality clashes with the teacher even without obvious evidence of dislike or antagonism. Simply put, if students do not like the teacher, they seem not to care much about the class. Students are human beings, and they often can "read" a teacher before the teacher

can "read" them. Maintaining warm relationships with students increases students' motivation to learn.

Teachers should use these measures to overcome the mindset ingrained in the hidden curricular ideology that some children deserve less and others deserve more. In a multicultural approach, all students deserve equal opportunity, and none should be relegated to the second-class education so frequently offered by the current educational system on the basis of deficient ideologies. New teachers must build positive teacher-student relationships to foster teaching and learning in a multicultural setting, where every child is accepted without regard to cultural background or SES.

Summing Up

This chapter highlighted the importance to new teachers of knowing and implementing principles of classroom management. There is no perfect classroom management technique or skill that works in all situations. To become effective managers in the classroom, teachers have to practice and apply management philosophies to different situations to gain confidence. Successful teachers are usually effective managers who can create a positive learning environment in which all learners are actively involved in the learning process. Maintaining good rapport with students is a must for all teachers; without good rapport, the way teachers manage and discipline students could be damaging to students' emotional, psychological, and academic development and growth.

Some teachers will not tolerate any little misdeed in the classroom, and this kind of expectation is virtually impossible for students because students are social beings, and they will make mistakes that can be corrected with gentle reminders from their teachers. Teachers who expect students to behave like their own children at home are not professionally equipped to teach because teachers are not surrogate parents.

With all the necessary rules, procedures, and preparations, teachers must create a positive learning environment to help all students learn new skills, feel safe, respect one another, engage in academic activities, have social interactions, and embrace cultural diversity. Classroom management has a common goal for all students: to enhance teaching and learning in a formalized process in a well-established multicultural setting.

CHAPTER FIVE

APPROACHES TO CLASSROOM DISCIPLINE

It is easier to build strong children than to repair broken men.
Frederick Douglass

Introduction

Classroom management and classroom discipline are terms often used synonymously; actually the two are slightly distinct but inseparable. Classroom discipline enforces the expectations set by classroom management principles. Even if classroom order is established, rules are crafted carefully, procedures are designed purposefully, and an effective management system is in place to handle student misbehaviors, without classroom discipline, the management system would not work. Just as civil society requires enforcement of the laws that are on the books, effective classroom management requires enforcement of classroom policies.

Discipline is something that some teachers dread. They do not want to deal with it because it takes time, energy, courage, patience, skills, and efforts. In some situations, teachers may lose control. Disruptive misbehaviors not only make teaching difficult, but they also intrude on the rights and freedoms of other students. In order to have effective classroom management, classroom discipline has to be effective as well. This chapter presents various aspects of the principles of classroom discipline to provide teachers with sound knowledge and help them develop skills for dealing with the causes and types of misbehaviors that are prevalent in today's classrooms.

What Is Classroom Discipline?

Unlike classroom management, classroom discipline is an ongoing process of responses issued by the teachers in dealing with or intervening in student behaviors and requires teachers to use fairness, consistency, flexibility, logical consequences, assertiveness, motivation, firmness, and modification. Each disciplinary action has a narrow focus; its focus is the timely direct response to the cause of misbehavior in the classroom. Teachers manage students and at the same time keep their eyes on student behaviors. Logical consequences for breaking rules are applied as part of discipline. In practice, discipline has been to be executed according to a hierarchy of consequences, or a sequential order of rules. Moreover, consider, for example, the use of *natural consequences* or *arbitrary consequences* instead of *logical consequences* is appropriate for dealing with some minor infractions.

Depending on the severity of the misbehavior or action, teachers may skip some steps, applying disciplinary actions that fit the misdeeds. For example, when a student talks during instruction, teachers can give a verbal warning, but when a student pokes another student with an object, teachers have to remove the object and restrain the abuser to protect the victim. Classroom discipline is the teacher's taking of any action to respond to misbehaving students in an effort to restore order and maintain control of the class. Keep in mind that teachers cannot rely on natural consequences under all circumstances happening in the classroom, and at the same time, they cannot apply arbitrary consequences because the disciplinary action does not align with the offense or misdeed. Figure 5.1 illustrates the foci of classroom discipline. Keep in mind that establishing and maintaining order and administering discipline are important parts of everyday classroom management.

Figure 5.1. Foci of classroom discipline.

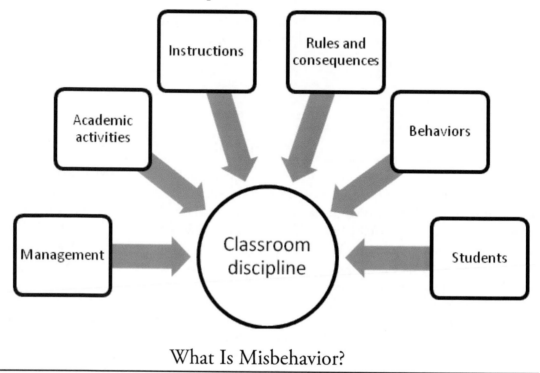

What Is Misbehavior?

There would be no need for rules, consequences, and discipline if all students were well behaved and free of psychological abnormalities. However, this is virtually impossible scenario because today's students bring a number of challenges to the classroom. One of these challenges is misbehavior. According to Charles and Senter (2012), Evertson and Emmer (2009), and Levin and Nolan (2007), misbehavior is a threatening action of an individual student that interferes with teaching, violates the right of other students to learn, creates an unsafe situation, destroys property, causes harm to others, or disrupts the flow of academic activities. Not every misbehavior requires discipline, and not every infraction of the rules is considered misbehavior. For example, being off-task is not necessarily misbehavior. But if a student is shooting paper through a straw, that student is misbehaving. Teachers need to deal with off-task students differently from misbehaving students. The context of the action can help teachers identify misbehaviors.

What Are the Causes of Misbehavior?

Some misbehaviors are predictable and expected, but most are unpredictable, uncontrollable, and unknown. For example, autistic children are expected to behave in certain ways because of their condition, but a sudden outburst of anger from another student is unpredictable. Table 5.1 lists some of the common causes of misbehaviors. Some misbehaviors arise from situational predicaments that come and go. For instance, Johnny may behave badly one day because he is upset with his older brother for some reason, but the next day Johnny may have a cheerful attitude and be willing to participate in academic activities. In other words, teachers should not label or mischaracterize students based on incidental behaviors.

Table 5.1. Common Causes of Misbehavior

Cause	Possible Contributors
Health conditions, diseases, surgery, medical issues	Allergies, lack of sleep, poor diet, sugar level, illness, side effects
Physical impairment	Vision, speech or hearing loss, paralysis, disability, handicap, disorder, mute
Neurological factors	ADD, ADHD, premature birth, fetal alcohol syndrome, mental disorder, crack baby, autism
Medication, drugs	Legal or illegal substance, over-the-counter remedies, allergy pills, homemade herbs
Familial factors	Parents, home, society, culture, traditions, divorce, separation, single-parent household, death, accident
Media influences	TV, games, movies, songs, society, pop culture
Gang-related activities	Violence, fighting, peer pressure, clothes, insignia, drugs, drinking, tagger/graffiti
Classroom factors	Teasing, bullying, peer pressure, teachers, curriculum, assignments, testing, expectations, conditions, hostility, learning climate, needs, failing, no assistance, administrators
Lack of support	Incomplete work, lagging, failing, frustration, anger, impulsivity

There are many types of misbehavior; however, all inappropriate behaviors of students can be classified into five major categories (Burden & Byrd, 2003; McNamara, 2007). Each category has a different set of misbehaviors as shown in Table 5.2. Furthermore, students who have emotional disorders require classroom management that provides emotional support, sensible structure, and procedures that decrease anxiety. On the other hand, students who have conduct disorders work well with teachers who can confront misbehaviors with warmth, but structure raises their anxiety level.

Misbehavior can be severe, moderate, or mild, depending on the cause. In most cases, classroom misbehaviors are mild or moderate; however, in rare cases, the incidents are so severe that immediate intervention and removal of students from class are required. Behaviors such as vandalizing school property or hurting oneself or others are examples of severe cases. Burden and Byrd (2003) recommended that mild misbehaviors be handled with attention, crowd control, directing, redirecting, and getting work done. Moderate problems are behaviors such as tardiness, cutting classes, talking, calling out, mild verbal and physical aggression, inattentiveness, having no supplies or books, and incomplete assignments. Severe misbehaviors include violence, vandalism, robbery, theft, drug use, alcohol abuse, and infliction of bodily injuries. Understanding the ranges should help teachers make wise decisions regarding the appropriate way to respond to disruptive behaviors.

Table 5.2. Categories of Common Misbehaviors

Category	Typical Behaviors
Hyperactivity	Unable to sit still, fidgets, talkative, impatient, demanding, hums, makes noises, excitable, anxious to please, poor coordination, neurological

	dysfunction, nonaggressive contact
Inattentiveness	Unable to complete work, distracted, wanders off, can't stay with games, can't complete work, can't follow directions, shy, withdraws from peers, fiddles, likes small objects, unable to sit still, fidgets, moves a lot, gets out of seat
Conduct disorder	Teasing, defying, can't stay with activities, can't accept correction, talks back, moody, fights, frustrated, can't handle problems, disobeys
Emotional disorder	Critical, unable to have fun, gullible, destructive, easily hurt, tense, fearful, withdrawn, unhappy, hyper, affective disorder, overly compliant
Impulsivity	Demanding, reckless, careless, accidents, gets into things, intrusive, unpredictable, uncontrollable

What Is Expected of Students?

Teachers cannot expect to see everything in their students, but one thing they should be able to expect of all children is good citizenship. They can reasonably expect all students to be good. No teacher expects students to misbehave or bring discipline problems to class. Most feel that school is a place where children should be educated, not a place where teachers should have to parent children while educating them. However, teachers should realize that not all children are properly trained and prepared at home before enrolling in school. Not all parents know how to parent their children well. The majority of children behave in ways that are appropriate for school, but some lack family structures, rules, parental control, and respect. Therefore, teachers should not expect all their students to possess middle-class values or have family and cultural backgrounds similar to their own.

Table 5.3. Characteristics of Achieving and Underachieving Learners

Achieving Learners	Underachieving Learners
▪ Arrive on time	▪ Late to class
▪ Come to class prepared	▪ Underprepared
▪ Follow directions	▪ Go off task
▪ Active	▪ Passive
▪ Attentive	▪ Not participating
▪ Enthusiastic	▪ Frustrated
▪ Willing to try	▪ Unsure
▪ Concerned and conscientious	▪ Complacent
▪ Motivated	▪ Irresponsible
▪ Well organized	▪ Poor risk taker
▪ Self-starting	▪ Procrastinating
▪ Task-oriented	▪ Daydreaming
▪ Go the extra mile	▪ Defensive
▪ Confident	▪ Distracted
▪ Competitive	▪ Bored
▪ Adaptive and flexible	▪ Have irritating behaviors

Note. Information from *Up from Under-achievement: How Teachers, Students, and Parents Can Work Together to Promote Student Success* by D. Heacox, 1991, Minneapolis, MN: Free Spirit Publishing.

Today's classrooms are like the colors of the rainbow. Children bring all kinds of cultures, traditions, values, and belief systems to class. They also bring all kinds of behaviors, attitudes, personalities, and ideas to school. Teachers are clinically and professionally trained to handle children's aca-academic misbehaviors, misconceptions, and misperceptions, but they are not always ready to handle religious and cultural differences. Teachers can modify children's behaviors but they cannot change who the children are. Even if students have destructive behaviors that need to be changed, teachers cannot expect them to change overnight. Table 5.3 illustrates the characteristics of two very different kinds of learners. Having some of both kinds in one classroom may pose challenges for instruction, classroom management, and discipline (Vang, 2010).

Teachers would love to have all students from the achieving group rather than the underachieving group. Nonetheless, teachers should not immediately assume that students in the underachieving group have behavioral problems. Perhaps teachers mischaracterize these students without careful consideration. Despite how teachers label and characterize students, every single student deserves to have equal opportunities in education, and the teachers' job is to provide all students with those opportunities to make sure that every student understands the golden opportunities available to them.

Sometimes the mischaracterizations and academic labels put on children not for academic reasons but because of psycho-social biases cause teachers to categorize students on the basis of wrong assumptions and misjudgments. Teachers must resist the tendency to predestinate students to a lower education based on these characterizations. Teachers should need to go beyond these undermining preconceptions.

Misbehavior is common among both achievers and underachievers regardless of how teachers may perceive them. Look at the common classroom disruptions and interruptions listed in Table 5.4. Students in either group are likely to display these misbehaviors. The point here is that teachers should not favor one group over the other in dealing with management and discipline concerns. If teachers show more tolerance toward achievers than underachievers, they are enforcing the classroom rules, procedures, and order unfairly, inconsistently, and capriciously.

Table 5.4. Common Classroom Disruptions and Interruptions

Disruption/ Interruption	Examples of Behaviors
Back talking	Defying, disobeying an order, challenging, talking, disrespecting, refusing
Teasing	Picking on, tattling, harassing, gossiping, making fun, inventing stories, insulting, disrespecting, singling out victims
Bullying	Hurting, teasing, harassing, gossiping, picking on, insulting, deriding, disrespecting, singling out victims, humiliating, threatening, tattling, stalking
Cheating	Looking over, copying, disobeying orders, disrespecting, don't-care attitude
Dawdling	Wasting time, taking too long, off-task, just sitting there, talking
Defiance	Back talking, disobeying orders, challenging, disrespecting, causing problems, distracting
Disrespectful	Defying, disobeying, back talking, dawdling, off-task, disrupting, distracting
Excessive talking	Paying no attention, off-task, distracting, disrupting, unable to complete work, dawdling, noisy
Gossiping	Tattling, sharing secrets, teasing, making fun, picking on others, concocting stories
Helpless hand raising	Blurting out wrong answers, cannot find answers, wanting to be called on, disrupting, being loud

Incomplete assignments	Turning in late, losing work, can't find work, work half done, taking too long, can't understand the work, too hard, too much
Racial remarks	Expressing remarks, being biased, being prejudiced, making race as issue, showing contempt, can't share, can't cooperate
Rough play	Pushing, pulling, shoving, horsing around, wrestling, chasing
Running	Disrupting, distracting, can't walk slow, tripping, bumping others, rushing
Classroom clown	Getting attention, making fun, being fun, disrupting, distracting, goofing off, entertaining, provoking
Stealing	Disrespecting, taking things, defying, disobeying, claiming, not admitting
Disruption	Causing, making, bothering, annoying, poking, pushing, tapping, yelling, throwing, thumping, complaining, whining, dropping things
Threatening behaviors	Hurting others, throwing objects, charging, inflicting injuries on self, fighting, disobeying, back talking, defying, disrespecting, violence, vandalizing, destructive
Throwing objects	Shooting paper through straw, tossing objects, disrupting, distracting, casting erasers, can't concentrate, annoying
Unprepared for class	Tardy, late, have no paper, no pencil, incomplete work, lost work, no book, bring nothing to class
Vandalism	Violence, destruction, threatening, hurting, scaring, breaking, disrespecting, defying, disobeying, back talking

Prevention of Student Misbehaviors

Preventing all misbehaviors in the classroom is impossible because most misdeeds are brought to the classroom from the outside. Students may have had a stressful day or night because of family or personal circumstances, such as getting up late, catching a cold, having a headache, having no time for breakfast, forgetting homework assignments, or forgetting to take medication. Teachers should anticipate misbehavior at any time so they are prepared to deal with problems whenever they come up. There will always be some students who will not turn in their homework assignments on the due date, and rules will always be broken. The teachers' responsibility is to take a proactive stance to prevent misbehaviors and, at the same time, find out why students misbehave in order to help them modify their unacceptable behaviors. Sometimes the misbehavior is directly related to the teaching modalities used in delivering instruction. Table 5.5 presents some causes of student misconduct.

Table 5.5. **Causes of Some Student Misconduct**

Misconduct	Possible Causes
Off-task or wander off	Not connected, unsure, lost, easy, hard, boring, finish early, repetitive, don't care
Inattentive, lost, uncertain	Seeking attention or assistance, question, doesn't understand
Giving up, quitting, stopping, do-not-care attitude	Cannot do, distracted, too difficult, not interested, irrelevant, not meaningful
Amusement, talking, poking, whispering	Too easy, finish early, boring, not enough work, free time
Excitement, loud, ecstatic	Over react, eager, emotion, feeling, easy, overjoyed

Waiting, sitting still, inactive, quiet	Not interested, lack ownership, feeling dumb, not feeling well, cannot hear, too much noise, unclear directions
Upset, angry, frustration, outburst, agitated	Outside issues, difficult, not understanding, need assistance, peer pressure, conflict
Not engaged, disobey, defiant, not listening, refuse to follow directions	Behavioral problems, ADD, ADHD, does not care, not understand, incompatible learning styles, attitude problems

Teachers should be prepared to handle misbehaviors at all times, and once they know the common causes of student misconduct they can more easily correct the misbehaviors without spending a lot of time directing and redirecting student attention. Developing effective prevention strategies will give teachers more time to teach and assist students who are in need of extra support. Also, prevention enables teachers to respond quickly and effectively when situations arise that require intervention.

Intervention Strategies

Not only do teachers have to know why students misbehave in class, but they must also use common sense strategies to intervene to resolve management and discipline problems. Some intervention strategies are private and some are public. Teachers might use verbal cues to calm students or they might use a timer to keep students on task. In some cases, teachers stop their instruction or a classroom activity until the misbehaving students cease their misconduct. No approach is perfect; however, some approaches are more effective than others.

Misapplication of intervention strategies can cause further disruptions. For example, if the teacher punishes the whole group or class for a single student's misbehavior, additional students may react inappropriately. If teachers unrealistically expect every single student to behave a certain way all day long, they may impose unwarranted consequences for minute infractions and in so doing damage their relationships with many students.

The first step in devising common sense strategies is to create and teach effective classroom rules that everyone will follow. The basic criteria for effective classroom rules are as follows:

1. They must be flexible and broad enough to deal with or cover a wide range of misbehaviors.
2. They should be expressed in positive terms.
3. They should be expressed in simple language that all students can understand and remember easily.
4. They must be consistent with school and district policies on discipline.
5. They can be enforced with logical, simple, reasonable, purposeful, appropriate, meaningful, valuable, and effective consequences.
6. The best number of rules for a classroom is between three and five.

Vang (2010) gave samples of classroom rules for Grades K–12; they are shown in Table 5.6. Keep in mind that the rules do not have to be perfect, but they must be enforceable; otherwise, rules mean little or nothing to the students. Teachers must enforce their classroom rules with professional attitudes according to the basic principles of classroom management and discipline. That is, enforcement must be firm, consistent, fair, flexible, logical, purposeful, motivational, situational, reasonable, and culturally appropriate.

Table 5.6. Examples of Classroom Rules, by Grade Level

Grades K–3	Grades 4–6	Grades 7–8	Grades 9–12
- Raise hands before speaking - Keep hands to self - Listen when someone speaks - Do not leave seat without permission - Follow orders to move in and out of class	- Be ready to learn - Follow directions - Keep hands and feet to self - Raise hands if need help - Be kind to others	- Be in seat before bell rings - Come to school prepared - Follow directions - Raise hands if have questions - Keep hands and feet to self - No foul language is allowed in class	- Be in seat before the bell rings - Follow directions - Be kind and responsible for personal actions - Wait for order to be dismissed - All assignments are due on time

The second step in devising common sense strategies is to develop effective logical consequences to deal with infractions of rules. These consequences should be carefully crafted based on the same premises as the creation of the rules. Table 5.7 presents examples of progressions of logical consequences at different grade levels, and Table 5.8 illustrates logical consequences for various infractions. Keep in mind that logical consequences must have as their aim behavioral modifications; the focus must be on the behavior, not on the student. Every time teachers focus on the students in discipline, the problem grows bigger and faster than the behavior because the approach is to change the individual student rather than address the cause of the action. Also, keep in mind that discipline can be frustrating, annoying, irritating, bothersome, and in some cases, uncomfortable. That is why teachers cannot lose their passion and patience; however, if they ever lose control, they may put their own career at risk.

Table 5.7. Examples of Logical Consequences, by Grade

Grades K–3	Grades 4–6	Grades 7–8	Grades 9–12
1. Verbal warning 2. Name on the board 3. Pull a card 4. Miss recess 5. Send note home	1. Verbal warning 2. Miss recess 3. Send note home 4. Contact parents 5. Conference	1. Verbal warning 2. Send to the office 3. Send note home 4. Contact parents 5. Conference	1. Verbal warning 2. Send to the office 3. Contact parents 4. Conference 5. Follow-up services

Table 5.8. Logical Consequences for Selected Infractions

Type of Infraction	Consequence
First offense	Verbal warning and teacher talks to student either privately or publicly, depending on the behavior and its severity
Second offense	Take away privileges and student loses one recess
Third offense	Take away privileges and student loses two recesses
Fourth offense	Take away privileges or lose all recesses for the day

Fifth offense	Take away privileges and call parent or guardian
Sixth offense	Take away privileges, send to the office, have meeting with parents, and evaluate for possible suspension.
Physical or verbal threats, severe disruption, or being rude to the teacher and classmates	Will not be tolerated and results in immediate referral to the principal, assistant principal, or appropriate administrator for intervention

Step 3 in devising common sense strategies is teaching the rules. Once Steps 1 and 2 are done, teachers need to teach the classroom rules to all students in the class. Keep in mind that the rules and the logical consequences may not be suitable for all students because of their different cultural backgrounds. Teachers need to make sure the rules and consequences are culturally appropriate and responsive to the needs of all students. For example, putting students' names on the board is considered humiliating and insulting in some cultures, and sending a note home to parents is culturally sensitive because some parents do not expect their children to misbehave in class at all. Here are some basic ideas that should be helpful to teachers in teaching classroom rules to all students:

1. Use simple terms and simple language to explain the rules and consequences to students.
2. Allow students to have a voice in creating the rules and consequences.
3. Build team spirit and student ownership of the classroom rules.
4. Give a copy of the rules and consequences to each student.
5. Send a copy home to parents.
6. Go over the rules and consequences until students understand and follow them.
7. Repeat the rules and consequences periodically to remind students.
8. Modify the rules and consequences if there are any problems with them.
9. Remind students that the purpose of rules and consequences is to guide them and their behaviors in and outside the class.
10. Understand that everyone will enforce the rules, but only the teacher can enforce the logical consequences.

It will be wise for teachers to share a copy of their classroom rules with school administrators to make sure they do not conflict with the school culture in general. Also, school administrators who review the rules and consequences can evaluate them for consistency with other teachers' rules and consequences. It is quite common for each classroom to have its own rules and consequences; they need not be the same for all classrooms except at the upper grade levels.

Step 4 is to print these rules and consequences on a poster and post them in a visible location in the classroom. The location of these rules and consequences posters is optional; however, the best location is next to the whiteboard or blackboard in front of the class. If the rules and consequences are posted on the back wall, they may be visibly accessible to students when the teacher wants to revisit them, but students have to turn around to see them. The best practice is to post them in a location where students can see them as they are looking at the teacher.

Lastly, Step 5 in using common sense strategies is the daily dealing with every infraction of rules in the classroom. Some teachers created great rules and appropriate consequences but fail to enforce them fairly, consistently, and wisely. However, strict enforcement of the rules and consequences may have a backlash and negative results if inflexibility precludes reasonable accommodations. Consider, for example, the age, culture, gender, and maturity of the child as well as the severity of the infraction. The following five-step process is crucial for dealing with management and discipline problems in the classroom:

1. Learn to ignore insignificant misbehaviors.
2. Learn to modify misbehaviors immediately and effectively.
3. Learn when to modify and correct misbehaviors privately or publicly.
4. Learn to take necessary action to protect the best interests of the class.
5. Learn when to refer students to the office right away to minimize the impact of their misbehaviors.

Both positive and negative behaviors are contagious. When teachers praise one student's good behavior, other students start to behave responsibly, but when teachers ignore one student's bad behavior, other students tend to copy the misdeed. When teachers reward one student for good behavior, other students want to earn the same reward for being good, but when teachers pay attention to one student's bad behavior, other students may act out to get the teachers' attention. In other words, teachers need to recognize the ripple effects of discipline. To have consistent daily management and discipline, teachers must not ignore any behavior. They must be flexible and appropriately address both anticipated and unexpected situations involving teaching, learning, and misconduct in the classroom.

Addressing misconduct appropriately means responding according to the severity of the behavior. Some minor misbehaviors can be ignored, some warrant a warning, and some require consequences. Table 5.9 categorizes some common student misbehaviors by the type of response that is appropriate.

Table 5.9. Appropriate Responses for Selected Misbehaviors

Ignore	Mild Warning	Consequences
Brief	Off-task	Inattentiveness
Self-corrected/self-controlled	Talking loudly	Rudeness, disobedience
Involving one or two students	Fail to complete work	Defiance
Not paying attention	Not following procedures	Talking back
Whispering to others	Not following directions	Refusal to work
Hushed Talking	Horseplay	Disrespect
Daydreaming	Tardy or late	Vandalism
Raising hand in the air	Have no materials	Violence
Putting work in folders	Dawdling	Eating or drinking
Taking initiative	Passing notes	Impulsive action, anger, upset

Some of the misbehaviors listed in Table 5.9 can be handled nonverbally, and some require a verbal response. Nonverbal responses include ignoring the behavior, using nonverbal signals, standing near the student, and touching the student mildly to control the situation (Burden & Byrd, 2003). Verbal responses teachers might use include the following: (a) call on the student during the lesson, (b) use humor to correct, (c) send an "I" message, (d) use positive phrasing, (e) remind the student of the rules, (f) give the student choices, (g) ask "What should you be doing?", (h) give a verbal reprimand, (i) issue a desist order, (j) give a direct appeal, (k) use a direct command, and (l) apply logical consequences. Both nonverbal and verbal responses are considered mild or moderate discipline. Mild discipline is nonpunitive, and moderate discipline progresses through the steps of logical consequences (Burden & Byrd, 2003).

Classroom Factors That Influence Student Behaviors

Teachers may wonder why students behave differently inside and outside the classroom. It is true that outside factors influence student behaviors positively and negatively, and students bring these factors into the classroom. However, inside the classroom there are factors that are influential as well. Some of the classroom factors that affect student behavior are the curriculum, the effectiveness of the teachers, methods of discipline, management skills of the teachers, teachers' attitudes, teachers' personalities, cross-cultural factors, administrators, school staff, school routines, adequacy of facilities, physical arrangement of the class, room temperature, noise, lighting, number of people, instructional factors, materials, delivery of instruction, student activities, instructional activities, group activities, peer pressure, temptations, social envy, and failure to meet the developmental needs of students. These factors are not hidden from the naked eye. Teachers are aware of them and should pay attention to them, making necessary adjustments to manage the classroom management and avoid discipline problems. In other words, misbehaviors sometimes reflect the nature of the classroom. The classroom is like a two-way mirror. Teachers should see themselves while managing and disciplining students for any misconduct. Otherwise, classroom discipline will become a social control mechanism that contributes nothing to quality teaching and learning.

To help teachers recognize classroom factors, twelve techniques for managing surface behaviors that occur in the classroom are shown in Table 5.10 (Burden, 2003; Burden & Byrd, 2003; Levin and Nolan, 2000; Redl & Wineman, 1957; Weinstein, 2003).

Table 5.10. Techniques for Dealing with Surface Behaviors

Techniques	Possible Actions and Remedies
Remove distracting objects	Privately tell students to put objects away, store them in a safe place, pick them up after school, inform students to keep them at home, not allow them in school
Provide support with routines	Provide students with a sense of security and direction by giving information about routines, schedules, activities, curricular changes
Reinforce appropriate behaviors	Use public praise, compliments, and encouragement for good behaviors, reaffirm appropriate behaviors, recognize and appreciate cooperation
Boost student interest	Recognize waxing and waning interests, offer assistance, monitor progress, check for understanding, provide guidance, keep students engaged
Provide cues	Use signals, prompts, perks, and engagement to prepare students; verbal and nonverbal warnings; smooth transitions, change tasks
Help students over hurdles	Provide hints, give clues, encourage, offer assistance, give guidance, show resources, use KWL, create graphic organizer
Redirect the behavior	Understand struggle, offer guidance, use different approaches, ask questions, give suggestion, reinforce with information
Alter the lesson	Recognize student interests, be aware of student curiosity, modify as necessary, accommodate needs, adapt activities, go with the flow
Provide nonpunitive time-out	Recognize frustration, anxiety, overwhelming challenges, and difficult situations; be flexible, allow time-out, use break time, allow cool off
Modify the classroom	Change seating chart, desks, tables, instructional equipments, and

environment	materials; rearrange; reorganize
Use enhanced technology	Include video clips, films, online resources; allow to search and browse the Web for information
Use cooperative learning	Put students to work in group, assign tasks, allow sharing, facilitate the process, allow group to process, work at own pace

In practice, use of these surface behaviors and management techniques is called the situational assistance approach. Teachers take actions to help students cope with the instructional situation quickly, making adjustments to get them back on task before the situation gets worse or escalates to other students. The goal is to put out the sparks before the flame starts.

Disciplinary Actions Teachers Should Avoid

When it comes to classroom discipline, U.S. teachers are subject to stricter limitations than teachers in most other countries. In some nations, teachers' use of harsh reprimands, threats, and physical punishment to discipline students is legally acceptable. However, in the U.S., these methods of discipline are considered abusive. Punishment as classroom discipline is an old concept whereby teachers respond to misbehavior by imposing harsh penalties with the intention of getting the student to stop or not repeat the undesirable behavior. Teachers are not permitted to use punishment in US schools today because punishment is associated with possible abuse. As mentioned previously, discipline is the term used in modern psychological contexts to address academic needs and appears to be more appropriate in terms of changing behavior.

In practice, teachers should be legally literate, academically wise, ethically prudent, and professionally trained. They need to be prepared to handle classroom management and discipline problems in a manner that exhibits proper conduct in all three domains depicted in Figure 5.2. This is important because discipline puts teachers in a risky position; if they ever "lose their cool" and abandon their professional demeanor, they may cross the line from discipline to abuse. Table 5.11 lists some practices teachers should avoid to protect their careers (Burden & Byrd, 2003; Kauchak & Eggen, 2005). Teachers walk a slim line of liability each and every day.

Figure 5.2 Standards of conduct domains for teachers.

These practices are not only harmful, but they do not work well with children. Teachers may need different kinds of disciplinary actions to handle individual students' misbehaviors; however, punishment should not be used on any children at all. Teachers must learn not to punish but to solve problems instead. That is the goal of effective and efficient managers.

Table 5.11. Disciplinary Practices Teachers Should Avoid

Practice	Examples/Problems
Harsh and humiliating reprimands	Negative verbal abuse, yelling, screaming, losing control, stern manner, intimidation
Threats, shouting	Direct attack, losing control, demanding, insulting, humiliating, intimidating, threatening
Nagging	Scolding, scorning, ongoing insults, ongoing humiliation, holding grudges, focusing on student
Forcing apologies	Lying, forcing, demanding, putting down, finding fault, admitting guilt
Sarcastic remarks	Deriding, taunting, ridiculing, making fun of, devaluing, demoting
Group punishment	Unfair, biased, ineffective, creating conflicts
Extra academic work	Punishment approach, unpleasant, irrelevant, ineffective, adding new layer of problems
Reducing grades	Irritating, mean spirit, undesirable, irrelevant, confounding, devaluing academics
Writing as punishment	Hostile approach, admitting guilt, lying, increasing anger, frustration, bad feelings
Physical labor or exercise	Hostile approach, unable to do, health issues, facing limitations, safety concerns
Corporal punishment	Abusive approach, spanking, paddling, slapping, pinching, bruising, abrasion, injury
Appeasement, cajoling	Bribing, promising, condoning, exchanging, buying, colluding, conspiring, swearing

Reinforcement of Good Student Behaviors

Teachers can find many meaningful ways to reinforce good behaviors in the classroom. Reinforcement is a disciplinary mechanism that motivates students to get back on task. Depending on grade level, reinforcement comes in different forms: a positive learning environment, clear expectations, equal opportunities, maintaining good rapport with students, effective communication, modeling, applying invitational learning, creating a healthy and safe learning atmosphere, being fair, being consistent, showing respect to students, displaying affection to students, an open-door policy, positive attitudes, pleasant personalities, and building team and group cohesiveness. A reward system is a common form of reinforcement in the classroom. Teachers can use stickers, pencils, certificates, stamps, a point system, a money system, and tickets to reinforce students to motivate them to behave well in the classroom.

Rewards can be of two types—contingent or non-contingent. Contingent rewards are things students have to earn from the teacher for doing something good, and non-contingent rewards are things students receive without having to do anything to earn them. Table 5.12 gives examples of contingent and non-contingent rewards.

Table 5.12. Examples of Contingent and Non-contingent Rewards

Reward	Contingent	Non-contingent
The teacher throws a pizza party for the whole class because of good API scores.	✓	
An announcement came through the intercom that all students are invited to see a Walt Disney show in the cafeteria at noon.		✓
The teacher tells the class how proud she is when they clean up after the project and thanks all of them for doing a great job.	✓	
The teacher prints out certificates of appreciation for all students and presents them on the last day of class.		✓
The teacher stamps all turned-in homework assignments.	✓	
The teacher gives free books to all students.		✓

Rewards are generally tangible items and reward systems work well to reinforce classroom behaviors. However, both contingent and non-contingent reward systems have disadvantages. The contingent system does not work when the teacher does not have any more rewards to give, and the non-contingent system does not work well when students receive free items even when they behave badly in class. Therefore, teachers have to choose and use these systems wisely to reinforce good behaviors.

Another form of reinforcement is praise, either public or private. Praise is the cheapest form of reinforcement available. It is a social reinforcer. Social reinforcements can be in verbal, nonverbal, and written forms. For instance, teachers can acknowledge good behaviors through facial expressions, thank-you notes, gestures, and physical contact. Keep in mind that feeling means everything to students, especially young children. The better they feel, the more energetic they are and the more motivated they become.

Table 5.13. Selected Student Privileges and Responsibilities

Responsibilities	Privileges
Answer the phone	Group leader
Answer the door	Classroom helper
Take notes to the office	Organize bookshelves, bulletin board, storage, etc....
Pass out papers	Freedom to choose books
Collect papers	Play a game
Take attendance	Use computer
Open the windows	Take initiative or be self-motivated
Adjust the shades or blinds	Record points
Erase the chalkboard	Earn bonus or free time

In addition, teachers can find and create alternative reinforcements that are beneficial to students inside the classroom; some can be used all year long. Burden and Byrd (2003), Charles and Senter (2012), and Kauchak and Eggen (2005) pointed out that students can earn privileges and responsibilities that reinforce their good deeds; some suggestions for these are listed in Table 5.13. Teachers should allow students an equal opportunity to earn these privileges and classroom responsibilities. Weekly rotations should be helpful in giving all students the opportunity to earn the reinforcement. However, teachers should not insist that students accept these privileges and responsibilities if they are not comfortable doing so or choose not to for any reason. Whatever reinforcements are selected, teachers must remember that it is their job to keep all students actively attentive, involved, and engaged in instruction, activities, and other aspects of the learning process.

Helping Students Practice Self-management

Before long teachers learn that they cannot control their students at all times even if they try to. Just as children learn how to live under their parents' rules and expectations, they learn how to behave in the classroom. Teachers ought to think about ways to encourage students to manage their own actions and behaviors in the classroom. The ultimate goal of classroom management and discipline is to move students toward self-discipline, self-management, and self-governance. Some teachers may find this concept hard to believe because they are more concerned with maintaining control than sharing responsibilities. Here are some tips to help teachers train their students to take charge of their own actions and behaviors:

1. Give clear, concise, and explicit directions to all students.
2. Make sure all students are clear about task expectations.
3. Explain exactly what students need to do for each task before beginning the next one.
4. Check for understanding and give clarification if needed to make sure all students are on the same page.
5. Make sure students are aware of their own actions and behaviors.
6. Allow students to correct themselves every once in awhile.
7. Model the good behaviors you expect to see.
8. Keep track of good behaviors and point them out to students.
9. Evaluate students' performance each day and share the results with them.
10. Each day ask students what they did well and expect them to do better tomorrow.
11. Teach social skills to all students and show them how to apply the skills.
12. Use social reinforcement to support self-management efforts.
13. Monitor students and give feedback frequently.
14. Be available, be accessible, be prepared, and be supportive.
15. Encourage cooperation, teamwork, and a positive learning community for all.

Student self-management is the ultimate goal for most teachers, and it is not easy to achieve. Each student is unique and some will take longer than others to learn how to manage their own actions and behaviors. But, as with anything else, if teachers allow students time to practice, they can achieve self-management. Remember, time and practice will help your students succeed.

Discipline Pitfalls

As explained previously, teachers can avoid certain practices that would put them in great jeopardy of losing their teaching privilege. Consider, for example, verbal, emotional, psychological, and mental abuses in the classroom are ethically and professionally unacceptable. However, it is not always easy for teachers to know what to do to prevent discipline problems. Some practices are clear cut, preventable, and avoidable, but there are pitfalls that teachers usually have to learn on the job. Some discipline pitfalls are inevitable. Here is a list of actions that good, experienced, and well-trained teachers will not do:

1. Use abusive approaches.
2. Intimidate students.
3. Use shouting, yelling, and hollering.
4. Apply parenting approaches.
5. Use blame to control students emotionally and psychologically.
6. Fail to state the rules positively.
7. Use complicated and complex rules.
8. Rely on natural consequences and arbitrary consequences.
9. Lack proper procedural guidelines.
10. Allow too much free time.
11. Deliver instruction without having students' attention.
12. Enforce rules inconsistently.
13. Rush to send students to the office.
14. Overreact to problems without knowing the causes.
15. Allow students to take a nap in class.
16. Lose temper in front of students.
17. Play favorites or show favoritism.
18. Embarrass students in front of the class.
19. Use inconsistent consequences.
20. Set up low expectations for students.
21. Take too long to solve problems.
22. Make discipline difficult for students to achieve.
23. Allow students to run them over.
24. Fail to handle difficult students.
25. Lack transitional activities.

Moreover, new teachers find classroom discipline to be quite difficult because they are not aware of the pitfalls, or perhaps they are afraid they will fall into these traps. Teachers have to create the kinds of rules, procedures, and order they feel comfortable enforcing in order to help students mature academically and socially.

Documenting Classroom Discipline

Teachers should always keep a disciplinary journal in their desks. Maintaining an up-to-date record of classroom discipline is a best professional practice. Documenting classroom discipline helps teachers reflect upon the effectiveness of their classroom management and at the same time helps them identify misbehaviors that are common, difficult, or problematic. It is hard to document every little thing that occurs in the classroom, but teachers should keep track of all moderate disciplinary actions. These records should not be used to track students but to help teachers learn what is working well and what is not working so well in order to adjust their methods of discipline accordingly. Moreover, documentation provides teachers with good opportunities to share their concerns with parents at parent/teacher conferences. Teachers can ask parents for specific suggestions as to how to handle recurring problems so they can better meet the students' academic needs.

Record keeping is also helpful when school administrators ask teachers for detailed information or explanations regarding incidents that have taken place in the classroom when dealing with concerns from parents. Documenting is not a requirement, but it is a good practice. It is helpful to have records when filing a report with children's protective services, submitting a report on injured students to the office of risk management, and keeping records of potential violence. The bottom line is that documentation protects teachers from being wrongfully accused of things they have not committed, and it is one of the ways to hold teachers accountable for their actions.

What Students May Expect of Teachers

Disciplining and managing students' behaviors are difficult tasks for teachers because unpleasant situations may arise unexpectedly. Neither teachers nor students want to have to meet with parents, school administrators, or other school staff to discuss behavioral problems that are sensitive and personal unless it is their last resort. Teachers expect students to behave in certain ways, and students have expectations of teachers. However, students' expectations may be unrealistic depending on their age, maturity level, ability level, and cognitive development. Regardless, teachers must understand that there are universal expectations all students can reasonably have of teachers. Table 5.14 lists examples of universal expectations of teachers no matter what individual students may expect. Teachers need to take into consideration the unique needs, abilities, and maturity level of each student when managing and disciplining students' behaviors.

Table 5.14. Selected Expectations for Teachers

Teachers Expected to Be		Teachers Expected Not to Be	
Welcoming	Engaging	Angry	Disorganized
Fair	Busy	Frustrated	Impatient
Firm	Meaningful	Hostile	Impulsive
Authoritative	Assertive	Violent	Put down
Friendly	Protective	Aggressive	Biased
Caring	Organized	Intimidating	Racist
Enjoyable	Entertaining	Mean	Prejudiced
Appreciative	Humorous and	Scary	Too difficult
Positive	upbeat	Stern	Perfectionist
Supportive	Prepared	Authoritarian	Too much work
Encouraging	Good listener	Spineless	Picky
Enthusiastic	Understanding	Stonewalling	Unprepared
Fun	Embracing	Disorderly	Permissive
	Rewarding		

In some Eastern cultures, teachers are viewed as clergymen, authority figures, public officials, and leaders. Children of minority backgrounds may bring this mindset to the classroom and expect teachers to have a lot of power in managing, disciplining, and teaching. In some cases, teachers are regarded highly.

Summing Up

This chapter examined the principles of classroom discipline to provide teachers with a comprehensive overview of student behaviors in the multicultural classroom setting. Discipline is a complex matter requiring teachers to respond to the cause of students' misbehaviors. However, discipline cannot stand alone; without management, order, procedures, and reinforcements, discipline will not work. Teachers need to combine all these ingredients into a unified whole that will help them manage and maintain control over their students' behaviors in the classroom. Punishment is not the same as discipline in psychological contexts or in academic contexts. Punishment refers to harsh penalties imposed because of students' misbehaviors.

There is no perfect form of classroom discipline. Teachers have to apply various disciplinary methods that best suit their students' needs. The goal of discipline is to further academics by directing and redirecting students' attention to the academic task at hand. Teachers cannot and will not use classroom discipline to change their students' cultural identity but to help modify the students' social behaviors in order for them to have equal opportunity in the learning process. Teachers should avoid bad practices that would jeopardize their professional careers and, at the same time, teachers should be aware of discipline pitfalls. Effective managers are effective disciplinarians. Teachers need to be legally literate, academically wise, ethically prudent, and professionally trained to handle classroom management and discipline issues.

CHAPTER SIX

MANAGING A POSITIVE PSYCHOSOCIAL ENVIRONMENT

School is not preparation for life, but school is life.
John Dewey

Introduction

Every once in a while, student teachers in the credential program are asked this question: Are teachers managers, leaders, facilitators, counselors, or supervisors? Many are stunned by this thought-provoking question. Student teachers feel that teachers are all the above because their jobs require them to do a little bit of everything. When asked if they felt well prepared and well trained to perform all these tasks, many student teachers shake their heads. Until they are placed in the classroom to do fieldwork experience they do not even realize that these responsibilities are theirs as well as delivering instruction. Teachers' daily lives are full with professional assignments and obligations, including planning, designing lessons, implementing instruction, evaluating student learning, managing, disciplining, and more. This chapter highlights the major components in creating a positive psychosocial environment for classroom management and discipline. It also explores how teachers maintain and manage their teaching responsibilities and the learning climate in the classroom.

Knowing the Classroom Environment

New teachers must not assume that a regular classroom will be loaded with everything they would need. One key to effective teaching is to create a good learning environment for the class. Students' health and safety come first. Teachers are responsible for a thorough visual inspection and evaluation of the physical environment of the classroom to make sure it is suitable for teaching and learning. Also, teachers must conduct a complete inventory to survey all furnished items and identify areas that have the potential for distractions or may pose health and safety concerns. Teachers must take notes and compile a list of items needing repairs. Besides counting desks, chairs, tables, and computers, teachers need to make sure essential items are in the classroom: keys to the door, locks for cabinets, heating and air conditioning manual, clean window blinds or curtains, adequate lighting, a screen, a projector, bookshelves, chair and desk for the teacher, pencil sharpener, trash cans, filing cabinets, classroom telephone, intercom system, clock, a TV monitor, a computer for the teacher, a flag post, emergency procedures guidelines, and a first-aid kit. Figure 6.1 illustrates that effectiveness of management, discipline, and teaching and learning are all part of the classroom environment. Remember, a productive environment for teaching and learning is the legal, ethical, and professional responsibility of the teacher even if schools are required to provide the proper environment to the teachers.

Figure 6.1. Essentials of the classroom environment.

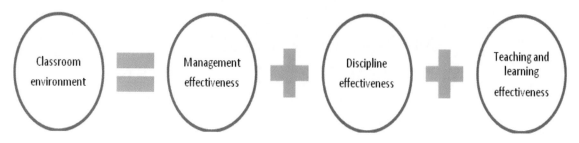

Professional Code of Ethics for Teachers

Teachers' professionalism determines the quality of classes they create for their students. A professional code of ethics should help teachers realize the importance of a suitable and appropriate learning environment.

Sometimes, experienced teachers share their daily responsibilities much like law enforcement officers work together. Teachers are held to a high standard in society because of their profession, and they have to act ethically, professionally, and legally to protect and supervise their students. They consider themselves the students' advocates as well as their protectors. Unlike law enforcement officers, teachers do not carry their badges to the classroom; but they do have their teaching licenses on file in the school office. In addition, teachers are expected to adhere to the professional code of ethics crafted by the National Education Association (NEA).

The NEA code of ethics for teachers has two main principles: Principle I is Commitment to the Student, and Principle II is Commitment to the Profession. The details of these two principles. In addition to expecting all teachers to follow the code of ethics, the NEA expects all beginning teachers to adhere to the model standards for beginning teacher licensing and development developed by the Interstate New Teacher Assessment and Support Consortium (INTASC). These are listed in Table 6.2.

Table 6.1. Teacher's Code of Ethics

PREAMBLE

- The National Education Association believes that the education profession consists of one education workforce serving the needs of all students and that the term "educator" includes education support professionals.
- The educator, believing in the worth and dignity of each human being, recognizes the supreme importance of the pursuit of truth, devotion to excellence, and the nurture of the democratic principles. Essential to these goals is the protection of freedom to learn and to teach and the guarantee of equal educational opportunity for all. The educator accepts the responsibility to adhere to the highest ethical standards.
- The educator recognizes the magnitude of the responsibility inherent in the teaching process. The desire for the respect and confidence of one's colleagues, of students, of parents, and of the members of the community provides the incentive to attain and maintain the highest possible degree of ethical conduct. The Code of Ethics of the Education Profession indicates the aspiration of all educators and provides standards by which to judge conduct.
- The remedies specified by the NEA and/or its affiliates for the violation of any provision of this Code shall be exclusive and no such provision shall be enforceable in any form other than the one specifically designated by the NEA or its affiliates.

PRINCIPLE I: COMMITMENT TO THE STUDENT

The educator strives to help each student realize his or her potential as a worthy and effective member of society. The educator therefore works to stimulate the spirit of inquiry, the acquisition of knowledge and understanding, and the thoughtful formulation of worthy goals.

In fulfillment of the obligation to the student, the educator:

1. Shall not unreasonably restrain the student from independent action in the pursuit of learning.
2. Shall not unreasonably deny the student's access to varying points of view.
3. Shall not deliberately suppress or distort subject matter relevant to the student's progress.
4. Shall make reasonable effort to protect the student from conditions harmful to learning or to health and safety.
5. Shall not intentionally expose the student to embarrassment or disparagement.
6. Shall not on the basis of race, color, creed, sex, national origin, marital status, political or religious beliefs, family, social or cultural background, or sexual orientation, unfairly
   a. Exclude any student from participation in any program
   b. Deny benefits to any student
   c. Grant any advantage to any student
7. Shall not use professional relationships with students for private advantage.
8. Shall not disclose information about students obtained in the course of professional service unless disclosure serves a compelling professional purpose or is required by law.

PRINCIPLE II: COMMITMENT TO THE PROFESSION

The education profession is vested by the public with a trust and responsibility requiring the highest ideals of professional service.

In the belief that the quality of the services of the education profession directly influences the nation and its citizens, the educator shall exert every effort to raise professional standards, to promote a climate that encourages the exercise of professional judgment, to achieve conditions that attract persons worthy of the trust to careers in education, and to assist in preventing the practice of the profession by unqualified persons.

In fulfillment of the obligation to the profession, the educator:

1. Shall not in an application for a professional position deliberately make a false statement or fail to disclose a material fact related to competency and qualifications.
2. Shall not misrepresent his/her professional qualifications.
3. Shall not assist any entry into the profession of a person known to be unqualified in respect to character, education, or other relevant attribute.
4. Shall not knowingly make a false statement concerning the qualifications of a candidate for a professional position.
5. Shall not assist a noneducator in the unauthorized practice of teaching.
6. Shall not disclose information about colleagues obtained in the course of professional service unless disclosure serves a compelling professional purpose or is required by law.
7. Shall not knowingly make false or malicious statements about a colleague.
8. Shall not accept any gratuity, gift, or favor that might impair or appear to influence professional decisions or action.

Source. Code of Ethics, National Education Association, 1975, retrieved from http://www.nea.org/home/30442.htm

Table 6.2. INTASC Standards and Expectations for Beginning Teachers

Standard	Expectations
Learner and Learning Domain:	Standards 1, 2, and 3
Standard #1: Learner Development	The teacher understands how learners grow and develop, recognizing that patterns of learning and development vary individually within and across the cognitive, linguistic, social, emotional, and physical areas, and designs and implements developmentally appropriate and challenging learning experiences.
Standard #2: Learning Differences	The teacher uses understanding of individual differences and diverse cultures and communities to ensure inclusive learning environments that enable each learner to meet high standards.
Standard #3: Learning Environments	The teacher works with others to create environments that support individual and collaborative learning and that encourage positive social interaction, active engagement in learning, and self-motivation.
Content Knowledge Domain:	Standards 4 and 5
Standard #4: Content Knowledge	The teacher understands the central concepts, tools of inquiry, and structures of the discipline(s) he or she teaches and creates learning experiences that make these aspects of the discipline accessible and meaningful for learners to assure mastery of the content.
Standard #5: Application of Content	The teacher understands how to connect concepts and use differing perspectives to engage learners in critical thinking, creativity, and collaborative problem solving related to authentic local and global issues.
Instructional Practice Domain:	Standards 6, 7, and 8
Standard #6: Assessment	The teacher understands and uses multiple methods of assessment to engage learners in their own growth, to monitor learner progress, and to guide the teacher's and learner's decision making.
Standard #7: Planning for Instruction	The teacher plans instruction that supports every student in meeting rigorous learning goals by drawing upon knowledge of content areas, curriculum, cross-disciplinary skills, and pedagogy, as well as knowledge of learners and the community context.
Standard #8: Instructional Strategies	The teacher understands and uses a variety of instructional strategies to encourage learners to develop deep understanding of content areas and their connections and to build skills to apply knowledge in meaningful ways.
Professional Responsibility Domain:	Standards 9 and 10
Standard #9: Professional Learning and Ethical Practice	The teacher engages in ongoing professional learning and uses evidence to continually evaluate his/her practice, particularly the effects of his/her choices and actions on others (learners, families, other professionals, and the community), and adapts practice to meet the needs

	of each learner.
Standard #10: Leadership and Collaboration	The teacher seeks appropriate leadership roles and opportunities to take responsibility for student learning, to collaborate with learners, families, colleagues, other school professionals, and community members to ensure learner growth, and to advance the profession.

Source: *The InTASC model core teaching standards*, Council of Chief State School Officers, 2010, http://www.ccsso.org/Documents/2011/InTASC %202011%20Standards%20At%20A%20Glance.pdf

Good teachers are not only reliable but also legally literate, ethically prudent, and professional. They are well-trained and knowledgeable about how to teach and how to maintain and manage the psychosocial environment in the classroom. Furthermore, good teachers understand the scope of their professional responsibilities as presented in Figure 6.2. This triangular representation of the three dimensions of teacher conduct should remind teachers of their professional responsibilities and commitment to the greater good of the entire community. These values are reinforced by the NEA's code of ethics and the InTASC standards of teaching. Teachers who possess these professional qualities are considered to be well trained and well prepared educators who are ready to enter the classrooms.

Figure 6.2. The domains of teacher conduct.

Professionally, these three dimensions are tightly interrelated. A teacher who is unethical is likely to be illegal or unprofessional as well. By the same token, a teacher who violates the law is probably also unethical. Careful adherence to high standards in all three domains enables teachers to provide students with a healthy and safe environment for learning and, at the same time, keeps teachers from giving into temptations that may jeopardize their professional careers.

What Is the Psychosocial Environment?

The classroom environment is the responsibility of the teachers because they hold the keys to the doors, and they are the managers who must maintain a healthy and safe learning atmosphere for all students at all times. As mentioned previously, the classroom is like a theatrical auditorium: teachers are the big screens and their personalities and attitudes are the pictures students see on the big screens. Teachers are leaders who make decisions and take action each and every day to keep the environment healthy and safe. The psychosocial environment is extremely important and perhaps is the prime factor contributing to quality teaching and learning.

Charles and Senter (2012) defined the psychosocial environment as including all human emotions; it is the overall climate, or "feeling tone," that exists in every classroom. The environment could be one of disappointment or encouragement; it could be a mixture of pleasure, distress, intrigue, boredom, happiness, sadness, excitement, love, fear, progress, and success. The psychosocial environment encompasses both positive and negative feelings as shown in Table 6.3.

The possibility that a classroom environment can be positive or negative is analogous to the idea that there are two sides to every story and the fact that every coin has two sides—head and tail. Teachers who understand the importance of psychosocial factors will create and maintain an environment that is conducive to teaching and learning. Those who lack understanding might put students in an environment that is academically detrimental and humanly depriving. In such an atmosphere, little or no quality teaching and learning can take place. Compare, for example, teachers who are well structured and have clean, organized, and neat classrooms for learning activities, with teachers who are messy, have poor organizational skills, and work in a cluttered and disorderly environment. The bottom line is that teachers who cannot keep the classroom environment up to required standards are probably not able to offer what is required for teaching and learning as illustrated in Figures 6.1 and 6.2.

Table 6.3. Positive and Negative Psychosocial Environments

Positive		Negative	
▪ Nurturing	▪ Conducive	▪ Frightening	▪ Punitive
▪ Understanding	▪ Welcoming	▪ Hostile	▪ Threatening
▪ Loving	▪ Enjoyable	▪ Scary	▪ Suppressing
▪ Friendly	▪ Caring	▪ Dark	▪ Oppressing
▪ Encouraging	▪ Warm	▪ Cold	▪ Cluttered
▪ Democratic	▪ Supportive	▪ Hot	▪ Messy
▪ Pleasant	▪ Promoting	▪ Harsh	▪ Disorganized
▪ Safe	▪ Motivating	▪ Aloof	▪ Bulky
▪ Healthy	▪ Rewarding	▪ Sarcastic	▪ Uncaring

The classroom must be a place where students can flourish academically, socially, and culturally. If placed in an environment where they cannot grow and glow, students are set up to fail because they cannot learn the skills they need in life. Teachers who can create positive learning climates have infinite impact on their students' learning, both immediate and long-term. An important learning outcome is retention of the information and skills gained, and the comfort of the students in the classroom environment influences their ability to retain what they have learned. Figure 6.3 shows that one of the components of retention is enjoyment of learning, which takes place in a positive psychosocial environment.

Figure 6.3. Components of student retention of information.

A positive feeling tone in a classroom should bring joy, comfort, pleasure, and energy that sustain academic progress and achievement. Teachers need to provide an environment in which students are free of physical, psychological, and mental suffering such as doubt, suspicion, fear, and anxiety. Students' states of mind affect their learning and retention. Figure 6.4 illustrates that the psychosocial health of both teachers and students as well as the learning process combine to form a positive psychosocial environment in the classroom.

Figure 6.4. Components of classroom psychosocial environment.

Physical Environment of the Classroom

Today's classrooms are varied in size, shape, and age. New schools have larger rooms with better equipment, furniture, tables, chairs, and desks whereas older schoolrooms are limited in space and have older tables, desks, and equipment. The physical environment of the classroom plays a major role in creating the overall psychosocial climate. Seating charts, storage units, closets, cupboard, windows, floor space, wall space, countertop space, shelf space, and other physical elements are all part of the classroom environment. Figure 6.5 displays several seating charts that may help teachers design their own classrooms to meet their own and their students' needs. Teachers are the architects who design their classrooms, and they must make the best use of what they have regardless of size or shape. A large room may seem preferable, but it does not give teachers a positive psychosocial environment automatically; they have to create that atmosphere. On the other hand, a smaller room does not prohibit teachers from producing a positive climate. The climate depends on the owner of the room, the teacher.

As mentioned earlier, teachers must bear in mind that their classroom designs must be (a) multidimensional—for multipurpose use, (b) event centered—for immediate and simultaneous activities, (c) flexible—for unexpected activities, and (d) public—so all students can share, socialize, use, enjoy, and learn.

Charles and Senter (2012) listed seven facets of the physical environment: floor space, wall space, countertop space, shelf space, cupboard and closet space, ambience, and ceiling space. Ambience is that aspect of the classroom environment that gives comfort, feeling, and enjoyment. One cautionary note concerns the use of the ceiling. Teachers should be extra careful when using the ceiling because of the possibility of hazard and injury; teachers risk accidents when they hang objects from the ceiling.

When arranging the room, teachers must consider the following factors: traffic patterns, visibility, auditory focus, accessibility, mobility, class participation, learning climate, engagement, transition, and rotation. Moreover, teachers must periodically adjust physical spaces to accommodate changes in academic activities and learning needs.

Social Context in the Psychosocial Environment

Human relations are the fundamental components of social context. School administrators usually look for quality professionalism and personal qualities in teachers. These traits have a lot to do with human relations skills and are important because teaching is a people business. Teachers deal with administrators, colleagues, parents, students, social workers, medical staff, office staff, and central office representatives. Professionalism may mean a number of different things to different people, but in practice, it means the teachers' reliability, interpersonal skills, and enthusiasm.

Figure 6.5. Selected basic seating arrangements.

Arrangements for independent work/tests/beginning of the year/lecture

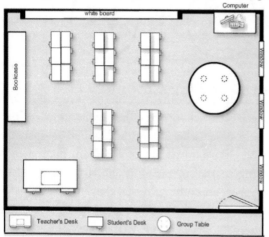
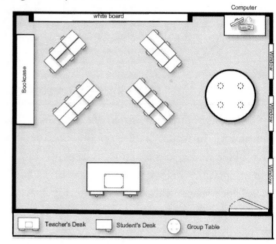

Arrangements for group work/stations

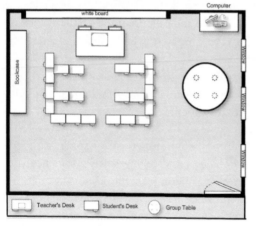
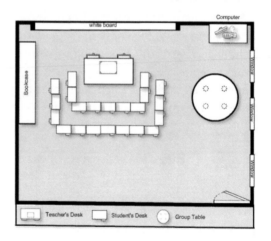

Arrangements for demonstration/discussion

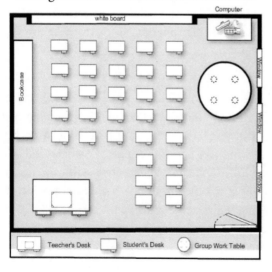
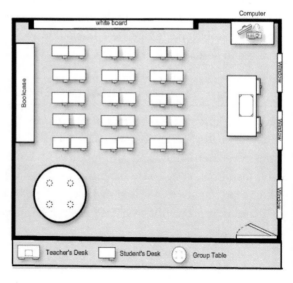

Reliability is a self-explanatory term that means that people can count on teachers to do their jobs. In other words, the teachers are present for their students, their colleagues, school administrators, and district personnel, and they perform their teaching assignments as required. Reliability also is evident in how teachers handle leaves of absence, sick leaves, preparation, planning, and team work. For new and probationary teachers, demonstrating reliability is extremely important.

Interpersonal skills are absolutely essential for teachers. Teachers must interact well with students, colleagues, parents, administrators, paraprofessionals, representatives of various social service agencies, and other district personnel. Building positive and cordial relationship is the key to connecting with people. Teachers' interpersonal communication skills tell others so much about their professionalism.

Human relations can be positive or negative, and human relation skills can be seen as serving two purposes: defense and offense. Politics does exist in the workplace, and it can be extremely dangerous for new and probationary teachers, especially if they have not yet developed defense skills. Cliques that are formed to protect the interests of their members can also be problematic. On the offense side, peers judge you by the enthusiasm they see in you as they get to know you, work with you, and talk with you. Your level of enthusiasm tells them how much you like your job. Teaching is stressful, and positive human relations help them as they struggle with dissatisfactions, frustrations, heath issues, and burnout.

In the social context, personal qualities play an even bigger role in teaching than in some other professions. Personal attributes such as passion, patience, organizational skills, commitment, perseverance, empathy, knowledge, expertise, and dedication are all important. However, in practice, the personal qualities administrators look for in teachers are oral communication skills, written communication skills, and commitment to the total school program. Both oral and written communication skills are essential because teachers communicate with and to students each and every day. In addition, writing skills are essential in designing lessons, communicating with parents, and conveying teaching and learning activities through texts. Teachers can correct their verbal communications as they speak, but once something is communicated in writing, it stands as written. Keep in mind that there is no such a thing as perfect communication, but teachers should always strive for excellent communication in both verbal and written forms.

Table 6.4. Selected Human Relations Skills

General Skills	Skills with Students	Skills with Colleagues	Skills with Parents
Professional composure	Positive attitude	Teamwork	Informing
Positive attitude	Positive character	Supportive	Communicating
Friendliness	Modeling	Sharing	Sharing
Active listening	Manners	Compromising	Notifying
Complimenting	Attention	Following	Conferencing
Honesty	Caring	Leading	Documenting
Integrity	Empathy	Collaborating	Following up
Supportiveness	Assistive	Collegiality	Contacting
Teamwork	Reinforcing	Cordiality	Suggesting
Group interests	Praise giving	Professionalism	Inviting
Cooperativeness	Rewarding	Ethics	Welcoming

As Tables 6.1 and 6.2 illustrated, commitment to the total school program is a way of committing to the students and the profession. For example, as teachers maintain good rapport with the students in their classes, they are at the same time strong advocates for the best interests of the entire student body of the school. The totality of the school program could include curricular activities, grant writing, student assessments, professional development, serving on committees, in-service activities, supervision, membership on student study teams, participation in the IEP process, and discipline-related activities. Simply put, commitment to the total school program means to be part of the school family.

It does not mean that all family members will agree on everything. Be careful because politics is everywhere, and try not to let politics interfere with teaching responsibilities. Overall, human relations skills such as those listed in Table 6.4 are significant contributors to the psychosocial environment of the classroom. Some teachers are territorial; however, they must learn that collaboration and collegiality will greatly strengthen their professional relationships and thus their success in the workplace.

Teacher Responsibilities in the Psychosocial Environment

The primary responsibility of teachers is to teach; however, teaching alone cannot be effective and beneficial to students if the psychosocial environment does not support it; classroom management is always a part of it. In other words, teaching can take place anywhere, but for learning to take place, teachers have to be proactive in establishing class structure, teambuilding, organizing the physical classroom, managing, disciplining, planning, and more. In practice, teachers must communicate and model the psychosocial interactions they wish to have. It takes time, energy, effort, leadership, responsibility, and decisions to develop a great psychosocial atmosphere. Some teachers may take years to learn how to build an environment they enjoy and love.

Regardless of how well trained and well prepared a teacher is, without a sustainable environment, the teaching and learning will go sour. The environment affects both teachers and students positively or negatively. In addition to guided practice, modeling, demonstration, delivery of instruction, and assessment, teachers hold the key to the development of a positive and safe class environment that boosts the psychosocial health of all.

Teachers need certain class building characteristics to build a positive, healthy, safe, and sound psychosocial and emotional environment in their class (Charles and Senter, 2012). As they build such an atmosphere, they can use the same characteristics to establish and maintain classroom structures that will provide academic benefits to students in the learning circle. Some of these traits are listed in Table 6.5.

Like people in any other profession, teachers develop their own attitudes, behaviors, personality traits, and conduct. Without a doubt, personality is the single most important factor that influences teaching and student learning in the classroom. Teachers must possess positive attitudes that foster learning; otherwise, maintaining a sound psychosocial environment in the class could be extremely difficult.

Furthermore, Ryan and Cooper (2001) observed that teacher competency may affect the psychosocial environment in the class. If teachers lack knowledge of subject matter, theoretical knowledge about learning and human behavior, and a repertoire of teaching skills, their performance is affected. One area that is significant in the development of a positive teaching and learning climate is the teachers' teaching style, as depicted in Figure 6.6. In addition to differences in emphasis on telling, showing, doing, and trying, there are different kinds of teachers according to personality; some are brick wall teachers, jellyfish teachers, backbone teachers, permissive teachers, mediocre teachers, great teachers, inspirational teachers, authoritative teachers, and authoritarian teachers.

Table 6.5. **Selected Class Building Characteristics**

Characteristic	Examples of Types of Actions
Positive attitude	Caring, fostering, nurturing, positive, supporting, sharing, fair
Enthusiasm	Motivating, promoting, encouraging, energizing, enjoying, fun, easy going, friendly
Student diversity	Unique, different, strengths, force, team, unified efforts
Belonging	Fit in, part of team, membership, sharing, inclusion, friendship, counting, ownership
Fairness	Even, positive, impartial, no favoritism, equal opportunity, reasonable, allowing to try, correcting
Responsibility	Ownership, in charge, teamwork, class action, cooperation, collaboration, action, consequences, commitment, trust, bond
Consistency	Fair, even, same, similar, predictable, preview, review
Friendliness	Pleasant, nice, kind, positive, encouraging, warm, supporting, caring, concerning
Progressing	Motivating, promoting, recognizing, praising, reinforcing, reassuring, affirming, improving
Success	Achievement, accomplishment, progress, improvement, rewarding, motivation, encouraging, promoting, earning
Understanding	Recognizing, supporting, assisting, motivating, promoting, encouraging, caring, empathy, compassion
Sense of humor	Funny, laughing, good time, sharing jokes, nice, kind, thought-provoking, flexible, understanding

Figure 6.6. **Four teaching styles.**

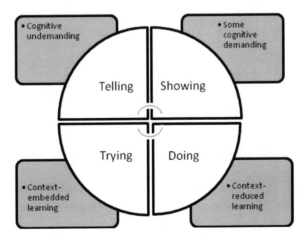

Most importantly, today's classrooms are filled with students of diverse socioeconomic backgrounds. Whether students are poor, rich, homeless, living in foster homes, or orphans, teachers need to exhibit the three professional attitudes described by Carl Rogers (1967): (a) be genuine or real with the students; (b) give positive, unconditional regard to the students; and (c) display professional empathy toward the academic struggle, difficulty, progress, and success of students.

Student Responsibilities in the Psychosocial Environment

Generally, teachers think students should be responsible and held accountable for establishing the psychosocial environment; however, students do not have the key to the door. Students are not legally responsible for what goes on in the classroom, but they are partially responsible for their learning while teachers are fully responsible to teach them and make sure they are receiving what is required by state law. Also, students' parents should be held accountable for the other half of their children's learning, the part that takes place outside the classroom. The responsibilities teachers may reasonably hold students accountable for are listed in Table 6.6. Keep in mind that not all children can perform these responsibilities because of their age, learning disability, special needs, language barriers, and gender; teachers need to take these factors into careful consideration.

Table 6.6. Selected Student Responsibilities

Responsibility	Examples of Dispositions
Preparation	Attendance, punctuality, habit, assignments, nutrition, basic needs, studying, supplies, medical needs
Social skills	Friendship, sharing, cooperation, asking, questioning, talking, seeking, communicating, working in groups
Behavior	Respect, manner, courteous, following directions, listening, patience, positive, self-control, pay attention
Positive attitudes	Can try, can do, can read, can share, can ask, can write, can speak
Learning	Practicing, trying, encoding, decoding, retaining, acquiring, applying, constructing, emulating
Contribution	Sharing, helping, exchanging, cooperation, grouping, socializing, participating
Take challenges	Do best, try hard, make effort, concentrate, study, take initiative, self-motivated, curiosity, desire, interest, ambition
Decision and choice	Learn to choose, think before action, considerate, careful, courteous, respectful, ask for permission
Dependable and independent	Cooperative, helpful, teamwork, self-control, take initiative, competitive, take charge, reliable, trustworthy, work alone
Consideration	Kind, nice, respectful, courteous, helpful, caring, supporting
Socializing	Playing, sharing, laughing, fun, excitement, amusement, interacting, singing, making friends, easy going, getting along
Respect	Nice, kind, courteous, helpful, supporting, listening, follow authority, follow rules, follow procedures

One area that is critical in boosting learning is increasing students' motivation toward learning specific subject matter in the classroom. Intrinsic and extrinsic motivations are equally important; however, students have different learning styles. Table 6.7 illustrates some of those differences according to Gardner's (1983) theory of multiple intelligences. Motivation comes and goes, and teachers need to make teaching and learning appealing to students by incorporating differentiating instructions, hands-on and minds-on activities, and cooperative learning.

Table 6.7. Multiple Intelligences

Type of Intelligence	Definition	Areas of Interest	Strengths	Possible Learning Styles
Linguistic	Word-smart or understand words and language easily	Reading, writing, memorizing, and telling stories	Memorization and reading	Reading, saying, hearing, or seeing words: The word player
Logical/ mathematical	Logical-smart, number-smart, or understand logical connections among different ideas, concepts, and theories	Experiments, numbers, asking questions, exploring patterns or relationships between objects, and inferring results	Math, reasoning, logic, problem solving, analogy, and details	Categorizing, ordering, sequencing, classifying, abstracting, and explaining patterns or relationships: The questioner
Spatial/ visual	Picture-smart or understand the expressions of arts, visual images, or mental images	Drawing, building, design, looking at pictures, examining objects, and creating images.	Imagination, visualization, sensing, reading mazes, interpreting charts, and solving puzzles	Visualizing, dreaming, mental imaging, drawing pictures, or photographic creation: The visualizer
Musical/ audio	Music-smart, sound-smart, rhythm-smart, or understand the patterns of sound system	Singing, humming tunes, listening, play to music, writing songs, responding to music, or creating rhythm	Memorization, picking sounds, understanding rhythms, or sensitivity to sounds	Sound, rhythm, melody, music, voices, or art: The music lover
Bodily/ kinesthetic	Hand-smart, body-smart, sports-smart, physical fitness, agility, or understand patterns of body movement	Moving, using body language, gesturing, touching and talking, or acting out	Physical activities, dance, sports, acting, crafts design, drafting, or hands-on activities	Touching, moving, interacting, processing, sensations of body movement, or feeling the physical appearance: The mover
Interpersonal	People-smart, friend-smart, social-smart, or understand grouping and social relationships	Making friends, liking people, talking to people, joining groups, sharing with people, depending on or player of team	Sharing, understanding, socializing, leading, following, organizing, communicating, listening, mediating, showing, or manipulating	Sharing, comparing, relating, cooperating, socializing, communicating, following, or leading: The socializer

Intra-personal	Self-centered, self-smart, self-propelled, or understand own ways	Be a loner, be isolated, pursue own interests, set up personal goals, or independent	Focusing on self, dealing with inward feelings, pursuing personal interests, like own ways of doing things, choose own goals, or follow instincts	Working alone, very independent, self-centered, having own space, creating own turf, liking individualized project, or being introverted: The individual
Natural	Flexible, adaptable, accommodating, considerate, or understand diverse needs and differences	Have flexible and adaptable patterns of thinking, feeling, understanding, or communicating with people	All forms of learning and interests, considering all things important, adjusting to needs accordingly, managing change well	Capable of adapting to different learning environments or subject matter, adjusting to needs accordingly, or controlling changes with flexibility: The flexible learner

Source: Information from *Frames of Minds: The Theory of Multiple Intelligences* by H. Gardner, 1983, New York: Basic Books.

Table 6.8. Five Domains of Student Learning

Domain	Associated Factors	Instructional Approaches
Cognitive	Comprehension, knowledge, skills, processing, and application	Knowing what and knowing how and expressing in written or verbal forms
Affective	Emotions, feelings, attitudes, personalities, behaviors, and values	Reflective responses to tasks, sharing with peers, interaction, communication, and expressing in verbal form
Psychomotor	Motor skills, coordination, comprehension, expression, and muscular control	Diagramming, mapping, manipulation, connection, idea web, and application
Social	Basic interpersonal communication skills, sharing, socialization, citizenship, and cooperation	Cooperative learning, teamwork, group activity, role and responsibility, and project
Academic	Cognitive academic language proficiency, literacy, constructivism, and context-reduction	Logical, arbitrary, social, physical, and constructive knowledge

Another element with direct and indirect influences on students' psychosocial dimensions is the instructional approach the teacher uses in the classroom. Table 6.8 lists the five domains of student learning and shows the factors and instructional approaches associated with each domain that may contribute to the emotional and psychosocial environment in the classroom. Vang (2010) cautioned:

These domains do not explicitly indicate how students feel in class; however, how students feel about a teacher plays a significant role in cognitive, social, and academic development. Whether the feelings are negative or positive could be critical in determining the extent of the child's engagement in academic tasks and the learning process. (p. 73)

Keep in mind that learning is the most important responsibility of students.

Everyday Maintenance and Management

It is easy to think about a typical day for teachers and imagine what they would be doing in the classroom. But it is very difficult to understand how each teacher feels about going to the classroom to teach each and every morning. Most teachers begin their daily routines around 7:00 a.m. and end at 5:00 p.m. These are typical working hours; however, most teachers spend at least 10 hours per day on the job because they have more teaching responsibilities than they can do in fewer hours.

Believe it, or not, most school principals expect teachers to work at least 10 hours a day. Why? Because the nature of the profession is such that teachers do not have enough time to do all the things in class that need to be done: prepping, planning, grading papers, cleaning the room, organizing the room, previewing lesson designs, reviewing materials, and most importantly, preparing instruction. So, they have to make the time, find the time, or borrow the time from somewhere else. Outside the classroom, teachers typically spend at least 20% of their own time on teaching assignments in order to adequately meet their obligations. Without this additional time, teachers would struggle and use improvised, impoverished, and capricious lesson plans in their teaching. The hours spent outside of instructional time directly impact the everyday maintenance and management of the psychosocial environment in the classroom.

Table 6.9. Typical Daily Schedule

Time	Samples of Routine Activities
8:00–8:15	Attendance, prepping, collecting and passing work, preparing, getting ready, introductory activities, ice breaker activities
8:15–10:00	Language arts (spelling, reading, writing, grammar, vocabulary words, read aloud, open court reading, pullout rotation
10:00–11:00	Math (addition, subtraction, multiplication, division, equations, expressions, number values, percent and decimal
11:00–11:15	Morning break (recess)
11:15–11:45	Science (life, earth, physical, or technology), hands-on and minds-on activities, experimentation, projects
11:45–12:10	Lunch
12:10–1:40	Reading (repeat morning lessons or new)
1:40–1:50	Afternoon break
1:50–2:15	Social studies (history)
2:15–2:45	Performance arts (arts, music, PE, songs, dance, etc....)
2:45–3:00	Clean up and dismissal

Usually the teachers' day follows a pattern such as that laid out in Tables 6.9 and 6.10. Teachers vary their class routines and schedules in accordance with the needs of the students, but they still operate according to a general pattern. In some schools, all teachers of the same grade level are expected to have similar or identical routines and schedules. Routines refer to regular ways or patterns of doing things in the classroom, and schedules are time allocations for the instruction of each subject matter. Moreover, assembly schedules and minimum days, on which students are dismissed early, shorten the time allocated for each subject area.

Table 6.10. Typical K–6 Schedules

Half-day K		Full-day K		Early dismissal		Full-day 1–6	
7:45–8:00	Attendance	9:00–9:45	Reading	9:00–9:45	Reading	8:30–9:00	Morning
8:00–8:15	Math	9:45–10:45	Writing	9:45–10:45	Writing		routine
8:15–8:20	Story time	10:45–11:45	Story time	10:45–11:45	Story time	9:00–11:00	Reading/
8:20–8:30	Writing	11:45–12:30	Lunch	11:45–12:30	Lunch		writing
8:30–9:30	Math/	12:30–1:15	Science	12:30–1:00	Science	11:00–11:15	Break/
	reading	1:15–2:00	Math	1:00–1:30	Math		recess
9:30–10:00	PE or snack	2:00–2:15	Snack/	1:30–2:00	Social	11:15–12:45	Math
10:00–10:15	Story time		break		Studies	12:45–1:15	Lunch
10:15–11:00	Centers	2:15–3:30	Social	2:00–2:15	Clean up,	1:15–1:30	Reading
11:00–11:30	Clean up,		studies		line up,		aloud
	line up, and	3:30–4:45	Clean up,		and dis-	1:30–1:45	Vocabulary
	dismissal		line up,		missal	1:45–2:15	Social
			and				studies
			dismissal			2:15–2:30	Science
						2:30–3:15	Arts/PE
						3:15–3:30	Clean up,
							line up, and
							dismissal

One of daily goals of teachers is to maintain order in the classroom at all times. To be in control of all situations, maintaining a sound emotional and psychological environment for teaching and learning, teachers need to enforce and reinforce classroom rules, logical consequences, and procedural guidelines developed for the class. Table 6.11 lists some basic rules, Tables 6.12 and 6.13 present some basic logical consequences, and Table 6.14 gives some basic procedural guidelines for academic activities in the classroom. Keep in mind that rules, consequences, and guidelines must be flexible; otherwise, teaching and learning would be too rigid. Teachers might go along with the flow every once in a while. Allowing students to take control of their academic tasks is not wrong unless the teacher fails to supervise or is not present in the room.

Table 6.11. Examples of Classroom Rules, by Grade

Grades K–3	Grades 4–6	Grades 7–8	Grades 9–12
▪ Raise hands before speaking	▪ Be ready to learn	▪ Be in seat before bell rings	▪ Be in seat before the bell rings
▪ Keep hands to self	▪ Follow directions	▪ Come to school prepared	▪ Follow directions
▪ Listen when someone speaks	▪ Keep hands and feet to self	▪ Follow directions	▪ Be kind and responsible for personal actions
▪ Do not leave seat without permission	▪ Raise hands if need help	▪ Raise hands if have questions	▪ Wait for order to be dismissed
▪ Follow orders to move in and out of class	▪ Be kind to others	▪ Keep hands and feet to self	▪ All assignments are due on time
		▪ No foul language is allowed in class	

Table 6.12. Examples of Logical Consequences, by Grade

Grades K–3	Grades 4–6	Grades 7–8	Grades 9–12
1. Verbal warning	1. Verbal warning	1. Verbal warning	1. Verbal warning
2. Name on the board	2. Miss recess	2. Send to the office	2. Send to the office
3. Pull a card	3. Send note home	3. Send note home	3. Contact parents
4. Miss recess	4. Contact parents	4. Contact parents	4. Conference
5. Send note home	5. Conference	5. Conference	5. Follow-up services

Table 6.13. Logical Consequences for Selected Infractions

Types of Infraction	Logical consequences
First offense	Verbal warning and teacher talks to student either privately or publicly, depending on the behavior and its severity
Second offense	Take away privileges and lose one recess
Third offense	Take away privileges and lose two recesses
Fourth offense	Take away privileges or lose all recesses for the day
Fifth offense	Take away privileges and call parents or guardians
Sixth offense	Take away privileges, send to the office, have meeting with parents, and evaluate for possible suspension
Physical or verbal threats, severe disruption, or rudeness to teacher and classmates	Will not be tolerated and results in immediate referral to the offices of principal, assistant principal, or appropriate administrators for intervention

Table 6.14. Basic Procedures for Classroom Management

Procedural Area	Possible Procedural Activities
Beginning of class/opening procedures	Roll call, absentees, tardy students, academic warm-up routines, behaviors, distributing materials, adjustment
Line up	Going out, coming in, outside the door, on the playground, going to assembly, dismissal
Room/school areas	Shared areas, teacher's desk, water fountain, bathroom, student desks, learning center stations, playground, lunchroom/cafeteria
Setting up independent work areas	Defining work alone, identifying problems, resources, solutions, scheduling, checkpoints
Instructional activities	Contact between teacher and students, student movement, signals for attention, signals for teacher, initiative, participation, group rotation, passing materials, behavior in group, behavior outside group, academic engaged time
Ending class	Putting things away, clean up, backpacks, homework, clothes, personal items, dismissing class
Interruptions	Rules, orders, conduct, delays, talk among students, out-of-seat policies, pencil sharpening
Work requirements	Heading papers, pencil or pen, neatness, legibility, incomplete work, late work, missed work, due dates, make-up work, supplies, coloring, drawing, cursive or manuscript
Communicating assignments	Posting, orally giving, turning, returning, homework, provision for absentees, incomplete work, collecting

Monitoring student work	Independent work, group work, presentation, completion in class, completion of homework, progress, challenges, difficulties
Checking assignments in class	Exchanging papers, going over answers, grading papers, turning in work, collecting work, correcting, practicing
Grading procedures	Assigning report grades, recording grades, extra credit work, grading criteria, grade contracts, record keeping
Academic feedback	Reward system, incentives, reinforcers, posting work, informing parents, record keeping, feedback on papers, progress, improvement
In case of emergency	Fire drills, health and safety, lockdown, poison, injury, choking, fire, flood, tornado, rain

On any given day, two very important things must happen in the classroom: teaching and learning. Learning is the most important responsibility for students, and teachers are responsible for making sure that learning is taking place. Student learning styles are described in Table 6.7. Classroom teaching is based solely on the instructional planning and student activities the teacher designs for the students to do in class. Teachers' attitudes and personalities play a major role in all instruction. Students can sense their teachers' attitudes toward the subject matter, lesson plans, learning objectives, instruction, student activities, and the class. Instead of simply using the direct instruction model, teachers should think creatively and incorporate different instructional modalities to make teaching and learning connected, congruent, compatible, accessible, comprehensible, and engaging. Consider, for example, the three tiers of instructional strategy depicted in Figure 6.7. These strategies are designed to be used sequentially to bring students to the specific goal and general objective of the lesson. Teachers should also pay special attention to how their behaviors, listed in Table 6.15 (Kounin, 1970), positively or negatively influence the psychosocial environment.

Figure 6.7. Three tiers of instructional strategies.

Activities and task strategies are used to support instructional strategies. However, teachers have many options for developing supportive activities to make instruction productive and effective. Use of group activities or cooperative learning is one of the most common task strategies because students enjoy working together as teams. One cautionary note: Group activities do not work well with students in Grades K–2 because students at that level have limited abilities in conversing, sharing, exchanging, and discussing. However, despite the negatives, students do enjoy the social process. For other grades, group activities should be productive if teachers prescribe them carefully with clear and concise directions and task responsibilities. The group process strengthens social cooperation, human relational skills, and interpersonal skills.

Table 6.15. Teachers' Instructional Behaviors

Behavior	Examples of Teacher's Actions
With-it-ness	Alert at all times to sights, sounds, movement, and interactions in the class
Overlapping	Engaged with or attending to two or more teaching events at the same to keep the processes of the classroom functioning and moving forward optimally
Smoothness	Preparing or preplanning the lesson so that extraneous matters are taken care of beforehand
Momentum	Plan well to keep the lesson plan moving briskly, avoiding over-emphasis on minor issues, and making adjustments to minimize fragmentation
Group alerting	Planning to call on students randomly, mobile, and applying response in unison.

Independent practice is the ultimate goal of learning because testing is based solely on individual students' ability to perform by retrieving information from their retention repertoire in the subconscious mind. In practice, nothing is more valuable than allowing students to practice all the concepts, skills, and ideas they are taught in class. Also, teachers must realize that most learning takes place in the classroom. Homework assignments are given to students for independent practice to reinforce what is learned in class, but these assignments should not ever be used to take the place of independent practice in class.

The bottom line is that the more time teachers allocate to academic engaged time, the more learning will take place because students must actively engage in the learning process. Getting all students to engage is the everyday job of teachers. If they do not perform this job effectively, some students will not learn what is expected of them in life. And that is how the psychosocial environment of the classroom is managed.

Daily Reflection on the Psychosocial Environment

Reflection is the key to becoming a successful educator. At the end of the day, teachers pack their personal belongings, check out in the front office, pick up their mail, and go home to join their families and loved ones. Taking one day at a time enables teachers to learn, relearn, thrive, grow, and glow academically and professionally. Expecting each day to be different but better fires teachers' passion, and implementing best professional practices enables them to become better and better practitioners. Whether teachers want to grade papers, organize desks, throw out the trash, record grades, read e-mails, or review the pace calendar before closing the blinds, lowering the curtains, turning the heater or air conditioner off, putting the lights out, and heading out the door, they need to spend just a bit of their time, perhaps 5 to 10 minutes, reflecting on what they accomplished during the day. They should forget any disciplinary problems and focus on the big things that matter the most to the students.

Reflective teaching helps teachers learn, grow, and glow and fuels their passions because reflection contains rich and practical tools that can sharpen teachers' actions in planning instruction. To inflame teaching passion, Vang (2010) explained the value of reflection to the teacher:

> There are two types of reflective teaching: reflection in action and reflection on action. *In action* means that the teacher reflects instantaneously and adjusts accordingly while teaching the lesson plan. *On action* means that the teacher reflects upon the overall effectiveness of a lesson plan after it is taught and uses the feedback to adjust so as

to improve curricular planning for future teaching. There is always room for professional growth, and growth comes through reflective teaching. (p. 311)

Reflective teaching improves teachers' preplanning, ongoing planning, and post-planning, as shown in Figure 6.8.

Figure 6.8. Cycle of planning instruction.

Moreover, keep in mind that one of the goals for having a positive learning psychosocial environment is to allow both students and teachers to experience class esprit de corps. As Charles and Senter (2002) explained:

> Esprit de corps is one of the best things that can happen in a classroom, because the work becomes joyful instead of onerous, and students active rather than lethargic. Days typically end with a satisfied glow instead of wretched fatigue…as students rally in spirit, they provide immense rewards to the teachers (p. 265).

At the end of the day, teachers may reflect upon the whole day and perhaps think to themselves about these two questions: What really energizes teachers and what really bothers teachers the most? Perhaps, the psychosocial environment will keep popping up in their minds because they can feel the esprit de corps, or perhaps they want to do things differently next time. The tone is a two-way mirror that determines how healthy, sound, and safe the psychosocial environment really is. At last, teachers can feel that their professional attitudes and personality do matter the most and are the most important ingredients of teaching and learning environment.

Summing Up

This chapter explained how teachers maintain and manage the psychosocial environment in the classroom. Establishing a sound, healthy, and safe psychosocial environment requires tremendous preparation, diligent work, and professional commitment. Some teachers may be born, but many are made, and they all are unique in teaching style, managerial skills, and human relations skills. Some are leaders, others are followers; and many are just teachers.

The NEA professional code of ethics and INTASC standards for teachers are valuable tools for professional growth. However, without a healthy psychosocial environment, these commitments and standards are difficult to follow. Teaching and learning go hand in hand; they are inseparable. The teachers' job is to teach and the student's job is to learn. But who should people blame if students are not learning what is expected of them? The answer is not easy. Perhaps a class's high or low API scores have something to do with the totality of the psychosocial environment of the classroom. Teachers need to be trained and well prepared to maintain and manage a learning environment that is emotionally, psychologically, and academically conducive to teaching and learning.

Most importantly, teachers must be legally literate, ethically sound, and professionally competent to provide a positive psychosocial environment in the classroom. Otherwise, their teaching would be wearing the wrong-size shoes: too tight, too loose, or too small. In other words, teachers have to create an environment that fits their and their students' needs so students are comfortable enough to learn and teachers are comfortable enough to develop professionally.

PART III

THE MULTICULTURAL STRATEGIES MANAGEMENT DOMAIN

CHAPTER SEVEN

UNDERSTANDING THE DAILY CLASSROOM STRUCTURE

The mediocre teacher tells; the good teacher explains;
the superior teacher demonstrates; and the great teacher inspires.
William Arthur Ward

Introduction

Today's classrooms are sophisticated in many ways. They are different in size, shape, and space. Newer schools have better and larger classrooms than older schools, which offer smaller and limited classroom spaces. The physical environment of the classroom may be the primary factor with short-term and long-term effects on the quality of teaching and learning. Most importantly, the classroom itself determines the psychosocial dimensions of teachers and students. Overcrowded classrooms are not necessarily the result of a high number of students. Sometimes, classrooms are crowded because the limited amount of space is disorganized. However, space constraints should not be the primary obstacles limiting teachers' ability to offer quality instruction. The teacher's creativity is what makes teaching and learning productive, fun, intriguing, entertaining, and engaging. This chapter gives teachers a conceptual framework for classroom structure to help them understand the scope of teaching responsibilities in the multicultural classroom setting.

What Is Classroom Structure?

Every hour of teaching has a beginning, a middle, and an end. Academic discipline requires procedural structure. Daily routines and structure are keys to effective teaching. The whole class as a unit is a solid structure, and the structure is made of different parts coming together. In order for teachers to have effective classroom management and discipline, classroom structure has to be well established, well organized, and properly implemented. Structure is a generic term and self-explanatory; however, classroom structure encompasses many practices in the classroom, including schedules, routines, rules, consequences, participation, instruction, student activities, management, and discipline. Classroom structure literally refers to the way teachers order, organize, establish, build, create, and prioritize the totality of the classroom environment for academic instruction on a daily basis.

How teachers begin the school year is crucial because setting the tone for the rest of the year, communicating clear expectations for all students, and laying out a plan of action are structures that form a solid foundation for other structures. Classroom structure also involves other areas, such as management, instruction, discipline, assessment, reinforcement, planning, and more. Without meaningful classroom structures, many things in the classroom can be out of compliance, and, for the most part, teaching and learning could be awkward, fragmented, disjointed, inconsistent, and chaotic.

As Figure 7.1 indicates, classroom structure encompasses two basic areas—instruction and management—and these two areas are further divided into their component parts. Good classroom structure contributes a great deal to the success of teaching, learning, management, and discipline if teachers understand and recognize the significance of its direct impact on the psychosocial environment in the classroom.

Figure 7.1. Components of classroom structure.

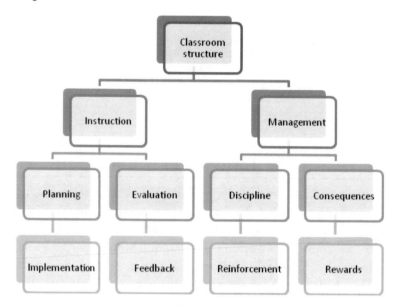

Good teachers who are responsible usually start developing classroom structure early enough to prepare students for academic teaching. For example, teachers set up behavioral expectations for all students. They use modeling; they give examples, and they explain how students should follow their orders in the classroom. It would be totally unfair to expect students to learn everything at once, but without a consistent approach, structure can fall apart easily. Moreover, classroom structure helps both teachers and students bounce back from difficulties throughout the year. Just like any other part of the classroom environment, practice makes perfect; therefore, teachers must train students in all structural areas.

The Process of Instruction

Teaching is the number one priority for teachers. Each day teachers make a number of decisions regarding academic curricular activities and how to deliver instruction. They also decide how to assess student learning, design tests to measure teaching and learning, and reflect on the effectiveness of teaching and learning at the end of the day. Management and discipline are important components of everyday life in the classroom, but teaching is the most important duty for teachers. Without quality instruction, students do not benefit from the managing and disciplining. Teachers must be clear about the instructional process, or their teaching could be just a recitation of superficial knowledge that students may not need. Figure 7.2 illustrates the five major stages of the instructional process (Cooper, 1999; Ryan & Cooper, 2001; Vang, 2010).

Figure 7.2. The instructional process.

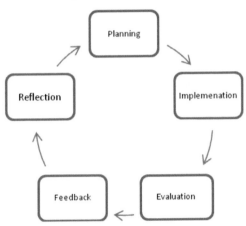

In addition, teachers must know *how to do lesson planning* for each lesson to be taught. Typically, lesson planning must include:

a. Content area standards
b. Time allocation
c. Grade level and age appropriateness
d. Learning objective (s) for each lesson plan
e. Materials or supplies required
f. Management strategies
g. Disciplinary approaches
h. Engagement level
i. Teaching methodology
j. Teaching style
k. Instructional presentation
l. Guided practices
m. Student activities
n. Independent practices
o. Make adaptations
p. Pedagogical skills, concepts, knowledge, and applications
q. Evaluation, closure, or assessment
r. Social interaction or socialization
s. Reviewing
t. Reflection

Regardless of the lesson plan format, teachers must include these components as much as possible to make the learning objective meaningful and purposeful for teaching and learning.

Student Diversity

The world has approximately 6.8 billion people who speak nearly 6,900 different languages. The U.S. has nearly 300 million people who speak approximately 425 dialects. K–12 schools have 54 million students. Of that number, 38 million are in Grades K-8 and 16 million are in Grades 9–12.

There are 5.2 million students with learning disabilities in American schools. And 3.2 million students speak primary languages other than English. California has 1.5 million limited English proficient (LEP) students and approximately 1 million fluent English proficient (FEP) students. All together, approximately 10 million U.S. students in K–12 grades speak a primary language other than English at home. Table 7.1 shows some of the California and national student demographics.

Table 7.1. Selected Student Demographics

Characteristic	California	Nation
White	31.9%	58.0%
Black	8.0%	16.9%
Asian/Pacific Islander	11.0%	4.4%
Hispanic	45.2%	19.5%
American Indian/Alaska Native	0.8%	1.2%
Economically disadvantaged	47.9%	36.7%
English-language learner	24.9%	7.8%

Note: Data from the National Education Association, 2006, and California Department of Education, 2005–2006.

Of the 54 million students in the U.S., minority students of diverse backgrounds make up 43%, up from 38% in recent years. Economically disadvantaged students make up 48% of California's 6 million students and 37% of all U.S. K–12 students. In California, migrant students make up approximately 3% of the total student population as compared to 0.6% of the U.S. student population. Students of color constitute a majority in 25 of the nation's largest school districts, including some in California. If these trends continue, in the next 20 years the number of students of color will outnumber the majority student population in the U.S. These students will pose instructional challenges to teachers.

Beginning the School Year

It does not matter whether a teacher begins in the classroom at the start of the year or on the morning of any given day, a pleasant tone of voice should be used to introduce students to the class to make them feel welcome. Teachers should go over daily learning expectations for each lesson plan, remind students of classroom rules and consequences and then go right into the daily routines and schedule. Preparing students' psychosocial environment, or the classroom's tone, is academically critical. Teachers should not start giving instructions if students are not ready because unready students are not actively engaged in the learning process. Taking the time to help students develop habitual attitudes toward classroom structures will pay off later as it will decrease time needed for preparation and discipline and therefore increase teaching time.

Good teachers usually incorporate various ideas and methods for engaging students spontaneously while simultaneously monitoring students' actions. Teachers must not ignore the need for special accommodations, modifications, and adaptations for students who require special assistance. In other words, the classroom structure has to be inclusive, considerate of all, and flexible to accommodate multicultural issues and other matters of diversity. Think of the classroom as comprised of three groups of students as illustrated in Figure 7.3: top, middle, and bottom. Every classroom should have structures that address the needs of students in all three groups.

Figure 7.3. Academic groups in every classroom.

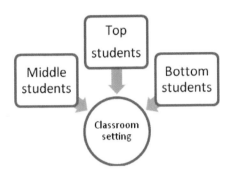

Opening Procedures

Teachers are the big screen in the classroom. Each morning students look at the screen, and whether the screen is colorful or black and white, that is the image to which students must adjust; that is the learning climate they feel in the classroom. Teachers' attitudes and personalities are contagious, and they affect students negatively or positively as depicted in Figure 7.4. The way they begin the day sets a tone for their students. Kind messages or welcome remarks gain students' attention in a pleasant way. Making sure students are in their seats, doing a quick visual check to see that everyone is alert and attentive, and having something fun for students to do when they first arrive begin their day with great energy and good feelings. While students are busy on task, teachers should perform daily routines such as taking roll or checking attendance, walking around to monitor students' on-task behavior, and provide assistance as needed. Some teachers like to sit while students are working, and although this posture is not bad, walking around demonstrates the desired trait of "with-it-ness."

Figure 7.4. The teacher as the "big screen."

Using signals is highly effective in the classroom. Teachers should train students to respond to classroom signals to save time and correct misbehaviors. For example, the following phrases can be used to gain students' attention quickly and pleasantly: "One, two, three; eyes on me" or "If you can hear me, touch your ear," "If you can hear me, touch your nose," and "If you can hear me, touch your chin." Some teachers use a high five, clapping, a bell, or a timer as signals. Keep in mind that every single academic activity does not have to be tightly structured, but most have to be structured to some extent because students are trained to practice activities that allow them to talk, share, move, and experience.

Normal Class Greetings

Social greetings should be used several times throughout the day. In the morning, teachers welcome students to class. After morning recess, teachers may greet students again to make sure they are feeling warm and included. After lunch, teachers should welcome students back to class. And after the afternoon recess, teachers should make no student is in any kind of pain or suffered an injury. Greetings could be very simple words, phrases, comments, or questions:

1.   Welcome back to class.
2.   How was recess?
3.   How were the games?
4.   Having any fun out there?
5.   Are you hot or cold?
6.   What did you learn out there?
7.   Are you ready for...?
8.   Any questions?

Use "I" messages, such as "I really like the way you guys.... Check to make sure students brought back all balls, jump ropes, rings, etc.... Most importantly, social greetings model social skills, encourage warm human relations, and provide comfort. Moreover, greetings could be public or private praise that helps create a productive, positive, warm, and welcome psychosocial learning environment for all. In most cases, class greetings have a direct influence on students' personal manners. The ultimate goal is to foster students' feelings of connectedness with their teachers and their peers. The importance of classroom interactions is pictured in Figure 7.5.

Figure 7.5. Classroom social relationships.

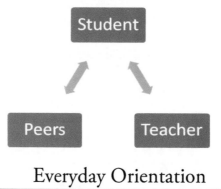

Everyday Orientation

Teachers should not be bored when they have to repeat some information to students over and over again. Repetition is part of reflective teaching. Most teachers repeat themselves to make sure students are clear, understand, follow, and "get it." Teachers must make sure that students are not only hearing them talking but are listening to what they are talking about. In other words, hearing is inattentive action, but listening is an attentive action. Consider, for example, students may hear their teachers talking but are not listening to them just as listening to the music is not the same as hearing the music.

Daily repetition is a useful way of improving recitation and rehearsal of anything that is not clearly understood. For example, teachers may have to remind students about the rules, consequences, homework assignments, testing dates, project due dates, and other academic information. They cannot expect students to remember everything in their heads. Some teachers use academic planners to help students keep track of important information, and they remind students to jot down information from the board. Others use daily notes to remind students of what is due the next day. These activities are part of daily orientation. Of course, students should be held responsible for their assignments, but keep in mind that taking responsibility may be new to some students, and training students to be responsible is one of the teacher's many duties.

Furthermore, orientation is often needed to convey information about changes, such as new seating charts, assignments, news, or school activities. Students may not fully understand something they heard outside the classroom, and they may need to ask the teacher for clarification. Or students may lack information about the school and school rules. Orientation is one of the ways to provide students with everyday information to explain or clear up misperceptions and misconceptions. Everyday orientation can provide clear guidance for students on classroom issues related to the psychosocial environment.

The Daily Schedule

Teachers should post the daily schedule and routine in a conspicuous location on the wall. Large-size print should be used to make the schedule visible to all students. Also, an early dismissal or minimum day schedule should be posted next to the daily schedule. If available, an assembly schedule should be posted in the same location for easy reference. Table 7.2 gives some samples of daily schedules. Many teachers write the daily schedule on the chalkboard, but that takes space that may be needed for instruction. The chalkboard should be used instead for academic purposes. Some teachers place a lot of information on the chalkboard because it is easy to do so. The best use of the chalkboard is for illustrating examples during instruction rather than for non-academic purposes.

The daily schedule does not usually include the procedural guidelines for student activities. Teachers need to create specific procedures for academic tasks in the classroom, and these guidelines need to be explained repeatedly to students to make sure they are clear and students understand them. Teachers in lower grades cannot expect students to memorize all classroom procedures. Instead, they must train students to practice them. The daily schedule will not work as well without clear, step-by-step procedural guidelines in place.

Table 7.2. Samples of Daily Schedules

Half-day K		Full-day K		Early dismissal		Full-day 1–6	
7:45–8:00	Attendance	9:00–9:45	Reading	9:00–9:45	Reading	8:30–9:00	Morning routine
8:00–8:15	Math	9:45–10:45	Writing	9:45–10:45	Writing		
8:15–8:30	Story time	10:45–11:45	Story time	10:45–11:45	Story time	9:00–11:00	Reading/ writing
8:20–8:30	Writing	11:45–12:30	Lunch	11:45–12:30	Lunch		
8:30–9:30	Math/ reading	12:30–1:15	Science	12:30–1:00	Science	11:00–11:15	Break/ recess
		1:15–2:00	Math	1:00–1:30	Math		
9:30–10:00	PE or snack	2:00–2:15	Snack/ break	1:30–2:00	Social Studies	11:15–12:45	Math
10:00–10:15	Story time					12:45–1:15	Lunch
10:15–11:00	Centers	2:15–3:30	Social studies	2:00–2:15	Clean up, line up, and dismissal	1:15–1:30	Reading aloud
11:00–11:30	Clean up, line up, and dismissal	3:30–4:45	Clean up, line up, and dismissal			1:30–1:45	Vocabulary
						1:45–2:15	Social studies
						2:15–2:30	Science
						2:30–3:15	Arts/PE
						3:15–3:30	Clean up, line up, and dismissal

Time Management in Class

One of the most critical elements in teaching is time management. Many teachers find managing time challenging for a number of reasons. They may forget about time when they are teaching, or they may spend too much time on one area and neglect others. Teachers are sometimes interrupted by students with questions and misbehaviors. Occasionally teachers digress from the subject matter and waste time on other topics. Finally, teachers have difficulty managing time if they lack organization, structure, good sequence in teaching, or focus. Teachers must realize they will never have enough time for everything they want to accomplish in the classroom. They have to make or find time to make instructional practices effective and, most importantly, to allow students to engage in academic tasks in class.

Teachers can strategize their teaching practices to improve time management. For example, the 20- to 30-minute lesson plans can be broken down in the following manner:

1. Use 5 minutes for introduction and engagement.
2. Spend the next 5 to 10 minutes in instruction and guided practice.
3. Use the rest of the period for academic engaged time.

With 45- to 60-minute lesson plans, teachers have more room for the various parts of the lesson. Teachers need to practice managing time until they can do it efficiently; otherwise, students may not grasp or master the concepts in a timely manner. Time is easier to manage when teachers are prepared, organized, and trained in how best to deliver instruction.

Teachers who lack classroom structure, procedural guidelines, routines, and smooth transitions often encounter time management problems because their way of managing the class is disorganized. Furthermore, good teachers will not give instruction until all students are ready. Some teachers deliver instruction without prepping their students, and that is ineffective and inefficient. Teachers have to execute their duties effectively and efficiently to achieve maximum output.

Providing Assistance in Class

Besides having procedural guidelines, teachers need to be creative in how they provide assistance to students in the middle and bottom groups during class. Making ways for students to engage in academic tasks during class on a daily basis is essential because students do not learn by listening to the teacher. Students learn by doing the work given to them in class. However, not all students are able to perform academic tasks independently. Some need extra assistance, especially ELL and SN students. Teachers must find extra time to provide instructional assistance; otherwise, there is no equity of instruction in class. In other words, students who lag behind will fall through the cracks without assistance. TPE standards and TPA tasks require teachers to make adaptations to accommodate the needs of ELL and SN students, and if they do not, there is a serious concern about their ability to provide fair instruction for all students.

Some teachers have instructional assistants or bilingual aides available for providing instructional assistance to needy students. Others use student peers in cooperative learning and group activities to help those students who cannot perform the tasks in class. Providing individualized instruction is quite difficult for most teachers because of time constraints; however, teachers need to make or find the time to help those students who need additional attention. Otherwise, needy students are left behind. Teachers can prescribe learning center instruction as an intervention strategy to help a small group of students who have similar needs, or they can use alternative approaches such as RTI, SIOP,

ELD, or SDAIE methodologies to target specific needs. These extra efforts need to be developed by the teachers or they will not take place.

Other types of in-classroom assistance include voluntary and involuntary activities such as the use of social reinforcement, classroom helpers, or privilege reinforcers. These activities should be used with caution and must be applied fairly. Teachers must follow classroom protocol to make sure all students have equal opportunity to participate in reinforcement activities.

Monitoring Medications

Today, many school children are on prescribed medications for medical conditions such as asthma, diabetes, heart problems, epilepsy, seizure, hyperactivity, hypertension, low blood pressure, and more. Also, some students are sensitive to certain foods and dairy products, and allergic reactions may occur in the classroom. Teachers should be on the lookout for allergies because they can be life threatening. Moreover, students who require daily medications for whatever reason should be properly noted. Teachers should not, at any time, administer insulin shots or medication doses to students in class. Only certified medical personnel, such as school nurses, are authorized to administer medications and injections.

Maintaining the Physical Environment

Today's classrooms are multicultural; students are culturally and linguistically diverse and come from many socioeconomic backgrounds. The student population is as diverse as the colors of a rainbow. Teachers must design classroom settings that respond to the diverse needs and abilities students bring to the classroom. If not, many students will be left to fend for themselves.

When designing the classroom, teachers should pay close attentions to these concerns: mobility, accessibility, academic achievement, visibility and auditory focus, patterns of class participation, social contact and interaction, positive learning climate, psychosocial environment, classroom management, transitional activities, classroom discipline, student work display, and centers. Moreover, classroom design has to meet most instructional demands. That means the classroom itself has to be a multipurpose environment where students can have full freedom to do all the activities prescribed by the teachers. On top of all these issues, the classroom must meet all health and safety standards as shown in Figure 7.6.

Figure 7.6. Classroom health and safety issues.

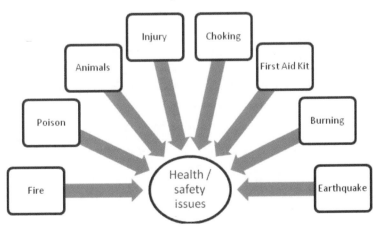

One area about which teachers should be concerned are the in-and-out traffic patterns of students. One goal of classroom management is to make sure all students are safe, and no one should be exposed to any kind of injury or health risk. Teachers are responsible for training students how to act responsibly inside the classroom at all times.

Increasing Discipline Problems

Teachers must recognize that discipline problems are increasing in public schools. Some students see school as a golden opportunity, but others are in school only because they are compelled to be. Teachers should anticipate misbehaviors and be prepared to handle any inappropriate student behaviors in a timely manner. However, teachers must address discipline problems professionally. The most common forms of school infractions are cheating, stealing, vandalizing, substance abuse, bringing a weapon to school, possessing illicit drugs, consuming or possessing alcohol, selling illicit drugs on school property, fighting, bullying, disobedience, and involvement in gang-related activities. Some discipline problems are typical, but others may be unusual. Maintaining constancy is a good approach to dealing with management and discipline problems as they arise; otherwise, some discipline issues may get out of hand.

Teachers are not always properly trained to handle difficult situations that may occur on school grounds or perhaps in the classroom. Recognizing the earliest signs of potential problems should help teachers to alert proper school authorities to deal with serious infractions properly and quickly. Keeping the classroom healthy and safe is the teachers' professional responsibility.

Establishing a Management Approach

As with classroom discipline, managerial matters require ongoing assessment and attention. There is no perfect form of classroom management, no one model that fits all. Teachers have to try different managerial techniques to discover what they feel comfortable with. The number one key is practice, followed by modeling of good behaviors. All managerial matters should be handled with respect for the parties involved, and teachers should hold themselves to high professional standards. Also, management needs to be flexible enough to accommodate students' needs. Teachers should not lose patience with their students even though classroom management and discipline problems are often emotionally and psychologically draining.

A sensible classroom management plan should include motivational strategies, a reward system, learning accountability, student activities, reinforcements, disciplinary procedures, and group activities. Teachers should set specific objectives for classroom management and continue working toward their ultimate goal. For example, if the goal of classroom management is to achieve effectiveness of teaching and learning in the classroom, teachers must set up objectives in different areas of teaching and learning that help them reach that goal. Figure 7.7 illustrates three areas in which establishing and achieving clear objectives contribute toward the goal of good classroom management. In some cases, teachers may have to let go of preconceived ideas in order to have the flexibility to execute an effective managerial approach.

Figure 7.7. **Management objectives.**

Keep in mind that without a sensible classroom management plan in place, the class can run wild. This is especially true when the psychosocial environment is not compatible with the ongoing instruction, academic activities, human relations, and learning expectations. Teachers must be vigilant at all times to keep managerial matters under control.

Establishing a Discipline Approach

Classrooms can be stressful and hectic, but one of the most important ways to control the activity is establishing classroom structures. Teachers need to craft classroom rules that are understandable, reasonable, purposeful, meaningful, sensible, and specific for all management needs. Rules that are difficult to understand or remember or expressed in negative language should be avoided; otherwise, teachers will spend a lot of time enforcing and reinforcing them. Most importantly, teachers must create only rules and consequences they feel comfortable using. Class rules should be explained to students on an ongoing basis because students are diverse in age, gender, socioeconomic background, language skills, and comprehension level.

Some teachers send a copy of class rules home to parents and have parents sign a form stating they have read the rules to their children. For upper-grade levels, teachers may use a contract as a binding mechanism to control students' behaviors; however, making contractual agreements with minors is a controversial issue. Parents may disagree with the rules and consequences their children are asked to agreed to in the contract. Class rules have to serve the best interests of the students, not the teachers. To have effective classroom discipline, teachers need to establish a systematic approach to discipline; they must be fair, firm, logical, consistent, and motivational. Figure 7.8 illustrates the components of classroom discipline.

Figure 7.8. Classroom discipline.

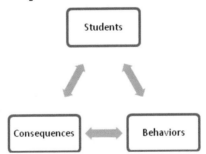

In the multicultural classroom setting, discipline should not be used to target any student's cultural identity and dignity; the purpose of discipline is to modify inappropriate actions. In other words, teachers must focus on the child's behaviors, not the child. Most importantly, teachers must model good and responsible behaviors in class; otherwise, classroom discipline can be a major structural problem.

Suspension and Expulsion Policies

School districts absolutely must maintain safe, healthy, and effective academic psychosocial environments for teaching and learning. That is why most school districts have zero-tolerance policies to deal with serious disciplinary breaches. However, in a multicultural context suspensions and expulsions are sometimes imposed in biased, unfair, and prejudicial ways. When it comes to suspensions and expulsions, schools have three options: (a) in-school suspension, (b) out-of-school suspension, and (c) expulsion. Which action is appropriate depends on the severity and duration of the actions and the cause of the misbehavior. Students who commit minor infractions are usually subject to option one, and students who commit serious offenses subject to option two or three.

However, schools and teachers cannot implement these options without providing students with due process; otherwise, students' constitutional rights could be violated as well as parental rights. Over the last 50 years, many schools have been entangled in court battles over the administration of school suspensions and expulsions. School Advisory Review Board members serve as a governance body that reviews these cases in the courts.

Curriculum Expectations

Most teachers enter the classrooms knowing how to teach from the teacher's manual using the direction instruction model, and so few really have a good grasp of the school's academic curriculum. The academic curriculum is based on state-adopted content area standards for all learners at specific grade levels. Most academic standards are state standards, and some are federal standards, such as those mandated by the NCLB Act of 2001. A district's curricular binders should include specifications regarding learning outcomes, learning objectives, curricular organization, curricular implementation, presentation of specific pedagogical skills for each subject matter, and the proliferation of applications that target students' needs. Also, curricular accountability guidelines are laid out to help teachers plan for each content area. In spite of so much information, these curricular designs do not fit all learners. Teachers must figure out how to adapt these academic curriculum guidelines for their students, and they should continue to make academic adjustments as necessary in order to implement the district's curricula effectively. In some districts, state and district curricula are aligned side by side with colored codes to help teachers meet all standards. Figure 7.9 illustrates three sets of curricular standards for which teachers are responsible.

Figure 7.9. Levels of curricular standards.

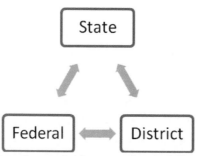

One cautionary note: Examine the teacher's manuals carefully and thoroughly to make sure the manuals address all required academic curricula. The text manuals may omit some of the knowledge or skills that must be taught according to federal, state, or district standards. Good teachers usually discover such lacks and add ingredients to the instructional applications as necessary. Moreover, some text manuals do not cover specific or in-depth content area knowledge. For example, ELD standards are specific about teaching ELLs, but very few textbooks or manuals offer the pedagogical skills that address the needs of these students. TPE and TPA require adaptations, but no text manual offers adaptation guidelines. It is always a good idea to check with the school's resource specialist or ELD coordinators for suggestions in meeting curriculum objectives and goals.

Lesson Plan Management

Teaching is a creative art. The more teachers teach, the better they become. However, even the most creative teacher begins with basic lesson plans. Common lesson plan formats are the five-step lesson plan, the three-step lesson plan, and the one-step lesson plan. Each format utilizes similar lesson strategies, activity strategies, and task strategies, depending on the nature of the learning objectives. Table 7.3 shows a typical five-step and three-step lesson plan format.

Table 7.3. **Five-step and Three-step Lesson Plan Formats**

Five-Step Plan	Basic Activities	Inductive (Three-step) Plan	Basic Activities
Step 1: Anticipatory set or introduction	Preparing, engaging, reviewing, previewing, taping, establishing purpose and learning objective	Step 1: Introduction or anticipatory set	Giving directions, procedures, demo, reviewing, previewing, engaging
Step 2: Instruction or gather input	Modeling, explaining, demo, illustrating, examples, samples, questions, answers, directions	Step 2: Activity, lesson development, or procedure	Giving detailed information, monitoring, questioning, answering, feedback, discussing
Step 3: Guided practices	Practicing, demo, monitoring, guiding, checking for understanding, doing exercises, drilling, giving feedback	Step 3: Wrap-up or debriefing	Closing, evaluating, assessing, questioning, answering, reviewing, reciting, reflecting
Step 4: Assessment, closure, or evaluation	Recapping, reviewing, giving more practice, checking for understanding, independent practice, worksheet, group work		
Step 5: Independent practice	Giving more practice, reviewing, applying, assessing, testing, timing, homework		

Lesson management usually involves these elements: content area standards, learning objectives, materials, engagement, instruction, guided practice, evaluation, independent practice, student activities, and assessment of student learning. Keep in mind that each lesson is implemented based on its learning objective(s); therefore, directions, group activities, explanations, modeling, guided practice, and independent practices may be different according to the specific learning objective. For example, an ELD lesson plan is different from an SDAIE lesson plan in many ways, and one major difference is the way the teachers pace the lesson. Pacing refers to how quickly or slowly the teachers engage students in the instructional process and how the teachers cover and uncover the entirety of the lesson's intended purposes.

Keeping Academic Records

Today storing academic records systematically is easier than it has ever been since technology is widely available, and most schools use a computer database for academic record keeping. Nearly every teacher has a laptop or desktop computer in the room for all academic functions, including recording attendance, assessment, discipline, behavioral issues, referral for services, contacts with parents, scheduling parent/teacher conferences, grades, progress, test results, ELD scores, proficiency level, and academic standing. However, technology should not be the teacher's only tool for accessing information for record keeping. Professional journals, academic planners, grade books, minutes of IEP meetings, and other academic records should be stored in proper places such as student folders, file cabinets, and sealed drawers.

Keeping up-to-date records is good professional practice and helps teachers keep abreast of the needs of all students. Academic records are used for many purposes, such as sharing information with legal guardians, school administrators, students, and teachers. However, some academic records are strictly confidential and may not be disclosed without proper authorization; these include those with information about the IEP process, medical conditions, suspicion of child abuse, psychological exams, and any records considered sealed. Teachers should keep a confidential file under lock and key. Teachers have the responsibility to report accurate academic information for each student in the class, and most reports are done electronically today. It is important to note that electronic devices are not designed to question the information but to simply store the information the teachers input into the system. Therefore, teachers must be cautious when they input student data.

Planning for Substitution

Good teachers have a subbing plan or a handbook ready in case of a personal absence. This plan can be kept near the teacher's desk or in a file cabinet that is easy to locate. It must have written instructions so the substitute can implement it properly. Good teachers prepare subbing plans in advance because that is in the best interests of the children. Subbing is a big business, and all teachers benefit from it. Teachers get sick occasionally and they have personal issues that require their absence from the classroom from time to time. However, state laws place limitations on subbing in the classroom, and school administrators are fully aware of the laws. For example, if subbing extends for 30 days in a single classroom, the parents of the students in that class must be notified of that fact.

More importantly, the law does not allow a sub to be in a class for 30 consecutive school days. Chronic use of subs should be addressed with school administrators. If parents question a teacher's frequent absences, they should have the right to pull their children from the class.

Many experienced substitute teachers can pick up the teacher's manual and improvise a lesson plans from scratch if there is no subbing plan in place. However, in practice, this is generally ineffective; every sub is not necessarily that capable. Besides, students deserve better and calling in a sub with no written lesson plan for that sub to follow is inexcusable except in an emergency or crisis. The bottom line is that in the absence of the classroom teacher, a substitute teacher should be able to continue the normal schedule and routines without serious interruption in the class. Anything less does students a great disservice.

Managing Student Groups

As with lesson management, curriculum management, and classroom management, teachers should be well trained and well prepared to manage student groups during instruction and at any other time in class on a regular basis. As mentioned previously, there are three basic groups of students in the classroom according to academic performance: top, middle, and bottom groups. Teachers can diversify instructions to meet the needs of students in all three groups; however, teachers must keep in mind that students cannot learn new concepts and skills by themselves. Teachers have to supervise, manage, instruct, monitor, and support all students' learning in all groups.

One of the ways to help students learn is grouping, or putting students in small groups for specific academic activities. But to have effective groups, it is extremely important that teachers know the principles of successful cooperative learning. These principles are: positive interdependence; individual accountability; equal participation; simultaneous interaction; collaboration; problem solving and group consensus; brainstorming, discussion, sharing, and selecting; specific group objectives; roles, responsibilities, and supports; and specific group goals. These are basic principles for group activity. Teachers do not have to apply all principles for every group activity; they apply them according to the nature of the group learning. In other words, the prescription for good groups varies with specific group objectives and activities.

Teachers can group students based on learning abilities, interests, and academic skills. However, if teachers do not provide consistent management and monitoring to ensure that the students in the groups are academically engaged in learning tasks, the prescription is meaningless. There is no magic formula for managing student groups successfully, but where there is a will, there is a way. Teachers should use intervention strategies as soon as they spot academic deficiencies in students to avoid a backlog of problems. Some teachers give up on students with special needs not because of time constraints but because of compounding problems.

Using centers or learning stations is another way teachers apply differentiating instruction to accommodate students who need extra support in grasping new concepts or skills. Again, the only way students who have learning problems are going to learn is for teachers to open the door to give them the right opportunity. Children will learn wherever and whenever teachers take time to teach and support them. As farmers say, crops will grow wherever water flows.

Making Homework Assignments Worthwhile

Classroom teachers must learn to design homework assignments that enhance student learning of specific academic skills and, at the same time, to hold students academically accountable for their learning outside the classroom. First, teachers need to let parents know and understand the expectations. Homework assignments are not for parents; however, parents must make sure students are doing the required work. Second, teachers must match homework assignments to their students' academic abilities. For instance, teachers may need to go over difficult problems in class before assigning the work. Third, teachers must establish clear routines or procedures for student submission and teacher evaluation of students' homework assignments on a daily basis. Fourth, teachers must monitor homework assignments to ensure students complete them on time and benefit from them. In other words, teachers must adjust, monitor, and evaluate homework assignments periodically in order to address students' academic needs. Table 7.4 gives an idea of appropriate time allocations for homework for each grade level. However, teachers must determine what is best for their students in accordance with each student's learning abilities. Remember, students may need different time alloca-allocations as well as different levels of homework assignments.

Table 7.4. Homework Time Allocations for All Grade Levels

Grade Level	Daily Time	Examples
Kindergarten	0–15 minutes	Select one of these: Spelling, writing, reading, math, coloring worksheets
First grade	0–20 minutes	Select two of these: Reading, spelling, math, writing journal entries
Second grade	0–25 minutes	Select two or more of these: Reading, spelling, writing, math, key concepts, or vocabulary words
Third grade	0–30 minutes	Select two or more of these: Reading, spelling, writing, math, key concepts, or vocabulary words
Fourth grade	0–40 minutes	Select three of these: Reading, writing, spelling, math, key concepts, practicing specific skills and knowledge, vocabulary words
Fifth grade	0–45 minutes	Select three or more of these: Reading, writing, spelling, math, key concepts, practicing specific skills and knowledge, vocabulary words, challenging problems
Sixth grade	0–45 minutes	Select three or more of these: Reading, writing, spelling, math, key concepts, practicing specific skills and knowledge, vocabulary words, challenging problems, creative and critical applications
Middle school	0–75 minutes	Select four or more of these: Reading, writing, spelling, math, studying for test, key concepts, practicing specific skills and knowledge, vocabulary words, challenging problems, creative and critical applications
High school	0–90 minutes	Select five or more of these: Reading, writing, spelling, math, studying for test, key concepts, practicing specific skills and knowledge, vocabulary words, challenging problems, creative and critical applications

Fifth, teachers must have an action plan to handle students who do not do their required work outside the classroom. Specific procedural guidelines must be followed to discipline such students; otherwise, homework assignments are not academically relevant or a significant part of learning. And lastly, teachers must make sure homework assignments reflect daily instructional practices; otherwise, there is no connection between homework assignments and what is going on in the classroom.

Collaboration and Human Relations

To collaborate with students, peers, parents, colleagues, school administrators, and other professionals, teachers must maintain open communication and positive public relations. Communication for teachers comes in two forms—oral and written. Teachers must be competent in these communications to convey messages to various parties in a professional manner. Maintaining a professional demeanor is a must, and providing honest and professional communication is necessary for establishing and keeping public trust.

In today's world, public trust in teachers is shaky because there have been incidents of improper acts and abuses involving young children and classroom teachers. Direct communication with parents and with the public if appropriate, especially regarding disciplinary issues, will help to restore trust. Parents who trust teachers will be less antagonistic when their children are disciplined for misbehaving in class, and teachers who have open communication with parents receive fewer parental complaints and expressions of dissatisfaction. Therefore, good public relations should make for good human relations through the medium of communication.

Religion in School

Here is a phrase teachers should contemplate: "As long as exams are required, there will be prayers in schools." Religion is an issue in public schools and an ongoing matter of controversy. Recently, a father brought a legal action against a public school for violating his child's religious freedom when the teacher asked students to recite the Pledge of Allegiance to the flag of the United States of America. The phrase, "one nation under God" triggered his action to sue the school district for failing to recognize his child's religious freedom. Even though the words "separation of church and state" do not appear in the U.S. Constitution, many people believe religion and all things public, or governmental, should be kept separate. The truth is, however, that some expressions of religious beliefs in public schools are permissible. Table 7.5 gives basic guidelines for dealing with religious issues in public schools.

Teachers must use these guidelines with caution and should not attempt to indoctrinate students with any religious value in the classroom. Teachers who are religious themselves need to recognize the conflicts and controversies surrounding academic freedom and school curricular applications. For example, teaching about religions is not the same as teaching someone to be religious. The United States does not have a national religion; however, its institutions and public practices appear to have some religious foundation. Although nearly 70% of Americans profess a belief in some form of Christianity, public schools should not interfere with or intrude on any family's religious beliefs.

Table 7.5. Guidelines on Religious Expression in Public Schools

Activity	Religious Rights in Schools
Student prayer and religious discussion	Students may pray in nondisruptive manner when not engage in school activities or instruction and are subject to the rules that normally pertain in the applicable setting.
Graduation prayer	Under current U.S. Supreme Court decisions, school officials may not mandate or organize prayer at graduation nor organize religious baccalaureate ceremonies.
Official neutrality	Teachers and school administrators are prohibited by the U.S. constitution from soliciting or encouraging religious activity and from discouraging activity because of its religious content.
Teaching about religion	Public schools may not provide religious instruction, but they may teach about about religion, the history of religion, comparative religion, the Bible or other scripture as literature, and the role of religion

	in the history of the United States and other countries.
Religious holidays	Although public schools may teach about religious holidays and may celebrate the secular aspects of holidays, public schools may not observe holidays as religious events or promote such observance by students.
Student assignments	Students may express their beliefs about religion in the form of homework, artwork, and other written and oral assignments; such home and classroom work should be judged by ordinary academic standards.
Religious literature	Students have the right to distribute religious literature to their schoolmates on the same terms as they are permitted to distribute other literature that is unrelated to school curriculum or activities.
Religious exemptions	Public schools enjoy substantial discretion to excuse individual students from lessons that are objectionable to the student or the student's parents on religious or other conscientious grounds.
Release time	Public schools have the discretion to dismiss students to off-premises religious instruction, provided that schools do not encourage or discourage participation, and public schools may not allow religious instruction by outsiders on school premises during the school day.
Teaching values	Though public schools must be neutral with respect to religion, they may play an active role with respect to teaching civic values and virtues.
Student garb	Students may display religious messages on items of clothing to the same extent that they are permitted to display other comparable messages.
The Equal Access Act	Student religious groups have the same right of access to school facilities as is enjoyed by other comparable students groups.

Note. Information from U.S. Department of Education, *Guidance on Constitutionally Protected Prayer in Public Elementary and Secondary Schools*, 2003, retrieved from http://www2.ed.gov/policy/gen/guid/religionandschools/ prayer_guidance.html

Extracurricular Activities

Some teachers are educators without borders, meaning they are altruistic, and their commitment to their students extends beyond the classroom. Even if their plates are full of teaching responsibilities, such teachers take their own time to support and enjoy extracurricular activities in order to promote students' overall psychosocial well-being. Some teachers are true mentors and should be commended for their efforts in school activities, such as sports events, plays and other performances, field trips, fundraising activities, fairs and carnivals, community events (blood drives, food drives, clothing drives, etc.), back to school nights, open houses, student clubs, assemblies, tutorial services, and more. In addition, some teachers are politically active in their community helping economically disadvantaged and other less fortunate individuals. Many teachers belong to professional organizations, such as teacher associations, charity organizations, religious organizations, and political parties.

Keep in mind that these are voluntary activities and are not be considered among teachers' daily functions. Moreover, teachers are contractual employees and should consult their teachers' unions for suggestions about extracurricular activities that may be helpful and warnings about those that may be inadvisable.

Home Visits

These days, teachers rarely visit students' families; the primary reason appears to be concern for the teacher's safety. Few parents, on the other hand, fear coming to their children's school for cultural and socioeconomic reasons. Legally, teachers can pay visits to their students' families if they have legitimate concerns about something in the best interest of the children. For example, if the only way to obtain a parent's signature on legal documents that permit school staff to provide necessary services to the child is to go to the student's home, teachers can make a home call to meet with parents for that specific reason. Or parents may request that the teacher come to the home in order to provide accurate information about something the parents do not understand, such as sports programs recruiting student athletes. Some preschool teachers who work for community programs make home visits to provide academic services to needy children.

Any teacher who plans to make home calls should discuss the situation with school administrators to make sure the trip is official, legally sound, and advisable. Otherwise, teachers who visit students' families can put themselves in physical or legal danger.

Sharing Personal Contact Information

Today, cell phones, computers, and internet services are very handy. Some teachers have no problems sharing their contact information with parents via these technological apparatuses. Parents can access teachers via e-mail or cell phone, and teachers can contact parents the same way. Academic records can be viewed on computer screen at home. Everything is so easy and convenient.

However, teachers need to keep their professional space; they must not allow themselves to get so close to students or their families that either is uncomfortable. Sharing too much information or having too much contact can impair teachers' professional judgment and decision making. In other words, teachers have to be extra careful about sharing contact information with parents and should consider setting basic policy guidelines as follows:

a. Make sure parents understand the purpose and boundaries of the policies.
b. If any violation occurs, contact is stopped immediately.
c. Teachers have a right to privacy.
d. Contact is to be made only for school purposes related to the child's needs.
e. No contact is to take place between teachers and their students.

Keep in mind that e-mails are not considered legally confidential, and when teachers use school computers for this kind of communication, schools have the legal authority to censure the content.

Figure 7.10. **Domains of teacher conduct.**

Remember, teachers must be legally literate, ethically prudent, and professionally wise as shown in Figure 7.10. If sharing contact information bothers teachers in any one of these areas, it is better to refrain from sharing the information. Teachers should never put themselves or their jobs in a questionable position.

School Violence

School grounds are not always free of violence, drug activity, sexual attacks, and physical altercations. Each year, millions of dollars are spent on school-based programs to prevent crime, reduce juvenile delinquency, combat hate crimes, lower substance abuse, and break up youth gangs. Deadly incidents and other violence have occurred in public schools, like the tragic Columbine shooting incident in 1999. Of the many deadly school shootings reported in the world, nearly 80% were in U.S. public schools. Each year, hundreds of thousands of schools across this nation are locked down to deal with potential violence and threats of violence. Although national statistics show that school violence is down, the statistics are not very convincing since deadly incidents still happen in schools.

Teachers must be prepared to handle violent acts properly and wisely; otherwise, they could be in great, even deadly, danger. Students have been known to target teachers, and some students' parents have been vindictive toward teachers. And students attack one another. Teachers have the responsibility of breaking up fights between students, but what happens if the teachers do not act in the right way?

Youth gangs have become increasingly dangerous, and gang-related activities are present in many schools. Teachers who report gang activities to police could be targeted for violence repercussions, and drug sales taking place on school grounds can pose imminent threats to everyone.

School bullying is a national crisis that is now widespread in American schools. Table 7.6 shows some statistics on bullying and some of the responses of the 30% of students in Grades 6-10 who reported being bullied at school on a moderate to frequent basis. Many teenagers are affected by this inhumane act. As role models, teachers must act quickly to protect students from being bullied and teased. At the same time, teachers must protect themselves from being the victims of bullying. Not only physical and verbal bullying, but cyber-bullying is also on the rise. Thousands of students are being cyber-bullied via cell phones, texting, emails, and social networking websites. Most schools have policies in place to handle bullying, but school personnel do not always stop the teasing that is so common in class and on the school grounds. Much still needs to be done to prevent teasing.

Table 7.6. **National Statistics on Bullying in Schools**

Statistic
1 out of 4 children is bullied
1 out of 4 children will be accused of bullying by another youth
77% of students who reported being bullied were bullied mentally, verbally, or physically
77% of students said they were bullied
1 out of 5 students admits to being a bully
8% of students fear being bullied
43% fear harassment in the bathroom
100,000 students carry a gun to school
28% of youths who carried a gun witnessed violence in school
282,000 secondary students were attacked each month

- More violence occurred on school grounds than on the way home
- 85% of students who reported being bullied were bullied on playgrounds
- 46% of male students were involved in physical fights
- 26% of female students were involved in physical fights
- 87% of students who reported being bullied sought revenge by shooting
- 86% of students who reported being bullied got picked on by other students
- 61% of students who reported being bullied were victims of physical abuse at home
- 54% of students said physical abuse led to school violence

There is no best way to handle school violence, and the truth is that most teachers are not trained to deal with violence. Nevertheless, teachers must always keep their eyes open and should alert school authorities of any suspicion of potential violence. Prevention is the best defense as intervention could be deadly. The bottom line is that school violence can happen anytime, anywhere, to any teacher. Be alert!

Reporting Child Abuse

Child abuse has been recognized as a serious threat against humanity ever since the late 1800s. Child abuse issues are growing, and many children are living in abusive homes. Each year millions of suspected child abuse cases are reported to Children's Protective Services. All 50 states have laws to protect children from being abused. Teachers are legally mandated reporters; they must report any reasonable suspicions of child abuse. It is not the teachers' responsibility to determine whether child abuse actually occurred; in fact teachers are legally barred from investigating their suspicions. Their job is to detect reasonable suspicion of child abuse and alert the child welfare authority and law enforcement agencies.

Failing to report suspected child abuse cases may prompt school administrators and state officials to revoke a teacher's credentials, and it may result in termination of employment. Sadly, many teachers have been accused of child abuse, especially sexual abuse. Some were found to be perpetrators while others were vindicated. To avoid the likelihood of false allegations, the NEA suggests that teachers not touch children. Remember that child abuse and neglect are crimes, and teachers must be vigilant to protect children at all times.

Summing Up

This chapter presented a comprehensive overview of classroom structure to introduce teachers to major areas in today's classroom environment. School structure is complex and teachers need to be aware of its many aspects. Proper attention to structure can keep teachers from being overwhelmed, frustrated, and burned out. Without classroom structure, the psychosocial environment in the class would be chaotic and put academic progress in jeopardy. Teachers who lack strategies for establishing structure have a difficult time with classroom management and discipline, essential elements for smooth, efficient, and effective teaching and learning.

Teachers should start early to plan their classroom structure and prepare to address student behaviors from the very beginning to set up the tone for the school year. Before school starts, teachers should explore the school facility to become familiar with the condition of the room; review the school curriculum and content area standards for teaching and learning expectations; organize a pacing calendar to put things in perspective; plan to organize the physical environment of the classroom to create a sound psychosocial environment that is conducive to teaching and learning; establish classroom rules, consequences, procedures, routines, and schedules; and make a check list of all items that should be in the classroom for personal inventory assessment. These basic preparations are crucial to the establishment of classroom structure. Understanding the classroom structure puts teachers ahead in the teaching game.

CHAPTER EIGHT

THE INCLUSIVE MULTICULTURAL CLASSROOM

*Wounds that can't be seen are more painful than
those that can be seen and cured by the doctors.*
Nelson Mandela

Introduction

The world has about 6.8 billion people in 226 different countries. Nearly 6,900 different native languages are spoken worldwide. In the American public school system, nearly 300 million people speak 425 different dialects. There are approximately 14,000 school districts with nearly 100,000 public schools. Of the 100,000 public schools, 4,700 are charter schools. In addition, the U.S. has nearly 33,700 private schools that offer kindergarten through the higher grades. The U.S. has nearly 54 million students in its public school system. Of that number, 38 million are K–8 students and 16 million are 9–12 students. Moreover, nearly 5.8 million students are enrolled in private schools. Of the 54 million students, nearly 10 million students speak a primary language at home other than English. These national educational statistics tell teachers how diverse the United States is and how important attention to multicultural education should be, especially in the areas of classroom instruction, management, and discipline. This chapter gives some multicultural perspectives and examines factors that are crucial for both public and private educational systems that serve students of color with diverse socioeconomic backgrounds.

What Is Cultural Diversity?

Literally, *diversity* is a generic term with multiple meanings in multicultural and multilingual society. Sometimes, when understanding and respect are absent, diversity is viewed in the academic context with negative connotations. As Vang (2010) explained, diversity literally means "differences," and the term *cultural diversity* traditionally has referred to differences in culture, race, ethnicity, language, class, religion, gender, and socioeconomic status. However, in today's schools, cultural diversity means different things and has academic designations, including low income, economic disadvantage, language minority, English language learners, limited English proficient, fluent English proficient, special needs, exceptionality, special education status, majority or minority. Teachers need to recognize that they may have students from any and all of these categories in their classrooms. The key to a successful culturally diverse classroom is a positive attitude toward and an appreciation for students who may not share the same socioeconomic backgrounds and middle class values as the majority of the students. Figure 8.1 illustrates the various psychosocial environments in which students find themselves in the U.S.

Figure 8.1. Psychosocial environments of students.

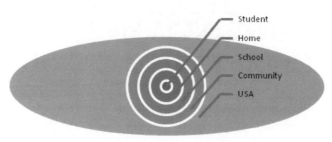

Sometimes the term cultural diversity is used to refer directly to minority groups such as women, students of color, the economically disadvantaged, those of a language minority, bilingual students, middle-class Americans, and more. Actually, all Americans are part of cultural diversity. All families are different in cultures, customs, traditions, values, religions, child rearing practices, gender roles, and socioeconomic status. Cultural diversity also means a mixture of different human characteristics, such as attitudes, personalities, emotions, reactions, acceptance, rejection, inclusion, exclusion, biases, prejudices, and stereotypes. The bottom line is that teachers should foster the positive aspects of cultural diversity and do provide a productive learning environment for all students.

The Salad Bowl Approach

The *e pluribus unum* motto of the United States—"out of many, one"—is an inclusive, pluralistic perspective that affirms the "salad bowl" and rainbow approaches to improving human relations in the academic and political arenas. It has replaced the old concept of America as a melting pot, which is an assimilationist approach. As explained previously, cultural diversity is NEVER a threat in the salad bowl society and, for the most part, the salad bowl mentality gives everyone the freedom and respect to preserve their unique cultures, traditions, languages, ethnicities, and belief systems. It is not only minority groups that wish to preserve their cultures and family traditions, all Americans should preserve their family cultures and traditions. All Americans must share with one another their differences in order for American children to embrace and feel a part of the nation's multicultural and multiracial fabric. The U.S. is one nation, under God, indivisible, with liberty, justice, freedom, respect, appreciation, and acceptance for all. This makes America a beautiful and colorful nation, just like the colorful arch of the rainbow.

Banks (2002), Burden and Byrd (2003), and Gollnick and Chinn (2008) suggested that teachers use sociograms or cultural activities to engage students in meaningful cross-cultural discussion to learn more about one another's cultures and traditions. If teachers fail to administer cross-cultural curricular activities to facilitate this learning, American children will not gain multicultural perspectives and may fail to show respect and appreciation toward one another. Despite the null and hidden curricula mindset in some schools, teachers need to think about this nation's place in the global community and prepare their students for it by helping them understand life from the perspectives of people from other cultures.

Teachers can establish a multicultural learning environment to help students understand the world they all share. Most importantly, teachers can also foster the value of inclusiveness as they help their students learn to accept one another's cultural differences.

Understanding the Multicultural Approach

As Vang (2010) wrote, the United States is a multicultural and multilingual nation and has the most diverse population of all nations in the world. The American fabric is made of diverse ethnicities, races, nationalities, languages, cultures, traditions, belief systems, values, customs, and creeds as shown in Table 8.1. The current educational system reflects the colorful arch of this rainbow because the student diversity encompasses children from many, many different families and socioeconomic backgrounds: European Americans, African Americans, Hispanic Americans, Native Americans, Arab Americans, Asian Americans, Americans of Asian Indian descent, Pacific Islanders, and Southeast Asian Americans. The American people are different in countless ways, and cultural diversity is an American value, ideal, and fact. Differences bring more strengths than weaknesses. The Olympic Games, World Cup Games, international sports programs, and the United Nations are perfect examples of the unity of the human race.

The great diversity of people in this country is what makes this nation unique. America is the richest nation on this planet because it was built on and continues to contain people, cultures, and languages from all parts of the world. No country in the whole world can be compared to the U.S. in the extent to which such a diverse population enjoys freedom, liberty, and justice.

Table 8.1. Major Racial Groups in America

Group	Number in 2000, in Millions	Projected Number 2009, in Millions
Whites	211.5	224.5
Hispanics	35.3	45.5
Blacks	34.7	37.3
Asians	10.2	13.2
Native Americans	2.5	2.4

Note. Data from U.S. Census Bureau, *Census 2000 Demographic Profile Highlights.* Numbers are rounded.

Teachers need to understand human differences in order to teach fairly in a multicultural classroom setting. Teachers must consider both differences in people and differences in people's environment. For example, in the classroom teachers will encounter diversity among their students with respect to gender, race, SES, age, height, weight, intelligence, sexual orientation, social status, learning styles, communication styles, confidence, cooperation, collaboration, and more. Some of these human variables are visible to the naked eyes and some are not. The hidden human differences require deeper probing to find and profound understanding to appreciate. These difficult-to-observe variables include self-esteem, respect, intelligence, learning styles, tolerance, regard, and empathy.

Furthermore, students are not the only ones in the school who are culturally and linguistically diverse; teachers are also diverse. Tables 8.2 and 8.3 illustrate the ethnic/racial diversity of both students and teachers. Teachers should count themselves as part of the diversity in the classroom. Some teachers exclude themselves from being part of cultural diversity, thinking they have been acculturated, assimilated, or are monocultural individuals. Figure 8.2 gives one depiction of cultural diversity—all Americans fit into the notion of *e pluribus unum*—one out of many. As role models, teachers should relate to all students with an inclusive attitude toward cultural diversity; otherwise, teachers' attitudes may not foster learning in the multicultural classroom.

Table 8.2. Ethnicity/Race of Students

Characteristic	California	Nation
White	31.9%	58.0%
Black	8.0%	16.9%
Asian/Pacific Islander	11.0%	4.4%
Hispanic	45.2%	19.5%
American Indian/Alaska Native	0.8%	1.2%
Economically disadvantaged	47.9%	36.7%
English-language learner	24.9%	7.8%
With disabilities	10.6%	12.8%
Migrant	2.5%	0.6%
LEP	1.5 million	3.2 million

Note: Data from the National Education Association, 2006, and California Department of Education, 2005–2006.

Table 8.3. Ethnicity/Race of Teachers, by Type of School

Ethnicity	Elementary	Secondary	Combined
White	82.1%	82.1%	82.1%
Black	8.4%	8.4%	8.4%
American Indian	0.4%	0.4%	0.4%
Asian	1.3%	1.4%	0.7%
Pacific Islander	0.2%	0.2%	0.2%
Hispanic	6.8%	5.5%	3.3%
Multiple race	0.8%	0.7%	0.6%
Minority	17.9%	15.7%	11.4%

Note. Information from US Department of Education, 2003-2004.

Figure 8.2. Spheres of cultural diversity.

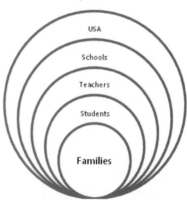

It is very important for teachers to explore multicultural approaches carefully to embrace individual differences and, at the same time, consider multicultural factors when selecting instructional methodologies, lesson strategies, activity strategies, task strategies, and cooperative learning for classroom management and discipline in the classroom. Teachers have a professional responsibility to provide a culturally responsive psychosocial environment for all learners.

Demystifying Multicultural Misperceptions

Despite how teachers may feel about the multicultural approach to education, nothing will change until teachers take the time to educate themselves about the academic intent of the multicultural education movement. This will give them a clearer understanding of the myths, misconceptions, and misperceptions associated with the movement. If teachers do not demystify the concept of multicultural education, they may reject the approach that is so crucial to providing equal opportunities to all their students.

Multicultural education is not an Eastern methodology for institutionalizing academic complexity into Western educational principles and theories. In fact, a multicultural approach is a Western idea that seeks inclusiveness to achieve equality, social justice, democracy, freedom, desegregation, non-discrimination, fairness, and balance in public education. Most proponents of multicultural education are Western scholars and educators.

Multicultural education has a legal basis in the ramifications of landmark decisions issued by federal and state courts against separation, segregation, discrimination, inequality, inequity, and unequal practices in public education. Consider, for example, the legal impacts of the rulings in *Lau v. Nichols* in 1974, *Brown v. Topeka Board of Education* in 1954, and *Plessy v. Ferguson* in 1896. Think of Public Law 94-142 (the 1975 Education of All Handicapped Children Act), the Civil Rights Act of 1964, the Bilingual Education Act of 1968, the 14th Amendment of the U.S. Constitution, the Equal Educational Opportunity Act of 1974, the Individuals with Disabilities Education Act of 1990, the Americans with Disabilities Act of 1990, and the No Child Left Behind Act of 2001. The ultimate goal of these court decisions and congressional legislation was to include, recognize, respect, appreciate, and accept all American children regardless of their SES, cultural background, and citizenship status and offer all of them an equal opportunity for a quality education.

Moreover, in California in recent years, Senate Bills 2042 and 1059 required that teacher preparation programs include college methodology courses that address the needs of English language learners and students with special needs. The California Commission on Teaching Credentialing (CCTC) requires that teacher preparation programs implement teacher performance expectations (TPE) standards and teacher performance assessment (TPA) tasks. CCTC guidelines for these standards and tasks mandate that new teachers design academic lesson plans to target all learners with special adaptations for ELL and SN students in instruction and assessment. Overall, all California's public schools are required by federal statutes to ask parents or legal guardians to identify any primary languages spoken at home for empirical data and funding purposes. This is done through a home language survey form.

The purpose of the multicultural approach is to advocate for all diverse learners in a pluralistic society. However, people with assimilationist attitudes may find demystification of the approach difficult because they lack the desire to honor the legal requirements to provide academic equality for the greater good of all the people. In other words, multicultural education is not just a humane idea; rather it is a legitimate approach to reforming and restructuring the public school system in a way that enables all learners to receive a fair, equal, and equitable public education. To demystify one's misperceptions about the subject is to accept the fact that multicultural education does not advocate for separate education but equal education.

Equal Opportunity for Minority Students

Teachers can make a big difference in the lives of all their students, and that should come from their big, caring hearts. Without genuine concern for their students, teachers' offering of equal opportunity is just lip service.

Over the last 50 years, Americans have struggled politically and socially to provide equality, social justice, and full inclusion in public education. Although gains have been made, equal opportunity for learners from diverse socioeconomic backgrounds is still lacking in many areas. The nation's educational values and ideals are based on a hegemonic ideology and Euro-centric approaches that offer minority students unclear opportunities in the system.

Attempts to create equal opportunity in public education have improved somewhat; students have equal access to public schools. However, in the classrooms of those schools, opportunities are not always equal. For example, many ELL, LEP, FEP, and migrant students are subject to capricious teaching, impoverished instruction, and legal segregation in public schools. Many schools use segregated curricula to separate these students into classrooms where little or no academic teaching is provided. In some cases, low achievers are treated with less attention and less respect by teachers as shown in Table 8.4 (Good & Brophy, 2000; Ryan & Cooper, 2001). The current LEP process does not work. The redesignation criteria used to reclassify LEP to FEP are egregiously flawed. More appallingly, LEP students are frequently taught by less qualified, non-credentialed, and underprepared practitioners. Meanwhile, schools continue to put academic labels on them for fiscal purposes.

Table 8.4. How Teachers Sometimes Treat Low Achievers

Type of Treatment	Possible Causes
Give little time for lows to ask questions	Assuming lows don't understand the question or don't know the answer or don't want to waste time
Allow no clue, no hint, or no opportunity for lows	Expecting lows to understand the question and to know the correct answer right away
Reward inappropriate behaviors or incorrect answers	Expecting lows to have middle-class values or focusing on the behaviors more than the needs
Criticize lows for failure	Blaming lows for not knowing or for not understanding
Praise lows for success less frequently	Failing to promote lows, lacking cross-cultural education, or holding prejudicial biases
Give less response and less public feedback	Holding stereotype, bias, prejudice, or rejecting
Pay less attention or interact less with lows	Avoiding lows for many reasons, focusing on other students, or ignoring lows' needs
Call on lows less	Expecting the right answers, presuming incompetent, or holding cultural grudges
Seat lows farther away	Focusing on loud, noisy, rowdy, or assertive students and avoiding quiet and polite students
Demand less from lows	Assuming lows don't have skills, have problems speaking Eng-

	lish, or won't know the answers
Give lows more private than public interactions	Putting pressure on lows to learn, expecting lows to adapt, or making sure assignments are done
Closely monitor lows in class	Focusing on lows' weaknesses, expecting lows to learn at the same rate, or having no time for lows
Give lows more structured activities	Expecting lows to learn specific skills, giving lows different activities, or using strict rules
Give lows no benefit of the doubt in borderline cases	Grading down instead of grading up, making errors too serious, expecting to be like other learners
Give lows less friendly interactions, fewer smiles, and less support	Presenting negative attitudes toward lows, shutting them off, or giving them no attention at all
Give lows shorter and less informative feedback	Failing to encourage lows; giving good, not good, or okay remarks; or sending "see me" notes.
Make less eye contact with lows and respond less attentively	Avoiding lows, considering lows to be "ghost like" students, or expecting nothing from them.
Use less effective lessons and less time-consuming instructional methods for lows	Giving content compatibility, not content obligatory, or watered-down instruction.
Give less accepted and lower use of their ideas and input	Assuming lows to be followers, not leaders, or expecting lows to be listeners, not actors.
Use impoverished and improvised curricula with lows	Using whatever can think of, giving lows easy assignments to please, expecting lows to do just enough, using lip services for lows, providing lows with cosmetic education, or offering lows nonacademic instruction.

As Table 8.4 shows, low achievers often become at-risk students in the psychosocial environment in which no quality teaching takes place. As Ovando, Combs, and Collier (2006) observed, language minority students are often innocent prisoners in the English-only classroom where no equal opportunity is given to them. Of the many factors Vang (2010) described that contribute to the poor education of at-risk students, poor instruction is the most single important one and it exacerbates all the others. The lack of quality instruction places at-risk students who lack academic skills needed for advancement at imminent risk of failure.

The hegemonic principles that have guided education for so long are likely to continue in today's practices as long as that socio-academic ideology continues to dominate the American philosophical and theoretical approaches to providing universal public education. The public school system uses socioeconomic status to determine the kind of schools minority children should be enrolled in, and that is totally unfair. Poor children get poor schools and rich children get rich schools. Perhaps this is due to the fact American society relies heavily on a "class warfare" philosophy in the distribution of wealth. Regardless of the reason, this mindset has got to change because there is only one public education system in America. Unless SES is replaced by equity in school placement, legal segregation will remain alive and well in the American education system.

The dilemma of poor schools for minority students is insurmountable for those students who are victims of the system. Teachers need to pay close attention to these issues and make changes to provide all students with quality education. Simply giving minority students universal access to schooling is not a sufficient condition to guarantee them equal opportunity to a quality education. Nor is providing them with universal access to schooling the same thing as enrolling them in schools that give them an education equal to what others receive. The instruction in the classroom is what determines the quality of the education. The American Institute of Research (2006) made an astonishing discovery after 5 years of study: the quality of learning is not based on the language of instruction but on the quality of instruction that the students receive in the classroom.

Keep in mind that the ultimate goal of multicultural education is to allow all students with diverse learning styles and abilities to receive quality instruction in the classroom, to engage in meaningful academic learning activities, and to acquire new knowledge, skills, and concepts through the process of constructivism.

Individual Cognitive Domain

In a multicultural classroom, teachers should be able to identify cultural characteristics of individual students in many academic areas. Children vary in their cognitive development, in how they understand, encode, decode, and process information. Their cognitive abilities determine how they perform academic tasks and assignments. Recognizing individual differences in cognitive development helps teachers pinpoint instructional strategies, activity strategies, and task strategies effectively. Knowing children's cognitive abilities enables teachers to determine how much time should be allotted for various tasks and how many questions or problems should be given to students for independent practice.

Also, problem solving, decision making, mental strategies, coordination, and analytical organization depend on the students' cognitive processes as well as their individual level of intelligence. The ways students reason, analyze, apply, relay, imply, abstract, extract, extrapolate, and interpret information are strong indicators or predictors of potential academic success or struggles. Keep in mind that students' cognitive ability depends on the subject matter. Some teachers are cognitively demanding and others are cognitively undemanding. In other words, some teachers engage students' critical thinking processes, but other teachers may present only superficial information to their students.

Individual Affective Domain

Teachers should bear in mind that feeling determines students' moods, attitudes, actions, and state of mind. The students' emotional attachment to lessons, activities, and tasks in class is related to their affective development. Affective perceptions deal with feelings, attitudes, emotions, and the egotistical nature of individual students. A number of factors may affect a child's feelings and attitudes toward school work: disputes, arguments, debates, friendships, teamwork, and socialization. Also, time management, organizational skills, self-esteem, self-discipline, self-confidence, cooperation, sharing, likes and dislikes, initiative, and self-direction may affect how students feel toward instruction, activities, and testing. Teachers should be able to sense how students feel and adjust teaching and learning accordingly.

Individual Psychomotor Domain

Besides the cognitive and affective domains, students should be evaluated on tasks involving psychomotor skills. Psychomotor skills are closely related to physical abilities, such as agility in sports. The psychomotor domain involves the use of gross motor skills and fine motor skills. Some tasks, such as cooking, for example, require skills in the psychomotor, cognitive, and affective domains. Children do not always develop in all three domains evenly. Students who are good in sports may lack cognitive skills at the same level but have affective and psychomotor skills at about the same level of development.

One area in which psychomotor skills is extremely important is driving. Maneuvering a car requires simultaneous and spontaneous coordination and control of the eyes, legs, hands, and mind. In class, students use psychomotor skills in writing, drawing, typing, and all the performance arts.

Students' physical differences are visible to the naked eye; their height, weight, appearance, color, size, expression, manner, and maturity level. Disabilities may affect students in the psychomotor domain; hearing impairment, vision problems, speech disorders, conduct disorders, and emotional disorders generally influence physical abilities. Teachers should take these factors into consideration while working in a multicultural and multilingual classroom.

Individual Social Domain

Friends are good medicine for children, especially when they are young, and when they are older, friends can be life savers. Also, friends apply peer pressure—good and bad—and they can shape a child's personality, attitudes, habits, and thinking. The social domain has to do with relationships with peers. It involves interactions, sharing, cooperation, communication, group activity, teamwork, and citizenship. The social domain also deals with people skills, such as asking questions, seeking assistance, reporting, talking in front of class, giving a speech, and speaking up. Keep in mind that students of color may refrain from some of these activities because of their cultural values, and teachers should not assume that they do not care or that they lack social skills. Reserved students may not question, speak up, or ask for assistance in class simply because they are timid or shy.

Socialization is healthy for all children, and teachers should encourage all their students to get involved in formal and informal social activities to sharpen their social skills. The social domain can overlap with the affective domain in some situations. For example, when children disagree or argue with one another, their feelings are affected by the social strain. Social behaviors greatly impact affect when students are teased or bullied by peers or strangers. For this reason, teachers should be concerned about student relationships in the class and work to create a sound psychosocial environment for all.

Individual Academic Domain

It is true that all children have skills in all the domains listed above, but not all children are good in all the domains. In other words, children may be strong in one or two domains and may be weak in other one or two other areas. For example, a student may be good in math but poor in English. Or a student is good in sports but struggles in science. These abilities affect students in the academic domain. The academic domain consists of five basic areas of knowledge and skill in children: social knowledge, physical knowledge, logical knowledge, arbitrary knowledge, and constructive knowledge.

Consider, for example, an assignment in earth science. If the teacher gives different kinds of rocks to students and asks them to classify the rocks based on the characteristics of each rock, students apply various kinds of knowledge and skills to complete the assignment. They would use social knowledge as they share information in a group and talk about the rocks. They use physical knowledge to describe the rocks, using adjectives or descriptive phrases. Logical knowledge is employed when students use their five senses to determine whether a given rock is igneous, sedimentary, or metamorphic. They use arbitrary knowledge to decide, compromise, and make inferences to support their conclusions regarding each rock. Finally, they use constructive knowledge as they process the information they receive and apply it to their personal understanding of rocks.

Furthermore, Vang (2010) pointed out that all five domains are essential for student learning in the classroom. Table 8.5 shows some of the factors associated with each domain with regard to learning, and it also shows the instructional approaches that are effective in each domain. However, students may present their knowledge and skills differently because of who they are and how they process information. Designing a variety of instructional approaches that arouse students' interests and curiosity appeals to the different learning styles and benefits all students.

Table 8.5. Five Domains of Learning

Domain	Associated Factors	Instructional Approaches
Cognitive	Comprehension, knowledge, skills, processing, and application	Knowing what and knowing how and expressing in written or verbal forms
Affective	Emotions, feelings, attitudes, personalities, behaviors, and values	Reflective responses to tasks, sharing with peers, interaction, communication, and expressing in verbal form
Psychomotor	Motor skills, coordination, comprehension, expression, and muscular control	Diagramming, mapping, manipulation, connection, idea web, and application
Social	Basic interpersonal communication skills, sharing, socialization, citizenship, and cooperation	Cooperative learning, teamwork, group activity, role and responsibility, and project
Academic	Cognitive academic language proficiency, literacy, constructivism, and context-reduction	Logical, arbitrary, social, physical, and constructive knowledge

Diverse Student Learning Styles

As Gardner (1983) discovered, learning style is directly associated with an individual student's type of intelligence. Some students learn best through linguistic methodologies, some through kinesthetic approaches, others through interpersonal means, etc. The learning styles that are most effective for each type of intelligence are listed in Table 8.6. Remember, teachers have their own preferred methods of teaching and learning styles. Teachers' styles are compatible with some students' learning styles but incompatible with others. However, adults' learning styles cannot be compared to students' learning styles because adults have more experiences and can vary their learning styles much more easily than students can.

Table 8.6. Multiple Intelligences

Type of Intelligence	Basic Definition	Areas of Interests	Areas of Strengths	Possible Learning Styles
Linguistic	Word-smart or understand words and language easily	Read, write, memorize, and tell stories	Memorization and reading	Reading, saying, hearing, or seeing words: The word player
Logical/ mathematical	Logical-smart, number-smart, or understand logical connections among different ideas, concepts, and theories	Do experiments, work with numbers, ask questions, explore patterns or relationships between objects, and infer results	Math, reasoning, logic, problem solving, analogy, and details.	Categorizing, ordering, sequencing, classifying, abstracting, and explaining patterns or relationships: The questioner
Spatial/ visual	Picture-smart or understand the expressions of arts, visual images, or mental images	Draw, build, design, look at pictures, examine objects, and create images	Imagination, visualization, sensing, reading maze, interpreting charts, and solving puzzles	Visualizing, dreaming, mental imaging, drawing pictures, or photographic creation: The visualizer
Musical/ audio	Music-smart, sound-smart, rhythm-smart, or understand the patterns of sound system	Sing, hum tunes, listen, play to music, write song, respond to music, or create rhythm	Memorization, picking sounds, understanding rhythms, or sensitivity to sounds	Sound, rhythm, melody, music, voices, or artful: The music lover
Bodily/ kinesthetic	Hand-smart, body-smart, sports-smart, physical fitness, agility, or understand patterns of body movement	Move, use body language, gesture, touch and talk, or act out	Perform physical activities, dance, sports, acting, crafts design, drafting, or hands-on	Touching, moving, interacting, processing, sensations of body movement, or feeling the physical appearance: The mover
Interpersonal	People-smart, friends-smart, social-smart, or understand grouping and social relationships	Making friends, like people, talk to people, join groups, share with people, depending on, or player of team	Sharing, understanding, socializing, leading, following, organizing, communicating, listening, mediating, showing, or manipulating.	Sharing, comparing, relating, cooperating, socializing, communicating, following, or leading: The socializer

| Intrapersonal | Self-centered, self-smart, self-propelled, or understand own ways | Be a loner, be isolated, pursue own interests, set up personal goals, or independent | Focusing on self, dealing with inward feelings, pursuing personal interests, like own ways of doing things, choose own goals, or follow instincts | Being a loner, working alone, independent, self-centered, having own space, creating own turf, liking individualized project, or being introverted: The individual |
| Natural | Flexible, adaptable, accommodating, considerate, or understand diverse needs and differences | Have flexible and adaptable patterns of thinking, feeling, understanding, or communicating with people | Focusing on all forms of learning, interests, considering all things as important, adjusting to needs, or being able to manage change well. | Having the ability and capability to adapt to different learning environment or subject matter, adjusting to needs, or controlling changes with flexibility: The flexible learner |

Note: Information from *Frames of Minds: The Theory of Multiple Intelligences* by H. Gardner, 1983, New York: Basic Books.

Differences in student learning styles can be looked at a number of different ways. One way of differentiating learning styles is to examine how students approach problem solving. Some students go right into solving problems without reading the questions or directions. Others read the questions, look at all possible answers, and reread the questions before answering. Many students do as they are told: read the directions, read the questions, and evaluate the possible answers before responding. These basic learning styles should guide how teachers design lessons, activities, and tasks for diverse learners.

Another way to differentiate learning styles is to contrast reflective and impulsive students. Reflective students who possess an analytical learning style tend to analyze and deliberate before answering, after considering the alternative. These students perform well in problem-solving activities (Kauchak & Eggen, 2005). On the other hand, impulsive students who react quickly often make mistakes, and these students may perform better on learning activities requiring factual information.

Learning styles can fall into two general categories: cognitive and sensory. Students with a cognitive learning style learn best through the thinking process, considering mentally how to solve, process, and strategize to answer questions, perform tasks or engage in activities. Those who learn through a sensory modality depend more on the five senses—hearing, sight, taste, touch, and smell. These senses are connected to sensory nerves located in the brain. For both types of students, learning depends on the level of cognitive development. Using the previous example of describing rocks, older and more experienced students can be expected to describe the rocks in detail with expressive terms, whereas younger and less experienced students may use simple words such as rough, round, angled, and hard.

In addition to cognitive development, study habits affect aspects of learning styles. Many students are night people, getting up late and going to bed late; others are morning people, getting up early and going to bed early. Some students can vary their sleeping patterns depending on their needs. Generally speaking, however, some students learn better in the morning and some learn better in the afternoon.

Right- and Left-Brain Learners

Learners fall into two main categories depending on which hemisphere of the brain is dominant: right-brain learners and left-brain learners. These two halves of the brain control behaviors, actions, perceptions, thinking, cognition, and communication. The right side of the brain controls the left side of the body, and the left side of the brain controls the right side of the body. In Hmong culture, in ritual-ceremonial communication with the spirits, we say, "Right crosses over left" and "Left crosses over right."

In teaching and learning practices, it is important to know that the dominance of the right or left hemisphere of the brain affects students' learning behaviors, performance abilities, and cognitive processing (Burden & Byrd, 2003). Table 8.7 illustrates some of the differences between right-brain and left-brain learners.

Table 8.7. Contrast of Right- and Left-brain Learners

Right-brain Learners	Left-brain Learners
▪ Visually oriented	▪ Analytical
▪ Spatially oriented	▪ Logical
▪ Demonstration	▪ Concrete
▪ Experience	▪ Sequential
▪ Open-ended questions	▪ Lecture
▪ Nonverbal approach	▪ Discussion
▪ Manipulation	▪ Verbal cues
▪ Divergent thinking activities	▪ Rules
▪ Flash cards	▪ Short questions and short answers
▪ Maps	▪ Yes or no approach
▪ Idea web	▪ Texts
▪ Films	▪ Word list or word bank
▪ Audiotapes	▪ Workbook exercises
▪ Crafts	▪ Readings
▪ Drawing activities	▪ Drills
▪ Wholistic approach	▪ Linear mode approach
▪ Broad thinking process	▪ Meaning and retention
▪ Intuitive thinking	▪ Question and answer exercises
▪ Guess-timating	▪ Vocabulary and definitions
▪ Testing ideas and principles	▪ Note taking
▪ Visual and spatial mode approach	▪ Recitation
▪ Use non-sequential mode	▪ Repetition
▪ Total physical response	▪ Memorization
▪ Integrate performance arts	▪ Review

Teachers also have either right- or left-brain dominance. Therefore, the way a teacher presents, delivers, engages, interacts, and designs lesson plans may have a direct link to his or her right- or left-brain hemisphere. The way a teacher explains problems, models, and guides students may have something to do with his or her right- and left-brain dominance. Dominance of either side of the brain has strengths and weaknesses.

Issues involving right- and left-brain dominance have been subjects of academic debate, so teachers should approach this topic carefully. Different instructional approaches should be tried, but students should not simply be labeled and taught with a methodology that seems appropriate to that label without making sure that methodology is actually effective with the student. Besides, brain chemistry is sometimes altered by the psychosocial environment; learning opportunities; medications; foods; stimuli; pain; and emotions such as pleasure, excitement, amusement, fear, shock, and surprise. Therefore, in a multicultural classroom, teachers cannot rely heavily on the concept of brain hemisphere dominance. In some cultures, people prefer right-brain learning over left-brain learning, and this kind of classification is sometimes considered harmful to individual students' self-esteem and cultural pride.

Students' Creativity

Teachers should recognize differences in students' abilities, knowledge, and skills; however, all students should be held to the same high expectations. One area of noticeable differences among students is creativity. Students may be creative in some areas, such as writing, and not creative in others, such as music or science. Or a student may be creative in thinking and writing styles that are not rewarded by the teacher because the styles do not meet the teacher's expectations. Teachers need to find ways to integrate the special creativity of these students into their learning. Otherwise, creative students can be penalized for their creative approaches. Some teachers are not creative thinkers themselves, and they may have difficulty dealing with creative students and inadvertently suppress the students' unique abilities.

Teachers should introduce lesson objectives that allow students to think creatively as well as critically. They can use task strategies, such as writing expository or narrative essays, allowing students to solve problems in more than one way, or prescribing hands-on and minds-on activities to engage students' imagination and creative thinking. Creativity is important for cognitive applications such as hypothesizing, asking questions, processing information, creating new ideas, testing, experimenting, using variables, sampling, communication, and modifying variables.

Student with Learning Disabilities

Nearly 5.2 million students in the nation's K-12 educational system have some kind of learning disability. In order to provide an education in the least restrictive learning environment for these students, teachers need to recognize different kinds of disabilities or exceptionalities. The most common student disabilities are mild learning disabilities, speech impairment, language disorders, mental retardation, emotional disorders, conduct disorders, physical disability, hearing impairment, visual impairment, orthopedic impairment, and other health conditions. Most teachers are not equipped with the skills and knowledge needed to deal with students with learning disabilities. To help teachers understand the basic needs of these students, Mercer and Pullen (2005) described some of the behaviors associated with learning disabilities, as shown in Table 8.8.

Table 8.8. Behaviors of Students with Learning Disabilities

Area of Concern	Characteristics of Behaviors	Behavior
Peer relations	Poor	Is a loner, plays alone
Adjustment to change	Poor	Easily upset or confused easily
Perseveration	Persistent	Spends too much time on a task
Emotional control	Poor	Easily angered or emotional
Dealing with frustration	Poor	Stamps foot or sulks
Asking for assistance	Poor	Sits quietly or delays assistance
Communication in general	Poor	Reserved, quiet, or self-centered
Physical comfort	Excessive	Needs hugs, touches, or comfort from others
Hyperactivity	Excessive movement	Has problems settling down
Learning style	Variable performance	Does well on one task and poorly on another
Task completion	Poor	Starts a task but cannot finish it on time
Maturity level	Immature	Behaves below age level
Learning new concepts	Poor or reduced vocabulary	Has understanding issues and prefers use of object labels
Responding to questions	Delays or needs wait time	Requires extra time to process thought
Situational behaviors	Inappropriate and funny	Laughs or talks to self
Dealing with dysnomia	Unable to recall words	Has difficulty recalling needed words
General attitude	Impulsive	Responds without thinking through
Following directions	Poor, unable to follow	Needs to be told to behave

Note. Information from *Students with Learning Disabilities* (6th ed.) by C. D. Mercer & C. P. Pullen, 2005, Upper Saddle River, New Jersey: Merrill/Prentice Hall.

McNamara (2007) identified the top 10 student learning disabilities as follows: hyperactivity, perception impairment, emotional lability, general coordination deficits, disorders of attention (short attention span and distractibility preservation), impulsivity, disorders of memory and thinking, specific learning disabilities (reading, arithmetic, writing, and spelling), disorders of speech and learning, and equivocal neurological signs and EEG irregularities. Dealing with students with learning disabilities can be a difficult challenge and sometimes stressful as well as frightening. Burden and Byrd (2003) suggested that teachers should concentrate on students' strengths, work as a team with special education teachers, make sure their expectations are reasonable, model appropriate behaviors, and try to understand their students' struggles.

Student Gender

Gender bias is alive and well in today's pluralistic society, and gender inequity has been part of this nation's culture for nearly 300 years. In some Eastern countries, women cannot drive a car, are not allowed to wear pants, and are excluded from leadership positions. In the United States, women did not have the right to vote before 1920, and still today, sex discrimination exists in many professions.

Today, gender inequity is found in many homes and is a part of everyday life for many students. Teachers, as role models, should recognize student gender differences and, at the same time, show respect for these differences in order to foster learning. All children, male and female, should be held to the same high standards and expectations. Boys and girls should be encouraged to learn all subject matter. The old stereotype that girls are not particularly good in math or science is not valid. This old mindset needs to be removed from the classroom; otherwise, female students may develop false perceptions about themselves in regard to specific academic subjects. In addition, teachers should create and provide equal learning opportunities for all students in all subjects. In practice, perhaps in some situations girls are subject to some physical limitations. However, teachers should recognize gender differences in abilities and offer meaningful lesson plans to teach students about limitations (lifting weight, leadership role, conducting experiment, debating, challenging authority, and playing sports) rather than portraying female students as less capable than male students.

Teachers may notice that students of certain cultures may find equal learning opportunities odd because they have not been brought up with gender equality. Many cultures are patriarchal. Therefore, teachers need to proceed cautiously as they attempt to foster gender equality in their classrooms. They need to do so in ways that do not discourage female minority students or others from engaging in what may seem to them to be male-like learning activities.

Language-Minority Students

As mentioned previously, the federal government requires public schools to identify the primary languages spoken in students' homes for the purpose of collecting empirical data for funding and other uses. The primary language is designated as L1 and English, the second language, as L2. Education experts and researchers disagree on how to best help students achieve L1 proficiency and how to best help them acquire L2. Despite the fact that at least 3 to 7 years are needed for language-minority children to learn English to the point where they are equal with their native speaking peers, no student should be subject to tedious and dubious academic testing that has no reliability or validity in proving English proficiency. Most students of diverse backgrounds are subjected to primary and secondary language testing and assessment for little or no academic purpose. Most instruments used to assess language-minority students are not designed for assessing English proficiency. Also, public schools are now using CST scores to determine language proficiency in LEP and FEP students. These practices are ludicrously ineffective and they must be stopped.

Some researchers and scholars have found that proficiency in a primary language other than English is not necessary for academic success. This means that teachers and public schools do not have to focus on getting language-minority students to be proficient in L1. After all, not all native-speaking students achieve academic success in school. However, for success, all students have to master the academic language, which is English.

Most schools use the Home Language Survey form to trigger the LEP process. The Home Language Survey form has misled and misguided minority parents for years. The LEP process is flawed with a myriad of problems, and the criteria for re-designating students from one level of proficiency to the next trap these students in a system that serves little or no academic purpose.

Moreover, student placement in bilingual education defrauds parents because few if any bilingual programs exist on many school sites. The parent notification letter sent to parents for LEP students generally describes bilingual programs, but most schools do not have the programs listed. Instead, LEP students are placed in transitional academic programs or mainstream English programs. They must take extra classes in secondary school as a LEP requirement. Very few LEP students are placed with properly trained teachers with BCLAD credentials.

The sad truth is that most public schools identify, classify, label, and group language-minority students for fiscal rather than academic purposes. In fact, almost no public school offers academic services to LEP or FEP students; they offer only lip service, cosmetic education, and surface assessment. These hegemonic practices need to stop; otherwise, public schools will continue to deprive language-minority students of equal and quality education solely on the basis of the language they and their parents speak at home.

Re-designation is the most problematic area for LEP students. Re-designation from LEP to FEP usually takes several years, and most LEP students are never re-designated. Students often remain in the same classification as originally designated throughout their years in school, their academic labels staying intact. Most schools ignore re-designation to keep state and federal funding for LEP services. If re-designation takes place, schools have 2 more years to monitor students in their regular courses of study in addition to imposing LEP requirements. In the end, most LEP students lump together as ELD V, so-called advanced or mainstream level of proficiency.

Table 8.9. The LEP Process

Time period	Assessment	Classifica-tions/Academic Labels	Reclassifica-tion	Re-designation criteria
0-3 months following parent's completion of Home Language Survey	School initiates oral and written assessments in primary and secondary languages	ELD I, II, III, IV, and V; or beginning, early intermediate, intermediate, early advanced, and advanced; or preproduction, early production, speech emergence, intermediate fluency, and advanced	Every 3-6 months or twice per year; or at least once per year assessment for reclassification. Most schools use CST scores; some use double and triple standards or several (scores from CST, CELDT, ELA CST, ROLA Level, SOLOM, etc....); most LEP students lump together in the end.	1. Reassessment 2. Teacher's recommendation 3. Overall "c" average grade 4. Parents' consent 5. Score at least 35 percentile on reading, writing, and math in on CST
After the first 3 months	Formal assessment at different times. Schools rely heavily on classroom teachers' informal and formal assessments of student progress	Same as above	Unlikely	Same as above

Not all parents are clearly advised about the LEP process and its criteria. Table 8.9 illustrates the timeline and some of the procedures of the LEP process.

Bilingual education started nearly 50 years ago in California and elsewhere. The intent of bilingual education was admirable; however, the implementation has been poor, inconsistent, capricious, and inadequate. Many models of bilingual education programs have been used, but none if any has proven successful in transitioning students from LEP to FEP in a timely manner. Most bilingual education programs were designed to meet federal and state mandates for focusing on basic interpersonal communication skills (BICS), but not cognitive academic language proficiency (CALP), and in most cases, for retaining school funding. The programs have had little oversight, supervision, or evaluation of their benefit for language-minority students. To date, the only bilingual program that has been shown to help language-minority students is transitional bilingual education (TBE); all others are unproductive school entitlement programs. In fact, the American educational system does not promote bilingualism in the K–12 grades but supports the conceptual frame that American students should experience second-language learning.

So, what does all this mean to teachers? It means that teachers should not use students' primary language as an excuse not to provide quality education for language-minority students. These students deserve no more and no less than any other student. Some may need primary language support here and there, and others may just need some assurance to boost their performance. So many children are falling through the cracks because some people working in the school system fail to fulfill their legal obligation to provide a quality education for all. Most language-minority children are in school to learn English—the academic language that will take them to success in America. They are not in school to be bilingual in Hmong, Spanish, Khmer, Lao, or Chinese. The bottom line is that teachers need to help ELLs become proficient in English. To achieve this academic goal, schoolteachers must stop using surface assessment, cosmetic education, lip service, and academic label for non-academic purposes.

Curricular Challenges

In an age when knowledge and access to knowledge are increasing at a rapid pace, the curriculum can pose challenges for the most seasoned teacher. New teachers in multicultural classrooms need not be intimidated by an expanding curriculum if they remember the three most "rules" about curricular challenges: (a) the way teachers teach still matters, (b) what the teacher believes about students still matters, and (c) how teachers use and apply the hidden curriculum still matters.

The way teachers teach should matter the most because learning is less dependent on *what* they teach than on *how* they teach all learners. Teachers who rely on verbal expressions and speaking ability use fewer hands-on and minds-on activities to engage students in the learning circle, and this limits students' opportunities for learning. On the other hand, teachers who incorporate hands-on and minds-on activities with their instruction benefit all learners regardless of their level of language proficiency. To help teachers remember that the way they teach matters greatly, they should examine the curriculum from the philosophical, educational psychological, and pedagogical points of view and answer the following questions associated with those perspectives:

1. *Philosophical question*: What should students learn in class?
2. *Educational psychological question*: How should students learn the academic content?
3. *Pedagogical question*: What form of instruction should be used to teach students the academic content?

Furthermore, the teacher's beliefs about students can also be examined from these three perspectives. Do they believe all students deserve their best practices regardless of their ability level or struggles (philosophical perspective)? Do they believe the content they are to deliver is important to each student despite students' positive or negative attitudes (educational psychological perspective)? Do they believe students are capable of responding to their instructional methodologies with appropriate learning (pedagogical perspective)? Teacher's beliefs about students influence their instructional practices positively or negatively and set students up for success or failure. Teachers must give quality instruction through meaningful activities to help students learn the content, and they should differentiate instruction based on their knowledge of students to enhance learning for individual students.

The ways teachers use or apply the hidden curriculum in instructional practice determine how students are going to be affected academically. Posner (1995) defined the hidden curriculum as instructional norms and values that are present but not openly acknowledged by teachers or school officials. The hidden curriculum is also known as the informal or implicit curriculum. Manning and Baruth (2009) observed a number of ways the hidden curriculum appears and impacts teaching, including the following:

1. Most school policies recognize only middle-class values and expectations.
2. School media are oriented toward the mainstream culture.
3. Instructional practices target the learning styles of the predominant culture.
4. Extracurricular activities are dominated by one race.

These hegemonic actions send negative messages to students of color. For example, some teachers expect language-minority students to fit to the book instead of using a book that fits the learners.

A Responsive Multicultural Curriculum

As Burden and Byrd (2003) suggested, teachers should create, offer, and provide a supportive, caring, and responsive multicultural curriculum to all students. However, this is not as easy as it sounds because teachers have to demystify their misperceptions about multicultural education. Here is what teachers need to consider in order for them to have a clear understanding of what is needed:

1. Multicultural education does not require anything new that the school system does not have or cannot offer.
2. Multicultural education does not advocate for separate curricular instruction for language-minority students or students of any minority.
3. Multicultural education does not require all teachers to be bilingual.

In other words, all that is necessary for teachers to provide quality multicultural education is to know that they have to pay close attention to all students in the classroom in order to offer meaningful teaching and learning that truly reflect all learning styles. For multicultural education to work, teachers must develop good attitudes toward working with multicultural students because teachers are the primary sources of inclusive and considerate pedagogical applications. Burden and Byrd (2003) offered the following guidance for teachers who wish to implement effective multicultural education in their classrooms:

1. Use fair and relevant curricula.
2. Consider differentiating curricular materials.
3. Vary your instruction.

4.   Challenge students' thinking and abilities.
5.   Use cooperative learning or grouping.
6.   Use alternative or differentiated assignments.
7.   Offer individualized study.
8.   Give learning opportunity to redo assignments.
9.   Allow class participation.
10. Use authentic and culturally relevant pedagogies.
11. Use authentic and fair assessments.
12. Provide assistance to students when needed.
13. Work with students with special needs.
14. Celebrate diversity in class.
15. Set high expectations for all students.
16. Encourage and empower all students to learn.
17. Show caring, respect, and appreciation.
18. Have positive attitudes.
19. Use flexible teaching approaches.
20. Adjust instructional methods.

This list does not require anything teachers cannot do in the classroom. These authors simply reinforce fair and relevant practices to remind teachers that they can benefit all learners if the content and curriculum materials reflect the diversity of learners in the classroom. Similarly, Vang (2010) offered multicultural approaches through the following measures:

1.   Develop integrated content instruction and curricula. For instance, students should be guided to make learning connections through the units or themes the teacher has developed to teach all students. At the same time, integrate language instruction and content instruction so as to keep all students on the same page, headed to the same objective or goal.

2.   Create social empowerment that promotes learning. For instance, engage students in meaningful and relevant communications during teaching to stimulate learning opportunities that allow students to use language as a medium of interaction to improve learning skills and social confidence. One useful strategy is to use cooperative learning or small groups to help students interact with one another while exchanging ideas.

3.   Prescribe more hands-on and minds-on activities. For instance, instead of using rote memorization to encode and decode facts and information, the teacher designs a hands-on activity that engages students in firsthand experience and allows students to digest what they have just learned through the activity before asking them to share how they understand what has happened in oral or written form or both.

4.   Set up clear, concise, and specific expectations for learning. For instance, for students with the family value of filial piety or with strict parental rules, teachers enforce their good and responsible behaviors in class by having clear classroom rules, routine procedures, assignment guidelines, and learning outcomes that keep students motivated. Consistency saves teachers time they can use to help students who need extra assistance. Classroom expectations should be reviewed on a regular basis as a disciplinary tool to hold students academically accountable.

5.   Deal with issues of cultural diversity. Teachers who take the time to learn about their students' cultural identities have a greater chance of helping their students improve their

self-concept, self-image, self-worth, and self-esteem because they build cultural connections with their students.

6. Combat prejudice in the learning environment. The teacher plays a vital role in reducing prejudice by modeling behaviors and attitudes and refusing to tolerate prejudicial or discriminatory remarks in the learning environment, demonstrating that all students are socially and culturally equal. Teachers can reduce or eradicate cultural misconceptions by introducing resources as well as instructional practices that help students learn from one another about their cultures and traditions.

7. Create equal opportunities for learning. For instance, teachers strategize teaching schemes that enable them to assist students who are having difficulty understanding assignments. This may mean devoting extra time in or out of class to certain students. Also, reflective teaching allows teachers to assess themselves based on student learning outcomes.

8. Provide equity of instruction. Some students may need individualized instruction regardless of how many times the teacher has covered or repeated a lesson. Individualized instruction is one of the most effective teaching modalities for helping language-minority students learn.

9. Use differentiated instruction modalities. For example, to accommodate the different learning styles of all students, the teacher needs to incorporate integrated content instruction as part of the instructional process and use a variety of instructional approaches to tap all students into the learning objective. One approach is to engage students' prior knowledge as much as possible in order to make the learning inspirational and relevant to real life situations.

10. Maintain good rapport with all students. Quite often students perform poorly in class because of personality clashes with the teacher even without obvious evidence of dislike or antagonism. Simply put, if students do not like the teacher, they seem not to care much about the class. Keep in mind that students are human beings, and they often can "read" a teacher before the teacher can "read" them. Maintaining warm relationships with students will increase students' motivation to learn.

Keep in mind that offering responsive multicultural curricula will be challenging to some teachers because it requires pedagogical skills, instructional planning, instructional strategies, student activities, assessment, adaptations, and relevant materials. However, without multicultural education approaches, the current educational system is failing to meet federal and state mandates in providing academic services to students of diverse backgrounds, especially for ELLs and students with specials needs. As reported on the *Fresno Bee* newspaper, under the current No Child Left Behind Act of 2001, top schools in California have failed to meet government-mandated growth goals in educating students of diverse backgrounds in any of the 46 subgroups as follows:

1. Only 9 of 92 California school districts with more than 10,000 students are not in program improvement.

2. Nearly 90 percent of California school districts with more than 10,000 students are not in compliance with federal mandates.

3. Nearly 90 percent of these school districts have failed to meet federal mandates in raising the level of student English proficiency.

4. Of the 46 subgroups in public education, these districts have failed to meet the federal mandated growth goals as follows:

a.   In math—low-income students, English learners, Hispanics, and students with disabilities.
b.   In English—African Americans, Hispanics, low-income students, and students with disabilities.

Becoming a Multicultural Educator

To all monolingual and bilingual teachers, the goals of multicultural education are (a) social empowerment, (b) integrated content for instruction, (c) prejudice reduction, (d) equal opportunity, (e) equity of instruction, (f) cross-cultural sensitivity, (g) awareness, (h) accommodation, (i) adaptation, (j) modification, and (k) understanding cultural diversity in the classroom.

In today's classrooms, all teachers do not have to be bilingual; however, they at the very least should try to be knowledgeable and skillful multicultural educators who can reach out to all learners in their classrooms. America is a nation of immigrants, languages, cultures, traditions, races, ethnicities, sexes, and religions. This country is so beautiful, and so are its people. The student body in the American educational system reflects the colors of a rainbow, and so many children are coming from the salad bowl communities that enrich the American fabric.

Teachers are educators of the future, and they have the professional responsibility to teach all children to become responsible, productive, and respectful citizens. Their goal is to reduce cultural biases, stereotypes, prejudices, and misjudgments, and to achieve this, teachers should at the very least be open-minded enough to acknowledge any personal ignorance in the area of multiculturalism. Such acknowledgment would aid them in finding ways to embrace cultural diversity. Without formal learning about America, students of color are confused in finding their cultural identity. To help their students overcome the psychological hurdles that so often come with minority status, teachers must recognize their own ethnocentrism. With this in mind, teachers can educate the world around them to view diversity as a great strength rather than as a weakness.

When American teachers become multicultural educators, America will once again become the land of the free, the home of the brave, and the country of *e pluribus unum*. Moreover, when all teachers can sing the same notes in harmony, American children will sing a harmonious song in chorus in the classroom. Becoming a multicultural educator strengthens one's mind and soul and brings professional development and growth that offers meaningful education to children of color coming from the salad bowl natio, the United States of America.

The ultimate goal for all teachers in this multilingual and multicultural nation is to become multicultural educators—the next generation of multicultural teachers.

Summing Up

This chapter reviewed multicultural aspects of cultural diversity to provide teachers with some knowledge to help them become multicultural educators for all vital of color. Teaching in a multicultural setting requires a passion for learning and an understanding that America is a complex world and its inhabitants are unique and diverse in so many ways. Learning to become a multicultural educator is similar to acquiring a taste for different foods and drinks. Teachers need a combination of knowledge and skills in order to recognize, respect, appreciate, and accept cultural differences in the classroom. Even if legal segregation is still in practice, teachers can help suppress the hegemonic ideology that drives teachers and students farther apart. Despite how anyone might feel, this great nation will always remain as one nation under God, indivisible, with liberty, justice, and education for all.

No American child deserves less of an education than anyone else. To achieve equality in education, teachers are the key to formally addressing incivility, injustice, discrimination, and segregation.

The LEP process continues to hurt LEP students in the school system. It is sad but accurate to say that LEP services have deluded many parents to believe that their children are getting the academic services they deserve; however, in reality, most LEP services are lip service, cosmetic education, and surface assessments. New teachers need to pay close attention to these pressing issues affecting minority students.

Lastly, multicultural education is not an Eastern plot for undermining the current educational system. Rather it is a Western methodology advocating for inclusiveness in education reform in an effort to protect all learners and their interests under the legal mandates of federal, state, and local government policies.

CHAPTER NINE

ESTABLISHING CLASSROOM MANAGEMENT STRATEGIES

Education's purpose is to replace an empty mind with a good one.
Malcolm Forbes

Introduction

The classroom is a complex place. Teachers are responsible for running classrooms crowded with students of diverse socioeconomic backgrounds. Not all students have American middle-class values, and each student brings a unique set of behaviors to the classroom. There is no one-model-fits-all approach to deal with all behaviors. Teachers who know their psychosocial environment appear to be able to manage classroom problems with flexibility and adaptability.

A typical classroom has several characteristics: multidimensionality, simultaneity, immediacy, unpredictability, lack of privacy, and joint history. Often, classroom management problems that teachers face are related to the teachers' lack of understanding of the complex setting in which they work each and every day. This chapter gives some ideas as to how teachers can enhance their practices with practical classroom management strategies to cope with everyday school life since the classroom is a curious, strange, and public place where students are expected to work together in social and academic harmony.

Philosophy of Education

Quite frankly, teaching and management all begin with the teacher' own philosophy of education. Each teacher is unique in so many ways that sometimes students are confused about how to meet teachers' behavioral expectations. A philosophy of education is a broad approach a teacher has about how to teach all students and expect all of them to learn and behave in class. Three fundamental questions should guide teachers in developing a philosophy of education:

1. What should students learn in class?
2. How should students learn the academic content?
3. How should students be taught instructionally and academically?

Teachers who can address these questions with professionalism, believing they can teach and students can learn, are better prepared to handle classroom management problems as well as instructional practices. Their answers provide a philosophy of education that guides their actions in managing students' behaviors during instruction. For example, teachers who start the school year with a poorly organized discipline plan set a precedent of allowing a lot of disruptions, misbehaviors, and managerial issues.

Teachers' beliefs in management, teaching, instruction, and students affect their professional practices positively or negatively. Teachers who expect students to understand and comply with their expectations at the outset should model the good behaviors they expect to see in class on a regular basis. On the other hand, teachers who lack consistent expectations are likely to face mountains of unexpected behaviors in class because student misbehaviors, in most cases, go hand in hand with the teacher's behaviors, attitudes, and actions in the classroom.

Table 9.1 compares three philosophies of education: the teacher-centered approach, the student-centered approach, and the humanistic approach. As the table illustrates, the philosophies differ in a number of ways and those differences affect teaching practice. Having a sound philosophy of education should help teachers get off to a strong start in teaching, managing, and disciplining.

Table 9.1. Three Philosophies of Education

Area of Impact	Teacher-centered Approach	Student-centered Approach	Humanistic Approach
Responsibility	Teacher	Student	Both, joint, or sharing
Handling management	Teacher	Student	Both, joint, or sharing
Time management	Wasting time or controlling	Self-managing, valuable, productive, efficient, and effective	Efficient, effective, productive, and valuable for individual students
Management objectives	Well planned, well prepared, well focused, and well organized	Sharing, caring, socializing, community approach, self-directing, and fun	Grouping, respecting, relationship, academic focus, cooperation, and teamwork

Philosophy of Management

All teachers do not share the same opinion about how best to handle classroom management problems. Each teacher enters the classroom with his or her own philosophy of management and his or her own ways of dealing with problems. Teachers who have a high level of tolerance can handle management problems in a variety of ways. But teachers who are bothered by any little distraction or disruption and expect the class to be nearly perfect spend a lot of time correcting, redirecting, and dealing with student behaviors they do not like. Philosophy of management is a broad approach to dealing with all kinds of management problems that occur in the classroom.

Teachers develop their professional philosophy of management based on (a) personal familial experiences; (b) prior schooling experiences; (c) educational experiences; (d) clinical experiences, academic development, growth, and training; and (e) real life experiences on the job. These experiences shape teachers' beliefs about classroom management and improve their theoretical approach to handling students' behaviors. Some teachers are assertive, stern, firm, and authoritarian and others are authoritative, consistent, fair, flexible, logical, and affirming. Some teachers are aggressive and mean and terrify their students. Table 9.2 depicts some of these management approaches.

Keep in mind that whatever teachers have in their mind about how to manage the class may not work as they expect. Therefore, teachers must be flexible enough to change their philosophy of management rather than expect students to change to fit the teachers' desires. Despite all previous infractions, for example, good teachers usually start fresh every day.

Table 9.2. Five Management Approaches

Problem based	Logical Consequences	Assertive	Aggressive	Punishment
Disciplining	Causes and effects	Privacy	Public	Power of authority
Tone of voice	Choices, options	Consistent, fair, firm, neutral, soft, slow	Stern, tense, loud, fast, irritating, angry	No choices, no options, power, authority, demanding
Eye contact	Signaling, communicating, expecting	Direct eye contact, signaling	Squirmy, sarcastic facial expression, blaming, frowning	Impulsiveness, resentment, power, authority
Body language	Signaling, looking, staring, waiting	Standing next to, walking close by, signaling	Gesturing, hands on hips, violating personal space, intrusive	Negative, resentment, power, demanding, controlling

Theoretical Guiding Principles

Wholistic approaches to classroom management look at many areas, including principles of management, principles of discipline, classroom structure, psychosocial environment, instructional strategies, student activity strategies, task strategies, and pedagogical applications. In developing a theoretical framework for classroom management, some teachers focus on Erikson's explanation of the personality development of students, as shown in Table 9.3, and others rely on Maslow's five hierarchies of human needs, as displayed in Table 9.4.

Table 9.3. Stages of Personality Development

Approximate Age	Stage of Development	Psychosocial Crisis or Conflict	Basic Strength or Capability	Core Deficiency or Personality Qualities
0–18 months	Infancy, or oral-sensory	Trust v. mistrust	Hoping, feeding, depending	Withdrawal, mistrusting, or trusting and warm
18 months–3 years	Early childhood, or muscular-anal	Autonomy v. shame and doubt	Will, basic skills, training, trial and error	Compulsion, physical abilities and skills, controlling, falling, shaming, doubting
3 years–6 years	Play age, or locomotor	Initiative v. guilt	Purpose, independence, self-exploration, self-correction	Inhibition, feelings, effort, making mistakes, blaming, misperceptions
6 years–12 years	School age, or latency	Industry v. inferiority	Competence, cooperation, skills, knowledge	Inertia, demanding, learning new skills, knowledge, understanding, experience, failure or success
12 years–18 years	Adolescence	Identity v. identity or role con-	Fidelity, peer relationships,	Prejudice, judgment, sex role, sense of iden-

		fusion	social beings, friendship	tity, personality development
19 years–40 years	Young adulthood	Intimacy v. isolation	Love, relationships, caring, companionship	Loneliness, isolation, confusion, personality disorder, conduct disorder
40 years–65 years	Middle adulthood or adulthood	Generativity v. stagnation	Caring, fostering, parenting, providing	Rejectivity, aging, ailing, supporting, providing
65 years–beyond	Late adulthood, or old age	Integrity v. despair	Wisdom, reflection, experiences, coaching	Disdain, fulfilling, failing, broken, despair, hopeless, death

Table 9.4. Hierarchy of Human Needs

Need	Basic Demands or Needs
Self-actualization	Fulfill potential, peace of mind, security, stability, knowledge, peace, self-fulfillment, oneness, religious values, belief system, faith, wisdom, principles, goals, success
Esteem	Feeling competent, recognized, respected, included, appreciated, accepted; having pride, strengths, proficiency, self-sufficiency, belief system
Love	The need to be loved, belong, be accepted, recognized, appreciated, respected, included
Safety	The need to feel safe, secure, loved, cared about, protected, unharmed, unthreatened
Physiological stage	Feeding, food, air, water, sex, protection, comfort, nurturing, caring

Whatever theoretical framework they choose, teachers need to understand the five guiding principles of classroom management based on two meaningful purposes. The two purposes are: (a) The classroom environment has to be a caring place where students can engage in positive and meaningful learning and (b) the teacher has to provide a productive psychosocial environment in which students can enhance their social, emotional, and cognitive development and growth. Weinstein, Romano, and Mignano (2011) listed the five theoretical guiding principles for today's teachers as follows:

1. Successful classroom management fosters self-discipline and personal responsibility.
2. Teachers foster positive student-teacher relationships, implement engaging instruction, and use good preventive management strategies.
3. The need for order must not supersede the need for meaningful instruction.
4. Teachers must become culturally responsive managers at all times.
5. Becoming an effective classroom manager requires reflection, hard work, patience, and time.

The bottom line for teachers is that they do not have to lose control or patience while dealing with students' behaviors in the classroom. Classroom management is complex and diligent leadership, knowledge, and skills are needed to handle intricate problems brought by students with diverse racial, ethnic, language, cultural, SES, and social class backgrounds. Once teachers take these issues into consideration, they can advance their practices in the many areas involving instruction, management, and discipline. Consider, for example, teachers' rules have to be clear, concise, consistent, fair, logical, firm, assertive, motivational, flexible, meaningful, purposeful, valuable, and simple.

Common Classroom Problems

To become effective classroom managers, teachers need to recognize some basic behaviors or misbehaviors common to the classroom. The earlier they recognize them, the easier it will be to stop them or intervene in a timely manner. Some student behaviors are preventable or avoidable if teachers are continually aware of the tone, or feeling, in the classroom. For example, teachers can adjust their instructional strategies if they feel that students are not interested in learning because of ineffective learning activities or an unhealthy psychosocial environment. Table 9.5 lists some common behaviors teachers should attend to on a regular basis.

Table 9.5. Common Classroom Behaviors

Behavior	Possible Management Strategies
Absenteeism	Talk to, find out, meet with parents
Acting out in class	Talk to, correct behaviors, send to the office
Angry, upset, mad	Give time off, cool down, talk to, send to the office
Annoying	Correct, talk to, give choices, send to the office
Argumentative	Give choices, send to the office, meet with parents
Attention-getting	Direct, redirect, correct, wait
Attention-seeking	Talk to, signal, correct, direct
Attitude change or swing	Talk to, motivate, engage, find out
Back talking	Give choices, send to the office, meet with parents
Boasting	Talk to, calm down, control self, give choices
Bullying, teasing, picking on, making fun of, harassing, insulting, threatening	Send to the office, document, talk to, meeting with parents
Calling out in class	Direct, redirect, correct, signal
Class clown	Correct, talk to, stop, give choices
Classroom rules breach	Give consequences, give choices, warn, correct, talk to
Cleaning up problems	Direct, redirect, monitor, talk to
Coping with death, grief, loss	Compassion, empathy, caring, comfort, talk to, understand, see counselor
Cursing	Warn, correct, talk to, give options
Daydreaming	Correct, talk to, find out, direct, redirect
Dawdling	Direct, redirect, encourage, motivate, talk to
Defiant	Give choices, send to the office, meet with parents, talk to
Demanding	Calm down, settle down, talk to, give choices, send to the office, meet with parents
Destructive, destroying property	Send to the office, meet with parents, document
Disrespectful	Give choices, warn, send to the office, meet with parents
Disruptive	Correct, direct, redirect, talk to, remove objects

Don't care attitude	Encourage, motivate, talk to, find out
Drawing on desks	Give choices, talk to, send to the office
Drinking in class	Correct, talk to, give choices
Drug abuse	Send to the office, meet with parents, professional help
Eating in class	Correct, talk to, give choices
Failure to ask for help due to shyness	Talk to, find out, encourage, motivate
Fighting, not getting along, name calling	Send to the office, correct, talk to, meet with parents
Frustration	Give choices, provide assistance, direct, redirect, calm down
Gossiping, rumors, tattling, conspiring	Correct, give choices, send to the office, meet with parents, talk to
Homework problems	Talk to, find out, do in class, meet with parents
Hyperactivity	Talk to, give choices, correct, keep busy, send to the office, meet with parents
Immature	Talk to, find out, meet with parents, motivate
Impulsive	Calm down, give choices, correct, direct, meet with parents, send to the office
Inappropriate behaviors during lunch or recess	Correct, talk to, direct, redirect
Incomplete work or assignments	Talk to, find out, do in class, meet with parents, send note home
Inconsistency	Direct, redirect, monitor, check
Interruption	Give choices, correct, talk to, send to the office, meet with parents, send note home
Lack of common sense	Talk to, prompt, correct, motivate, encourage
Lack of interest	Motivate, encourage, find out, talk to, curiosity
Lack of motivation	Find out, motivate, encourage, talk to
Lack of self-esteem	Motivate, encourage, know interests and strengths
Late to class, tardy	Talk to, correct, send notes home, meet with parents
Lying	Talk to, correct, give choices, send notes home, send to the office, meet with parents
Name calling	Give choices, correct, talk to, send to the office, meet with parents
Negative responses	Correct, talk to, give choices
Nervous habits in class	Encourage, motivate, support, talk to, find out
Noisy work habits	Correct, signal, talk to, find out, give choices
Off-task behaviors	Direct, redirect, check, monitor, talk to
Playground issues	Address, talk to, correct, supervise
Poor attitudes	Motivate, encourage, talk to, correct, find out
Poor work habits	Talk to, correct, encourage, motivate, monitor, organize
Quietness, loner, isolated, independent	Talk to, encourage, motivate, find out, support
Rebellious	Give choices, correct, talk to, send to the office, send notes home, meet with parents
Rivalry toward others	Talk, correct, give choices, send to the office, send notes home, meet with parents
Rushing in and out, not in	Direct, redirect, talk to, supervise, correct

line	
Short attention span, short temper	Give choices, control self, talk to, find out, signal
Silent, quiet, not participating	Encourage, motivate, support, talk to, correct, find out
Not sitting in seat	Find out, correct, support, give choices, talk to, send to the office, meet with parents
Stealing	Send to the office, meet with parents, talk to, correct, find out
Stubborn	Talk to, correct, give choices, find out
Talking in class	Correct, direct, redirect, signal, talk to
Tantrums, upset, mad	Give choices, control self, calm down, send to the office, send notes home, meet with parents
Tardy, late	Talk to, find out, correct, send notes home
Teasing, picking on, kidding	Talk to, correct, send to the office, send notes home, meet with parents, warn
Throwing objects, shooting objects	Remove objects, talk to, give choices, send to the office, send notes home, meet with parents, correct
Truancy, absenteeism	Talk to, find out, send notes home, meet with parents

Of course it is impossible to handle every single misdeed in the classroom. Teachers must employ their professional judgment to deal with each situation. Keep in mind that not all student behaviors are bad and not all require disciplinary action. Teachers have to pay close attention and listen actively and carefully to the whole environment in order to respond to students appropriately. Having a quiet classroom does not mean that students are learning, and having a noisy classroom does not mean that students are off-task. Learning depends not on noise level but on what activities are going on in the classroom.

Furthermore, good teachers are always prepared to handle students and their behaviors professionally and ethically. In some cases, being vigilant can minimize unnecessary management problems. Monitoring whether students are on task, providing assistance as needed, and pacing the room to check on students keep students focused on task activities. Regardless of what strategies are used to manage students, teachers have to be actively involved in the teaching and learning process at all times. Students, especially students who are not paying attention or cannot read the directions and so engage themselves in the given task, need their teachers' undivided attention in order to concentrate on assigned tasks.

The key to achieving effective management is to be aware of the classroom environment and students' behaviors at all times. Effective managers understand that classroom management is a process rather than a product. Prompt response and action should help teachers handle most interruptions and minor misbehaviors. Sometimes students take the responsibility to correct their own misdeeds if the teachers remind them of the rules, consequences, and procedural guidelines. Consider, for example, teachers must teach all students accountability, regardless of age, to be responsible for their own learning and expect them to use their class time for improving learning as much as possible.

Classroom Management Strategies

There are many problems teachers have to deal with every day in the classroom, as listed in Table 9.5, and there are many classroom management strategies teachers must learn to apply practically, ethically, and professionally. It is hard to imagine every single little thing that teachers will face in the classroom and how they are going to resolve all problems without causing disruptions to the class. No classroom is free of problems. Similarly, there is no child who has perfect attitudes and behaviors. Nor is there any teacher who is a perfect manager. In other words, teachers must anticipate management and discipline problems in order to prepare for them. Moreover, teachers must keep in mind that classroom management cannot be perfect but has to be meaningful and sensible.

To help teachers get off to a good start in managing their classrooms, 10 major strategies, or practical areas all teachers must at the very least learn, understand, and recognize, are presented below. Without a good grasp of these strategies, classroom management problems can pile up and unsolved issues will compound exponentially to give teachers insurmountable stress and distress. Many experts and scholars suggest that new teachers take a proactive stance to prevent misbehaviors by forging positive relationship with students in a productive learning environment (Charles & Senter, 2012; Evertson & Emmer, 2009; Henley, (2006); Herrell & Jordan, 2006; Levin & Nolan, 2007; Manning & Bucher, 2007; Nissman (2006); Weinstein et al., 2011. Following are the primary managerial strategies:

Practical strategy one is: Organize the physical classroom environment and instructional supplies. The classroom should be designed to create a productive, positive, and sound psychosocial environment for academic learning. A number of different arrangements are possible, as shown in figure 9.1. The items that need to be considered in the arrangement are the following:

- Wall and ceiling space
- Floor space, floor plan, or floor diagram
- Arrangement of student desks or seating charts
- Small-group instruction areas or stations
- Computer workstations
- Teacher's desk, filing cabinet, projector, computer, and other equipment
- Bookcase or bookshelves
- Storage areas
- Centers
- Countertops
- Pets, animals, aquarium, artifacts, souvenirs, or special displayed items
- Textbooks and instructional materials
- Student work
- Portfolio files
- Frequently used classroom materials and supplies
- Teacher's supplies and resources
- Other extra materials
- Student belongings
- Equipment such as TV, VCR, CD player, headphones, pencil sharpeners, extension cords, adaptors, small whiteboards, markers, erasers, etc.
- Seasonal or infrequently used materials, supplies, textbooks, and crafts, such as posters, bulletin boards, colored blocks, calculators, protractors, balls, templates, handouts, outlines, transparencies, laminated items, special project materials, etc.

Figure 9.1. Selected samples of classroom designs.

Arrangements for independent work/tests/beginning of the year/lecture

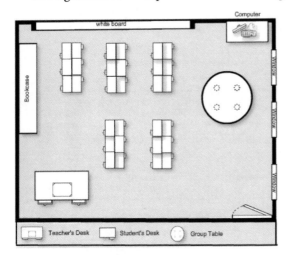
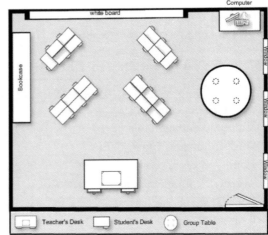

Arrangements for group work/stations

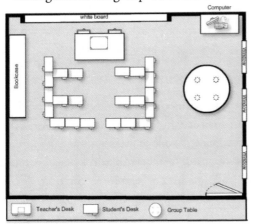
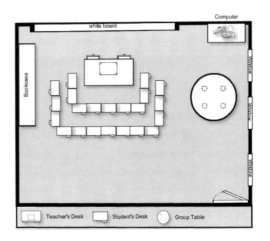

Arrangements for demonstration/discussion

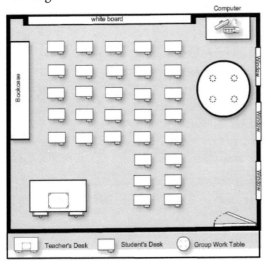
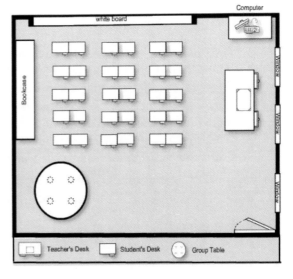

Table 9.6 is a checklist teachers can use to make sure essential items have been organized efficiently and in a way that creates a caring, supporting, and productive learning environment for all students. Keep in mind that teachers can use the walls to teach, communicate, celebrate, honor, and display academic successes of students.

Table 9.6. **Classroom Design Checklist**

Floor, Wall, and Ceiling Spaces	Supplies and Storage Spaces
• Teacher's desk and tables	• Student supplies area
• Student desks and tables	• Student work
• Small-group areas, mat, floor	• Textbooks and trade books
• Computer desks or work stations	• Portfolio files or journals
• Teacher's equipment and storage	• Frequently used materials and supplies
• Bookcases or bookshelves	• Infrequently used materials and supplies
• Centers	• Teacher's supplies and materials
• Countertops	• Classroom supplies and materials
• Pet and animal areas	• Student belongings, coat racks, back packs, etc.
• Traffic patterns	
• Classroom library or supply rooms	• TV monitor, big screen, VCR, CD recorder, etc.
• Bulletin boards, posters, laminated materials, etc....	

Practical strategy two is: Establishment classroom rules, consequences, and procedures. Rules, consequences, and procedural guidelines must be laid out for the whole class. Teachers must set behavioral expectations along with short-term and long-term goals as well as learning objectives for the class. Whether these objectives or goals will be met each day or not, teachers should be geared toward these target aspirations, using them to determine the daily actions in the classroom. Sharing, discussing, and brainstorming learning expectations with students before setting up the rules and procedures is critically important to the effectiveness of classroom management. Some guidelines for establishing classroom rules and consequences are as follows:

1. There must be at least three rules, but it is best to have not more than five.
2. Each rule must be stated clearly with positive words or language.
3. Each rule must be enforceable and able to be implemented.
4. All rules must be accompanied by a set of logical consequences.
5. There must be at least three not more than five consequences.
6. Each consequence must be enforceable and able to be implemented.
7. Both rules and consequences must be age- and grade-level appropriate.
8. Both students and teachers must adhere to the rules and consequences
9. Rules and consequences can be changed by the students and teachers in the class together.
10. Rules and consequences should be reviewed periodically to ensure effectiveness and fairness.

Areas and activities for which classroom procedures must be established are as follows:

- Student desks, tables, and storage areas
- Teacher's desks, tables, and storage areas
- Storage and countertops
- Drinking fountain and sink

- Pencil sharpener
- Restrooms and restroom pass
- Centers
- Equipment usage and areas
- Computer stations
- Feeding animals, watering plants, or changing water, etc.
- Student attention
- Student participation
- Talk among students or think-pair-share
- Obtaining assistance
- Finishing work early
- Taking initiative
- Transitions into and out of the room
- Small-group instruction
- New procedures for future new areas

Tables 9.7, 9.8, 9.10, and 9.11 give some examples of classroom rules, consequences, and procedures.

Table 9.7. **Selected Classroom Rules, by Grade**

Grades K–3	Grades 4–6	Grades 7–8	Grades 9–12
✓ Raise hands before speaking	○ Be ready to learn	➤ Be in seat before bell rings	☐ Be in seat before bell rings
✓ Keep hands to self	○ Follow directions	➤ Come to school prepared	☐ Follow directions
✓ Listen when someone speaks	○ Keep hands and feet to self	➤ Follow directions	☐ Be kind and responsible for personal actions
✓ Do not leave seat without permission	○ Raise hand if need help	➤ Raise hand if have questions	☐ Wait for order to be dismissed
✓ Follow orders to move in and out of class	○ Be kind to others	➤ Keep hands and feet to self	☐ All assignments are due on time
		➤ No foul language is allowed in class	

Table 9.8. **Examples of Logical Consequences, by Grade**

Grades K–3	Grades 4–6	Grades 7–8	Grades 9–12
▪ Verbal warning	▪ Verbal warning	▪ Verbal warning	▪ Verbal warning
▪ Name on the board	▪ Miss recess	▪ Send to the office	▪ Send to the office
▪ Pull a card	▪ Send note home	▪ Send note home	▪ Contact parents
▪ Miss recess	▪ Contact parents	▪ Contact parents	▪ Conference
▪ Send note home	▪ Conference	▪ Conference	▪ Follow-up/services

Table 9.9. Logical Consequences for Selected Infractions

Type of Infraction	Consequences
First offense	Verbal warning and teacher talks to student either privately or publicly, depending on the behavior and its severity.
Second offense	Take away privileges and lose one recess.
Third offense	Take away privileges and lose two recesses.
Fourth offense	Take away privileges or lose all recesses for the day.
Fifth offense	Take away privileges and call parents or guardians.
Sixth offense	Take away privileges, send to the office, have meeting with parents, and evaluate for possible suspension.
Physical or verbal threats, severe disruption, or being rude to teacher and classmates	Will not be tolerated and results in immediate referral to the principal, assistant principal, or appropriate administrator for intervention.

Table 9.10. Selected Procedures for Room Use

Situation	Possible Procedural Activities
Beginning of class/ opening	Roll call, absentees, tardy students, academic warm-up routines, behaviors, distributing materials, adjustment
Line up	Going out, coming in, outside the door, on the playground, going to assembly, dismissal
Room/school areas	Shared areas, teacher's desk, water fountain, bathroom, student desks, learning center stations, playground, lunchroom/cafeteria
Setting up independent work areas	Defining work alone, identifying problems, resources, solutions, scheduling, checkpoints
Instructional activities	Contact between teacher and students, student movement, signals for attention, signals for teacher, initiatives, participation, group rotation, passing materials, behavior in group, behavior outside group, academic engaged time
Ending class	Putting things away, clean up, backpacks, homework, clothes, personal items, dismissing class
Interruptions	Rules, orders, conduct, delays, talk among students, out-of-seat policies, pencil sharpening
Work requirements	Heading papers, pencil or pen, neatness, legibility, incomplete work, late work, missed work, due dates, make-up work, supplies, coloring, drawing, cursive, manuscript
Communicating assignments	Posting, orally giving, turning in, returning, homework, provision for absentees, incomplete work, collecting
Monitoring student work	Independent work, group work, presentation, completion in class, completion of homework, progress, challenges, difficulties
Checking assignments in class	Exchange papers, go over answers, grading papers, turning work in, collecting work, correction, practicing
Grading procedures	Assigning report grades, recording grades, extra credit work, grading criteria, grade contracts, record keeping
Academic feedback	Reward system, incentives, reinforcers, posting work, informing parents, record keeping, feedback on papers, progress, improvement
In case of an emergency	Fire drills, health and safety, lockdown, poison, injury, choking, fire, flood, tornado, rain

Table 9.11. **Areas Needing Procedures**

Transition	Small-group Instruction	Other Areas
■ Beginning of the day	■ Centers and stations	■ Passing out papers or distributing materials
■ Leaving the room	■ Intervention strategies	
■ Returning to the room	■ Learning objectives	■ Interruptions
■ Between tasks	■ Prepping students for activity	■ Delays
■ Top of the hour		■ Restroom pass
■ Bottom of the hour	■ Student movement in and out of the group	■ Library
■ Before lunch	■ Cooperative expectations and behaviors	■ Resource room
■ After lunch		■ School front office
■ Ending the day	■ Expected behaviors outside the group	■ Cafeteria
		■ Playground areas
	■ Sharing and using materials and supplies in group	■ Recess
		■ Sports equipment and balls
	■ Group process and learning activities	■ Fire and disaster drills
		■ Classroom helpers
	■ Time on task	■ Student leaders
	■ Completion of work	

Practical strategy three is: Establish ongoing monitoring strategies for managing student work. Teachers need to figure out how to hold students accountable for their learning. Teachers are responsible to make sure student learning takes place and the learning process is productive and meaningful. Basic guidelines for monitoring students and student work are as follows:

1. Clearly communicate assignments and work requirements.
2. Devise clear instructions for assignments.
3. Model how assignments could be done.
4. Provide clear and concise standards or examples for form, neatness, and due dates.
5. Communicate clear procedures for absent students.
6. Monitor student progress on task and in progress.
7. Make sure students complete given assignments.
8. Maintain records of student work.
9. Create and manage student portfolios.
10. Keep track of and manage paperwork.
11. Provide opportunity for making up or redoing work to enhance learning
12. Give feedback on a regular basis.

Teachers can help students monitor their own work by establishing accountability, encouraging reflection, and insisting on progress and responsibility. For example, if teachers have ways to let students know what is missing or not turned in and provide opportunity for redoing the work, students can motivate themselves to catch up. If teachers give quick or instant feedback, they encourage students to improve their work habits, and better work habits lead to improved student learning. Table 9.12 gives some ideas as to how teachers can monitor students as they progress and work toward completing their assignments.

Table 9.12. Monitoring Strategies that Enhance Learning

Clear Communication of Assignments and Work Requirements	Monitoring in Progress and the Completion of Assignments	Providing Quick Response or Feedback on Assignments
▪ Post assignments in conspicuous location ▪ List clear standards, expectations, and instruction, such as pencil, disc, paper, headings, due dates, erasers, neatness ▪ Post procedures for absent students to make up the work ▪ Consequences, penalty, deduction, and minus for late work ▪ Provide opportunity for assistance ▪ Monitor and check for progress on regular basis	▪ List clear procedural guidelines for monitoring and assessing student work ▪ Give clear guidelines for short- and long-term assignments and special projects ▪ List step-by-step how to complete each assignment before the next one ▪ Post due dates for each assignment ▪ Maintain a systematic record of student work ▪ Provide directions for students helping or supporting one another ▪ Allow sufficient time for the work	▪ Meet requirements and expectations ▪ Explain grading policies and procedures ▪ Give quick feedback to motivate students ▪ Encourage students to track their own progress and work ▪ Expect report on regular basis ▪ Provide clear guidelines for parent help ▪ Designate location for displaying student work ▪ Make journal entries or encourage students to keep records ▪ Create portfolio or file folder for student work ▪ Use rubrics or scales for grading to avoid disputes

Practical strategy four is: Create a productive, positive, sound, and inclusive psychosocial learning environment. A positive climate promotes student learning and appropriate student behaviors. Creating the right environment at the beginning of the year sets a clear platform for the rest of the year. Teachers can reinforce appropriate behaviors by praising students, reassuring them, complimenting, affirming, and encouraging. To get off to a good start, teachers may consider doing the following:

1. Be creative and artful when designing the classroom.
2. Create a positive learning climate for all.
3. Be inclusive and considerate about students' feelings.
4. Teach rules and procedures early.
5. Explain teacher's roles, responsibilities, and authority.
6. Plan for a great start with fun, excitement, entertainment, and joy.
7. Make the first day sparkling, memorable, and spectacular.
8. Be aware of social, emotional, psychological, and mental factors (See Table 9.13).
9. Have formal and informal communication with parents and legal guardians.

10.   Be aware of cross-cultural issues in the multicultural classroom (See Table 9.13).
11.   Cope with problems, issues, and unexpected circumstances (See Table 9.13).
12.   Set up a plan or a handbook for substitute teachers (See Table 9.13).
13.   Reflect throughout the first 4 weeks.

Table 9.13. Factors to Consider in Establishing a Positive Environment

Social Factors	Cross-cultural Factors	Unexpected Factors	Substitution Factors
<ul><li>Greeting students</li><li>Welcoming remarks</li><li>Introductions</li><li>Description of room</li><li>Show students around</li><li>Get to know students' names</li><li>Go over rules, procedures, consequences, and infractions early</li><li>Design meaningful lesson plans based on content knowledge</li><li>Prepare transitional activities to be used as time fillers</li><li>Decide when to distribute textbooks</li></ul>	<ul><li>Practical difficulties—hardship, low income, poverty, work schedules, child care, transportation, language barriers, limited educational background, feeling inferior</li><li>Psychological barriers—unhappiness, dissatisfaction, negative feeling, false assumptions, mistreatment, struggles, bad experience</li><li>Cultural barriers—lack of language skills, no translator, respect teachers as authority</li><li>Socioeconomic barriers—refugee, immigrant, illegal, new arrival, migrant worker</li><li>Legal barriers—lack of understanding of parental and student rights</li></ul>	<ul><li>Walk-in visitors, interrupt by school staff, drop-in incidents</li><li>Late arrivals, tardy</li><li>New students</li><li>Forget lunch money</li><li>Paperwork</li><li>Taking school bus issues</li><li>Insufficient supplies, materials, books</li><li>Disabled and handicapped students</li><li>Weeping, crying, whining, tantrum</li><li>Wetting pants, accidents</li><li>Sick students</li><li>Hurt or injured students</li><li>Fighting, pushing, pulling</li><li>Can't follow routines, procedures, rules</li></ul>	<ul><li>Class roll</li><li>Seating chart</li><li>Rules and logical consequences</li><li>Daily schedules and routines</li><li>List of students on medications and medical alerts</li><li>Instructional resources and lesson plans</li><li>Classroom emergency procedures</li><li>Map of the school</li><li>Emergency phone numbers</li><li>Student work assignments</li><li>Instructions for reporting injuries, serious behaviors, fights, etc.</li></ul>

Figure 9.2 illustrates that the relationship between students and teachers is affected by the learning climate. Therefore, creating a positive environment is important in getting off to a good start at the beginning of the year. The first few days and weeks of school prepare students for the rest of the year by ensuring them of positive learning and academic successes. For students to achieve a high lev-

el of academic learning, teachers must help them follow classroom rules and procedures and meet classroom expectations and, at the same time, engage them in meaningful learning experiences.

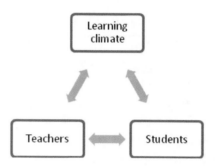

Figure 9.2. Relationships among students, teachers, and learning climate.

Practical strategy five is: Plan for the instruction in the classroom. Teacher planning consists of seven stages of curricular pedagogy and academic activities: (1) daily, (2) weekly, (3) monthly, (4) term, (5) unit, (6) semi-annual, and (7) yearly. Planning consists of three phases: preplanning, ongoing planning, and postplanning. All types of planning should be done consistently and at the right time. A pacing calendar is helpful for logging all curricular pedagogy and academic activities. Sometimes, changes must be made, and planning ahead can provide the flexibility and the time needed for future changes.

Instructional practice is a process that consists of five steps: (1) planning, (2) implementation, (3) evaluation, (4) feedback, and (5) reflection. These are illustrated in Figure 9.3. As teachers follow this process, they will notice that not all students learn the same way, and not all students comprehend the same thing the same way. Teachers must take these differences into account as they plan their instructional practice.

Figure 9.3. Process of instructional practice.

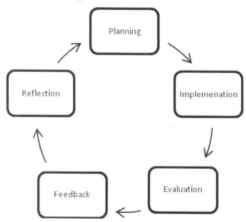

The different ways students learn, comprehend, and process information through coding, encoding, and decoding are referred to as learning modes. Students' learning modes reflect their learning styles or learning preferences. Evertson and Emmer (2009) organized student learning modes into four major categories as follows:

1. Sensory/logical—using a step-by-step approach to gather, rehearse, and explain information.
2. Sensory/emotion—using interpersonal relationships to help review and master information.
3. Intuitive/logical—using natural curiosity to solve problems and understand big ideas.
4. Intuitive/emotion—using opportunities for creative projects to deepen understanding.

Because any classroom probably contains students who learn by each of these different learning modes, it is extremely important for teachers to vary academic activities and use differentiating instruction to accommodate all learning needs in the classroom. In other words, it is better for teachers to design curricular pedagogy and academic activities to fit the ways students learn than for teachers to expect their students to fit the ways the teachers prefer to teach. Teachers must design detailed lesson plans and employ instructional formats appropriate for all students in the classroom. Instructional formats may include the whole group, small teacher-led groups, small cooperative groups, student pairs, individualized instruction, centers and stations, intervention/remediation groups, groups of new arrivals, ability groups, and gifted and talented groups. If teachers can set up the room to offer these formats to meet all the different groups of learners, the students will benefit immensely.

Furthermore, normal instructional planning and daily instruction should be carefully considered to include other components, such as content development, class discussion, recitation, reinforcement, reflection, feedback, review, and testing. Table 9.14 lists the advantages and disadvantages of the most common instructional formats. Keep in mind that the teaching goal for each lesson plan is to deliver clear instruction to maximize student learning. The following suggestions will help teachers keep their instruction clear:

1. Have clear learning objectives.
2. Keep communication and directions clear.
3. Use a clear sequence in teaching.
4. Utilize technological support.
5. Check for understanding.
6. Prevent misbehaviors.
7. Manage group work.
8. Manage student movement.
9. Maintain group focus.
10. Keep transitions smooth.

In practice, clarity of instruction is enhanced by good organization, a coherent sequence of presentation, modeling, illustrations, examples, direct and explicit expressions, precise and concrete information, making the connection between teaching and learning, checking for comprehension, and achieving content mastery. The bottom line is that teachers have to provide clear, consistent, and convincing detailed information to hold students accountable and responsible for knowing the learning objectives and goals and performing the work as expected.

Table 9.14. **Advantages and Disadvantages of Common Instructional Formats**

Format	Advantages	Disadvantages
Whole group	Saves time, efficient, all benefit and hear same information	One-model-fits-all approach, not beneficial to all learners
Cooperative group	Social interactions, student centered	Not all students learn, not all benefit from activity
Centers and stations	More practice, enrichment, focused	Limited time, quick fixes, fast

learning	but ineffective, dependency

Practical strategy six is: Manage cooperative learning groups in the classroom. Teachers can establish strategies and routines that support cooperative learning activities to maximize student participation and learning. The elements of cooperative learning are (a) positive interdependence; (b) individual accountability; (c) equal participation; (d) simultaneous interaction; (e) collaboration; (f) problem solving and group consensus; (g) brainstorming, discussion, sharing, and selecting; (h) specific group objectives; (i) roles, responsibilities, and supports; and (j) specific group goals.

For a group to be productive, teachers must ask themselves why they put students in groups. Grouping must serve learning purposes. The learning purposes served well in groups are: (a) completion of assignments, (b) mutual assistance, (c) strategizing to solve problems, (d) sharing materials, (e) group discussion, and (f) increasing student involvement and productivity. Teachers can help students achieve these meaningful learning objectives and goals in their groups by doing some of the following:

1. Arrange the room appropriately.
2. Set procedures for talking and movement in the groups.
3. Explain routines and expectations.
4. Set clear objectives and goals for the groups.
5. Train students on group attention signals.
6. Promote interdependence.
7. Clearly expect individual accountability.
8. Monitor group work and behavior.
9. Intervene frequently to resolve minor problems.
10. Encourage group efforts and skills.
11. Promote social skills.
12. Promote leadership skills.
13. Offer group and individual rewards to motivate learning.

A cooperative group has a number of roles students may play. Common roles are lead person, recorder, speaker, member, and initiator. The teacher also plays several key roles in order to supervise, control, and monitor the group process. These roles are shown in Figure 9.4.

Figure 9.4. Teacher's roles in cooperative group.

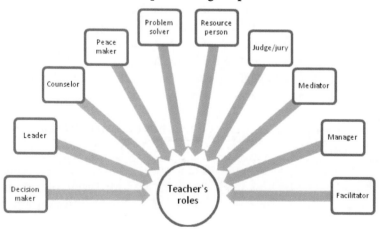

Practical strategy seven is: Maintain appropriate student behaviors in the classroom. To be prepared for handling student behaviors is to anticipate the unexpected in the classroom because students are predictable and classroom behaviors come and go. Each day of the week and each hour of the day are different. As Henley (2006) explained, people are social beings and everyone needs companionship. Student behaviors reflect this human reality; students are social beings who need companionship, engage in parallel and interactive play, and have their feelings affected by the psychosocial environment.

If teachers expect students to be good every day, they will find student misbehaviors unacceptable and think of the class as out of control. Teachers should not be easily lulled into complacency by the good behavior of their students at the beginning of class, in the middle of the day, at the end of the day, or at the beginning of the year because external and internal factors can influence how students behave in response to psychosocial stress and distress (Evertson & Emmer, 2009). In other words, teachers must be vigilant at all times to detect problems; be consistent in dealing with student behaviors; and be assertive in enforcing classroom rules, consequences, and procedures to eliminate problems instead of allowing unresolved problems to escalate over time.

In practice, teachers can follow a few basic principles to maintain appropriate student behavior as follows:

1.   Provide ongoing monitoring of student behavior.
2.   Monitor and supervise students' academic progress.
3.   Remind students of rules, consequences, and procedures.
4.   Be consistent, firm, and assertive in enforcing rules, consequences, and procedures.
5.   Detect and deal with problems early and promptly.
6.   Set clear expectations for learning each day.
7.   Clearly communicate assignments and work requirements.
8.   Provide assistance as needed.
9.   Manage student progress.
10. Facilitate the group process.
11. Build a productive, positive, sound, and inclusive learning climate for all.
12. Use alternative reinforcements—privileges, recognition, rewards, incentives, tangible activities, etc.

Teachers can use reward systems or incentives to encourage student behaviors; however, these actions have negative and positive effects. For example, students may refuse to listen or pay attention when teachers are out of rewards, and these positive and negative reinforcements become meaningless when students' only motivation is get the rewards. Teachers must use and choose these reinforcements wisely and carefully. As Figure 9.5 illustrates, use or non-use of rewards has different effects on students.

Figure 9.5. **Effects of use of incentives for reinforcement.**

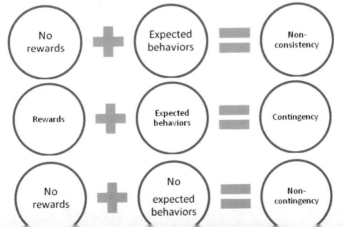

Practical strategy eight is: Use clear communication in teaching, managing, ordering, controlling, patrolling, supervising, monitoring, and engaging students at all time in the classroom. A teacher's way of communicating, conveying, instructing, and directing students reflects the teachers' attitudes, personalities, and enthusiasm toward the psychosocial environment. And more importantly, the teacher's tone of voice can affect whether students feel positive or negative. Some teachers speak in a low tone of voice, and students may have a hard time hearing or understanding. Others are clear, loud, pleasant, and engaging. Communication skills directly affect how teachers teach and how students learn and behave in the classroom.

Teachers can always practice preventive management skills as well as proactive management skills; however, there is no perfect way of predicting student behaviors, and no known technique, strategy, or plan works all the time or every time. Teachers must learn how to approach problems and employ appropriate strategies to alleviate the cause of the problems. Communication works pretty much the same way as management. Teachers have to find meaningful and effective communication skills for handling students professionally without turning them off, being mean to them, being aggressive, being intimidating, or making them feel scared.

Some of the forms of communication that are effective in the classroom are listed in Table 9.15 (Alberti, 1977; Everston & Emmer, 2009; Glasser, 1975; Kottler, 2002; Zuker, 1983).

Table 9.15. Selected Forms of Communication

Form	Examples
Constructive assertiveness	Stand up for one's rights to advocate for students' best interests
Identify the problem	Have a clear statement of the problem or concern, identify the cause and effects of behavior right away
Body language	Direct eye contact, alert posture, facial expression, attentive to listen
Insisting on behavior	Intend to obtain appropriate behavior right away, not giving up, make correction instantly
Empathic responding	Show understanding, compassion, feeling, sympathy toward students; accommodate; give regards
Listening	Be attentive, wait, be patient, calm down, control
Processing	Repeat, summarize, recap, review, go over
Problem solving	Step-by-step process—identify, select, commit, and resolve

Regardless of how little a problem is, teachers must bear in mind that their role is to modify the exhibited problem behaviors and at no time try to change the student's cultural identity or persona. In other words, teachers must focus on the behaviors, not on the students, in order to modify the situation. Also, miscommunication can be very sensitive in some cultures. For example, the phrase "I don't care" means different things in different cultures and subcultures, and the word "assertive" could be considered rude, impolite, mean, or inappropriate in some cultures. Therefore, teachers must be professionally, ethically, and culturally literate when communicating with parents of multicultural and diverse backgrounds.

Practical strategy nine is: Manage problem behaviors in the classroom. Teachers can strategize techniques, ideas, and plans as to how to deal with minor disruptions, interruptions, and misbehaviors as well as major problems that may arise in the classroom. As mentioned previously, classroom management and discipline are ongoing events, and teachers should not expect to be relaxed and kicked back at any time. Think of a teacher as being like a responsible driver, always watchful of everything when behind the wheel, ready no matter what might happen on the road, thus averting otherwise inevitable accidents. Teachers drive the classrooms all day long, providing healthy and safe learning environments for all their students.

Table 9.16 lists some samples of intervention teachers can use to respond to problem behaviors. To become effective in using management and disciplinary interventions, teachers need to practice. They need to keep their management skills sharp.

Table 9.16. Interventions for Classroom Problems

Minor problems	Moderate problems	Extended problems	Serious problems
▪ Use nonverbal cue ▪ Ignore ▪ Get activity moving ▪ Use proximity: move closer, stand nearby ▪ Use group focus ▪ Redirect behaviors ▪ Provide needed instruction or directions ▪ Use brief order desist, stop, pause ▪ Give choices, options ▪ Correct in private ▪ Logical consequences	▪ Take away privileges, ▪ Remove activity ▪ Isolate or separate ▪ Use penalty ▪ Assign detention ▪ Miss recess ▪ Refer to the office ▪ Send note home ▪ Contact parents for conference ▪ Notify administrators ▪ Document behavior	▪ Use problem solving strategies ▪ Step-by-step process ▪ Identify problems ▪ Select actions ▪ Commit to action ▪ Propose solution ▪ Resolve ▪ Refer to administrators for further services ▪ Conference with parents ▪ Document resolution	▪ All these must be dealt with by school administrators: ▪ Teasing incidents ▪ Bullying ▪ Tattling ▪ Gossiping ▪ Fighting ▪ Chronic avoidance ▪ Disobeying authority ▪ Defiance ▪ Talking back ▪ Power struggle ▪ Making threats ▪ Self-endangering ▪ Attempting suicide ▪ Gang-related activity ▪ Vandalism ▪ Substance abuse

One cautionary note is in order: Some problems cannot be solved in the classroom and need to be referred to the school office or administrators for intervention. Teachers must focus on protecting other students' health, safety, and rights and, at the same time, teachers must protect themselves from being harmed. Also, dealing with problem behaviors takes extra precautions; teachers must not lose their patience, and that is the bottom line.

Practical strategy ten is: Manage special groups in the classroom. Teachers can develop special instruction and academic activities that enhance the learning of students with special needs, language barriers, disabilities, and other special conditions. These students pose instructional challenges, and without extra assistance, they fall through the cracks easily. Keep in mind that special groups include students from the top, middle, and bottom academic groups. Gifted and talented students need special attention from teachers to keep the class work from being too easy and boring for them. On the other hand, students in the bottom group often seem to drown in the class because they cannot swim and sink to the bottom of the barrel. Table 9.17 lists some groups of students who need extra attention in the classroom.

Table 9.17. Selected Special Groups of Students

High Achievers	Low Achievers	Students with Special Needs	English-Language Learners
▪ Gifted and talented ▪ High abilities ▪ Exceptional ▪ Above grade level ▪ Creative ▪ Divergent needs ▪ High achievers ▪ Proficient ▪ Independent learners	▪ Language learners (L1) ▪ Lack reading ▪ Lack writing ▪ Lack speaking ability ▪ Lack basic skills ▪ Lack organization ▪ Lack language skills ▪ Lack support ▪ Below grade level ▪ Struggling ▪ New arrivals ▪ At-risk ▪ Problem behaviors ▪ Poor, low SES	▪ ADD ▪ ADHD ▪ IEP ▪ 504 ▪ IDEA ▪ Autism or ASD ▪ Seizure ▪ Epilepsy, convulsion ▪ SED ▪ CD ▪ PDD ▪ Vision impaired ▪ Hearing impaired ▪ Mute ▪ Deaf ▪ Retarded ▪ Multiple disabilities	▪ LEP ▪ FEP ▪ ELLS ▪ New arrivals ▪ Refugee ▪ Immigrant ▪ Undocumented ▪ Bilingual ▪ Minority ▪ Students of color ▪ Diverse SES ▪ Poor native children

In California, TPE standards and TPA mandates require teachers to provide inclusive instruction to all students with specific accommodations, modifications, adaptations, and interventions for special groups of students who will not benefit from regular instructional practices. These requirements are legal mandates, not based on multicultural approaches or humanistic advocacy. Teachers must do their job to fulfill these requirements; otherwise, the needs of students in special groups will be neglected and overlooked as has been done for the past 50 years. Table 9.18 lists some teaching practices that may be practical in helping to meet the needs of these students.

Table 9.18. Selected Co-teaching Models

Model	Basic Activities	Types of Lesson Plans or Classes
One teaches and one observes	One provides instruction while the other observes students for specific reasons	Useful in any class with any lesson plan when monitoring student progress or behavior.
One teaches and one drifts	One provides instruction for the whole class while the other moves around the class to assist students with problems or understanding.	This is a common practice in K–1 grades, where teachers work together as a team.
Team teaching	Meshing instruction by two teachers at the same time, sharing different parts of lesson plan	Works well with specific subject matter, perhaps for science or math in Grades 4–6 or higher. This model is also used in

	or dividing lesson for coverage, depending on the nature of teaching.	ELD/SDAIE classes where an instructional aide instructs bilingual students while the teacher is delivering whole-class instruction.
Alternate teaching	Reteaching or reflective lesson plan in a small group, also called center or individualized instruction.	Works well with a group of students with similar needs, interests, and academic levels. This model is similar to individualized instruction.
Parallel teaching	Instruction on the same lesson plan delivered by two teachers in the same room.	Works well with all subject areas but usually used in lower grades or large classrooms with diverse needs and abilities.
Station teaching	One or two teachers work at different locations, or centers, with different groups of students.	Typical practice in Grades K-6 where teachers group students and assign them to different stations for specific instruction.
Monolingual and bilingual teaching	Monolingual teacher and bilingual instructional aide or teacher assistant work simultaneously in ELD class where translation is needed to help language-minority students comprehend the content covered in the lesson plan	Works well with ELD lesson plans with EL adaptations or with students with special needs adaptations targeting language-minority students or students with learning disabilities.

The Goals of Classroom Management

So much has been said about preventive management, proactive management, classroom discipline, classroom structure, and management strategies, and now it is time to stress keeping classroom management simple and focused. Classroom management and discipline have several goals: (a) to enhance teaching and learning; (b) to provide a productive, positive, sound, and inclusive learning environment; (c) to foster a good psychosocial environment, or tone, for students and teachers in the classroom; (d) to accommodate all learning preferences and learning styles in the multicultural classroom; (e) to maximize time efficiency and time management; (f) to offer quality instruction to all students; (g) to improve student learning outcomes; (h) to empower positive and academic social interactions among students and teachers; (i) to facilitate different instructional practices, formats, and strategies in response to diverse needs and abilities of student groups; and (j) to achieve the ultimate goal of effective teaching and learning. If teachers can remember all these and continue to work toward the ultimate goal, all students will benefit every step of the way toward achieving great successes in school and in life.

Despite all the best things the best teacher does, management and discipline problems will not disappear any time soon. There is no end, and every day is a new beginning for new problems. Teachers will deal with management problems as long as they remain in teaching.

Summing Up

This chapter addressed several major practical management strategies teachers can apply directly in their classroom. The ongoing process of classroom management has a beginning but no ending because management and discipline are continually needed. The more teachers practice management and discipline skills, the better they will become at it. The more they solve problem behaviors, the more problem behaviors they will see. The more students are rewarded, the better they will act to earn more rewards. The more teachers give, the more students will take; the better teachers behave, the more students will emulate them; and the better teachers teach, the more students will learn. All these are part of everyday life for teachers in the classroom.

Classroom management strategies are complex and teachers cannot learn everything overnight. It takes time, practice, diligent effort, development, trial and error, persistence, and perseverance to build a solid foundation. There is no perfect way of managing or disciplining students, but there are sensible and meaningful ways to handle student behaviors professionally, ethically, and legally. Classroom management and discipline are not about training students to meet the teachers' personal needs and wants but about modeling good and appropriate behaviors that comply with classroom rules, procedures, and routines that guide the process of teaching and learning.

Teachers are drivers of their classrooms and students are passengers in their cars. Teachers must create a positive learning environment to ensure the health and safety of all students all the time. As drivers, teachers cannot take risks or be reckless. The bottom line is that teachers are solely responsible for everything going on in the classroom, and that is why the strategies described in this chapter prepare teachers to take charge of all teaching and learning in their classrooms.

PART IV

THE BEST PROFESSIONAL PRACTICES DOMAIN

CHAPTER TEN

BEST PROFESSIONAL PRACTICES

A good teacher is like a candle; it consumes itself to light the way for others.
Unknown

Introduction

Teachers are independent individuals with unique differences in teaching styles, learning styles, philosophy of education, leadership skills, philosophy of classroom management, disciplinary techniques, professional growth, and personal qualities. Their uniqueness brings diverse qualities to the schools and classrooms where they educate students of color each and every day. Schools are complex places and require teamwork, professional relationships, proper communication, professional courtesy, partnership, collegiality, and socialization. Teachers, by nature, are social beings. They must learn how to work well with their supervisors, colleagues, students, and parents. Developing productive relationships with mentor teachers should help new teachers gain valuable life experience on the job. New teachers should learn how to dodge issues and people who are demanding and negative, such as difficult colleagues who want to control their professional lives. There are professional practices new teachers have to learn on the job. This chapter covers different aspects of best professional practices that new teachers must learn to equip them with the knowledge and skills needed to become great teachers.

What Makes Teaching and Learning Fun?

Teaching might be difficult for some teachers, and learning could be a highly demanding task for many students. Teachers who understand and employ best professional practices can make the job easier for both teachers and students. They can usually find creative ways to teach, engage, and promote quality teaching and effective learning simultaneously. Creativity is what makes teaching special; teaching is an art and teachers must learn how to express the beauty and craftsmanship of the art. Consider two basic questions: What is teaching? What is learning?

All new teachers learn *what* to teach, but many have not learned *how* to teach mandated content area standards. Teaching is more than just giving out the information in the textbook, lecturing students, presenting new ideas, or following scripted instruction. Teaching is a process of designing ongoing academic instruction that involves integration, innovation, creation, interaction, and transference of knowledge and skills from teachers to students in a formalized setting. Teaching is not the same as preaching. Academic instruction requires engagement of the thought process and critical thinking of students, and engagement is best obtained with hands-on and minds-on activities that affirm the teaching components stated in the learning objective.

By the same token, learning is not simply the retention of information. Learning is an ongoing process of encoding and decoding information that involves comprehension, acquisition, retention, and construction of knowledge and skills gained from formalized instruction. Learning is a complex process that is different for different students. This is also true for teaching since each teacher is unique in style, management, discipline, and application. Sometimes new teachers are asked: How do you know your students are learning from you? In most cases, teachers test students on retention of information rather than construction of knowledge and skills.

As Ornstein and Levine (2006) explained, *constructivism* is a philosophical learning theory that emphasizes the ways in which learners actively create meaning by constructing and reconstructing ideas about reality. Constructivism is based on the premise that students learn better when teachers engage them in self-directed learning activities, or hands-on and minds-on prescriptions, rather than when they inactively and passively receive information from the teachers through lecture, seatwork, scripted instruction, or meaningless activities designed to focus more on the teachers' role of controlling than on student responsibility to learn new ideas and concepts. Teachers can help students construct new knowledge and gain new skills based on their previous life experiences by including hands-on experiments, collaborations, problem-based learning, cooperative learning, small-group activities, class discussions, think-pair-share, research activities, student projects, and fieldtrips.

Both teaching and learning are fun if both teachers and students enjoy one another inside the psychosocial environment. Moreover, teaching and learning can be more fun if teachers are creatively innovative and understand their students' interests, curiosities, and needs. In addition, teachers must believe that all students can learn, can achieve, and that students progress at different speeds. Believing in students can shape professional practice because it reduces prejudice, bias, and hegemonic ideology. Most importantly, teaching and learning are beneficial to both teachers and learners if the teachers possess positive attitudes that foster learning. A teacher's personality in front of the students could be deadly contagious and poisonous or could be as sweet as the honey of bees. Teachers should contemplate this phrase: "Attitude is everything and is the best medicine to treat the emotions, the psyche, and feelings."

Teachers' attitudes toward themselves, the subject matter, the classroom, their students, lesson plans, and instruction directly affect teaching and learning outcomes. The covert and overt messages teachers send to students determine the students' levels of enthusiasm, excitement, enjoyment, energy, and collaboration. Sadly, bad attitudes can stir fear, intimidation, and consternation in students. To apply best practices, teachers must adhere to their professional code of ethics.

What Are Best Professional Practices?

Most teachers know the term *best professional practices* because it is widely used in the teaching profession today; however, not so many teachers know what constitutes best educational and professional practices or what the term really means in practice. When asked, "What are best professional practices?" student teachers compile their own lists of values, beliefs, skills, knowledge, and experiences that are to their own liking. For example, most new teachers think patience, passion, organization, management, discipline, teaching, and assessment in the classroom are their best professional practices.

One way to help new teachers contemplate best professional practices is to examine these five thought-provoking questions:

1. What are the obstacles to teaching?
2. How does a teacher overcome these obstacles?
3. What keeps teachers teaching?
4. How do teachers learn, grow, and glow?

5. What makes teaching and learning worthwhile?

Perhaps the answers to these questions will help new teacher elicit the practices that best enhance their professional development and teaching repertoire.

Simply put, best educational practices refer to the daily actions teachers take, based on their professional decision making, to ensure that their academic instruction is efficient, effective, appropriate, productive, sensible, meaningful, purposeful, and conducive to the ongoing learning of all students. Experienced teachers know that best professional practices heavily rely on the daily academic activities or well-planned curricular activities used in the classroom to facilitate the teaching and learning process. Table 10.1 lists some classroom-tested activities that are considered best educational practices.

Table 10.1. **Selected Best Tested Classroom Activities**

Activity	Possible Uses
Teachers are coaches and facilitators	Mentoring, guiding, enabling, supporting, providing, encouraging, motivating, inspiring, engaging
Recognizing multiple intelligences	Accommodating, reaching out to, engaging, adapting, modifying, varying, differentiating, using different approaches
Recognizing learning styles	Knowing strengths and weakness in learning, accommodating, engaging, varying, adapting, modifying, differentiating, using different strategies
Using interdisciplinary approaches	Integrating science, social studies, language arts, math; using across academic disciplines; using idea web; applying mapping concepts
Differentiating instruction	Grouping, center or station instruction, individualized instruction, special group instruction, whole group
Engaging prior knowledge/background knowledge	Building on life experiences, repeating previous learned knowledge, reciting past lessons, reviewing embedded ideas
Following standards-based curricula/academic standards	Using academic content area standards, adopted standards, district standards
Benchmark testing	Using pre- and posttests, using ongoing assessment to guide instruction, using district standards
Using data-driven instruction/measurement-driven instruction	Applying assessment results, test results, student learning outcomes
Integrating technology content	Incorporating technology in instruction and student activities to enhance teaching and learning
Using graphic organizers	Detailed approaches, specific learning objectives, explicit instruction, study guide, giving highlights, focal points
Assessing	Using portfolio, authentic, alternative, journal, rubrics, diagnostics, formal, informal
Using tiered instruction/sequence of instruction	Using step-by-step process, five-step lesson plan, three-step lesson plan, ELD format, SDAIE format, scaffolding, reciprocal teaching
Cooperative learning	Grouping, teamwork, project-based learning, think-pair-share
Using inquiry-based instruction, guided inquiry, or problem-based instruction	Using investigative approaches, questions, thought provoking ideas, curiosity, extrinsic approach, intrinsic approach

Different teachers could have different best practices because teachers may not all agree on the effectiveness of the same practices for teaching, learning, management, and discipline for their particular students. However, lack of experience and professional training may keep new teachers unaware of some potentially best practices. Therefore, be open minded when sharing the activities you have found to be best professional practices. Building the quality traits of best professional practices takes time. It normally takes at least 3–5 years for new teachers to develop themselves professionally and discover what they like best, do best, and feel comfortable with on the job. Experienced teachers usually settle down to teach a specific grade after a few years on the job because they have found their comfort zone in which they believe they can handle, manage, discipline, and most importantly, teach at ease.

Building Professional Confidence

Teachers must learn how to build professional confidence, and they must find a stronghold to which they can retreat, something that will lift them from pitfalls and boost their self-esteem and allow them to persevere; otherwise, the tasks of teaching—managing, disciplining, assessing, and organizing—will create an acrimonious working environment. The teaching profession has a high level of stress, and the impact of that anxiety on their personal and professional lives can be great. Teachers must find mentors with whom they can share and who can guide them through the first two years of teaching. Many teachers are left to fend for themselves in the classroom with no one knowing how they really feel inside. New teachers are often in a catch-22 situation: they are afraid to ask school administrators or co-workers for assistance because they do not want to be labeled as incompetent, unknowledgeable, unprepared, unskilled, and a nuisance. Keep in mind that no one knows everything, and no one learns everything in the first week, month, or year. Teachers do not have to feel they are intrusive or bothersome if they ask someone for assistance. As mentioned earlier, teachers must be assertive in seeking help when they need it; help is not likely to come to their doorstep.

Building confidence takes time, persistence, effort, and diligence. Mistakes are not inevitable, but some mistakes are costly, dangerous, and unacceptable. For example, letting frustrations turn into anger and anger escalate into outbursts is unprofessional and unethical. Teachers can assess their strengths and weaknesses professionally and privately in order to understand what they need to improve right away, in the short term, or in the long term. Areas that would need teachers' attention right away if they are problematic are (a) teaching effectiveness; (b) management issues; (c) disciplinary problems; (d) consequences; (e) assessing student learning; (f) engaging students in the learning process; (g) providing clear and concise directions and instruction for academic tasks; (h) providing assistance as needed during class; (i) dealing with ELLs or students with special needs; (j) having adequate resources or materials to support instructional practices; (k) organizing the classroom for all academic activities; and (l) having a daily schedule, formal routines, procedural guidelines, and classroom structure in place. Table 10.2 lists some procedures that might be used for specific academic activities or areas. Teachers should plan ahead of time to check off these areas early to make sure the classroom is ready, appropriate, and productive.

Teachers build confidence in a number of different areas, as shown in Table 10.3. The fundamental principle in building confidence is to believe in yourself; believe that you can overcome barriers, obstacles, and problems; believe that if there is a will, there is a way to solve problems and improve situations. The second principle is to realize that teachers do not have to know everything or have all answers and therefore seek assistance before it is too late. The third principle is to accept the fact that stress or distress is part of life but not all life. Accepting stress as normal and inevitable but not controlling should give teachers confidence to cope with the demands and any unexpected circumstances on the job. The fourth principle is that a basic knowledge of human development enables teachers to understand how children behave in the classroom. The fifth and final principle for building confidence is to take one day at a time, focusing on successes, the big picture, or progress instead of concentrating on little, unimportant things. Just putting an end to idle contemplation, procrastination, and complaining should motivate teachers to strive for greater success each day. Most importantly, all these principles help new teachers understand their self-efficacy.

Table 10.2. **Procedures for Basic Academic Activities**

Academic Activity/Area	Possible Procedural Activities
Beginning of class/opening procedures	Roll call, absentees, tardy students, academic warm-up routines, behaviors, distributing materials, adjustment
Line up	Going out, coming in, outside the door, on the playground, going to assembly, dismissal
Room/school areas	Shared areas, teacher's desk, water fountain, bathroom, student desks, learning center stations, playground, lunchroom/cafeteria
Setting up independent work areas	Defining work alone, identifying problems, resources, solutions, scheduling, checkpoints
Instructional activities	Contact between teacher and students, student movement, signals for attention, signals for teacher, initiative, participation, group rotation, passing materials, behavior in group, behavior outside group, academic engaged time
Ending class	Putting things away, cleaning up, backpacks, homework, clothes, personal items, dismissing class
Interruptions	Rules, orders, conduct, delays, talk among students, out-of-seat policies, pencil sharpening
Work requirements	Heading papers, pencil or pen, neatness, legibility, incomplete work, late work, missed work, due dates, make-up work, supplies, coloring, drawing, cursive or manuscript
Communicating assignments	Posting, orally giving, turning in, returning, homework, provision for absentees, incomplete work, collecting
Monitoring student work	Independent work, group work, presentation, completion in class, completion of homework, progress, challenges, difficulties
Checking assignments in class	Exchange papers, going over answers, grading papers, turning work in, collecting work, correcting, practicing
Grading procedures	Assigning report grades, recording grades, extra credit work, grading criteria, grade contracts, record keeping
Academic feedback	Reward system, incentives, reinforcers, posting work, informing parents, record keeping, feedback on papers, progress, improvement
In case of emergency	Fire drills, health and safety, lockdown, poison, injury, choking, fire, flood, tornado, rain

Lastly, teachers should build confidence on their strengths and stop worrying too much about what they lack, do not know, or do not have. Finding their niche or their strong points and using those to develop their professional repertoire should ignite their passion and build greater confidence.

Table 10.3. Checklist for Building Teacher Confidence

Teaching	Managing	Discipline	Assessment	Resources
▪ Preparation	▪ Patience	▪ Ignoring	▪ Teacher-made	▪ Textbooks
▪ Organization	▪ Passion	▪ Correction	tests	▪ Workbooks
▪ Lesson plan	▪ Assertiveness	▪ Moderate	▪ Pop quiz	▪ Worksheets
design	▪ Persistence	approach	▪ Independent	▪ Handouts
▪ Time man-	▪ Firmness	▪ Refer to the	practice	▪ Blank paper
agement	▪ Fairness	office	▪ Thumbs up or	▪ Construction
▪ Daily schedule	▪ Logic	▪ Contact par-	down	paper
▪ Routines	▪ Reasonableness	ents	▪ Small white	▪ Manipulatives
▪ Procedural	▪ Modeling	▪ Conferences	boards	▪ Blocks
guidelines	▪ Reinforcement	▪ Logical con-	▪ Yes or no ques-	▪ Board
▪ Clear direc-	▪ Reward system	sequences	tions	▪ Erasers
tions	▪ Motivation	▪ Reasonable	▪ Guided prac-	▪ Pencils
▪ Sequence of	▪ Sense of hu-	▪ Purposeful	tice	▪ Crayons
teaching	mor	▪ Valuable	▪ Demonstration	▪ Story books
▪ Creativity	▪ Positive atti-	▪ Motivational	▪ Illustrations	▪ Laminated
▪ Hands-on and	tude	▪ Sensible	▪ Modeling	materials
minds-on ac-	▪ Humanistic	▪ Humanistic	▪ Recitation	▪ Posters
tivities	approaches	approach	▪ Review	▪ Placards
▪ Cooperative	▪ Focus on be-	▪ Modeling	▪ Reflection	▪ Flashcards
learning or	haviors, not		▪ Reading	▪ Easel
grouping	students		▪ Response	▪ CD recorder
▪ Differentiating			▪ Exercises	
instruction			▪ Worksheets	

Factors Influencing Student Learning

To strengthen their use of best educational practices, teachers need to understand the factors that influence student learning in the classroom. When teachers think of those factors, they usually think about intrinsic and extrinsic variables that influence individual students' learning. However, teachers need to look beyond these simple factors. For example, some students may not be motivated by an intrinsic desire to learn, but perhaps they could be motivated by a productive psychosocial learning environment. Some students' limitations may suggest limitations on their learning potential, but a creative teacher may be able to lift them to a higher level of learning. Figure 10.1 displays the factors with the greatest influences on student learning (Haselkorn & Harris, 1998; Ryan & Cooper, 2001).

Best educational practice is not all about the resources the teachers have available in the classroom; rather it is about the ongoing actions that teachers take to make teaching and learning effective and efficient. Students do not avail themselves to learn when teachers cannot deliver meaningful instruction through creativity, integration, adaptations, and interdisciplinary approaches. As Figure 10.1 shows, the quality of teachers is the factor that most influences student learning, followed by academic standards and achievement testing. New teachers must be clinically trained to be well prepared for the classroom. No child deserves less when it comes to education. Every child should have a great and inspirational teacher who affects student learning positively. For a child, education is a golden opportunity in life.

Figure 10.1. **Factors influencing student learning.**

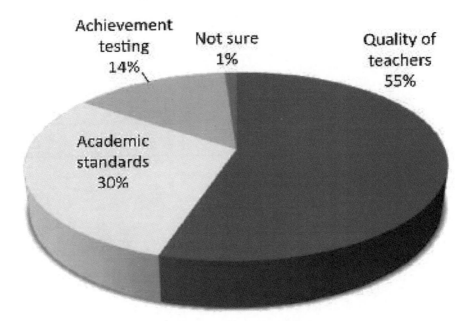

The School Curriculum and Instruction

To employ the best practices, new teachers must at the very least understand the fundamental values of the school curriculum and instruction and what teaching and learning are about. Sometimes these terms are overlapped in definitions and applications in teaching. These are basic terms, and for the most part, teachers appear to know what they mean, but in practice, not all teachers understand or use these terms in the same ways. Therefore, there is no accepted single definition for each of them.

Academically, in practice, *school curriculum* refers to designed academic activities based on content area standards that teachers use to teach and students learn in the classroom. *School instruction* refers to the methods of delivery by which the school curriculum is taught by the teachers in a formalized setting. The school curriculum directly involves the content, skills, knowledge, values, concepts, and attitudes students learn in school, and school instruction is the academic medium teachers used to convey the school curriculum through a process that takes place inside the classroom involving creativity, organization, selection, arrangement, guidance, and strategy. Both school curriculum and school instruction should be based on academic standards.

As Eisner (1994) and Valance (1995) explained, schools have five different academic curricula: (a) the explicit curriculum, (b) the implicit or hidden curriculum, (c) the null curriculum, (d) the extra curriculum, and (e) integrated curriculum. Similarly, Posner (1995) described the school concurrent curricula in five ways—(1) the official curriculum, (2) the operational curriculum, (3) the hidden curriculum, (4) the null curriculum, and (5) the extra curriculum. Table 10.4 compares these school curricula.

School curricula are set as learning goals for teachers and students, and teachers have the responsibility to design academic curricula to guide the instructional process to reach these ultimate goals. Sometimes teachers are confused about teaching objectives and goals. As explained earlier, each goal may have many objectives; or, in other words, many objectives equal one goal. The number of specific objectives depends on how the teacher plans to meet each curricular goal required for each academic subject matter.

Table 10.4. Comparison of School Curricula

Eisner's Categorization	Basic meanings	Posner's Categorization	Basic meanings
Explicit curriculum	Curriculum found in books, guides, courses of study, formal educational experiences	Official curriculum	The curriculum described in formal documents
Implicit, or hidden, curriculum	Informal curriculum, the kinds of learning students acquire from the nature and organization of school and attitudes of the teachers	Hidden curriculum	Instructional norms and values not openly acknowledged by teacher or school officials
Null curriculum	Topics left out of the course of study, not taught, not available	Null curriculum	The subject matter not taught
Extra curriculum	Learning experiences extending beyond the core of students' formal studies, such as clubs, sports, school plays, non-academic credit activities	Extra curriculum	Planned experience outside the formal curriculum
Integrated curriculum	Skills, concepts, and ideas of various disciplines are combined and related, a mixed bag of teaching, a multiple approach	Operational curriculum	Curriculum embodied in actual teaching and tests

School curricula are set as learning goals for teachers and students, and teachers have the responsibility to design academic curricula to guide the instructional process to reach these ultimate goals. Sometimes teachers are confused about teaching objectives and goals. As explained earlier, each goal may have many objectives; or, in other words, many objectives equal one goal. The number of specific objectives depends on how the teacher plans to meet each curricular goal required for each academic subject matter.

Teachers should take curricular challenges into careful consideration when planning instruction and activities. Figure 10.2 shows some of the factors and forces that may influence curricular activities in the classroom. Most teachers are alone in the classroom with students, and whatever they teach will greatly influence students' cognitive development positively or negatively. One challenge is *standard-based education.* This is the use of curricula and instructional practices focused on predetermined standards. *Academic standards* are mission statements that specifically address what students should know, learn, and understand and what skills and knowledge students should have upon completing the goal of each standard. Meeting academic goals is not all that easy these days since teachers have so many responsibilities on their plates.

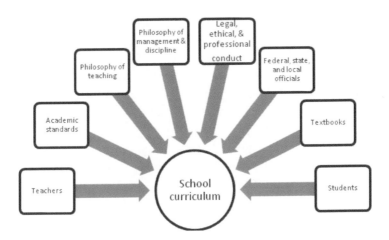

Figure 10.2. **Forces influencing school curriculum.**

Teachers are generally pressured by their school leaders and program coordinators to follow the school's curriculum guides and testing schedules. The purpose of these guides and schedules is to ensure that teachers are helping students meet academic standards. However, meeting academic standards is quite challenging, and sometimes teachers teach to the standards instead of using standard-based curricula for instruction. Without using the pedagogical approaches listed in Table 10.5, most teachers have great difficulty helping ELLs and students with special needs or learning disabilities meet state, local, and district academic performance standards. Most importantly, one model of instruction will not enable all students to excel in the skills and knowledge required for each academic standard. Teachers need to design sensible and meaningful instruction that engages students in the learning process and helps them master the key concepts, knowledge, and skills. Research shows that a quality education is not dependent on the language of instruction but on the quality of instruction.

Table 10.5. **Selected Pedagogical Approaches for ELLs and SNs**

Lesson plan objective	Accommodations	Modifications	Adaptations	Interventions
Life cycle	Use technology, video clips, animation, picture books, transparency, overhead projector	Simplify life cycle, give short directions, step by step instruction, modeling, samples, visual aids, regalia, pictures	Parts-to-whole approach, label each stage, connect pictures to life cycle, hands-on activity, bridge, key terms, chart, organizer	Think-pair-share, small-group activity, extra practice, more time on task, review, reflection, KWL, scaffolding
Basic math	Assign specific homework, review, problems, overhead projector, independent practice	Limit number of problems, limit correct answers, model, use examples, practice incorrect problems	Use study guide, more practice, focus on specific skills or problems, guided practice, use manipulatives, extra time, skill development	Review, more practice, pair up, use differentiating instruction, process v. product approach, comprehension
Reading	Ask questions, use	Slow pace, clear	Study guide, focus on	Pair up, word

clear and concise directions, put questions on the board, limit problems, peer tutor, partnership	enunciation, adjust the level of difficulty, choice of book, extra time, pair up, use graphic organizer, pictures	specific skills, vocabulary words, regalia, transparency, overhead projector, comprehension, reciprocal teaching, details--action, plot, scene, character	bank, review key concepts, extra time, KWL, organizer, short questions, short answers
Personal timeline	Pair up, give examples, model, cooperative learning, bilingual books	Sentence frames, specific details, use outline, bilingual resources, practice, extra time	Appropriate resources, focus on ability, monitor progress, feedback, extra time, use guide or outline, pair up	Monitor progress, pair up, sentence frames, focus on specific details, outline, chart

Instructional Practices

The pedagogical framework includes the instructional approaches teachers plan to employ when designing lesson plans. The primary goal for teachers is to instruct, and the teaching responsibility is the single most important legal obligation required of teachers by federal, state, local, and school district guidelines. There are many instructional approaches, strategies, methodologies, modalities, and schema that teachers need to know. However, teachers will use only a few of these instructional practices in the classroom. Most public schools use the direct instruction (DI) model for whole class instruction. Some use the Sheltered Instruction Observation Protocol (SIOP), and others use Response to Intervention (RTI). SIOP and RTI are basically the same but some teachers prefer one over the other. No method of instruction, no matter how well it works for some students, meets all learners' needs in the classroom. Therefore, teachers must learn more than one or two teaching techniques and applications in order for them to provide flexible instruction. A rigid teaching style should be avoided if possible because it does not benefit most learners.

Table 10.6. **TPE Standards**

Domain	TPE Standards
Domain A: Making subject matter comprehensible to students	TPE 1: Specific pedagogical skills for subject matter instruction
Domain B: Assessing student learning	TPE 2: Specific pedagogical skills for subject matter instruction TPE3: Interpretation and use of assessment
Domain C: Engaging and supporting students in learning	TPE 4: Making content accessible TPE 5: Student engagement TPE6: Developmentally appropriate teaching practices TPE 7: Teaching English learners
Domain D: Planning instruction and designing learning experiences for all students	TPE 8: Learning about students TPE 9: Instructional planning
Domain E: Creating and maintaining effective environments for student learning	TPE 10: Instructional time TPE 11: Social environment
Domain F: Developing as a professional educator	TPE 12: Professional, legal, and ethical obligations TPE 13: Professional growth

In California, new teachers must know how to use the Teacher Performance Expectation (TPE) standards and must meet all Teacher Performance Assessment tasks (TPA) in teaching. Table 10.8 details the TPE standards and Table 10.7 displays the four tasks of TPA for easy reference. The TPE standards are state mandates; they are required for a preliminary teaching credential. Vang (2010) listed many instructional approaches for new teachers for consideration while planning instructions, student activities, and task activities; these are shown in Table 10.8.

Table 10.7. **Tasks of TPA**

Task	Assessment Expectations
Task 1: Subject-specific pedagogy	Using subject-specific pedagogical skills (TPE 1), planning for instruction (TPE 4, 5, 6, 9), planning for assessment (TPE 3), making adaptations (TPE 4, 6, 7)
Task 2: Designing instruction	Establishing goals and standards (8, 9), learning about students (TPE 8, 9), planning for instruction (TPE 8, 9), making adaptations (TPE 4, 6, 7), using subject-specific pedagogical skills (TPE 1), reflection (TPE 13)
Task 3: Assessing learning	Establishing goals and standards (TPE 8, 9), planning for assessment (TPE 3), learning about students (TPE 8, 9), making adaptations (TPE 4, 6, 7), analyzing student learning evidence (TPE 3), reflection (TPE 13)
Task 4: Culminating teaching experience	Establishing goals and standards (TPE 8, 9), learning about students (TPE 8, 9), describing classroom environment (TPE 10,11), planning for instruction (TPE 4, 5, 6), making adaptations (TPE 1, 4, 5, 6, 7), using subject-specific pedagogical skills (TPE 1,4,5,6,7), analyzing evidence of student learning (TPE 2, 3, 13), reflection (TPE 13)

Table 10.8. **Comparison of Traditional and Modern Instructional Approaches**

Traditional Approach	Modern Approach	Recommended Approach
Whole language	Phonics	Need both approaches, depending on the nature of the lesson plan.
Whole group	Small group or centers	Both approaches are equally crucial to student learning; however, varying instruction helps teachers focus on specific learning needs.
Learners are passive in the learning process	Learners are active in the learning process	Learners should learn to be both passive and active, depending on the learning objective.
Product is the most important part of learning	Process is the most important part of learning	Both are essential to learning because students need procedural knowledge as well as application to real life experiences.
Part to whole is emphasized	Whole to part is emphasized	Both concepts are equally valuable, depending on the nature of the lesson plan.
Learning relies on sequence of skills	Learning depends on relevant, real, and prior experiences	Both approaches equally important because learners need to develop both in order to compete academically.

Extrinsic motivation is best in learning	Intrinsic is best in learning	Depends on the learner's personal desire to learn each subject; however, both approaches are critical in the development of well rounded-knowledge and repertoire of learning skills.
Ability grouping	Interests, needs, or desires grouping	Depends on grade level and age of learner.
Competition stressed	Cooperation stressed	All learners need both in order to perform academically and socially.
Teacher centered	Student-centered	Teacher centered saves time but creative student centered is better.
Teacher as leader	Teacher as facilitator	Both roles equally important.
Textbook	Children's literature and portfolio	Both approaches are needed in order to broaden students' personal understanding of multicultural society and cultural diversity.
Tests used to assess student learning	Portfolio and progress used to assess student learning	Both approaches are appropriate, depending on grade level.
Book-centered setting	Child-centered setting	Both approaches are important because learners need the right tools as well as sufficient attention in order to excel academically.
The child must fit to the book	The book must fit to the child	Both approaches important; however, ELLs will not be able to read difficult texts if they are not prepared academically. Appropriate reading materials necessary.
One model fits all	Multiple approaches to deal with diverse learners	Depending on learners' academic ability and comprehension level, teachers need to incorporate different teaching methodologies to accommodate different learning needs.

As Vang (2010) explained, *teaching methodologies* refer to instructional approaches, teaching styles, and instructional strategies. The term *methodology* refers to how teachers teach and how students learn, not what teachers teach. The terms *approaches* and *methodologies* are used interchangeably in academia. The term *strategy* is often used to refer to instructional practices, approaches, and methodologies as well. However, strategy has a narrower focus than does approach. *Pedagogy* is another term used by educators in academia, and it has multiple meanings. Distinctions between the technical terms *critical pedagogy, multicultural pedagogy,* and *pedagogical skills* can confuse teachers. The word *pedagogy* simply refers to how students learn. Moreover, the terms *instructional strategy* and *teaching strategy* are frequently used interchangeably in teaching practice. Basically, these terms have the same meaning. New teachers must learn how to decipher this academic terminology to better understand the nature of teaching and learning.

Many teaching strategies have been developed over the years by scholars and educators. Some are more effective than others. Many of these techniques are unknown to new teachers because only a few have been introduced in the course of studies for new teachers. Table 10.9 lists some lesser-known teaching strategies that are currently in practice. Keep in mind that all strategies are useful if teachers know how to apply them appropriately and wisely. Each has strengths and weaknesses, or advantages and disadvantages, depending on their purpose. For example, ELD and SDAIE methods of instruction benefit all learners; however, direct instruction is suited for students fluent in English.

Table 10.9. **Selected Teaching Strategies**

Acronym	Strategy	Example of Use
TI	Thematic instruction	Organizing or framing instruction around key areas, concepts, or ideas to make connections
CALLA	Cognitive Academic Language Approach	Involve topics, academic language skills, and language acquisition
ILA	Integrated language arts	Whole-language approach to learn new language
5w's + H	What, when, where, who, why, and how	Question-based instruction, inquiry instruction, or investigative approach
DI/EDI	Direct instruction/explicit direct instruction	Systematic approach, one model fits all, use in all subject matter teaching
ELD	English Language Development	Transitional bilingual education programs without primary language(L1) support
ESL	English as a second language	ELD or SDAIE instruction or whole-language approach
K-W-L	What I *know*, what I *want* to learn, and what I *learned*	Student-centered approach
LEA	Language experience approach	Used mostly in language arts for writing and reading based on student's experiences and prior knowledge
PQ5Rs	Preview, question, read, recite, reflect, review, and respond	Used in all subject matter teaching and with any instructional methodologies
PR	Preview and review	Engage prior knowledge and tap into lesson plan objective
CL	Cooperative learning	Groups, centers, or stations
PW	Process writing	A process of writing or POWERS: Prewrite, organize, write, edit, rewrite, and submit
RT	Reciprocal teaching	Question-based approach used mostly in language arts for reading: 4-step process: Summary, clarification, question, and prediction
RTI	Response to intervention	Intervention strategy to identify at-risk students, SIOP components, 2-tier approaches, adaptations, modifications, accommodations, and intervention
SIOP	Sheltered Instruction Observation Protocol	RTI components, ELD components, SDAIE components, SMART Plan, and intervention
Scaffolding	Backing out or withdrawal strategies, or building skills as layers or levels	Use in all subject matter teaching, ELD, SDAIE, TESOL, ESL, SEI, and others
SDAIE	Specially designed academic instruction in English	ELD instruction with primary language support (L1)
SEI	Sheltered English instruction	ESL, TESOL, ELD, or SDAIE instruction

TESOL	Teach English to speakers of other languages	ESL , ELD, or SDAIE instruction
TNA	The natural approach	Used mostly in language arts
TPR	Total physical response	Music, dance, physical education, or body movement
GI	Guided inquiry instruction	Student centered, investigative instruction, question based

Teachers need to be familiar with a wide variety of instructional activities that support and enhance learning for all students. These activities can be used as activity strategies or task strategies depending on the lesson plan learning objectives. Table 10.10 presents several instructional strategies that are practical for everyday use (Herrell & Jordan, 2006). Table 10.11 illustrates modeling techniques that teachers can use to enhance guided practices. There are three basic tiers of instruction: instructional strategy, student activity strategy, and task strategy. Together, these tiers form a sequence of instruction.

Table 10.10. **Selected Activity and Task Strategies**

Strategy	Key Concepts
Predictable routines and signals	To reduce anxiety in learners, early prepping, engage prior knowledge, easy approach
Visual scaffolding	To provide language support through visual images such as pictures, video clips, regalia
Interactive read aloud	To read out loud, recitation, repetition, expression, prediction
Advanced organizer	To get the mind in gear for information, engagement, hooking up, connection of concepts
Expository organizer	To bridge concepts, to connect ideas, to engage, to contextualize
Comparative organizer	To compare and contrast information, to differ, to classify, to differentiate, to separate, to sort out
Skills grouping or ability grouping	To gather students with similar needs, abilities, skills, or interests for group instruction, target needy areas, intervene
Shared reading, guided reading, or choral reading	To model reading, read in unison, model reading, guided reading, practice reading
Leveled questions	To break down questions to student levels of comprehension, easy vocabulary words, short question, yes or no approach
Partner work or peer tutoring	To practice verbal skills, talk to peer, share with peer, interact with peer
Culture studies	To allow students to conduct study on their cultures and share cultural values in class, exchange ideas
Learning centers or learning stations	To provide extra practices for reinforcement of verbal skills, activity skills, social interaction
Collaborative reading	To select different books for different reading levels, flexible approaches, equal opportunity
Word walls	To organize lists of words for study, whole-language approach, vocabulary word building, word bank
Cloze techniques	To fill in the blanks, sentence frames
Dictoglos	To practice listening skills, followed by reading skills, recalling

	information, details, facts
GIST-generating interaction between schemata and text	To summarize reading through discussion, reciprocal teaching components—evaluation, prediction, summary, question, and clarification

Table 10.11: **Modeling Techniques to Enhance Guided Practices**

Modeling one	Modeling two	Modeling three	Modeling four
1. Tell me, I will forget 2. Show me, I will remember 3. Involve me, I will understand	1. Watch me as I do it 2. Follow me as I do it 3. Help me as I do it 4. I help as you do it 5. You do it.	1. I do, you watch 2. I do, you help 3. I do, you tell 4. You do, I tell 5. You do, I help 6. You do it yourself	1. Telling how to do 2. Showing how to do 3. Trying how to do 4. Doing how to do 5. Learning how to do

Doolittle (2002) divided instructional strategy into lesson plan strategy, activity strategy, and task strategy, as shown in Table 10.12. In practice, instructional strategy is broad and can be used over one or several class periods. Activity strategy is generally applied in a single class period, and task strategy is rather short, about 5 minutes long, and can be used within lesson or activity strategies. Again, remember that teachers can employ these techniques where they feel they best fit their students' needs and academic abilities.

Table 10.12. **Three Types of Instructional Strategies**

Instructional Strategies		
Direction Instruction	**Group Instruction**	**Inquiry Instruction**
▪ Advanced organizer ▪ Expository and comparative organizer ▪ Question and discussion techniques ▪ Concept development ▪ Direct presentation ▪ Lecture ▪ Programmed instruction ▪ Mastery learning	▪ Jigsaw ▪ Cooperative learning ▪ Question and discussion techniques ▪ Reciprocal teaching ▪ Synectics ▪ Graffiti ▪ Jurisprudential inquiry	▪ Problem-based learning and instruction ▪ Question and discussion techniques ▪ Concept development ▪ Concept attainment ▪ Discovery learning ▪ Free and guided learning ▪ Simulation and role playing ▪ Case-based learning and instruction
Task Strategies		
➢ Whip around ➢ Minute reflection ➢ Entry slips ➢ Response cards ➢ Focused learning ➢ KWL ➢ Best choice debate	☐ Outcome sentences ☐ Think aloud ☐ Read aloud ☐ 3,2,1 processor ☐ Sudden brainstorming ☐ Connect 12 ☐ PMI	✓ Think-pair-share ✓ Entry assignments ✓ Exit slips ✓ 3-minute conversation ✓ Background probes ✓ Vote your conscience ✓ Questions and answers

The engagement level of students depends on the types of activities teachers use to involve students during the instructional process (Howe, 2002). For example, teachers who use hands-on and minds-on activities engage students at a high level as compared to teachers who depend on note taking, lecture, and verbal interactions. Table 10.13 depicts engagement level by activity type. Most students do not learn by listening but by doing. Therefore, teachers should think about integrating more hands-on and minds-on activities for students; these types of activities are beneficial to all students, especially those who lack language skills. No matter how effective an instructional practice is said to be, teachers need to assess student learning on an ongoing basis. Employing sound instructional strategies does not guarantee student learning; periodic assessments will let teachers know how effective the strategies they have chosen to use are.

Table 10.13. **Engagement Level by Activity Type**

Activity Type	Engagement Level	Sample of Tasks
Minds-on activities with concrete materials	High	Writing or jotting down thoughts and reflections in journal after conducting an experiment
Hands-on activities with concrete materials	High	Doing firsthand experience, observing an experiment, or conducting an investigation in a group
Visiting school garden	High	Observing different plants or vegetables, picking some leaves for experiment, or harvesting some fruits
Computer lab activities	Medium to high	Logging onto websites to find out more about a specific topic or finding answers from computer
Guided discussions	Medium to high	Students participate in learning activities, ask questions, listen to peers, take a role in the learning process, and work responsibly. Teacher is a guide or facilitator, not the leader and controller.
Reading activities	Low to medium	Reading aloud, silent reading, or teacher reads and students listen
Listening and watching the teacher	Low	These types of activities barely engage students or hold their interest.
Listening only	Very low	These types of activities are considered disengaging.
Lecturing or preaching	Very low	These types of activities are not academically appropriate for Grades K–12.

Assessment of Instruction

Teachers spend nearly two months every year preparing students for testing and administering academic assessments such as benchmark tests, high-stakes tests, standardized tests, and other empirical tests. The real purpose of assessment is to measure the effectiveness of instruction. In some cases, however, assessment is used to measure the teacher's effectiveness. Most new teachers do not learn how to assess or test students until they are in the classroom. School districts use different assessment instruments. In California, many teachers are haunted by the Academic Performance Index (API), mandated by the California's Public School Accountability Act of 1999, which is used to rank student performance and schools. Table 10.14 lists some of the instruments used in California's public school districts and elsewhere in the U.S. California's Standardized Testing and Reporting (STAR) Program, one of the more widely used instruments in the state, is comprised of four major exams as follows (California Department of Education, 2010):

1. California Standards Tests (CSTs) are standards-based tests that measure the achievement in state content standards in English/language arts, mathematics, science, and history/social science.

2. The California Modified Assessment (CMA) is designed for students with disabilities whose individualized education program (IEP) team determines that the CMA is appropriate. Students must also meet State Board of Education-adopted eligibility criteria. The CMA is designed to provide eligible students an accessible assessment for measuring achievement in California content standards.

3. The California Alternate Performance Assessment (CAPA) is for students who have significant cognitive disabilities.

4. Standards-based Tests in Spanish (STS) are for students who either received instruction in Spanish or were enrolled in a school in the United States for fewer than 12 months. Students who complete the STS also complete the grade-level CST and/or the CMA. Results from the STS are not included in state or federal accountability reports.

Moreover, the California English Language Development Test (CELDT) is a required state test for English language proficiency, given as an initial assessment to newly enrolled students whose primary language (L1) recorded on the Home Language Survey form is other than English and as an annual assessment to students previously identified as English learners (LEP and FEP students) enrolled in K–12 grades in California's public schools. In recent years, California has tested all students in all academic subject matters at various points in their schooling as follows:

- English-language arts (ELA): Grades 2 through 11
- Mathematics: Grades 2 through 9
- Science: Grades 5, 8, and 10
- History/social science: Grades 8 and 11

According to the California Department of Education, in 2010, ELLs and students with special needs were tested as follows:

1. Students took end-of-course tests in mathematics (Grades 7–11), science (Grades 9–11), and history/social science (Grades 9–11) if they were scheduled to complete the corresponding courses by the end of the school year.

2. Students who had an IEP and met the State Board of Education-adopted eligibility criteria were able to take the CMA for ELA in Grades 3–9, the CMA for mathematics in Grades 3–7, the CMA for Algebra I and for science in Grades 5, 8, and 10 (life science) instead of the corresponding grade-level and content-area CSTs. Students in Grade 8 who took the CMA for ELA and/or science were also required to take the CST for history/social science.

3. Students with disabilities who were unable to take the CSTs with accommodations or modifications or were unable to take the CMA with accommodations took the CAPA in ELA, mathematics, and science (approximately 1% of the tested population).

4. Spanish-speaking English learners (ELs) who either received instruction in Spanish or were enrolled in a school in the United States for fewer than 12 months were required to take the STS. At the option of the school district, schools may have also tested Spanish-speaking ELs who had been in school in the United States 12 months or more who were

not receiving instruction in Spanish. Students who completed the STS also completed the grade-level CST and/or CMA (if designated in the student's IEP).

Table 10.14. Examples of Assessment Instruments by Type

Achievement Tests	Aptitude Tests	Language and Speech Tests
• BEST—Basic Educational Skills Test	• WISC I,II, III—Wechsler Intelligence Scale for children	• BSM I,II,III—Bilingual Syntax measure
• CAT—California Achievement Test	• Stanford-Binet—Stanford-Binet Intelligence Scale	• LAS—Language Assessment Scale
• CTBS—California Test of Academic Skills	• SOMPA—System of Multicultural Pluralistic Assessment	• IPT—Idea Placement Test
• ITAS—Individual Test of Academic Skills	• Raven—Raven's Progressive matrices	• QSE—Quick Start to English
• SABE—Spanish/California Test of Basic Skills	• BWPE—Bateria Woodcock Pisco Educateria	• PPVT—Peabody Picture vocabulary Test (English/Spanish)
• WRAT—Wide Range Achievement Test	• MAT—Matrix Analogies Test	• SOLOM—Student Oral Language Observation Matrix

Which tests are used depends on the school district and school site. Some schools use the QSE to assess kindergarteners' proficiency in English, for example, and others use the BSM or the LAS for the same purpose. The tests listed in Table 10.14 are used for *diagnostic evaluation, formative evaluation, and summative evaluation* of student learning. Diagnostic evaluation is used to determine the individual's level of competence; formative evaluation is used to measure student learning outcomes, providing feedback reflecting instructional effectiveness; and summative evaluation is used at the end of each unit to examine student learning outcomes based on a broader measure of student ability and competence in the content areas taught.

One note for teachers: The terms *diagnostic assessment, formal assessment, informal assessment,* and *summative assessment* are also used interchangeably in academia with diagnostic evaluation, formative evaluation, and summative evaluation.

Teachers need to know the differences and similarities between the terms *evaluation, measurement, and assessment.* These terms are interrelated. Measurement refers to the process of academic testing used to obtain data concerning learning outcomes or about student learning of specific content standards. Assessment is similar to measurement; however, it examines the learning outcomes from norm-referenced tests, not tests designed or made by schools. Evaluation is a broad based process for obtaining data about learning outcomes from different sources to help teachers arrive at a value judgment, decision, or conclusion based on measurement data, formal/informal evaluation, and other gathered information. Measurement is the criterion used for determining the final grade, and evaluation is the final grade the teacher assigns to the students.

Teachers should not be confused between *norm-referenced* test and *criteria-reference* test. Simply, a norm-referenced test is an assessment used to compare learning outcomes of one group of students with another group of students, and a criteria-reference test compares specific criteria in the test, such as performance standards, math skills, vocabulary skills, and more. Assessment or measurement rely heavily on the validity, reliability, and practicality in testing (Airasian, 2001; Burden & Byrd, 2003).

Validity has to do with how an instrument measures what it purports to measure. Teachers design test questions to measure students on achieving the learning objectives of each lesson taught in class; how well the questions measure achievement of those objectives determines the content validity. A test with low content validity does not provide a good gauge of student learning. *Reliability* refers to the consistency of test results. If teachers assess student learning with a particular instrument and receive the same or nearly the same results each time, the instrument is reliable; if the results are inconsistent, the instrument is unreliable. *Practicality* has to do with all other factors involved in administering tests: preparation, location, testing climate, directions, instructions, test anxiety, time, grading, complexity of test questions, and more.

Most importantly, teachers must use rating criteria to measure or assess student learning. Numerical rating scales of 1, 2, 3, 4, and 5, or numerical rubric scales of 1, 2, 3, 4, and 5 are useful for scoring student work. Teachers can use alternative measures, such as checklists, anecdotal records, participation charts, observation scales, performance scales, portfolios, and other criteria. Teachers might also use products or performances as rating criteria because in a multicultural classroom some students are good at presenting their products rather than demonstrating their learning through performance. Howe (2002) listed multiple assessments teachers can use to measure student learning as shown in Table 10.15.

Table 10.15. Uses of Selected Types of Assessment

Type of Assessment	Form/Usage
Traditional	Paper and pencil tests, multiple choice tests, true/false test
Authentic	Applying learning experiences and knowledge to real-life situations, connecting learning with real-world experiences
Performance	Demonstrating understanding and knowledge by doing what the student has been learning to do, can do vs. know
Product	Hands-on activities, constructing, inventing, creating, etc...
Workbook	Recording thoughts, actions, understandings, writings, discussions
Concept map	Creating diagrams representing knowledge of concepts, drawing, art work
Essay	Allowing students to express understanding and knowledge in written form, short answers
Open-ended question	Encouraging students to demonstrate what they know and relate to experiences
Behavior checklists	Observing students and their behaviors in action, sharing with others, discussing with peers
Portfolio	Collection of work, records, journal, workbook
Short answer	Paper and pencil tests with short answers, multiple choices, true/false, cloze, word bank
Matching	Using words, phrases, statements, sentences, frames

Assessment of instruction holds both students and teachers academically accountable for learning and teaching. Teacher-made tests are often better than standardized measures for assessing what students have learned, can do, and know. Perhaps assessment of student learning can determine teaching effectiveness, but it can provide even more information on the teacher's competence in delivering the content knowledge of each academic subject.

Becoming a Reflective Educator

Using best educational practices requires professionalism, professional development, and personal growth. Teachers often formally or informally mull over their successes, failures, mistakes, or struggles, and this reflection causes growth. Professional development begins with the teacher's good attitudes, knowledge, skills, and personal qualities; these are the hallmarks of professional educators and role models for all learners. Professional reflection is the key to becoming a successful educator. Wise and knowledgeable teachers reflect and focus on their strengths to stir up their passion rather than procrastinating because of obstacles that seem to hold them back. Reflective practitioners actively think about how instruction, management, assessment, student activities, and task strategies enhance student learning. They use the feedback and experiences of the learners to evaluate their practices and improve their teaching.

Self-reflection should be a daily exercise, and its formalized practice will become a professional habit that constantly reminds teachers to consider the effectiveness of their teaching practices. In other words, with practice, reflective teaching can become a natural daily activity that is practical and informative. To help teachers develop a habit of reflecting on their teaching practices, the following basic guidelines for reflection are offered:

1. Use in-action and on-action reflection on a daily basis.
2. Set aside quality time each day for reflection.
3. Apply self-reflection, examining the strengths and weaknesses of each lesson taught during the day.
4. Share ideas with colleagues and ask questions about changes or improvements.
5. Use notes, journals, voice recorders, or technological devices to help with reflection.
6. Think creatively when reflecting.
7. Focus on what is working well first.
8. Identify what is not working so well second.
9. Plan to add, delete, or improve areas of interest.
10. Include instruction, guided practices, student activities, and discipline as part of reflection.
11. Ask what students like, dislike, struggle with, or enjoy the most.
12. Keep this in mind: Learning + enjoyment = retention.

Self-assessment is a part of reflection. However, it is hard to assess oneself without a checklist. Some teachers use a teaching inventory guide to help them reflect on daily teaching practices. Table 10.16 lists examples of teaching inventory guides. Regardless of what teachers use to help them reflect, the key is to demonstrate personal honesty, commitment, and dedication toward teaching, development, and growth.

Teachers can create their own teaching inventory checklist guide. Professional reflection not only helps teachers plan better to advance their teaching practices and enhance student learning but also guides teachers in how to set their teaching objectives and goals for the class. Teachers should be goal-oriented, task-oriented, and organized professionals in order to make challenging tasks, teaching assignments, and professional responsibilities manageable, doable, and enjoyable all year long.

Table 10.16. **Teaching Inventory Checklist**

Content Area Standards	Learning Objectives	Instruction	Guided Practices	Independent Practices
• Use specific content area standards • Grade level and age appropriate • Key concepts • Pedagogical skills • Focus on specific learning outcome	• Frame learning objective(s) from content area standards • Use sustainable, measurable, and achievable learning objective • Go over with students • Modify and adapt for all learners	• Prior knowledge • Contextualization • Preview/review • Engagement level • Model, guide, illustrations, examples, samples, try out activities • Materials or supplies • Apply modifications, adaptations, and accommodations • Check for understanding • Practice	• Use overhead projector • Model, demonstrate, illustrate • Use manipulatives • Hands-on and minds-on activities • Video clips • Worksheets or handouts • Small whiteboards • Thumb up or down • Questions • Check for understanding	• Put problems on board or overhead projector • Worksheet or handout • Allow time for academic engagement • Group students for activity • Go over problems and answers • Recap learning objectives

Summing Up

This chapter presented a variety of approaches to help teachers cultivate best professional practices and equip them with well-rounded knowledge and skills to enhance their teaching practices in the multicultural classroom. Use of best professional practices requires professional commitment, leadership, dedication, perseverance, and growth. Teachers must have patience, passion, positive attitudes, a good personality, and people skills to cope with the daily demands, pressures, and unexpected circumstances on the job.

Building confidence takes efforts and sacrifice. Teaching is not for everyone, and not everyone can be a good teacher. Many teachers lack competence and confidence in some areas because of many factors, such as inadequate clinical training, insufficient teaching experience, and capricious subject matter preparation.

Instructional practices are complex because one model does not fit all learners. Teachers must be adequately prepared to employ different methodologies or instructional strategies to benefit all kinds of learners. For most, assessment is the weakest area because they do not learn how to assess student learning prior to entering the classroom. Most teachers learn how to conduct assessments when they are in the classroom. Finally, reflective teaching should help teachers become better educators. Self-reflection is a powerful tool, and if teachers use this tool carefully and wisely, their teaching practices could become among the best of professional practices.

CHAPTER ELEVEN

DEVELOPING STRATEGIC MANAGEMENT ACTION PLANS

A master can tell you what he expects of you....
A teacher, though, awakens your own expectations.
Patricia Neal, actress

Introduction

Although classroom management and discipline problems are unpredictable and unanticipated, teachers must be prepared to handle these unexpected misbehaviors professionally, ethically, and legally. Teachers who successfully respond to classroom management problems are able to identify the causes of the problems and assess the situations quickly. Teachers vary in their responses; some punish students rather than solve the problems. Wise and experienced teachers usually do not react to problems in anger and with punishment. Instead they examine the situation and select a problem-solving approach to bring a meaningful solution that helps involved students learn from their mistakes. For some students, consistent reinforcement is not enough to create a lasting change in behavior. Therefore, teachers need to be well prepared to handle all kinds of management problems that may arise in class. This chapter examines a variety of management problems and shows teachers how to devise a strategic management action plan to deal with most of the typical student behaviors with workable approaches that solve problems instead of punishing students for misbehaving.

Why Punishment Is Unsuccessful

Teachers have to understand why punishment does not work well with students even though it may work for their own children at home. Punishment is the infliction of a penalty to control, command, and reprimand wrong doing such as criminal behaviors, civil disobedience, breaking curfew, and penal code violations. Students are not criminals, and their misdeeds are not considered felonies or misdemeanors under school policies and education codes. Therefore, for academic discipline, punishment is a poor choice because of its negative consequences. Table 11.1 lists some of the reasons punishment does not succeed in disciplining students. Punishment has connotations of harshness, inhumanity, and brutal penalties such as hard labor, torture, beating, tormenting, deprivation, and humiliation.

Why Problem Solving Is Successful

Teachers must keep in mind that the objective of discipline is to help affected students change their behaviors, and the goal of management is to modify the behaviors, not the students, through logic, understanding, and responsibility. In other words, teachers discipline students academically to help build their self-discipline as well as self-control. Problem solving works because teachers involve all parties, helping them realize and recognize the impact of their actions and understand the nature of their misbehaviors as they address the cause formally and professionally. Table 11.2 presents examples of problem solving approaches that should be helpful to teachers and students in dealing with management problems. Teachers have to adjust these strategies to the students' level of understanding, age, and cross-cultural sensitivity.

Table 11.1. Reasons Punishment Does Not Work

Wrong Approach	Reasons for Not Working
Focus	Focuses on the past, profiles students, connects to previous behaviors, based on wrong assumptions
Insidious side effects	Cause ripple effects, negative feelings, unpleasant emotions, insulting, hostile climate
Teacher-student relationship	Poor, broken, scarred, painful, strained, negative
Illogical	Commanding, controlling, demanding, humiliating, reprimanding, belittling, scolding, putting down, forcing
Un-educational	Not for modification, positive learning, responsible behavior, and correction; does not build self-discipline, improve skills, teach conflict resolution or problem solving
Tone of voice	One-way approach, poor interaction, predetermined solution, rush to judgment

Table 11.2. Reasons Problem Solving Works

Right Approach	Reasons for Working
Positive cooperation	Focuses on both sides, teambuilding, cooperation, finds common ground, solves problem together
Logical understanding	Improves responsibility, holds students accountable, is responsible for own action
Empowerment	Encourages cooperation, improves skills, learns conflict resolution, builds confidence, gains competence
Lasting change	Learns from mistakes, applies to other problems, makes adjustment, improves coping skills
Reaction to problems	Knows how to react, act, respond to, deal with, solve problems and cooperate
Step-by-step process	1-find the cause, 2-propose a solution, 3-solution and prevention, 4-Learn now to deal with same or similar problem, 5-Reach agreement and execute action plan, and 6-Review and evaluate the completion of action

Designing a Personal Classroom Management Plan

As part of their strategic management action plan, teachers must develop a personal classroom management to help them plan ahead of time, prepare early, and think through the many activities they want to include in their classroom. The components of this plan must be appropriate for all students in order for teachers to create a productive, positive, and sound academic learning environment. Once the plan is created, teachers can always modify it as they go along. They can adjust, add to, or subtract from the plan for any grade level they are assigned to teach. Teachers can develop a personal classroom management plan that is specific to their classrooms, using the components shown in Table 11.3 as a guide (Manning & Bucher, 2007). The managerial plan must be flexible, and there is no one-model-fits-all approach. Teachers have to design a plan that fits their students, instead of expecting all their students to fit into some general plan. A classroom management plan cannot be a fixed action plan.

Table 11.3. **Components of a Personal Classroom Management Plan**

Components	Examples
Philosophy of management	Write a brief stanza describing personal belief in management—e.g., I believe in fair, logical, firm, assertive, and consistent discipline to motivate my students to learn to the best of their abilities.
Philosophy of education	Write a brief paragraph telling personal belief in education—e.g., I believe all students should have equal opportunity in education and deserve quality education in pursuing their potential to become successful in school and in life.
Behavioral expectations	Write a few expectations for students—e.g., I expect my students to be attentive, active, curious, well-behaved, able to follow directions, cooperative, able to learn
Pre-school check-off list	Create an inventory check-off list or a procedural guideline check-off list for all areas needing procedures in the classroom.
Classroom slogan or motto	Use keywords (respect, cooperation, teamwork, community, etc.) for motto or choose catchy phrases (TEAM—Together Everyone Achieves More; RESPECT—Respect Every Student's Privacy, Exceptionality, Culture, and Talent; RSVP-Responsible, Supportive, Valuable, and Purposeful; VIP—Very Inspiring Personality; MVP—Most Valuable Pupil; etc.)
Classroom arrangement	Make an inclusive floor diagram or floor map showing seating chart, storage, countertops, computer, big screen, teacher's desk, etc.
Class rules	Establish 3–5 norms or rules for the class.
Hierarchy or logical consequences for rule infractions	Establish 3–5 logical consequences for rule infractions.
Motivational strategies	Create intrinsic, extrinsic, contingent, and/or non-contingent reward systems to motivate students.
Management procedures and routines	Develop a daily schedule with time allocations for each academic subject matter, list specific routines for students to do, include procedural guidelines for different areas.
Instructional practice	Use five-step lesson plan format (anticipatory set, instructions, guided practices, evaluation, and independent practice); sequence of teaching; instructional process (planning, implementation, evaluation, feedback, and reflection).
Adaptations	Explain specific accommodations, modifications, adaptations, and interventions for ELLs and SNs; give examples, like ELD, SDAIE, Hands-on, Minds-on.
Reflective teaching	List three areas for reflection (e.g., instruction, engagement, and assessment); or identify strengths and weaknesses of each lesson

Strategic Action Plan to Deal with Management Problems

Teachers will encounter a myriad of management problems throughout their professional careers. Some problems are common and typical, and others are unpredictable and unexpected. The unexpected is to be expected when dealing with students with ADD/ADHD, conduct disorders (CD), or emotional disorders (ED). Teachers must be prepared and, at the very least, should anticipate management problems before they happen. Teachers who anticipate problems tend to react more positively in solving the problems. If teachers expect all students to control their own actions and behaviors, their reactions to students' misbehaviors are likely to be negative because of their predetermined mindset that students should never misbehave. Best educational practice is having a strategic action plan in place.

In this section, many situational management problems are presented, and each is addressed by examining the teacher's approach, possible solutions, and the goals. Looking carefully at these situations will help teachers develop comprehensive responses to daily management problems so they have meaningful and effective ways of solving problems. The issues presented here do not cover all the problems that may arise, and the possible solutions should not be seen as the panacea for all management problems. They are given here as guides. Teachers have to craft their own management tools for handling classroom problems and arrive at the solutions they desire for their classrooms.

Moreover, teachers must take students' age, cognitive development, maturity level, and cultural factors into consideration when they approach solutions to management problems. As a start for new teachers, Nissman (2006); Charles and Senter (2012); and Herrell and Jordan (2006) gave the following teacher-tested classroom management tools as troubleshooting applications and practical ways of dealing with everyday management and discipline in the multicultural classroom:

Area of concern:	Establishing classroom rules
Teacher's approach:	What should teachers do to make sure students follow the rules in the classroom?
Possible solutions:	1. Take time to teach, review, and remind about rules; go over any complex situations, make necessary adjustments; use RSVP approaches. 2. Enforce rules with logical consequences, allow flexibility, apply rules appropriately. 3. Use constant and periodic review of rules; teach students rules; be firm, consistent, assertive, motivational.
Goals:	Ensure all students follow rules, understand logical consequences, take responsibility for their actions; improve self-discipline, self-control, self-motivation, self-management; follow orders, procedures, routines; maintain control of class; improve learning opportunities.

Area of concern:	Poor attendance or truancy
Teacher's approach:	What should teachers do to address absenteeism, chronic absences, and related factors preventing student attendance?
Possible solutions:	1. Keep attendance record up to date, talk to in private, find out issues, explain school policies. 2. Discuss concerns with school administrators for guidance, document concerns. 3. Contact parents via formal letter, follow up with courtesy telephone calls, and schedule a conference with parents to address attendance.

Goals:	Improve attendance; improve student learning; advocate for student's best interest; improve self-control, self-management, self-discipline; motivate students.

Area of concern: **Classroom routine violations**

Teacher's approach:	How can teachers help students make adjustments to the everyday routine?
Possible solutions:	1. Post and practice routines with students. 2. Model consistent routines and make modest adjustment to accommodate difficult situations. 3. Plan well, use organized lesson plan, and model smooth transitions.
Goals:	Increase smooth transitions; improve self-control, self-management, self-discipline, self-correction; improve cooperation; minimize disruptions and distractions.

Area of concern: **Annoying distractions**

Teacher's approach:	How can teachers prevent annoying and/or irritating behaviors in class?
Possible solution:	1. Apply moderate discipline (verbal warning, pull a card, lose privilege, etc.). 2. Private correction, intervention, monitoring. 3. Be mobile, proactive, give early warning before activity.
Goals:	Stop the behaviors; reduce disruptions and distractions; improve self-discipline, self-management, self-control; create positive learning environment.

Area of concern: **Disobedient toward authority**

Teacher's approach:	What can teachers do to help students change or improve their interactions with authority figures, especially teachers?
Possible solution:	1. Meet with students to address concerns and find out reasons. 2. Refer students to talk with school administrators. 3. Seek suggestions from school administrators, parents, and others.
Goals:	Respect teachers; improve self-control, self-discipline, self-management; show acceptable behaviors; follow directions; obey authority.

Area of concern: **Argumentative students**

Teacher's approach:	How can teachers deal with argumentative students in class?
Possible solution:	1. Be assertive, firm, clear, pleasant, and consistent. 2. Use no threat, appeasement, promise, accusation, negativity, confrontation. 3. Meet with students to find out their side of story, provide clarification, refer to the school administrator for further assistance.
Goals:	Respect teachers and other students; improve self-control, self-discipline, self-management; show acceptable behaviors; follow orders; obey authority.

Area of concern: **Attention seeker or getter**

Teacher's approach:	What can teachers do about students who exhibit attention-getting or -seeking behaviors during class?
Possible solution:	1. Use mild discipline (ignore, verbal warning, pull a card, etc.) 2. Talk to in private, make corrections, pause. 3. Be assertive, firm, clear, pleasant, and fair; give options.

Goals:	Improve cooperation, self-control, self-discipline, self-management; show acceptable behavior; minimize disruptions and distractions; be patient; ask for help.

Area of concern:	**I don't care attitude**
Teacher's approach:	How do teachers get students who have an "I don't care attitude" to change?
Possible solution:	1. Find out student's interests, curiosity, and problems to motivate. 2. Modify instruction, activity, group activity. 3. Talk to in private; use reward system; make learning fun, relevant, intriguing.
Goals:	Change personal attitude; motivate to learn; improve self-management, self-control, self-discipline; show respect; display acceptable behaviors.

Area of concern:	**General behavior problems**
Teacher's approach:	What should teachers do to eliminate constant misbehaviors?
Possible solution:	1. Review rules and logical consequences, explain unacceptable behaviors, and model good ones. 2. Make a list of acceptable behaviors for modeling, explain consequences, use mild to moderate discipline. 3. Talk to in private, make correction, refer to school administrators, contact parents.
Goals:	Show acceptable behaviors; improve self-control, self-discipline, self-management; improve cooperation; create positive learning environment for all.

Area of concern:	**Blurting answers in class**
Teacher's approach:	What can teachers do with students who blurt out or call out answers during class?
Possible solution:	1. Give clear directions, expectations, and procedures. 2. Give warnings before activity about calling out answers without following the rules, apply consequences, change methods of reviewing, call on specific students. 3. Ignore calling out answers, put answers on a screen, talk to in private, make correction.
Goals:	Improve cooperation; improve self-control, self-discipline, self-management, self-confidence; follow directions, rules, procedures.

Area of concern:	**Class clown**
Teacher's approach:	How do teachers handle or deal with students who are acting like class clowns?
Possible solution:	1. Talk to in private to find out reasons, acknowledge unacceptable behaviors, make corrections. 2. Apply moderate discipline and consequences. 3. Refer to school administrators, contact parents, document what really happened.
Goals:	Stop acting like class clown; improve self-discipline, self-management, self-control; improve cooperation; show acceptable behaviors; reduce disruptions and distractions.

Area of concern:	**Does not follow rules**
Teacher's approach:	What should teachers do when students cannot follow rules and constant repetition or reminder is needed?
Possible solution:	1. Model good behaviors, review rules to make sure they are relevant and enforceable, make changes as necessary. 2. Teach students rules and consequences, post rules and consequences in conspicuous location, create procedures. 3. Praise good behaviors, apply mild and moderate discipline, use reward system.

| Goals: | Keep classroom under control; have smooth transitions; improve work habits; model acceptable behaviors; improve self-control, self-management, self-discipline; improve learning opportunities |

Area of concern: **Cleaning up work areas or room**

Teacher's approach:	How can teachers teach students to clean up work areas when they are finished with their learning activities?
Possible solution:	1. Establish clean-up rules and procedures, model to students, allow time for clean up. 2. Preplan activity, use cutouts or premade materials, limit messy activity. 3. Monitor students on task, provide empty trash cans, use smooth transitions.
Goals:	Be responsible; improve time management; have smooth transitions; keep room organized and neat; improve self-discipline, self-control, self-management.

Area of concern: **Grieving a loss of life**

Teacher's approach:	How can teachers help students who are grieving the loss of a family member, a friend, a fellow student, or a teacher?
Possible solutions:	1. Acknowledge the loss with compassion, empathy, and sorrow; provide emotional and psychological support to the individual and family members; and refer student to counselor, school psychologist, or other professionals. 2. Allow time off to cope with grief; watch for depression, confusion, anxiety, psychological abnormality. 3. Understand and respect cultural differences; be prepared to deal with the child's capacity, questions, or misunderstanding regarding loss of a life.
Goals:	Provide emotional, psychological, cultural, academic support to the child; recognize the child's grief, agony, pain, suffering, confusion, depression; provide professional assistance to the student to allow time for coping; improve coping skills.

Area of concern: **Daydreaming in class**

Teacher's approach:	How can teachers aid a child who is constantly daydreaming during class?
Possible solutions:	1. Check for understanding of directions, assignments, problems. 2. Talk to in private to find out more about personal needs, assess learning issues, provide strategic plan for improvement. 3. Evaluate teaching methods, student activity, task activity, engagement level.
Goals:	Improve work habits; follow directions; do the work; ask for assistance; improve self-discipline, self-management, self-motivation; improve concentration.

Area of concern: **Verbal cursing or Non-verbal cursing**

Teacher's approach:	What should teachers do when a student curses at a teacher or a fellow student in the classroom?
Possible solutions:	1. Denounce it right away, temporarily ignore it, use mild discipline, give warning. 2. Use moderate discipline, talk to in private, make correction. 3. Contact parents, refer to school administrator, hold conference.
Goals:	Improve self-control, self-management, self-discipline; be responsible for acceptable behaviors; improve interpersonal relationship; stop cursing; cooperate; follow authority.

Area of concern:	**Vandalism in the classroom**
Teacher's approach:	How can teachers deal with carelessness or malicious acts toward other students' personal and school property?
Possible solutions:	1. Talk to in private, apply mild and moderate discipline, make corrections, expect improvement. 2. Document incidents, provide close supervision, refer to school administrators, contact parents. 3. Hold conference with parents, set up plan for improvement, file report with law enforcement.
Goals:	Stop careless or malicious attitude and behavior; respect personal and school property; improve self-discipline, self-control, self-management; improve personal responsibility; show acceptable behaviors.
Area of concern:	**Demanding student during class**
Teacher's approach:	How can teachers deal with students who constantly demand attention during class?
Possible solutions:	1. Vary methods of instruction, student activity, task activity. 2. Use cooperative learning grouping, pair up. 3. Use simplified activities, find out reasons, talk to in private.
Goals:	Improve self-management, self-discipline, self-control; improve completion of task, activity, work; be responsible for work; improve motivation; be patient.
Area of concern:	**Disrespectful in the class or lack of respect**
Teacher's approach:	How can teachers deal with students who show disrespect toward other students or the teacher in the classroom?
Possible solutions:	1. Model acceptable behaviors, set up expectations, apply mild discipline, warning. 2. Talk to in private, make corrections, give choices or options, apply moderate discipline. 3. Refer to school administrators, contact parents, hold conferences.
Goals:	Improve self-control, self-management, self-discipline; improve interpersonal interactions; create a positive learning environment; obey authority; follow directions.
Area of concern:	**Displaying disruptive behaviors in class**
Teacher's approach:	What do teachers do with students who cannot get along with other students and continue to display discontentment or rivalries?
Possible solutions:	1. Review seating chart, methods of instruction, student activity, task activity, cooperative learning, grouping. 2. Talk to in private, find out personal issues, make corrections, set expectations, apply mild and moderate discipline, warning, give choices. 3. Refer to school administrators, document incidents, contact parents, hold conferences.
Goals:	Improve self-management, self-control, self-discipline; be responsible for own actions; respect others; display acceptable behaviors; improve social and interpersonal relationships; reduce disruptions and distractions.
Area of concern:	**Drawing or writing on desks**
Teacher's approach:	What should teachers do to deal with students who write or draw on desks instead of working on assignments or doing work?
Possible solutions:	1. Make sure directions are clear and rules explained, set high expectations for work, monitor students on task. 2. Apply mild and moderate discipline, find out issues, make corrections, set improvement standards. 3. Talk to in private,

document incidents, refer to school administrators, contact parents, hold conference.

Goals:	Improve self-management, self-discipline, self-control; improve personal responsibility; stop minor vandalism; follow directions; complete work.

Area of concern: **Suspicion of substance abuse**

Teacher's approach: What should teachers do when they suspect students of substance abuse—drugs, alcohol, smoking, etc.?

Possible solutions: 1. Acknowledge concerns in private, find out about suspicion, refer students to school administrators, document incidents, contact parents. 2. Offer professional assistance, provide coping skills, offer substance abuse information. 3. Offer relevant curricular activity to curb substance abuse, discuss peer pressure, acceptable behaviors.

Goals: Be free of substance abuse; enforce drug-free education; cope with peer pressure; get treatment or professional assistance; show abstinence; improve self-discipline, self-management, self-control.

Area of concern: **Shy, timid, reserved, and alone students**

Teacher's approach: What can teachers do about students who are shy, timid, reserved, and alone and do not ask for assistance during class?

Possible solutions: 1. Give clear and concise directions, set clear expectations, check for understanding, completion of work. 2. watch for struggle, anxiety, frustration, depression, confusion; provide assistance; talk to in private, find issues. 3. Vary instruction, use cooperative learning, grouping, accommodation, adaptations.

Goals: Be active learner; ask for help; participate in activity; cooperate with peers; engage in learning activity; build learning confidence; increase social skills; improve motivation.

Area of concern: **Frustration over assignments**

Teacher's approach: How can teachers help students cope with frustration over assignments, missing assignments, make-up assignments, and due dates?

Possible solutions: 1. Check for understanding, offer assistance to students, talk to in private, make a list of things to do, give opportunity with timetable or deadlines, find out issues. 2. Use intervention strategies, refer to tutorial services or after-school program, schedule private conferences. 3. Contact parents, hold conference, discuss alternatives.

Goals: Improve self-control, self-management, self-discipline, self-confidence; improve work habits; reduce frustration; improve concentration; provide learning opportunities.

Area of concerns: **Homework accountability**

Teacher's approach: What can teachers do to get students to do assigned homework or to hold students accountable for homework assignments?

Possible solutions: 1. Review homework policies and procedures, check the relevancy of homework assignments, level of difficulty, connection to covered content, number problems, time allocation. 2. Review purposes, meanings, connections, relationship. 3. Methods of correction, review, grading, feedback, strategic plan to deal with incorrect answers, difficult problems.

Goals:	Improve learning, practices, skills, and knowledge; hold students accountable for completion of homework; improve mastery of concepts; improve study habits, self-management, self-discipline; improve practice; sharpen skills.

Area of concern: **Shifting attention and interests**

Teacher's approach:	What can teachers do to help students who shift their attention or interests during class?
Possible solutions:	1. Give clear directions; set clear expectations; review methods of instruction, student activity, task activity, engagement level, presentation. 2. Find out issues, talk to in private, check level of difficulty of assignments, modifications, adaptations. 3. Vary activities, use alternative reinforcements, apply motivational strategies.
Goals:	Improve learning opportunities; motivate; encourage; be engaged; improve self-discipline, self-management, self-control; show cooperation.

Area of concern: **Hyperactivity and distractibility**

Teacher's approach:	How can teachers manage the hyper students who can be distractive to others in the classroom?
Possible solutions:	1. Prescribe hands-on activities; use a timer to time activity; shorten activity or assignments; keep hands, eyes, and mind busy; allow varied pace. 2. Keep area free of objects, use controlled exposure approaches. 3. Apply reinforcements, use reward system, motivational strategies.
Goals:	Improve work habits; improve self-discipline, self-management, self-control, self-confidence; minimize distractions and disruptions; show cooperation; display acceptable behaviors.

Area of concern: **Misbehaviors outside the classroom**

Teacher's approach:	How can teachers help reduce students' inappropriate behaviors during lunch or recess?
Possible solutions:	1. Reinforce and enforce rules, procedures, and expectations outside the classroom; model behaviors; supervise, monitor. 2. Apply mild and moderate discipline, be assertive, talk to in private, make corrections. 3. Provide various activities, rotations, seating arrangements.
Goals:	Improve self-management, self-discipline, self-control; minimize accidental incidents; improve outside behaviors and responsibilities; improve social skills; improve student relationships.

Area of concern: **Inconsistency in routine**

Teacher's approach:	What can teachers do with students who are inconsistent in or have problems with routine matters?
Possible solution:	1. Teach and review rules and procedures constantly, check for understanding, monitor student activity, use consistent and positive reinforcements. 2. Review routine issues; make adjustments, modifications, accommodations; be patient, reminding. 3. Talk to in private, make corrections, avoid rigid structure or routine.
Goals:	Improve self-management, self-discipline, self-control; improve smooth transitions; improve responsibility; be consistent; follow directions.

Area of concern:	**Individualization or individual attention for special needs students**
Teacher's approach:	How can teachers personalize instruction or how can teachers give individualized attention in the classroom?
Possible solution:	1. Vary instructional practice, use a variety of teaching materials, prepare individual academic tasks or plans. 2. Use modifications, adaptations, accommodations; organize complex tasks; provide hands-on and minds-on activities; use cooperative learning; grouping. 3. Use self-correcting materials; use instant and constant feedback; use team teach, aide, flexible instructions.
Goals:	Reach out to special needs students; improve learning opportunities; promote student learning; motivate learning; empower multicultural approach; improve learning opportunities.

Area of concern:	**Lack of interest in academics**
Teacher's approach:	How can teachers deal with students who place emphasis on sports and technological apparatuses rather than academics?
Possible solutions:	1. Understand single-sided learners, recognize students' interests, use reward system, motivational strategies, understand learning styles, make learning fun and enjoyable, emphasize value of education. 2. Use integrated content or activities; use a variety of teaching resources, make students curious, use various student activities, grouping, find interesting topics. 3. Talk to in private, find out issues, offer strategic interventions, set expectations, inform parents.
Goals:	Motivate students to learn; promote self-confidence and self-esteem; modify learning habits; inspire learning passion; improve learning for all academics; improve work habits.

Area of concern:	**Lack of motivation to learn**
Teacher's approach:	What can teachers do to motivate students who lack motivation to learn in the classroom?
Possible solution:	1. Use motivational strategies; use reward system; employ a variety of teaching methods; use various activities; make learning fun, enjoyable, entertaining, intriguing. 2. Use accommodations, adaptations, modifications, appropriate teaching materials. 3. Use cooperative learning, hands-on and minds-on activities; make learning interesting, curious, stimulating.
Goals:	Motivate learning; promote self-confidence; improve learning opportunities; improve self-esteem; inspire learning; improve self-control, self-management, self-discipline.

Area of concern:	**Lack of self-esteem**
Teacher's approach:	How can teachers make students feel better about themselves inside the classroom?
Possible solutions:	1. Build a positive learning environment, provide support, use praise, give encouragement, provide learning opportunities. 2. Promote progress and success, understand feelings, motivational strategies, use reward system. 3. Talk to in private, find out issues, make corrections, inform parents, refer for services.
Goals:	Improve feelings about self; motivate to learn; promote self-worth, self-concept, self-image, and pride; improve self-confidence; improve self-reliance; increase learning opportunities.

Area of concern:	**Not listening or not paying attention**
Teacher's approach:	What can teachers do for students who will not listen or pay attention during class?
Possible solutions:	1. Prep, tape, engage, hook up, prepare, and direct for instruction; set clear expectations; model listening skills; use clear and pleasant voice; check instructions for clarity and relevancy. 2. Talk to in private, find out issues, make corrections, engage students constantly, shorten instructions. 3. Use hands-on and minds-on activities, cooperative learning, grouping; give few directions, modify activities, etc....
Goals:	Improve participation; promote acceptable behaviors; show cooperation; improve self-management, self-control, self-discipline; follow directions; increase learning potential.

Area of concern:	**Students who seek assistance constantly**
Teacher's approach:	What can teachers do when students constantly come up to them for assistance during class?
Possible solutions:	1. Set clear rules and procedures, tell student to raise hands for help, give clear directions, model appropriate behaviors, set clear expectations, use timer to time assignments. 2. Talk to in private, find out issues, make corrections, redirect. 3. Use grouping activity, provide assistance, use praise, apply motivational strategies, use reward system.
Goals:	Improve self-management, self-discipline, self-control; promote self-reliance, self-confidence, self-motivation; improve work habits, personal responsibility, concentration; show acceptable behaviors.

Area of concern:	**Name calling in class**
Teacher's approach:	What can teachers do with students who call other students names in the classroom?
Possible solutions:	1. Set rules and consequences for name calling, show intolerance for name calling, use moderate discipline, warning, give options, use assertive approach. 2. Talk to in private, find out issues, make corrections, model acceptable behaviors. 3. Intervention strategies, document incidents, refer to school administrators, contact parents, hold meetings.
Goals:	Improve student relationships; stop racial remarks or name calling; create a positive learning environment for all; embrace multicultural classroom; have inclusive classroom; improve self-management, self-control, self-discipline.

Area of concern:	**Nervous habits in class**
Teacher's approach:	What can teachers do with students who have a habit of chewing on rulers, erasers, crayons, pencils, nails, and objects?
Possible solutions:	1. Review activity or task for appropriateness, talk to in private, find out issues, make corrections, offer assistance, give alternatives. 2. Use cooperative learning, grouping, pairing; modify activity; shorten task; use hands-on and minds-on activity. 2. Observe for emotional and psychological abnormality, academic issues, cultural issues; refer for services; contact parents.
Goals:	Improve work habits; engage in learning activity; find out issue; improve self-discipline, self-management, self-control, self-dependence; improve self-confidence and self-esteem.

Area of concern:	**Noisy work habits or talking while working**
Teacher's approach:	How can teachers control or monitor students who have noisy work habits or talk loudly while working on task during class?
Possible solutions:	1. Give clear directions early, set clear expectations early, remind students of independent work, concentrate on task, seatwork rules and procedures. 2. Use mild discipline, verbal warning, mild consequences, talk to in private, keep busy, use hands-on and minds-on activities. 3. Modify seating chart, play music, monitor students on task, put stimuli on the board, emphasize completion of work.
Goals:	Improve self-management, self-discipline, self-control, self-independence; improve work habits; improve independent practices; show acceptable behaviors; show respect for others.

Area of concern:	**Off-task behavior**
Teacher's approach:	What can teachers do with students who are off-task or are not doing what they are supposed to do during class?
Possible solutions:	1. Set clear expectations, give clear directions, check for understanding, monitor students on task, provide assistance. 2. Write specific task on board or overhead, find out the cause, make corrections, talk to in private. 3. Use mild and moderate discipline, issue warning, give choices, apply consequences.
Goals:	Improve personal responsibility, self-discipline, self-management, self-control; improve learning opportunities; improve work habits; improve acceptable behaviors; to improve cooperation; pay attention

Area of concern:	**Playground issues**
Teacher's approach:	What can teachers do to help students understand playground behaviors such as taking sides, complaining, aggressive play, social turmoil, conflict, picking one over the others, etc...?
Possible solutions:	1. Set and review rules and procedures for playground, supervise students, monitor group activity, prescribe specific games, explain rules. 2. Use mild and moderate discipline; be firm, assertive, consistent; ensure health and safety; talk to in private; make corrections. 3. Time out, cancel game activity, document behaviors, discuss in class.
Goals:	Improve health and safety; improve self-control, self-management, self-discipline; improve teamwork, collaboration, social skills; show cooperation; improve game activity; have fun.

Area of concern:	**Adaptability or adjustment problems**
Teacher's approach:	How can teachers improve students' ability and flexibility to deal with unfamiliar situations and tasks or new ideas in the classroom?
Possible solutions:	1. Explain new situations to students, respect their ability to adapt, expect students' questions and confusion, instill the process, take time to make gradual adjustment. 2. Model changes; show new rules, procedures, and routines; practice together; use public praise; encourage for making efforts. 3. Be patient, talk to in private, find out issues, make corrections, modify complex issues.
Goals:	Improve smooth transitions, improve work habits, improve adaptability and adjustment, improve self-confidence, improve learning environment, be flexible.

Area of concern:	**Poor attitude in the classroom**
Teacher's approach:	What can teachers do to help students who have poor attitudes in the classroom?
Possible solutions:	1. Apply early engagement; use motivational strategies; prompt students with enthusiasm, excitement, intriguing ideas; vary instruction; use different activities. 2. Use positive reinforcements, prescribe hands-on and minds-on activities, use cooperative learning and grouping. 3. Talk to in private, find out issues, set expectations, offer assistance, make corrections, monitor work habits.
Goals:	Improve self-control, self-reliance, self-management, self-discipline; improve work habits; improve learning opportunities; improve cooperation; improve productivity; improve personal responsibility.

Area of concern:	**Taking pride in work to boost learning**
Teacher's approach:	What can teachers do to encourage students to take more pride in their work to boost their learning?
Possible solutions:	1. Use constant verbal and public praise, promote progress and success, apply reward system, use motivational strategies, give instant and constant feedback, acknowledge well-done work, recognize students' hard work to boost their ego. 2. Use reflective teaching, plan well, make learning fun and enjoyable, allow learning opportunities. 3. Use cooperative learning and grouping, display student work, show honesty and enthusiasm.
Goals:	Improve self-control, self-management, self-discipline, self-reassurance; improve learning outcomes; improve motivation; improve productivity; boost self-esteem; encourage self-confidence.

Area of concern:	**Putting proper identification on assignments**
Teacher's concern:	How can teachers teach students to put proper identification on assignments or papers before turning them in for grading?
Possible solutions:	1. Use verbal reminder to put name on paper before doing activity; remind students to check their papers before turning them in; develop a process and put it on the board; set clear rules, procedures, and expectations; emphasize the importance of putting name on papers. 2. Make sure all handouts or worksheets have space for student's name, review materials, allow students to identify their papers without name, give opportunity to put proper identification. 3. Talk to in private, find out issues, make corrections, reaffirm proper practice, use public praise.
Goals:	Improve personal responsibility; improve self-management, self-control, self-discipline, self-confidence; improve practice; improve quality of work; improve academic discipline.

Area of concern:	**Taking initiative for independent work**
Teacher's approach:	What can teachers do to help students who finished work early take initiative while waiting for other students to finish work during class?
Possible solutions:	1. Establish clear rules, procedures, and routines for taking initiative; make learning materials available for independent work; provide transitional activities for practice; have extra handouts or worksheets; offer interest corners or activities. 2. Have social and activity reinforcements ready, give privilege as-

signments, use classroom jobs. 3. Writing journal entries, reading books, doing homework, being classroom helpers.

Goals:
Improve personal responsibility; improve self-control, self-management, self-discipline; improve cooperation; improve motivation; increase learning opportunity; boost pride and self-esteem; improve work habits; minimize disruptions.

Area of concern: **Rivalry toward peers or not getting along well**

Teacher's approach:
How can teachers help students improve in their cooperative behavior with peers, or how can teachers promote students' getting along well?

Possible solutions:
1. Set clear rules, procedures, routines, and consequences; expect cooperative behaviors at all times; stress teamwork, group work, collaboration; explain cooperative and competitive activities. 2. Apply moderate discipline, identify possible factors and discuss them with students, explain problem-solving skills, use conflict resolution process. 3. Supervise students at all times, monitor students on task, provide immediate response to concerns, keep eyes on students.

Goals:
Improve social and interpersonal relationships; create a positive and productive learning environment for all; improve self-control, self-management, self-direction, self-discipline; improve conflict resolution and problem-solving skills; improve cooperation and collaboration.

Area of concern: **Short temper or short attention span**

Teacher's approach:
How can teachers deal with students who have very short attention spans and cannot concentrate on completion of tasks during class?

Possible solutions:
1. Talk to in private, find out issues, make corrections, offer assistance, make adjustments. 2. Check student activity or task for appropriateness, use adaptations and modifications to accommodate student needs as necessary, vary activities, use hands-on and minds-on activities. 3. Use cooperative learning, recognize learning styles, check for health issues, vary engagement level, make learning interesting, use curiosity as guide.

Goals:
Improve work habits; improve completion of tasks; improve self-control, self-management, self-discipline; improve productivity; improve learning outcomes; take personal responsibility.

Area of concern: **Silent or quiet students**

Teacher's approach:
How can teachers relate to or reach out to silent students who do not react or respond to instructional practices in the classroom?

Possible solutions:
1. Get to know the students, talk to in private, find out issues, make corrections, encourage to participate, allow opportunities, offer assistance. 2. Find out about interests; use motivational strategies, reward system, cooperative learning, group work. 3. Check for cultural issues, language barriers, health-related issues; contact parents; document concerns.

Goals:
Improve self-confidence, self-discipline, self-esteem, self-motivation; improve cooperation; improve learning opportunities; improve work habits; improve social and interpersonal skills.

Area of concern:	**Getting out of seat or not sitting in seat properly**
Teacher's approach:	What can teachers do with students who are out of their seats, put their feet in the aisle, stretch their legs across the aisle, stand up while doing work, or are not sitting properly in their seat?
Possible solutions:	1. Set clear rules, procedures, and consequences; set clear expectations for work habits; remind students of proper seating; make corrections. 2. Talk about health and safety issues, show respect to others, enforce rules and consequences, use public praise, apply mild and moderate discipline. 3. Talk to in private, find out issues, make corrections, set expectations, give options or choices, check for other issues.
Goals:	Improve self-discipline, self-management; self-control, self-motivation; improve work habits; improve cooperation; improve health and safety; reduce disruptions; show respect to others.

Area of concern:	**Social adjustment or social inclusion of new students**
Teacher's approach:	What can teachers do to help new students or new arrivals make social adjustments so they are included?
Possible solutions:	1. Welcome students to class, get to know the students, use multicultural activity to help students learn about one another, use sociogram, introduce students to class, use sharing activity. 2. Use cooperative learning, grouping, teamwork; show immediate acceptance; be friendly; be sensitive; respect personal space. 3. Do not pressure to adjust, allow time to fit in, encourage students, praise students, use motivational strategies.
Goals:	Improve self-confidence, self-esteem, self-worth, self-concepts, self-image; improve student relationships; improve acceptance; be inclusive; improve social adjustment process.

Area of concern:	**Stealing in the classroom**
Teacher's approach:	What can teachers do to deal with stealing in the classroom when students find their personal items missing?
Possible solutions:	1. Set clear rules and consequences for stealing, discuss matters at hand, allow items to be returned without question, declare when item is lost or found, stress that sticky fingers are not tolerated, emphasize respect for property. 2. Monitor student activities, provide better storage for valuable items, document incidents, teach and model good behaviors, have a basket in which recovered lost items are to be returned. 3. Take appropriate steps to solve stealing incidents, talk to in private, make corrections, document incident, contact parents, refer for assistance.
Goals:	Stop stealing; improve student relationships; improve self-confidence, self-control, self-discipline; show respect; increase moral responsibility; create healthy and safe classroom for all.

Area of concern:	**Students taking sides or student criticism**
Teacher's approach:	What can teachers do when students take sides or criticize one another during class?
Possible solutions:	1. Mediate right away, allow students to express feelings, listen to both sides, encourage compromise, use conflict resolution process, discuss issues at hand with honesty and respect, model good behaviors, walk students through the

process. 2. Monitor student actions, allow no putdown, encourage students to solve issues, promote civility through multicultural education. 3. Make certain all students are in good spirits, work with students to find consensus or compromised solution, set clear rules and procedures for handling criticism, be open-minded, make sure situation is under control

Goals: Improve student relationships; solve problems together; improve conflict resolution process; show respect; improve self-discipline, self-management, self-control; create a positive learning environment for all, etc....

Area of concern:	**Students with personal problems**
Teacher's approach:	What can teachers do to help students with personal problems?
Possible solutions:	1. Respect personal space and privacy, talk to in private, find out issues, offer appropriate assistance if necessary, make corrections, provide accommodations, document relevant issues, etc. 2. Monitor student behaviors and actions, observe changes or progress, allow time to heal, contact parents, refer for services. 3. Pay attention to health issues, use informal and formal approach to help students cope, keep eyes on sensitive issues, take appropriate steps to alert parents, refer to school administrators.
Goals:	Protect students; provide assistance; get help for personal problems; improve self-esteem, self-control, self-image, self-concept, self-discipline, self-management; improve learning opportunities; alleviate potential health problems.

Area of concern:	**Students who work fast and finish early**
Teacher's approach:	How can teachers cope with students who complete assigned work in a minimal amount of time?
Possible solutions:	1. Evaluate activity right away to see if work is too easy; check for accuracy, neatness, completion; review relevancy of work, appropriateness, level of difficulty; provide more challenging work; have alternative assignments available. 2. Take initiative, use transitional activities, have books and other materials available, allow independent work. 3. Refer to interest corners, perform classroom assignments, be class helper.
Goals:	Minimize disruptions, distractions, boring tasks; improve learning opportunities; improve self-management, self-control, self-discipline, self-motivation; improve personal responsibility; motivate learning.

Area of concern:	**Students who do poor work and rush to get done**
Teacher's approach:	How can teachers deal with students who often do poor work and rush to get it done without following directions properly?
Possible solutions:	1. Evaluate whether amount of work is too little or too much, check for accuracy, set clear expectations for each task, allow enough time, stress neatness. 2. Explain quality and quantity, set procedural guidelines for review and revision, apply mild and moderate consequences for rushed work, use reward system, promote completion and quality, motivate students to follow directions. 3. Talk to in private, find out issues, set expectations, give directions.
Goals:	Improve quality of work; improve accuracy; improve work habits; improve self-discipline, self-control, self-management, self-confidence; improve learning opportunities; improve practice.

Area of concern:	**Students pack up to leave before bell rings**
Teacher's approach:	What can teachers do to stop students packing up to leave the room before the bell rings?
Possible solutions:	1. Make rules clear, clarify that pack-up is not allowed until told to do so, monitor time carefully; model good behaviors, keep students on task, warn students five minutes before the bell. 2. Apply mild and moderate discipline, stress no early dismissal unless necessary; allow enough time for tasks. 3. Use consistent procedures and routines, practice with students, have clear reasons for not packing up early, encourage cooperation.
Goals:	Improve personal responsibility, self-control, self-management, self-discipline; promote good behaviors; follow orders; show respect to authority; minimize disruptions.

Area of concern:	**Student stress**
Teacher's approach:	How can I deal with students who exhibit lots of learning stress in the classroom?
Possible solutions:	1. Evaluate the cause of stress right away, find out issues, make corrections, offer assistance, review assigned work, check for understanding, vary instruction, modify assignments, provide support, make sure student has adequate sleep. 2. Be aware of cultural factors, observe self-esteem, check feelings, monitor progress, allow formal and informal evaluations, use cooperative learning, grouping, refer to school administrators, contact parents, etc. 3. Refer to services, seek professional assistance.
Goals:	Reduce impact on learning; improve self-confidence, self-management, self-control, self-discipline; increase productivity; improve self-esteem; get help; seek professional assistance; iincrease learning opportunities.

Area of concern:	**Substitution/preparation for substitute**
Teacher's approach:	How can teachers be assured that the substitute performs, reads, and follows the plans teachers have left for them to do?
Possible solutions:	1. Prepare a complete folder for substitute; set clear expectations; use step-by-step process; provide copies of daily schedule, routines, procedural guidelines. 2. Give clear directions and instructions to the substitute, list specific activities and tasks for students to do, put instruction in sequence, explain rules and consequences. 3. Provide specific information about special needs students, ELLs, and special accommodations; offer alternative activities; give direction where to find additional resources, etc.…
Goals:	Improve quality teaching, make smooth transitions, maintain constant implementation, reduce confusion, minimize negative impact on students, improve consistency.

Area of concern:	**Suspicion of abuse of students**
Teacher's approach:	What can teachers do if they have reasonable suspicion a student has been or is being abused?
Possible solutions:	1. Teachers are mandatory reporters and must report suspicion, talk to in private, evaluate the situation quickly, gather preliminary information about the abuse, ensure the child that abuse is not allowed, document concerns, take appropriate action if abuse appears to have occurred. 2. Refer the child to the school nurse or school administrator for second opinion, confirm story, decide

whether to contact proper authority, file a referral or report. 3. Provide emotional and psychological comfort for the child, reduce anxiety and trauma as much as possible, involve law enforcement, involve social worker.

Goals: Prevent abuse to any child, protect children from abuse by anyone, report possible abuse to proper authority; document incident, follow state laws, advocate for the best interest of the child, make a referral.

Area of concern:	**Talking in class**
Teacher's approach:	What can teachers do with students who talk during class when they should be listening, working, concentrating, or attending?
Possible solutions:	1. Give instant and constant signals, monitor students on task, provide assistance, give verbal warning, set clear expectations, give clear directions, offer learning opportunities when work is finished. 2. Apply mild and moderate discipline, give choices, use public praise, promote good behaviors, use reward system, apply motivational strategies. 3. Talk to in private, find out issues, make corrections, set clear expectations, refer to school administrators, contact parents.
Goals:	Improve self-control, self-management, self-discipline, self-motivation; reduce disruptions and distractions; increase productivity; show cooperation; display acceptable behaviors.
Area of concern:	**Temper tantrums**
Teacher's approach:	How can teachers deal with students who show outbursts, throw temper tantrums, or are upset in the classroom?
Possible solutions:	1. Evaluate isolated incident, intervene right away, talk to in private, find out issues, make corrections, give warning, give options, calm down, separate from the rest. 2. Apply moderate discipline, refer to school administrators, document incident, model appropriate behaviors, discuss concerns with class. 3. Contact parents, hold conference, offer services.
Goals:	Minimize impact on the rest of students; remove disruptions and distractions from class; safeguard the class; provide healthy and safe learning environment; improve self-control, self-discipline, self-management; show acceptable behaviors.
Area of concern:	**Tardiness or showing up late**
Teacher's approach:	What can teachers do with students who frequently show up late and disrupt classroom routines?
Possible solution:	1. Talk to in private, find out issues, make corrections, set expectations, explain rules, go over class schedule. 2. Apply mild discipline, document incidents, refer to school administrators, contact parents, hold conference, offer assistance. 3. Evaluate family situations, transportation problems, cultural issues; seek alternatives.
Goals:	Improve school attendance; prevent future incidents; alleviate more problems; improve self-discipline, self-management, self-confidence; increase learning opportunities; arrive on time.
Area of concern:	**Television addiction**
Teacher's approach:	What can teachers do to help students who watch too much television on a regular basis?

Possible solutions:	1. Introduce a lesson in class that discusses issues related to watching television, brainstorm with students how to make TV an effective source of learning. 2. Allow students to devise a plan to help others learn how to watch TV, make a list of good programs to watch, give options, offer choices, be aware of influences. 3. Send a note home to parents sharing what students learn in class, discuss TV's influence, share concerns formally.
Goals:	Reduce time watching TV; improve self-discipline, self-control, self-management; educate about TV programs; understand media influences; improve study habits; increase productivity; concentrate on school; promote good behaviors.

Area of concern:	**Truancy or absence**
Teacher's approach:	How can teachers reduce students' truancy, absences, and negative attitudes toward school such as boredom, laziness, don't care attitude, homeboy attitude, ditching, or skipping?
Possible solutions:	1. Talk to in private, find out issues, stress the importance of getting an education, use motivational strategies, make adjustments to instruction and student activities, offer assistance. 2. Seek professional assistance, offer counseling, use reward system, offer alternatives. 3. Contact parents; enforce attendance policies; send notice home to parents.
Goals:	Improve attendance; improve self-discipline, self-management, self-control; motivate to learn; provide learning opportunities; emphasize the importance of education; enforce attendance policies.

Area of concern:	**Internet addiction**
Teacher's concern:	What can teachers do to help students who spend too much time on the internet surfing or playing games?
Possible solutions:	1. Introduce lesson that stimulates dialog about internet services, allow students to discuss what is important and what is not, make a list of constructive things they can do with the internet, brainstorm ideas to help other children learn and use the Internet as a tool. 2. Allow students to propose a policy for how to use the Web for educational purposes, make a list of websites that are educational resources. 3. Share with students about school policies on surfing the web, send copies home to parents, encourage parents to keep eyes on internet use.
Goals:	To reduce time on the web; to concentrate on study; to improve study habits; to improve self-control, self-discipline, self-management, self-concept; to improve personal responsibility; to focus on education; etc....

Use Balanced Management and Discipline

Quite often, teachers want to control everything happening in the classroom, and they expect all students to behave well in all learning situations during academic activities. But having complete dominance and control of students is not the best approach to providing quality classroom management and student discipline. For example, using a zero tolerance approach to disciplining students often causes resistance, challenges, and disruptions in class because students may not like the way the teacher demands their attention. Moreover, students could be afraid to ask questions, respond to questions, or participate in discussion because the teacher may overreact to any little thing, even unimportant behaviors. Teacher authority has to be balanced with careful consideration of these circumstances: (a) the whole class, (b) individual students, (c) type of instructional activity, (d) type of student activity, (e) situational events taking place in the classroom, (f) students' excitement and enthusiasm, (g) student engagement, (h) inquiry-based approach, (i) student-centered approach, and (j) teacher-centered approach. Dominating the class without considering these circumstances is detrimental to students' academic progress and their freedom to receive quality instruction in a learning environment that is positive, caring, nurturing, empowering, stimulating, and inspiring.

To develop a balanced management and discipline approach, teachers must understand different types of teacher authority. *Traditional authority* is the approach of teachers who view themselves as their students' parent figures and expect the students to behave as they should under the presence and supervision of an adult. *Bureaucratic authority* is the approach of teachers who use their legitimate prerogatives to reward students using contingent applications such as performance, grades, logical consequences, and incentives, to deal with appropriate and inappropriate behaviors. *Professional authority* is that of teachers who use their knowledge, skills, and expertise to design lesson plans, instructional activities, student activities, and assessments to control student behaviors and stimulate learning. *Charismatic authority* is wielded by teachers who use their social and interpersonal skills to engage students in teaching and learning through interactive and communication styles that are attractive to students.

Besides type of teacher authority, teacher leadership plays a key role in classroom management and student discipline. *Permissive leadership* is the style of teachers who lack structure, organization, control, supervision, and guidance for their students; they frequently allow students to run wild. *Optimistic leadership* is practiced by teachers who believe teaching and learning can take place in any situation, and all students can learn at different level, if the opportunity is given to each student to try his or her best. *Authoritarian leadership* is the style of teachers who approach students with relentless dominance and control and provide little or no reason for rules, at the same time assigning harsh punishments or consequences that are arbitrary and inappropriate for disciplining students. *Authoritative leadership* is the style of teachers who provide students with proper guidance, appropriate modeled behaviors, and expectations that help students understand, learn, and grow through the course of maturity, responsibility, and self-management.

Keep in mind that no teacher authority or teacher leadership is perfect for dealing with all student behaviors because each style has its own challenges, resistances, and disappointments as well as cooperation, fear, and consternation. Therefore, teachers must be flexible and open to feedback from their students and, at the same time, seek administrative assistance whenever possible.

The Role of School Administrators

Teachers need strong administrative support in order to deal with serious and difficult management and discipline problems in the classroom. There is no way teachers can solve all the problems that occur while they are teaching, managing, disciplining, directing, monitoring, supervising, and assisting students in the classroom. Teachers' multiple responsibilities put them at a disadvantage because some problems are bigger and require more time to resolve or need immediate attention. New teachers are often afraid to refer students who have serious behavioral problems to the office to see school administrators because they do not want to be labeled as incompetent teachers. This reluctance makes new teachers vulnerable to a great deal of stress and puts them over their limit for coping with chronic managerial problems.

School administrators have a very heavy caseload also, and they cannot realistically spend a great deal of their time dealing with students to discuss their behavioral problems. However, they should see students as the prime source of their income and the clientele for the whole school. In other words, students should be their priority—period. In fact, nearly 80% of school administrators' time should be spent in managerial duties and responsibilities, and of that time, the majority should be devoted to helping teachers deal with student behaviors and serving the overall needs of both teachers and students. Today, most students who are referred to the office for disciplinary issues are watched by school secretaries in the front office rather than by administrators. Students spend hours waiting to see school administrators. In most cases, this is not the proper course of action for these students. It wastes time. Instead, these students should use their time doing something meaningful. Generally, students are not disciplined consistently or quickly, and that is a disservice school administrators have to step up to change. Otherwise, sending students to the office is meaningless and ineffective.

It is true that most school administrators are former classroom teachers; however, not everyone is an effective manager. Some administrators have the ability to influence students positively and cause them to change their behaviors, but very few have an effective systematic approach to addressing student behaviors. Some teachers find this appalling because in the end they are the ones who must rectify the situation with the misbehaving student.

Legal Guardians or Parents

Teachers have to respect the rights of the parents or legal guardians of the students they have in their classes. With respect to students, parents can move mountains, but teachers cannot. School policies and procedures have to be followed in order to protect all parties—students, teachers, parents, and school administrators. Discipline is sensitive and teachers have to take precautions. Table 11.4 gives some suggestions for working with parents.

Table 11.4. **Do's and Don'ts for Working with Parents**

Do's	Don'ts
1. Concentrate on abilities	1. Do not use students as translators or interpreters
2. Focus on behavior as problem	2. Do not focus on the child as problem
3. Respect the culture and language of students and parents	3. Do not concentrate on what parents lack
4. Use cultural brokers, paraprofessionals, or educators who know the cultural background when dealing with cross-cultural issues	4. Do not assume all parents of an ethnic groups are the same
5. Provide specific guidance or ideas for parents to do at home to boost learning	5. Do not assume parents understand when they nod
6. Believe all parents care very much about education regardless of their cultural background and SES	6. Do not overlook their concerns
7. Listen to parents' concerns	7. Do not defraud parents by having them sign papers
8. Inform parents about positive things about their children	8. Do not assume parents' ethnicity before asking
9. Use writing as formal communication with bilingual or monolingual parents	9. Do not give grades to satisfy parents
10. Be honest with parents	10. Do not discipline with shame or humiliation
11. Deliver what is promised	11. Do not call the mother to make decision without involving the father
	12. Do not expect a handshake from the mother
	13. Do not expect to meet both parents

Summing Up

This chapter covered comprehensive strategic action plans teachers should find helpful in dealing with management problems. Teachers should develop their personal classroom management plan to fit their own needs. At the same time, they should adjust their plan to accommodate their students' emotional and psychological differences. In the early days, teachers practiced harsh discipline, including corporal punishment, humiliation, and physical labor. Today, however, teachers appear to prefer problem-solving approaches to dealing with management problems and disciplinary issues. Punishment does not work in today's schools, but a problem-solving approach does.

Many strategic action plans were presented in this chapter to help teachers design their own comprehensive responses to management problems. There is no panacea that will solve all problems, and the plans presented here may work in some cases but not in all. Teachers must modify and adjust them to find what fits in their managerial practice. Examples were given for a number of areas of concern—each with the teacher's approach, possible solutions, and goals. These are practical examples of typical approaches to solving some of the most common classroom problems.

Teachers need to have strong administrative support in handling management and discipline problems because they cannot do everything in the classroom while teaching, assessing, managing, interacting, assisting, directing, monitoring, and supervising. School administrators can help rehabilitate students in a timely manner. Leaving disciplinary problems to the school secretaries does not help teachers eliminate chronic misbehaviors. Discipline is sensitive in nature, and teachers have to administer discipline because of their role *in loco parentis*. However, they must respect the rights of their students' legal guardians and parents. All parties have legal rights, and all parties—students, parents, and administrators as well as teachers—performing their respective roles promote a safe and productive classroom experience.

CHAPTER TWELVE

HELPFUL TIPS FOR THE FIRST FEW YEARS

Education is not filling a bucket, but lighting a fire.
William B. Yeats

Introduction

Teaching is not only a tough job, but a highly demanding career. The first few years of teaching are challenging for most new teachers because there so many things teachers have to know before entering the classroom; most beginning teachers enter the classroom with limited knowledge and skills, and some cases, teachers have mixed perceptions. Some new teachers who lack clinical training and preparation sink faster than they thought they would. Those teachers who can swim well in the critical first three years of teaching survive the mental anguish and emotional distress. Teaching is not for everyone, and not everyone can be a good teacher. All teachers who leave the teaching profession do not go through the exact same difficulties before they leave, and not all teachers who remain in teaching do so for the same reasons. Each teacher is uniquely different. This chapter addresses some key areas in teaching and offers suggestions to help beginning teachers better prepare themselves for dealing with the first few years of teaching.

Teachers Are Ordinary People

First and foremost, in teaching, all teachers give some, but some teachers give all. Still, no one is perfect in this world, and life is a process of trial and error. Teachers are ordinary people whose profession is subject to much scrutiny and criticism. Teacher turnover is high in the first few years of teaching as the result of a number of factors: (a) poor classroom management skills; (b) a myriad of disciplinary problems; (c) teaching incompetency; (d) dissatisfaction with employment; (e) a high level of work-related stress; (f) lack of parental involvement; (g) too many professional responsibilities; (h) high expectations resulting from mandates, policies, and regulations; (i) constant testing to measure teaching accountability; and (j) financial matters related to funding and low salary. Any one of these factors demonstrate that teachers, like everyone else, are imperfect, and teachers are expected to do well in most if not all of these areas. Because of this impossible-to-meet expectation, teachers are frequently perceived by others to be part of the problem as well as the solution. However, people do not realize that some teachers decide to leave teaching because they just cannot do enough to earn the public trust they really deserve. In other words, the public today not only has little trust in teachers but often fails to show them respect.

Whether one believes new teachers are born or made, it is totally impossible to find perfect teachers who can perform everything without making mistakes. New teachers should hold themselves to high standards of professionalism and ethics, but they just cannot expect themselves to be perfect. Teachers teach, learn, re-teach, grow, and glow all at the same time. What the public, parents, and school administrators expect of new teachers should be realistic, sensible, and measurable. Some expectations that are reasonable for all teachers are as follows:

1.　Design appealing instruction.
2.　Use state content-area standards to inform instruction.
3.　Set learning expectations for all learners.
4.　Demonstrate pedagogical skills.
5.　Use a variety of teaching strategies and modalities to engage students.
6.　Differentiate instruction.
7.　Apply sound judgment.
8.　Treat all students with dignity and respect.
9.　Use technology to enhance teaching and learning.
10.　Provide a healthy, safe, and risk-free learning environment for all students.

Although teachers are not perfect, they should do all that is in their power to avoid making professional mistakes. Some mistakes are understandable and can be excused, but some mistakes are unacceptable, such as child abuse, substance abuse, loss of patience, child pornography, cyber sex, a violent temper, and sexual relationships with students. Most importantly, teachers should consider themselves as role models for the children they are teaching, coaching, mentoring, and guiding each and every day.

Go Beyond Highly Qualified Teachers

Today, laws in most states require teacher preparation programs to recruit, prepare, and train highly qualified student teachers to become classroom teachers. However, in practice, school districts are looking for quality teachers who are well rounded in knowledge and are clinically trained to be able to handle the teaching workload each and every day. New teachers must prepare themselves to become high-quality teachers and even go beyond the highly qualified expectations because today's classrooms are linguistically and cultural diverse. Students of color bring diverse abilities, needs, demands, and challenges to the classrooms. The law may only require teachers to meet only minimum qualifications (MQ); however, to become quality teachers, new teachers must take extra steps to increase their knowledge and sharpen their skills in these areas of teacher competence: (a) professional, positive attitudes that foster learning; (b) content knowledge in all academic subject matter; (c) fundamental and theoretical knowledge about human behaviors related to teaching and learning; (d) a rich repertoire of teaching skills; (e) methods in multicultural education; (f) teaching methodologies; (g) pedagogical skills and applications; (h) leadership skills; (i) instructional planning; and (j) student assessment.

Moreover, quality teachers are professionals who always want to do their very best for all; they strive for best professional practices to promote teaching and learning excellence. Quality teachers work at *being the best of the best*. Quality means different things to different individuals, but for teachers, quality falls under these categories:

- personal qualities—oral communication skills, written communication skills, and professional commitment
- professionalism—reliability, dependability, interpersonal skills, and professional enthusiasm
- pedagogical creativity and innovation—instructional planning, technology, and student activities

- fundamental teaching skills—sequence of teaching, learning, and assessment
- principles of teaching and learning—what to teach, how to teach, and how students learn
- classroom management skills—managerial skills, structure, routines, procedures, modeling, daily schedules, order, managing student work, and monitoring
- differentiating instructions and teaching methodologies—guided practices, mapping, idea web, thematic unit, grouping, pairing, and independent practices
- organizational skills—physical environment, instructional materials and resources, and instructions
- time management skills—using time efficiently and effectively
- planning skills—daily, weekly, monthly, unit, term, and yearly activities

Keep in mind that the employability of quality teachers appears to be high because there will always be high demand for quality instruction. The quality of teacher has a greater influence on student learning than the language of instruction. In other words, quality teachers who provide students with quality instruction give the best benefits to students, parents, administrators, and ultimately the community.

Who You Know and Who Knows You

New teachers should have learned much from their clinical training before they enter the classroom. Passing the fieldwork experience or student teaching practicum verifies that new teachers have acquired adequate knowledge, skills, and practical experience to become good classroom teachers. However, the short duration of clinical training is not sufficient to prove that new teachers are equipped with all the teaching tools needed to teach all the academic subject matter they may be assigned. New teachers will have to spend at least a few years developing and sharpening their practice. It usually takes at least 4 to 5 years working full-time for teachers to find out what grade level, subjects, and activities they really enjoy. New teachers generally settle on a specific grade level after teaching for a few years, and that is their comfort zone.

The practical training teachers receive as part of their education gives them the privilege of obtaining their preliminary teaching credentials from the state so they can begin teaching, but they still have 5 years to clear their preliminary teaching credentials unless the process is delayed or extended for some reason. This two-step credentialing process means they get one foot in the door of the teaching profession immediately after their training ends and they have a few years to get both feet in the door. To do that, new teachers must make themselves marketable—both employable and desirable— and they must adapt to the job market because they will be competing with many other teachers who have more or less experiences than they have. In addition to having a professional portfolio or credential files as they seek employment, new teachers must make connection with people in the school "business," such as principals, teachers, administrators, and friends who are teachers. Eighty percent of new teachers are hired because they know someone or someone knows them through personal and professional connections—who you know and who knows you makes a big difference.

What Keeps Teachers Teaching?

If new teachers are to grow and glow, they must keep looking for any opportunity to practice teaching. Shortly after completing their fieldwork experience, some student teachers may not be able to obtain a teaching position with a local school district right away. If that is the case, they must make themselves available to continue practicing teaching by subbing, volunteering to work in the class-room, or engaging in school activities to get to know people. Continuing to practice effective teaching is one of the ways to keep tuned and up to date on teaching skills. Getting involved not only helps new teachers gain more experience in teaching, but it also enriches their resume, professional portfolio, or credential files. To make oneself marketable, one has to be willing to go out and hunt for a job instead of merely browsing the Web for a job opening. Today, most school administrators prefer to hire people they have known, have seen teaching, or with whom they are acquainted.

For new beginning teachers, teaching is the number priority; however, without effective management and sound discipline, quality teaching is just a plan, not an action. New teachers must understand the nature of effective teaching practices. Research indicates that the quality of instruction matters regardless of the language of instruction used in the classroom. Instructional approaches and strategies play a vital role in designing meaningful and quality instruction for all learners. Consistent routines and classroom structure are essential to effective teaching. Consider, for example, the three guiding principles for designing a lesson:

1. What should students learn in class?
2. How should students learn the academic content?
3. How should students be taught instructionally and academically?

These principles should lead teachers to examine the instructional process, shown in Figure 12.1. Teachers must know how to apply lesson plan design to guide instruction systematically so their teaching practices are not disorganized and fragmented. Table 12.1 illustrates basic teaching practices for new teachers through a five-step lesson format.

***Figure 12.1.* Instructional process.**

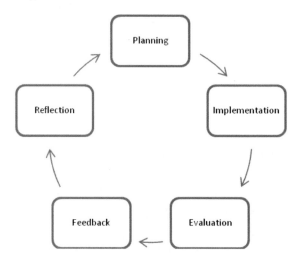

Keep in mind that it is not what the teachers do that matters the most, but it is what the teachers get the children to do. Children do not learn by listening to something being read out loud, hearing a lecture, or hearing a story. Most children learn when they are shown, guided, and involved. To improve teaching practice, Vang (2010) and Vosniadou (2001) presented some examples of academic plans for various instructional models as illustrated in Table 12.2.

***Table 12.1.* Five-Step Lesson Plan Format Activities for Basic Teaching Practices**

Practice	Activities
Assessing and engaging prior knowledge or background knowledge	Anticipatory set, introduction, hook up, engaging, pumping ideas, thought-provoking questions
Prepping and gaining attention	Preparing, tapping, directing, engaging, cooing mindset
Giving clear directions, instructions, guidance	Instructional practices, modeling, guiding, showing examples, demonstrating, illustrating, interacting, checking for understanding
Guided practice	Modeling, illustrating, showing, demonstrating, practicing problems, trial and error, checking for understanding, drilling, quizzing, guessing, involving, predicting
Maintaining momentum, brisk pace, active participation	Collaborative activities, independent practice, hands-on and minds-on activities, group activities
Assessing learning, checking for understanding, recapping, review	Evaluating, questioning, recapping, reviewing, practicing, reciting, repeating, checking, reaffirming, bringing to closure
Above and beyond activities, homework assignment, enrichment activities	Selecting specific content skills for practice, giving more practice, independent work, study guide

***Table 12.2.* Instructional Models with Academic Plans**

Model	Focal Point	Examples of Academic Plan
Active and attentive instruction	Keep students awake and academically accountable. Learning requires active, attentive, constructive, and enthusiastic involvement of the learners.	Provide hands-on and minds-on activities, such as writing, sharing, experiment, observation, group project, and collaborative activities.
Collaborative and cooperative instruction	Interaction and communication are essential to learning since learning is primarily a social activity and participation in the social life of the school is central for learning.	Put students in groups; facilitate the process; and provide guidance, modeling, coaching, and supervision.
Multicultural instruction	Connecting experience with learning increases motivation since students learn best when they participate in activities they perceive to be useful in real life and culturally relevant.	Give students opportunities to share their experiences in real life situations in authentic contexts and prescribe activities that reflect their cultural values.
Preview and review instruction	Engage students by relating new information to prior knowledge since new knowledge is constructed on the basis of what is already understood and believed.	Preview key concepts with students to demystify false conceptions and beliefs before tapping them into the learning objective, and later review with students what they learned.
Strategic instruction	Enhancing study skills increases productivity since students learn by employing effective and flexible strategies that help them to understand, reason, memorize, extrapolate, and solve problems.	Teaching study skills, organizational strategies, coping skills, and access to resources helps students learn by developing personal strategic plan of action.
Autonomous instruction	Promoting self-management and self-regulation increases personal responsibility since students must know how to plan, or-	Allowing students to set learning goals; making sure they are working toward those goals in a timely man-

	ganize, and monitor their learning by setting learning goals for themselves and correcting their personal mistakes.	ner; showing how to develop effective strategies and when to use them; and promoting self-management, self-confidence, and self-regulation.
Retrospective instruction	Besides preview and review, going back to basics to restructure learning is necessary since prior knowledge can stand in the way of learning new concepts, and students must learn how to solve internal inconsistencies or restructure existing conceptions.	Allowing students to ask questions about any misconceptions, recognizing prior beliefs and incomplete understanding of concepts, building on existing knowledge, and prescribing meaningful hands-on and minds-on activities to validate learning.
Cognitive process instruction	To minimize memorization and maximize understanding, students need to learn how to find answers since learning is better when material is organized around general principles and explanations rather than based on the memorization of isolated facts and procedures.	Teaching students how to find the answers rather than giving them the answers is critical in developing cognitive academic skills since the process is more important than the product.
Transferring instruction	Connecting learning to experience makes learning fun and enjoyable since learning becomes more meaningful when the lessons are applied to real life situations.	Helping students transfer learning experience to real life situations or vice versa, such as a personal timeline, family traditions, favorite food, and personal childhood story. Transference can be either implications or applications, like moving from simple to complex.
Apprenticeship instruction	Spending time to practice is key to successful results since learning is a complex cognitive activity that cannot be rushed and requires considerable time and periods of practice to start building expertise in an area.	Allowing time for academic engagement increases student learning, spending time showing and modeling increases comprehension, and practicing over and over again helps students learn.
Differentiating instruction	Recognizing developmental and individual differences promotes learning in multicultural settings since students learn best when their individual differences are taken into consideration.	Using multiple approaches or differentiating instruction benefits diverse students, and introducing a wide range of materials creates learning opportunities, allowing students to pursue areas of interest and encouraging students to be who they are.
Motivational instruction	Motivating students to learn is key to successful results since learning is influenced by learner motivation, attitude, and personality and modifying these behaviors can create an academic breakthrough.	Recognizing extrinsic motivation or intrinsic motivation, acknowledging accomplishment, giving praise, encouraging learning, and promoting progress and success motivate students to succeed.

Note. Information from *How Children Learn* (Educational Practice Series-7) by S. Vosniadou, 2001, Brussels, Belgium: International Academy of Education, and *An Educational Psychology of Methods in Multicultural Classroom*, by C.T. Vang, 2010, New York: Peter Lang Publishing.

Also, keep in mind that teaching is a process that requires teachers to do ongoing planning, preparation, routine, structure, organization, lesson plan design, student activities, assessment, independent practice, and closure. Of all of these, organization is the key to making a lesson plan successful and teaching practices effective. It is important to remember that teaching has ups and downs, and teachers must learn how to weather these fluctuations to smooth out their practice.

Effective Guided Practices

Effective instruction relies heavily on the instructional process and the guided practices teachers use to convey new concepts, ideas, skills, and knowledge to the students. Learning objectives state specific learning outcomes and expectations; however, instruction and guided practices are the vehicles the teachers must use to help students attain the content area knowledge required by each academic standard. Instruction may involve a step-by-step process, a sequence of teaching, tiers of teaching, illustrations, demonstrations, instructional strategies, student activities, and examples. Guided practices are specific teaching schemes and modalities teachers use to impregnate new ideas and concepts in students. Keep in mind that creativity is what makes teachers innovative. To create meaningful instruction, teachers must know how to use detailed and concrete examples. Modeling is a process of guiding instructions through a series of graphic demonstrations and illustrations to enhance student learning. Table 12.3 presents four modeling techniques teachers can use to augment the guided practices.

Table 12.3. **Selected Modeling Techniques**

Modeling One	Modeling Two	Modeling Three	Modeling Four
1. Tell me, I will forget	1. Watch me as I do it	1. I do, you watch	1. Telling how to do
2. Show me, I will remember	2. Follow me as I do it	2. I do, you help	2. Showing how to do
3. Involve me, I will understand	3. Help me as I do it	3. I do, you tell	3. Trying how to do
	4. I help as you do it	4. You do, I tell	4. Doing how to do
	5. You do it.	5. You do, I help	5. Learning how to do
		6. You do it yourself	

Challenges of First-Year Teaching

Teaching is a process of growth, success, and survival. It is a sink or swim process. Not every new teacher will go through the exact same process or sequence in their professional development; however, most will have similar experiences as they teach and live the process. Moir (2007) described the first year or so of teaching as having five distinct phases, as shown in Figure 12.2 and explained in Table 12.4. According to Moir, new teachers move through anticipation to survival, disillusionment, rejuvenation, reflection, and then back to anticipation. Making the transition from student to becoming a teacher is critical. New teachers should learn these phases so they are not taken by surprise, and they can develop a strong framework to make their first year of teaching a positive experience rather than feeling they must sink or swim.

Figure 12.2. **Phases of first-year teaching.**

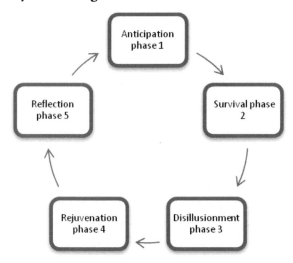

Table 12.4. **Phases of First-Year Teaching**

Anticipation (Aug.–Sept)	Survival (Sept.–Oct.)	Disillusion-ment (Oct.–Dec.)	Rejuvenation (Dec.–Apr.)	Reflection (Apr.–June)
▪ Transition from student to teacher ▪ Simulated experience to in charge person ▪ Excited and anxious to teach ▪ Expectations ▪ Management and discipline problems ▪ Real teaching ▪ Student engagement	▪ Rapid pace ▪ Bombard with issues and problems ▪ Realities of teaching ▪ Struggle to keep head above water ▪ Focused and consumed ▪ Overwhelmed with demands ▪ What really works and what does not ▪ Unfamiliar with curriculum ▪ Handle turmoil	▪ Question commitment and competence ▪ Stressful time ▪ Health issues ▪ School events, parent/teacher conferences ▪ Teacher evaluation ▪ Communication with parents ▪ Distress ▪ Self-doubts ▪ Low self-esteem ▪ Doubt professional commitment ▪ Face tough times	▪ Slow rise ▪ Improvement and adjustment ▪ Increased enjoyment ▪ Focus more on professional life ▪ Better planning ▪ Become organized and structured ▪ Leave problems behind and move on ▪ Great sense of relief ▪ Under the system better ▪ Find excitement and enjoyment ▪ See strengths and weakness in self ▪ Question and reflect on effectiveness ▪ Curriculum development ▪ Long-term planning	▪ Reflect on successes and failures over the year ▪ Plan for next year ▪ Organize curriculum, management and teaching strategies ▪ Vision emerges and think about next year ▪ Reenter the anticipation phase ▪ Expectations ▪ Plan, implement, evaluate, give feedback, and reflect ▪ Make changes or adjustments ▪ Engagement ▪ Fun activities

Beating the Probationary Period

Besides knowing the teacher contract and tenure, new teachers must learn to beat all odds during the first 2 years of probation. As mentioned earlier, coaching and mentoring are critical for new teachers. Once new teachers are hired, they must find veteran teachers to be their coaching and mentoring partners during the first 2 years. In most school districts in California, BTSA or induction programs are available and they provide invaluable support to new teachers; however, not all teachers receive supportive services.

The way probationary teachers are treated varies from district to district and state to state. In most states, collective bargaining laws protect non-tenured and tenured teachers through the course of the evaluation of their teaching performance. Becoming a member of the teacher's union is optional for newly hired teachers. Teachers should know that unionized efforts send strong messages to school districts concerning hiring, terminating, firing, and employment related disputes. Also, legal fees can be expensive; newly hired teachers may not able to afford legal counsel but unions can. Therefore, new teachers should weigh these factors when they decide whether to join the teacher's union.

During the probationary period, school principals and other administrators are required to conduct formal and informal evaluations of new teachers throughout the year as specified in their hiring contracts. Typically, school principals evaluate probationary teachers once or twice per year or every six months. The year-end evaluation is the most important one. The timeframe for evaluations should be given to probationary teachers when they begin work.

Most evaluations are formal; however, informal evaluations may be conducted in special circumstances. Formal evaluations are announced visits to the classroom and informal evaluations need not be announced. Each formal evaluation takes 20 to 25 minutes at the most. New teachers should get a copy of evaluation forms and pay close attention to all the criteria before the evaluation takes place. The criteria usually cover a range of teaching responsibilities such as management, discipline, engagement, guided practices, evaluation, closure, and independent practices. The evaluators and/or union representatives advise new teachers about their formal evaluations in writing.

Typically, school principals or administrators look for many things during the evaluation, but their professional focus hones in on three major areas: the beginning of the lesson plan, the lesson plan's instructions and guided practices, and the ending of the lesson plan. New teachers should always be ready to deliver a carefully prepared lesson plan, demonstrating that their instructional strategies and student activities are academically sound. The implementation of the plan must be well organized and well delivered.

Following each evaluation, a required formal meeting takes place of the evaluator and the probationary teacher. This meeting should be cordial and informative as well as supportive. The evaluator will discuss with the new teachers the highlights of his or her observations. The scores will be shared and supported with detailed information. The overall rating is extremely important. Even if scores are low in some areas, the overall rating may still be satisfactory. Usually, the evaluator gives the probationary teacher several constructive suggestions or recommendations to help the teacher improve. Whether the evaluation is at mid-year or at the year's end, the process is pretty much the same. New teachers may request that a union representative be present during these meetings with the principals or administrators; however, this could be a double-edged sword unless there are issues that need union involvement at the time of the evaluation.

A decision to renew the contract of or rehire a probationary teacher could be easy or difficult, depending on the results of all evaluations, the professional relationship between the teacher and the school administrators, and in many schools, compatibility of personalities and attitudes. Keeping it simple: If the school principal likes and trusts the new teacher's abilities and leadership skills, rehiring or renewal of contract is likely. However, if unresolvable personnel issues are involved in the process and the annual contract is unlikely to be renewed, the union representative will notify the probationary teacher about the decision through written or verbal communication. Sometimes, the school principal will inform the individual teacher directly.

Second-year probationary teachers should do everything they can to earn tenure; otherwise, they have to start all over in a new district. Giving someone tenure is a big decision because tenure is a life-long reward for credentialed teachers. As mentioned previously, tenured teachers are protected by due process. So, to help new teachers succeed in their probationary period, here are some suggestions:

1. Work well with the site principal.
2. Ask for his or her guidance.
3. Be flexible on the job.
4. Take the job seriously.
5. Show professional enthusiasm.
6. Be a player on the team.
7. Be aware of collegiality and teacher's roles.
8. Have a mentor or coach on the job.
9. Practice quality teaching.
10. Promote academic excellence.
11. Learn to be a follower.
12. Understand the school culture.
13. Maintain good rapport with students.
14. Work well with parents.
15. Show pleasant personal qualities.
16. Be aware of professionalism, ethics, and legal mandates.
17. Show your teaching art with creativity.
18. Demonstrate organizational skills and keep room tidy.
19. Be a good planner.
20. Be a life-long learner—teach, learn, and grow.

Keep in mind that education and politics are inseparable, and politics is part of human nature. Probationary teachers should learn to curb politics in the workplace as much as possible during the first 2 years of teaching until they are tenured.

Politics aside, it is site principals who make the final decision to hire, retain, or transfer teachers. Therefore, probationary teachers should seek coaching and mentoring from their site principals as much as possible. However, too much courting of the attention of school administrators could backfire. The best course of action is to be careful with people, choose wisely, and protect your interests by learning what is going on around you at all times. Following are some survival tips:

1. Learn to work with other educators.
2. Schools require teamwork and all kinds of players.
3. Cultivate professional relationships.

4. Learn how to fit it into the school culture.
5. Use effective communication skills.
6. Use professional courtesy.
7. Work well with colleagues and supervisors.
8. Avoid difficult people who are demanding.
9. Learn to weather ups and downs professionally.
10. Master workplace skills.

Bear in mind that the first step toward professional development and advancing one's teaching career has to be taken by the teacher. In other words, new teachers must take charge of their careers as soon as they get both feet in the door.

Managing Stress Productively

New teachers should have learned from their fieldwork experience or student practicum how stressful teaching really is. Figure 12.3 illustrates some of the pressures teachers face on a daily basis. Teaching is now considered by experts in educational psychology to be one of the most stressful occupations (Charles & Senter, 2002; Kauchak & Eggen, 2005; Evertson & Emmer, 2009; Vang, 2010). Charles and Senter (2002) differentiated between *eustress*, which they said is good for teachers, and *stress*, which is bad. They defined *eustress* as a positive pressure that occurs in the presence of interesting, challenging, yet resolvable problems, it energizes, enlivens, motivates, promotes, empowers, and excites teachers to develop professional passion in teaching. On the other hand, the researchers noted that *stress* causes distress with negative and undesirable side effects, such as an unhappy state of mind and tension.

Figure 12.3. **Pressures on teachers.**

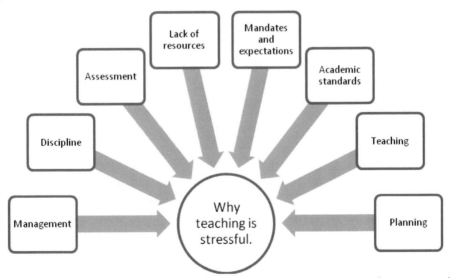

As soon as they feel stress, new teachers should take quick steps to manage the stress productively; otherwise, the number of stressors will increase exponentially. Here are some steps new teachers can take to reduce stress:

1. Plan.
2. Prepare.

3.   Organize.
4.   Prioritize.
5.   Get enough sleep.
6.   Take time to rest.
7.   Do some exercises, jog, or run.
8.   Eat healthy food.
9.   Adopt a positive attitude.
10. Take good care of your health.
11. Manage time wisely.
12. Set objectives and goals.
13. Have self-esteem, self-efficacy, and self-reliance.
14. Have a support system at home and at work.
15. Manage both personal needs and professional needs.
16. Focus on strengths, not weakness,
17. Ask questions or ask for help.
18. Be open-minded.
19. Take criticism positively and constructively.
20. Expect high performance but not perfection.
21. Learn to avoid unimportant things.
22. Learn to say no the first time.
23. Allow for privacy, quiet time, or time alone.
24. Reduce time robbers.
25. Increase time savers.

A tidy room reduces stress. A high level of stress can cause a number of negative events and feelings such as burnout, fear, dissatisfaction, demotion, powerlessness, helplessness, anxiety, impatience, impulsive behaviors, and mental incapacitation. These symptoms could be directly related to job performance and other negative side effects that may jeopardize new teachers' careers. If they notice any of these symptoms, new teachers should consider seeking professional assistance immediately before the stress becomes too much to handle.

Short-term and Long-term goals

New teachers should look for any opportunity to advance their careers. Being a classroom teacher is good and rewarding, but for some, teaching may not be a permanent career. Career changes happen all the time in the school system. Some teachers return to graduate school to earn advanced degrees in instruction, curriculum, management, and/or leadership. Others, who have earned their graduate degrees, move up to be part of the management and administrative staff, becoming coordinators, assistant principals, principals, counselors, learning directors, and grant writers.

To move up the career ladder, new teachers need to set personal and professional goals. They should think about 5 years and 10 years from now. As mentioned previously, new teachers have 5 years to clear their preliminary teaching credentials for life. Many teachers earn graduate degrees, and some earn postgraduate degrees. Setting short-term and long-term goals helps teachers become educational leaders, managers, principals, and administrators.

Just as teaching is not for everyone, neither is management. However, earning an advanced degree not only opens doors to career advancement, but it also helps teachers earn higher pay. The pay for someone with a bachelor's degree + 20 postgraduate units is lower than the pay for someone with a master's degree regardless of number of years in teaching. This is one of the reasons many teachers take college courses for professional development—not only to acquire skills and knowledge but also to qualify for a pay raise.

Furthermore, establishing professional goals should help new teachers deal more effectively with career challenges. Having goals makes it easier for them to make decisions regarding issues related to everyday life. A goal-oriented approach makes difficulties more manageable and solvable and makes the teacher more flexible and adaptable. New teachers can set goals by making lists of the things they want to learn, brainstorming the challenges or obstacles they need to overcome, and organizing specific steps to take to improve their repertoire of teaching skills. Professional growth does not happen by chance, and new teachers must take charge of their careers by developing strategic action plans to improve their teaching skills needed in the classroom. Going back to school does not have to be the goal; perhaps, one goal could be to master some simple task the new teachers need to do to take charge of their careers in order to learn how to weather the career ups and downs.

The following may provide some ideas of goals that will improve teaching practice and thus further teaching careers:

1. Perform routine tasks efficiently to prevent falling behind in teaching responsibilities.
2. Set up daily, weekly, monthly, and yearly goals.
3. Set up career goals and take specific steps to achieve them.
4. Keep up to date and informed about current issues, trends, changes, and policies in education.
5. Make a personal plan of action to manage one's stress, distress, and struggles to prevent potential burnout, turnover, voluntary resignation, and career pitfalls.
6. Maintain a professional portfolio to measure one's own progress, growth, and success throughout the year.
7. Use problems as opportunities to learn from and become a better teacher without dwelling on mistakes that can cause tremendous stress.

Figure 12.4. **Areas for establishing professional goals.**

Short-term and long-term goals could also have to do with everyday life situations, such as taking one day at a time, leaving all school problems at school but taking successes home, keeping things in perspective, taking a sensible approach to advancing and enhancing everyday activities, or keeping problems small and solving them quickly. The bottom line is to keep motivated toward achieving self-actualization as shown in Figure 12.4. Without having professional goals it is hard to imagine how new teachers can progress professionally, ethically, and academically.

Becoming a Professional Educator

It takes time and lots of professional development and growth to fulfill the role of a professional educator. The process of becoming a professional educator involves more than just acquiring skills in instructional practice, lesson plan design, management, grading papers, and prepping students for high-stakes testing. TPE standards 12 and 13 place the following legal and ethical obligations on teachers: Professional educator:

- Take responsibility for student learning outcomes
- Be aware of personal biases and values that can affect teaching and learning outcomes
- Manage time spent in teaching to ensure that academic goals are met
- Understand federal and state educational laws and procedures pertaining to the needs of ELLs, SNs, and students with disabilities
- Know child welfare laws and report reasonable suspicion of child abuse
- Maintain a non-hostile learning environment
- Understand federal and state laws to deal with violent behaviors
- Demonstrate openness to supervision and assessment of progress
- Evaluate own teaching practices and subject matter knowledge
- Seek feedback from colleagues, supervisors, and administrators
- Engage in cycles of planning, teaching, reflecting, and discerning problems
- Use feedback to improve teaching effectiveness
- Set short-term and long-term goals for professional development and growth
- Demonstrate punctuality and reliability
- Make plans for instruction, activities, and substitution during absences

Moreover, as mentioned previously, today's teachers have to be legally, ethically, and professionally literate. Professional development is the responsibility of the teachers. They should know the guiding principles of being good educators. Each teacher should ask himself or herself this question and answer it thoughtfully: What is expected of me in the classroom? Professional expectations for teachers are high. Most teachers set professional short-term and long-term goals. Teachers who are goal oriented fare better because their planning helps them clarify their thinking, their career path, and their decision making. Teachers who plan well develop a professional demeanor, master workplace skills, use time management strategies wisely, and utilize best practices in the classroom.

Teachers should learn to weather the ups and downs of education early in their careers. For example, they can plan ahead to strategize an action plan to help them get ready for evaluations by administrators. They can build their teaching confidence, use reflective teaching as a key to becoming a successful teacher, learn how to work with other educators, become a team member, and cultivate professional relationships that foster professional growth as well as career advancement.

Professional educators learn how to fit in at school and adapt themselves to be part of the cultural community. They show professional courtesy toward one another, learn how to work well with school administrators, select excellent mentors for help, watch out for difficult people and demanding individuals, and join other educators in professional affiliations. Moreover, good teachers create links between home and school. Teachers as well as students benefit from having a positive relationship with parents and legal guardians. If parents believe in and trust their children's teachers, those teachers receive fewer complaints about their management and discipline than teachers with little or no relationship with parents or legal guardians. Interestingly, parents who have good relationships with teachers are more open to ask or answer questions at parent/teacher conferences. Parents can expect many things from teachers, and without productive school-home relationships, tension can build up and communication can turn sour. Parents expect teachers to keep them up to date on items such as the following:

- School and class policies, rules, and logical consequences
- Field trips
- Guest speakers
- Curricular changes
- Homework and projects
- Grading concerns and issues
- Reading lists or books for children
- Testing dates or assessment schedules
- Student progress and success
- Behavioral problems or incident reports

In addition, professional educators should learn how to notify parents appropriately via phone calls, notes, or e-mails. In some cultures, the mother may not want to speak with teachers over the phone, and the father is the primary communicator for the family. When making a phone call to such a student's home, teachers should at least attempt to speak to the father first. Also, not all families have e-mail and not all can read English. Bilingual materials and translations should be available for bilingual parents who cannot speak English well. Dealing with parents can be sensitive, and teachers need to be courteous and professional at all times. It does not matter whether the communication is about the student or about a conflict between parents and teachers; parents always win the argument. That is the bottom line.

A Positive Multicultural Environment for All

Today's teachers must learn to be multicultural educators because the student body is like the colors of a rainbow. As mentioned previously, there are 425 dialects spoken by K–12 students in U.S. schools. In California, over 100 different languages are spoken by families of K–12 students. Nearly 80% of our public school classrooms have students who speak at least two primary languages other than English. These cultural factors are essential for teachers to understand if they are to create a multicultural classroom for all learners. Having a positive multicultural class is vital in successful teaching and learning. When students and teachers work together in a productive, sound, and cooperative learning environment, the psychosocial synergy of that positive cultural atmosphere transcends daily concerns and challenges and allows teachers to focus on student achievement and success from multicultural perspectives.

Figure 12.5. **The cultural iceberg.**

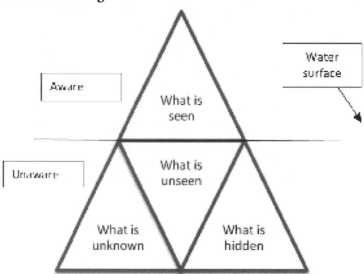

Professional educators can create a culturally responsive classroom for all learners. Wood (1999) suggested several approaches to their responsibilities that help teachers create such an environment:

1. The social curriculum is as important as the academic curriculum. This inextricable connection is essential for cognitive development and emotional growth for all children.
2. How children learn is as important as what children learn. This approach includes teacher-centered instruction and student-centered activities.
3. The greatest cognitive growth occurs through social interaction. This approach suggests the use of cooperation and competition as well as cooperative learning to foster learning.
4. There is a set of social skills that children need in order to be successful academically and socially. This approach allows teachers to teach other skills besides academia, such as CARES: cooperation, assertion, responsibility, empathy, and self-control.
5. Knowing the children we teach is as important as knowing the content we teach. This approach suggests making connections between teaching and learning with real life experiences.
6. Knowing the parents of the children we teach is as important as knowing the children. This approach links the school and the home to work together.
7. Teachers and administrators must model the social and academic skills they wish to teach their students. This approach explains the importance of providing quality education to all learners regardless of their socioeconomic backgrounds.
8. The quality of education must be as important as the quality of language of instruction. This approach emphasizes that it is not the quality of education that matters most but the quality of instruction.
9. Children's coping skills are as important as the study skills they need. This approach suggests that teachers should teach both coping and study skills to children.
10. The goal of learning is as important as the goal of teaching. This approach emphasizes the fact that the quality of teaching and learning go hand in hand.

What teachers learn about most of the cultures of their students is just the tip of the cultural iceberg. In other words, teachers may be aware of cultural issues "above the water" but unaware of all cultural matters hidden beneath the surface as illustrated in Figure 12.5. There is so much to be learned, and teachers should take the time to learn as much as they can; creating a culturally responsive classroom can be challenging.

Making the Classroom a Productive Place for Learning

Each teacher is assigned to a single classroom for the entire year and, perhaps, for many years to come. The teacher must make that classroom conducive to learning. A productive learning environment serves many purposes; the three most important purposes, regardless of the grade level, subject matter, or nature of the class, are that it facilitates quality teaching, student activity, and health and safety. Teachers must create a well-organized, tidy, and orderly classroom to give students and teachers a pleasant and decent work place. They do so when they do the following:

1. Evaluate the physical features of the room.
2. Arrange the room to meet teaching and learning needs.
3. Create effective seat arrangements.
4. Organize work areas.
5. Carefully check for teaching and other supplies.
6. Create student-centered space.
7. Save space for a bulletin board.
8. Decorate the room academically.
9. Find a space to display student work.
10. Check for storage, bookshelves, countertops, etc.
11. Designate a place for student supplies, teaching supplies, etc.
12. Designate a place for unused materials.

To make the classroom a more productive place, teachers need to forge positive relationships with all students. They need to learn students' names as quickly as possible, model good behaviors right away, create rules and logical consequences, clearly communicate their expectations, and establish norms for daily routines. Developing positive and warm relationships with students and maintaining good rapport with them save time and energy later on. Students have certain expectations of teachers; however, teachers must set high expectations for all students. Teachers should gather academic information about each student early to learn about their academic abilities.

Remember that cultural differences and ability differences affect teaching and learning in the multicultural classroom. Teachers must prepare strategic action plans to deal with reluctant learners, struggling students, ELLs, SNs, students with ADD and ADHD, and disabled students early in order to avoid potential problems. The higher the students go academically, the greater the challenges teachers will face. To minimize disruptions and distractions during class, teachers need to teach good citizenship and model acceptable behaviors that make all learners feel valuable. They can create learning opportunities that help all learners improve their self-discipline, self-management, self-control, and self-image.

Teachers who respect their students earn respect from their students. Respect grows as teachers recognize the meanings of student diversity given by prospective student teachers, shown in Table 12.5.

Table 12.5. **Meanings of the Word *Diversity***

	D	I	V	E	R	S	I	T	Y
1	Different	Individuals	Value	Each other	Regardless of	Skin	Intellect	Talents or	Years
2	Different	Independent	Views that	Everyone	Respects	Supports and	Idolizes to	Teach	Youngsters
3	Direct	Individuals to	Value	Education with	Respect	Support	Integrity	Toward	Young & old
4	Dynamic	Intelligence	Values	Embracing and	Reaching out to	Students'	Insatiable needs for the	Total	Yarn
5	Diverse	Individuals	View	Everyone with	Respect to	Strengthen	Ideas	Toward	Yourself & others
6	Develop	Ideas	Values and	Establish	Respect	Support for	Individuals	That are different from	You
7	Direct	Impact by	Voicing	Equality	Respect and	Sensitivity	In	To	Yourself
8	Develop	Individual tolerance	Value	Equality for all that includes	Religions	Social awareness	Ideas	Traditions to fulfill the hearts	Yearning
9	Display	Inner	Value	Especially	Regarding	Someone's	Ideas	Talents and	Youth
10	Division	Is	Very	Expensive and will	Revive	Serious	Injustice	Toward	Yourself

A productive classroom should have clear guiding principles regarding motivation to encourage students to try their very best. Teachers can motivate students to work hard by using extrinsic and intrinsic rewards, praise, and appealing and tangible rewards that inspire students to learn. Along the same line, teachers must exhibit positive attitudes that foster learning and student success. As mentioned previously, teacher attitudes and personalities are the most important factors influencing student learning outcomes. Most teachers today employ teacher-centered instruction and have little or no time for questioning during teaching. But questioning helps students improve their understanding and comprehension, provides opportunities for success, and provides opportunities for enjoyment. Of course, teachers can do more to improve the learning climate, and the more creative teachers are, the more students feel a sense of belonging in a positive and productive learning environment, the more eager they will be to learn.

Taking a Proactive Approach Toward Management

Management and discipline are an ongoing process rather than product, and problems will always be challenging for most teachers no matter how many years they have taught in the classroom. There is no single solution to all management problems, but there are solutions. Each year a teacher receives a new group of students, and each student brings different challenges, needs, and demands to the classroom. As early as possible, teachers must determine why their students misbehave. Students misbehave during class for a variety of reasons: poor instruction, lack of engaging student activity, too much free time, too noisy a room, too boring a lesson, and lessons that are too fragmented.

Besides rules, consequences, and procedural guidelines, common sense strategies can be used to prevent student misbehaviors. For example, teachers' actions should be firm, pleasant, assertive, straightforward, logical, motivational, and fair. At the same time, teachers must learn to avoid management and discipline pitfalls. Keep this saying in mind: "Pain is temporary, but pride is forever." In other words, misbehaviors come and go, but inappropriate disciplinary actions could cost teachers a career. Of course, teachers will make mistakes, but the severity of the consequences depends on what kind of mistakes teachers make. Some mistakes are unacceptable: losing patience, making threats, using corporal punishment, attacking students, and abusing students sexually. Teachers must maintain their composure at all times. To get off to a good start, teachers should follow the basic steps for developing their managerial approach outlined in Table 12.6.

Table 12.6. **Steps for Developing Classroom Norms**

	Step	Examples
1.	Create a classroom discipline plan	Choose general rules that apply all day: rules for following directions, reinforcements, tangible rewards, privileges, logical consequences, hierarchies for rule infractions (mild warning, moderate criteria, and negative consequences), age and grade appropriateness
2.	Share classroom discipline plan with school administrators	Seek administrative support and feedback, prevent future inconsistencies, comply with school and district policy, fair, reasonable, enforceable, logical, educational, motivational
3.	Teach classroom rules to students	Review rules and consequences with students, model good examples, make sure students have clear understanding of the general expectations, stress rules as guiding principles for all, make a discipline plan poster and post it in visible location
4.	Implement classroom discipline plan	Daily schedules, daily routines, specific directions, procedural guidelines, group activities, task activities, transitions, areas needing procedures; remind students of rules and consequences; apply, adjust, and make changes
5.	Review classroom discipline plan	Do ongoing assessment of discipline plan to ensure effectiveness, make periodic changes to accommodate students' needs, allow flexibility, evaluate rules and consequences criteria, review infraction problems

The goal of management and discipline is to enhance the effectiveness of teaching and learning. To achieve this goal, teachers must learn how to allow students to improve their self-control, self-discipline, self-management, and self-motivation. Teachers should enforce all codes of conduct, classroom rules, and procedural guidelines to maintain order in the classroom and, at the same time, they must make sure things are running smoothly and efficiently. For example, they must have effective transitional activities whenever there is a gap between lessons, rearrange the seating chart if there is an ongoing problem, and monitor students to avoid off-task behaviors as well as cheating. Many teachers spend a large amount of time disciplining, managing, and controlling the class, but they fail to spend time with students to enjoy the work and have fun with them. As mentioned previously, teaching must be enjoyable and produce positive learning if teachers are to remain in their professions. Laughter relieves stress; it is a natural medicine. That is why people go to comedy clubs to listen to jokes and laugh with friends. Teaching is not a comedy club, but it should be fun and enjoyable, too.

Nonetheless, teachers who think they can have zero problems in their classes will find their days full of stress, disappointment, and agonies because children play, talk, fight, argue, and disagree; these behaviors are in their nature. Teachers cannot stroke students like animal trainers stroke animals to induce positive behaviors. If teachers were allowed to give perks or strokes like animal trainers, all students would be waiting for such perks, but both children and animals misbehave if teachers or trainers run out of treats. To minimize disruptions and distractions caused by misbehaviors, teachers need to develop sound discipline principles and strategic action plans to deal with problems. Teachers can identify three basic types of behaviors—behaviors they can ignore, behaviors that require a mild warning or reminder, and behaviors that require moderate or negative consequences.

At the same time, teachers must control their reactions and maintain a professional demeanor when disciplining students. The ripple effect can be either negative or positive, and the aversive consequences could be substantial when teachers lose their composure in front of students. So, in other words, teachers must solve problems instead of punishing children. Teachers may put themselves in harm's way if they fail to take proper action to break up a fight or prevent potential violence in the classroom. Some situations can get out of hand and need to be referred to school administrators for proper action. Teachers cannot deal with all problems and all students because they have so much to do in the classroom. Their plates are always full of responsibilities. Teachers are not masters of students; they are teachers and learners at the same time. They must reflect on what makes students misbehave in class. Questioning oneself is not bad at all; actually self-assessment that reflects upon one's successes, failures, strengths, and weaknesses is helpful. Remember, the more teachers practice, the more effective and strong they will become.

Using Sound Discipline to Minimize Disruptions in Class

It takes time to practice what is working and to know what is not. New teachers should start as soon as possible establishing sound disciplinary techniques in the classroom to minimize disruptions. As mentioned previously, natural consequences, arbitrary consequences, and logical consequences are practical tools teachers can use to support their management and student discipline needs. However, it is not what tools teachers use that matters; it is how teachers use these tools that matters the most.

Teachers should design sound discipline principles or approaches based on the specific needs in the classroom. As they apply the Golden Rule, teachers must take all factors involving student diversity into careful consideration when devising any type of discipline. The following approaches will help establish sound discipline:

1. Health and safety in the classroom is the number one priority.
2. Be proactive to prevent misbehaviors at all times.
3. Try to manage, correct, modify, and handle most student discipline effectively in class.
4. Serious problems, issues, situations, or incidents must be referred to the administrators.

5. Provide careful supervision to students with special needs, such as those with ADD, ADHD, ED, CD, and young students who may not understand all expectations.

6. Enforce and reinforce classroom rules, policies, procedures, and expectations with consistency, fairness, logical consequences, purposeful approaches, reasonable efforts, explanations, and simple forms of communication.

7. Apply appropriate consequences for the offense.

8. Maintain accurate records of behavior incidents, disciplinary actions, interventions, and referrals for all students for future reference.

9. Keep personal property and valuable items away from students.

10. Student discipline could become a legal matter, and all students have rights to due process.

11. Work for the best interests of the child by cooperating with all involved parties.

12. Never abandon the classroom at any time.

13. Never leave students unsupervised at any time.

14. Never fail to report injuries involving a child.

15. Never conceal valuable information to cover up student misdeeds for personal gain.

Sound discipline protects both the students and the teacher at the same time. One ingredient new teachers can add to sound discipline is character education. The six pillars of character education are illustrated in Figure 12.6. Understanding these pillars is a valuable source for improving student behaviors, but no one actually teaches them directly to students. Teachers should look for ways to incorporate them in their own behavior and in their teaching.

Figure 12.6. The six pillars of character education.

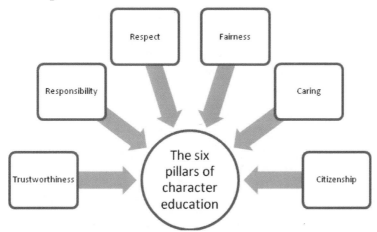

New teachers must learn to differentiate four categories of student misbehaviors: (a) behaviors they can ignore, (b) behaviors for which they must give a mild warning or reminder, (c) behaviors to which they must apply logical consequences, and (d) behaviors for which they must refer students to the office in order to protect other students. Teachers cannot prevent all disruptions and misbehaviors in class. But teachers who are acquainted with the basics of school policies, laws, and education codes know how to handle student misbehaviors and how to discipline students in ways that are beneficial to all involved parties.

Becoming a Knowledgeable and Skillful Teacher

New teachers want to become dynamic and authoritative educators. Of course, that is not easy and cannot happen overnight. But nothing is impossible if teachers believe in themselves and set high professional goals. As the Chinese philosopher Lao-tzu once said, "A journey of a thousand miles begins with a single step." This quotation should inspire teachers to put their minds and hearts into becoming the best they can be. George S. Counts once explained, "In the course of history, education has served every purpose and doctrine contrived by man.... If it is to serve the cause of human freedom, it must be explicitly designed for that purpose."

Only those who teach will appreciate these quotations because becoming dynamic and authoritative teachers is an odyssey, a quest to achieve a noble goal. Reaching the ultimate dream of teaching does not happen by accident but through a course of deliberate action. It takes a series of intentional acts to create a productive, active, and positive learning environment in which students can self-manage their learning actions, academic progress, and learning opportunities as they work with purpose that supports their cognitive development and emotional well-being. Of course, to reach their goals teachers must be clinically trained in how to design, deliver, and assess effective teaching and learning with the appropriateness of academic instruction that is beneficial to both teachers and students.

Dynamic teachers plan effective instruction ahead of time, laying out a blueprint for teaching practices that will bring the highest quality to their students. Wise teachers set as a goal that all learners will actively participate in an active learning community, and they plan instructional practices in a step-by-step fashion so students will learn through the sequence of teaching. As mentioned previously, teachers plan daily, weekly, monthly, by the unit, by the term, and yearly. Each plan serves a purpose in teaching and learning. For example, good teachers develop teaching plans to assess and engage students' prior knowledge; to adapt instruction to accommodate the needs of ELLs, SNs, and students with learning disabilities; and to devise activities that are appealing to students. TPE standards and TPA tasks require that new teachers know how to use resources that take students beyond the text, such as realia, visual aids, placards, manipulatives, hands-on and minds-on activities, and online resources. In their planning, teachers have to think of how they can reach out to less-proficient learners, ELLs, SNs, and new arrivals, each of whom poses unique challenges to instructional practice. Wise teachers develop back-up plans ahead of time for meeting the needs of these kinds of students.

After planning, the next step is to deliver effective instruction that will benefit all learners. As mentioned previously, teacher's attitudes toward the subject matter, students, lessons, content area, and delivery are crucial in the implementation process. A teacher's enthusiasm may motivate students to learn; a teacher's approach can make instruction relevant to learning; a teacher's ability to engage background knowledge helps instructional practice; a teacher's creativity can incorporate and integrate high-level thinking skills; and a teacher's adaptability enables the teacher to meet students' learning styles in meaningful ways. As Charles and Senter (2002) explained, the correlation between a student's active learning role and retention of information received during instruction is significant in determining the effectiveness of teaching as shown in Table 12.7.

In delivering instruction, teachers may want to examine Bloom's (1956) taxonomy as it relates to thinking processes. In the cognitive domain, the taxonomy has six levels, as displayed in Table 12.8, progressing from lower to higher orders of thinking. At each level, students respond to instructional practices with actions, products, academic skills, and vocabulary skills. Not all instruction is geared to all six levels, and in most cases, teachers bring students to only the three lowest levels. However, this does not mean that students cannot achieve at all six levels, and teachers should gear their practices toward helping students achieve at all levels of thinking.

Table 12.7. **Correlation Between Active Learning Role and Retention**

Role	Retention	Possible Explanation
Reading	10%	Students retain only what is relevant to their real-life experiences or interests.
Listening, or hearing	20%	Students retain only what is interesting, amazing, and exciting.
Seeing, or vision	30%	Students retain only the highlights of scenes, actions, and episodes they like.
Combining listening and seeing or hearing and vision	40%	Students retain only their favorite parts that are relevant to their personal life experiences and what they can remember by encoding and decoding the messages.
Engaging in discussion	70%	Discourse, conversation, or discussion allows students to retain more information by engaging in critical thinking and analysis of the situation.
Experiencing, practicing, or doing hands-on activity	90%	Experiencing, doing, practicing, engaging in hands-on activity or firsthand experience enhances students' knowledge, skills, critical thinking, analysis, and logical application.

Note. Information from *Elementary Classroom Management* (3rd ed.) by C. M. Charles and G. W. Senter, 2002, Boston: Allyn and Bacon.

Table 12.8. **Bloom's Taxonomy Cognitive Domain Levels**

Level	Basic Skills	Word Skills	Student Activities
Knowledge	Prior knowledge, experiences, context-embedded approach, real life experiences, personal ideas	Telling, showing, describing, knowing, identifying, seeing, listing, collecting	Naming, recalling, knowing places, sharing, concluding, evaluating, classifying, communicating
Comprehension	Context-reduced approach, predication, evaluation, questioning, translating, logical, arbitrary, social, physical, construction	Concluding, summarizing, evaluating, interpreting, translating, analyzing, comparing, contrasting, estimating, discussing, inferring, differentiating, sorting	Engaging in process, using critical thinking, classifying information, making inferences, translating ideas, analyzing differences, comparing similarities, describing results
Application	Approaches, methods, strategies, modalities, contextualization, styles, process, products, schema	Examining, solving, applying, completing, experimenting, classifying, relating, showing, illustrating, modifying, investigating, strategizing, sorting	Puzzling, assembling, sequencing, constructing, combining, diagramming, mapping, webbing, solving, justifying, criticizing

Analysis	Parts to whole approach, investigation, discovery, examination, conclusion, generalization, context-embedded approach, context-reduced approach	Organizing, ordering, explaining, elaborating, analyzing, separating, connecting, dividing, comparing, selecting, classifying, inferring, examining, criticizing, disputing, refuting	Experimenting, sequencing, dissecting, categorizing, classifying, charting, graphing, spreadsheet, outlining, diagramming, mapping, concept, comprehending, understanding, acknowledging
Synthesis	Constructivism approach, application, creativity, evaluation, predication, generalizing, conclusion, knowledge base	Testing, examining, proving, planning, designing, inventing, composing, preparing, combining, generalizing, arranging, performing	Composing, compiling, combining, constructing, inventing, predicting, assembling, solving, concluding, comparing, evaluating, extrapolating, separating
Evaluation	Theoretical approach, principles, application, assessment, analysis, differentiation, discerning, reasoning, rationalizing	Applying, deciding, assessing, testing, measuring, elaborating, interpreting, translating, recommending, suggesting, judging, selecting, combining, discriminating, ranking, rating, grading	Categorizing, evaluating, justifying, concluding, criticizing, prioritizing, investigating, recommending, classifying, sorting, communicating, relating, proving, discriminating, characterizing

One way to stimulate learning is to use technology for part of instruction. Most classrooms today are equipped with a number of technological devices such as a computer, wireless internet service, and smart boards. Teachers can easily access online resources to enhance instructional practice. They can make effective electronic presentations that include video clips, animation, or real people. Students like electronic applications because they are entertaining and intriguing, and they stimulate their critical thinking. However, electronic lesson plans or technology cannot take the place of a real teacher. Students need to have human interactions to stimulate real and long-lasting learning. Electronic teaching is temporary, but real learning from real teachers lasts a lifetime. Moreover, teachers can design independent practices to enhance learning. Wise teachers usually prescribe independent work, worksheets, or handouts that are appealing to students and inspire learning. They use collaborative activities to boost cooperative learning and assign meaningful homework for further practice to sharpen content area skills.

As part of guided inquiry instruction, teachers can capture students' thoughts with questions and answers by engaging prior knowledge and real life experiences before tapping into the lesson plan's learning objective. Playing games, such as bingo, double jeopardy, wheel of fortune, and hangman, makes students curious and excited. Academic games can also be used to retain information through the process of reviewing main ideas. Wise teachers strategize action plans to help students master or grasp concepts by teaching study skills that promote academic success and, at the same time, create helpful study guides to maximize learning potential. The bottom line is that the teacher's creativity will benefit diverse learners in the multicultural classroom.

Assessment of Students' Progress

To consistently deliver quality teaching, beginning teachers, at the very least, must know how to assess students' progress. If teachers have not assessed their students regularly, they may find them behind at the end of the term and discover that it is very difficult to catch them up. Ongoing assessment is challenging, but it is also necessary. The only way teachers know how much their students have or have not learned, how well they have mastered the concepts, is through assessment. Many forms of assessment are available to teachers. New teachers must know two main types of assessments: formative and summative assessments.

Formative assessment is used primarily to provide meaningful information on student learning that teachers can use to adjust their instructional practices and enhance student learning. Formative assessment can be done either formally or informally. Informal assessment consists of practices such as questioning during instruction, thumbs up or down, yes or no answers, check lists, or simple observation. On the other hand, formal assessment is conducted through paper-and-pencil tests, quizzes, small white board drills, exercises, independent practice, and homework assignments.

Summative assessment is used to evaluate student learning, progress, and acquisition of content knowledge from the lessons taught to students. The purpose of summative assessment is not to give teachers information to help them improve instruction but rather to measure students' learning of the material the teachers delivered in class. Summative assessment focuses on student retention of information.

New teachers should also be familiar with different instruments used in assessments, particularly authentic assessments and alternative assessments. Basically, authentic assessments have to do with activities associated with real life content or experiences. A student may be asked to perform a task that demonstrates acquisition of a skill. Academic alternative assessments are measures that are not traditional tests; they include portfolios, journals, holistic grading, student products, performances, group tests, presentations, peer evaluations, self-evaluations, case studies, individual projects, and extracurricular activities.

Although ongoing assessment is extremely important, teachers must at the very least understand why students fail tests. They may fail for any number of reasons other than lack of knowledge or competence, such as language barriers, poor study skills, low comprehension level, inadequate language skills, and cognitive factors. Teachers may be responsible for some test failures if (a) the assessment is poorly designed, (b) the students are poorly prepared, or (c) the instructional practices were poor. If new teachers can fix these three items, their students will perform better on tests.

Assessing is time consuming. However, without knowing how students are faring in class, teachers can easily be off target and therefore not align instruction with learning needs. That would leave students who are falling behind to fend for themselves. Many of the students who fall through the cracks cannot help themselves—they are the victims of disservice. Just as crops will grow where water flows, students will learn where teachers teach, show, and involve them.

In terms of summative assessment, CST prepping and testing are quite common in today's schools, especially in California. The Academic Performance Index (API), with its rankings based on students' total scores on the CST, drives school curricula. Normal API rankings range from 200 to 1,000 with a state medium of 800. STAR program results, which are reports of results from California standardized tests, indicate a student's academic standing and success and predict the student's language proficiency level—far below basic, below basic, basic, proficient, or advanced. Scores that indicate these proficiency levels in the different content areas of the CST are shown in Table 12.9.

New teachers must learn how to interpret these psychometrics; otherwise, the results could be misleading to teachers as well as students and parents.

Table 12.9. CST Proficiency Level Scores

Proficiency Level	Language Arts	Mathematics	History	Science
Advanced	392–600	418–600	400–600	399–600
Proficient	350–391	350–417	350–399	350–398
Basic	300–349	300–349	300–349	300–349
Below basic	263–299	247–299	275–299	269–299
Far below basic	150–262	150–246	150–274	150–268

In addition, new teachers must be familiar with the CELDT scores for ELL, LEP, and FEP students. Tables 12.10, 12.11, and 12.12 show the scores used by school districts in California to determine the proficiency levels of these students in the tested areas of listening and speaking, reading, and writing at the different grade levels. The CELDT scores for each proficiency level are much higher than the STAR scores for the corresponding level; however, the constructs of the two tests are different.

Table 12.10. CELDT Listening and Speaking Proficiency Level Scores, Grades K-12

Proficiency Level	K	1	2	3-5	6–8	9–12
Beginning	220–408	220–419	220–452	220–437	220–437	220–433
Early intermediate	414–456	424–467	456–491	442–479	441–480	438–481
Intermediate	460–504	471–515	495–535	483–522	484–521	484–522
Early advanced	509–544	521–555	544–568	529–558	528–557	526–562
Advanced	556–710	587–710	587–710	571–710	571–710	571–710

Source: California English Language Development Test (CELDT): Explaining and using 2010–2011 summary results, California Department of Education, 2011, pp. 14–16.

Table 12.11. CELDT Reading Proficiency Levels, Grades 2–12

Proficiency Level	2	3–5	6–8	9–12
Beginning	340–434	340–460	340–459	340–455
Early intermediate	440–474	466–496	487–498	466–498
Intermediate	479–509	501–529	503–529	502–532
Early advanced	515–538	536–554	534–560	537–563
Advanced	556–630	567–640	567–650	569–650

Source: California English Language Development Test (CELDT): Explaining and using 2010–2011 summary results, California Department of Education, 2011, pp. 14–16.

Table 12.12. CELDT Writing Proficiency Levels, Grades 2–12

Proficiency Level	2	3–5	6–8	9–12
Beginning	280–405	280–441	280–439	280–441
Early intermediate	418–462	448–486	447–483	448–483
Intermediate	468–506	492–528	488–522	488–528
Early advanced	512–536	537–571	530–572	536–568
Advanced	544–640	587–690	588–700	587–700

Source: California English Language Development Test (CELDT): Explaining and using 2010–2011 summary results, California Department of Education, 2011, pp. 14–16.

Trends in Teaching

New teachers should be aware of current trends in K–12 education. Right up front, new teachers may have some information on pressing issues and topics that are of particular concern in public education, such as bilingual curricula, sex education, religion, diversity, disabilities, history of gays and lesbians, and multicultural education. But when they enter the classroom, they encounter more immediate matters, such as management and discipline problems, individualized education programs, testing, assessing, reporting, curriculum design, resources, standards, and preparation. There are so many things of which teachers should be aware, but not all of them have direct impact on their instructional practices. New teachers should pay more attention to those items that relate to or may interfere with their daily professional obligations.

Today's teachers face nearly insurmountable challenges when they try to provide quality education to students who are not native speakers of English. In fact, the majority of teachers are monolingual. The current budget crisis has eliminated many paraprofessionals who speak different languages and dialects, and that leaves teachers with the tough assignment of dealing with this group of students. Of the 3.2 million LEP students in the U.S., nearly 1.5 million attend public schools in California. And California houses another 1 million FEP students. On top of that, 5.2 million students in the country have some kind of learning disability, and nearly half are in California. Neither California nor the nation at large has enough special education teachers to satisfy the requirements of the federal Individuals with Disabilities Education Improvement Act (IDEIA). Nearly 70 percent of students with disabilities are being taught by unqualified teachers who seriously lack clinical and professional preparation for the task. The lack of adequately trained educational personnel to meet the needs of language-minority students and students with disabilities has direct negative impacts on teaching.

Multicultural education is going to continue to be a huge concern in K–12 education because state mandates seem to recognize more of the needs and challenges of ELLs and SNs. Especially in California, parents of minority students contend for equality in public education for their children and bring legal challenges demanding better education for children of low socioeconomic status. Currently, the California Commission on Teacher Credentialing (CCTC) requires pedagogical adaptations for ELL and SN students. Table 12.13 lists some of the most important multicultural issues new teachers are likely to face. The table frames each issue as a true or false statement so new teachers can consider the matter carefully and think of how they are going to address the academic needs of ELL and SN students in order to meet state mandates.

Table 12.13. **Selected Multicultural Issues**

True	False	Issue
		1. Generally, cultural differences are apparent in how children of diverse backgrounds learn, interact, communicate, and behave in the classroom.
		2. It is a public perception that discontinuity between home and school cultures has a significant effect on school success for students of color.
		3. In some cultures and/or some families, literacy is an acculturating factor embedded in their daily lives to promote the value of education.
		4. Parental goals and attitudes toward learning have a significant effect on school success for children of diverse backgrounds.
		5. Contemporary school curricula, classroom environment, teaching strategies, management, and discipline relate well to the academic needs and cultural learning styles of students from diverse socioeconomic statuses.

		6.	It is a public perception that the home language has a significant influence on school dropout.
		7.	Parental poverty level is still considered the primary factor in school success for children of diverse backgrounds.
		8.	The learning styles of students of diverse backgrounds may be at odds with those of the traditional U.S. school because of cultural mismatches and deficits.
		9.	Nationally, all children should learn about the beliefs, values, traditions, social norms, and contributions of other people in a pluralistic society.
		10.	Practically, school teachers should be colorblind and become multicultural educators for all children of diverse backgrounds.

In the U.S., literacy is a growing national concern, and federal, state, and local government officials put great pressure on teachers to raise literacy rates. Expectations are high for teachers as well as students. More testing is being required for students in public schools. Each year, teachers spend nearly two months preparing students for taking high-stakes tests. In addition, teachers are required to perform benchmark testing and instructional assessments. The goal is to improve literacy; however, pockets of low literacy have been present for years, and they will not change overnight. Nevertheless, teachers share the blame for low literacy and the responsibility to increase literacy. The No Child Left Behind Act of 2001 put tremendous pressure on state policy makers to narrow the academic achievement gap between the highest and the lowest students. This act fails to provide sufficient funding to schools but requires schools to recruit, train, and hire highly qualified teachers for the classrooms. So far, the legislation has not resulted in equitable distribution of resources and quality teachers in the current system.

As mentioned previously, the nation is facing a national crisis in meeting the needs of minority students, retaining teachers, and stopping teacher turnover. Teacher turnover is increasing, and a teacher shortage is looming. That means this nation needs teachers, perhaps hundreds of thousands of new teachers. Without them, public education will crumble as students are taught by less qualified teachers, underprepared paraprofessionals, and interns who lack the necessary clinical training. All this leads to one solid conclusion: public education in this nation badly needs reform. Restructuring is needed in the areas of finance, governance, accountability, teacher preparation, academic excellence, and literacy.

Technology is going to be a big factor in public education. In higher education, more online courses are being offered from the perspective of doing business. K–12 education is one of biggest businesses in the nation. Each year billions of dollars are spent on public education. America has the richest system in the world but not the best system in the world. If the current trends in K–12 education hold, online courses soon will be considered to reduce the costs of public education. In other words, although more teachers are needed now, in the future, perhaps, fewer teachers will be needed when technology is widely available to students.

Current budget crises in California and elsewhere have caused teachers fear and consternation. Funds for K-12 education have been cut substantially, by hundreds of millions across the board. Many school districts are struggling financially. In California alone, thousands of teachers have received lay-off notices, and many are out of a job because of tax revenue shortfalls. This trend is likely to continue at least for the next few years.

Furthermore, the theory of constructivism has been around for decades and is making its way to the classroom. Today's practices pretty much reflect the direct instruction model; however, that model does not fit all students. Millions of students do not benefit from this teacher-centered instruction model. Now some schools are considering replacing direct instruction with SIOP or RTI. The real problem is not the fault of teachers who have been told to do their jobs with a failing method of instruction, but teachers share the responsibility to find solutions that work. Keep in mind that public education is driven not only by federal, state, and local mandates and requirements but also by data- or research-based policies.

In the early 1980s, Gardner's landmark book *Frames of Mind* introduced the idea of multiple intelligences to the world; since then, that concept has shaped teaching, learning, management, and discipline. New teachers, at the very least, should take the notion of multiple intelligences into careful consideration when teaching in a pluralistic society. They must discard the Bell Curve concept that undermines equality and equal opportunity in public education.

America has changed over time, moving from the concept of a melting pot to multiculturalism, to a pluralistic society, to a salad bowl, and finally to the concept of a rainbow. Just as American life has undergone a myriad of changes and problems, so has the American public school system. The proliferation of violence and gang-related activities in society has made its way into the educational system. Schools are not free of gangs, drugs, violence, and abuse. Each year, teachers are arrested for committing crimes against children, and many children are affected by violence and gang activities. Today, bullying is a national crisis and teasing is a school crisis. Hundreds of thousands of children are hurt by inhumane acts. Teachers, as role models, must protect children from harm from others or themselves.

Perhaps, this section has provided some intriguing 21st-century issues for new teachers to consider in preparing themselves to look to the future as they become the next generation of teachers. Good luck!

Summing Up

This chapter discussed survival tips for beginning teachers to help prepare them for the classroom. The tips give teachers a quick reference to teaching practices, phases of first-year teaching, multicultural issues, assessment, professional teaching, and issues affecting public education. Much more is required of teachers today than in the past because of new laws and mandates and the diverse needs and abilities of students. The information in this chapter is meant to reassure teachers about what they really need to know to prepare themselves for real teaching. Transitioning from simulated experiences to real life teaching can be frightening and nerve-wracking because of high expectations and difficult challenges.

New teachers are not expected to know everything, but at the very least, they must know what it takes to be a real teacher in front of diverse learners who may not know how to read or understand how to obey rules. It takes time to train students, and training children is not like training animals to behave. Teachers' hands are tied with obligations and legal responsibilities. Moreover, teachers cannot expect students to behave like their own children at home. Being a parent is not the same thing as being a professional teacher. The parental role is based on natural and biological rights and restricted by state laws. On the other hand, the teachers' role is based on privileges given by the state. Teachers cannot play the parents' roles in the classroom.

Public education is a rather complex field in which to work. New teachers must maintain their professional, ethical, and legal standards as they prepare themselves to become professional educators, part of the next generation of teachers.

REFERENCES

Airasian, P. W. (2001). *Classroom management: Concepts and applications* (4th ed.). New York: McGraw-Hill.

Alberti, R. L. (1977). *Assertiveness: Innovations, applications, issues.* San Luis Obispo, CA: Impact.

American Institute for Research. (2006, February 21). *Five-year study of Proposition 227 finds no conclusive evidence favoring one instructional approach for English learners* (Press release). Washington, DC: Author.

Andrew, M. D., & Jelmberg, J. R. (2010). *How teachers learn: An educational psychology of teacher preparation.* New York: Peter Lang Publishing.

Banks, J. A. (2002). *An introduction to multicultural education* (3rd ed.). Boston: Allyn & Bacon.

Blair, J. (2000). AFT urges new tests, expanded training for teachers. *Education Week, 19*(32), 11.

Bloom, B. (1956). *Taxonomy of educational objectives: Handbook I: Cognitive domain.* New York: McKay.

Bronfenbrenner, U. (1989). Ecological systems theory. In R. Vasta (Ed.), *Annals of child development* (vol. 6) (pp. 187–249). Greenwich, CT: JAI Press.

Bruner, J. (1966). *Toward a theory of instruction.* Cambridge, MA: Harvard University Press.

Burden, P. R. (2003). *Classroom management: Creating a successful learning community* (2nd ed.). New York: Wiley & Sons.

Burden, P. R., & Byrd, D. M. (2003). *Methods for effective teaching* (3rd ed.). Boston: Pearson Education.

California Department of Education. (2005–2006). *Number of teachers by ethnicity 1981 to 2004.* Retrieved from http://www.cde.ca.gov/ds/sd/dr/ethteach.asp

California Department of Education. (2010). *Standardized Testing and Reporting (STAR) program: Summary of 2010 results.* Sacramento: Author.

California Department of Education. (2011). *California English Language Development Test (CELDT): Explaining and using 2010–2011 summary results.* Retrieved from http://www.cde.ca.gov/ta/tg/el/ documents/celdtsmryrslts2011.pdf

Centers for Disease Control and Prevention. (2008). School-associated student homicides—United States, 1992–2008: *Mortality and Morbidity Weekly Report, 57*(2), 33–36.

Centers for Disease Control and Prevention. (2010a). Youth risk behavior surveillance—United States, 2009: Surveillance summaries. *Mortality and Morbidity Weekly Report, 59*, SS-5

Centers for Disease Control and Prevention. 2010b. *Youth violence: Facts at a glance.* Retrieved from http://www.cdc.gov/violenceprevention/ pdf/yv-datasheet-a.pdf

Charles, C. M., & Senter, G. W. (2002). *Elementary classroom management* (3rd ed.). Boston: Allyn and Bacon.

Charles, C. M. & Senter, G. W. (2012). *Elementary classroom management* (6th ed.). Boston: Pearson Education.

Cooper, J. M. (1999). The teacher as a reflective decision maker. In J. M. Cooper (Ed.), *Classroom teaching skills* (6th ed.) (pp. 1–19). Boston: Houghton Mifflin.

Council of Chief State School Officers. (2010). *The INTASC model core teaching standards.* Retrieved from http://www.ccsso.org /Documents/2011/INTASC%202011%20Standards%20At%20A%20Glance.pdf

Cummins, J. (1981). The role of primary language development in promoting educational success for language minority students. In California State Department of Education, *Schooling and language minority students: A theoretical framework* (pp. 3–49). Sacramento: Office of Bilingual Education, California State Department of Education.

Darling-Hammond, L. (1996). *What matters most: Teaching for America's future.* Washington, DC: National Commission on Teaching and America's Future.

Darling-Hammond, L., & Sclan, E. (1996). Who teachers are and why: Dilemmas for building a profession for twenty-first century schools. In J. Sikula (Ed.), *Handbook of research on teacher education* (2nd ed., pp. 67–100). New York: Macmillan.

Data from Center for Disease Control (CDC) and Prevent School-Associated Student Homicides-United States, 1992-2006. MMRW 2008; 57(02): 33-6, and www.CDC.gov/violenceprevention.

Dewey, J. (1956). *The child and the curriculum. The school and society.* Chicago: University of Chicago Press.

Doolittle, P. E. (2002). *How people learn: Practical strategies for teaching and learning.* Blacksburg, VA: Virginia Polytechnic Institute and State University Press.

Doyle, W. (1986). Classroom organization and management. In M. C. Wittrock (Ed.), *Handbook of research on teaching* (3rd ed.) (pp. 392-431). New York: Macmillan.

Eisner, E. (1994). *The Educational imagination: On the design and evaluation of school programs* (3rd ed.). New York: Macmillan.

Erikson, E. (1950). *Childhood and society.* New York: Norton.

Evertson, C. M. & Emmer, E. T. (2009). *Classroom management for elementary teachers* (8th ed.). Upper Saddle River, NJ: Pearson Education.

Freud, S. (1935). *New introductory lectures on psychoanalysis.* New York: Norton.

Gardner, H. (1983). *Frames of mind. The theory of multiple intelligences.* New York: Basic Books.

Gesell, A. (1925). *The mental growth of the pre-school child.* New York: Macmillan.

Glasser, W. (1975). *Reality therapy. A new approach to psychiatry.* New York: Harper & Row.

Gollnick, D. M., & Chinn, P. C. (2008). *Multicultural education in a pluralistic society* (8th ed.). Upper Saddle River, NJ: Pearson Education.

Good, T. L., & Brophy, J. E. (2000). *Looking in classrooms* (8th ed.). New York: Addison–Wesley Education.

Haselkorn, D. & Harris, L. (1998). *The essential profession: A national survey of public attitudes toward teaching, educational opportunity and school reform.* Belmont, MA: Recruiting New Teachers, Inc.

Heacox, D. (1991). *Up from under-achievement: How teachers, students, and parents can work together to promote student success.* Minneapolis, MN: Free Spirit Publishing.

Henley, M. (2006). *Classroom management: A proactive approach.* Upper Saddle River, NJ: Pearson Education.

Herrell, A. L., & Jordan, M. (2006). *35 Classroom management strategies: Promoting learning and building community.* Upper Saddle River, NJ: Pearson Education.

Howe, A. C. (2002). *Engaging children in science* (3rd ed.). Upper Saddle River, NJ: Pearson Education.

Ingersoll, R. (1997). *The status of teaching as a profession: 1990–91.* Washington, DC: U.S. Department of Education.

Ingersoll, R., & Smith, T. (2003). The wrong solution to teacher shortage. *Educational Leadership, 60*(8), 30–32.

Jones, V. F., & Jones, L. S. (2001). *Comprehensive classroom management: Creating communities of support and solving problems* (6th ed.). Boston, MA: Allyn & Bacon.

Kauchak, D., & Eggen, P. (2005). *Introduction to teaching: Becoming a professional* (2nd ed.). Upper Saddle River, NJ: Pearson Education.

Kohlberg, L. (1969). Stage and sequence: The cognitive development approach to socialization. In D. A. Goslin (Ed.), *Handbook of socialization theory and research.* Chicago: Rand McNally.

Kottler, J. A. (2002). *Students who drive you crazy: Succeeding with resistant, unmotivated, and otherwise difficult young people.* Thousand Oaks, CA: Sage & Corwin.

Kounin, J. S. (1970). *Discipline and group management in classrooms.* New York: Holt, Rinehart & Winston.

Labaree, D. (1992). Power, knowledge, and the rationalization of teaching: A genealogy of the movement to professionalize teaching. *Harvard Educational Review, 62,* 123–154.

Lawson, K. (2007). *Business buddies: Coaching and mentoring.* New York: Barron's.

Lessow-Hurley, J. (2000). *The foundations of dual language instruction* (3rd ed.). New York: Addison Wesley Longman.

Levin, J., & Nolan, J. F. (2000). *Principles of classroom management: A hierarchical approach* (3rd ed.). Boston: Allyn & Bacon.

Levin, J. & Nolan, J. F. (2007). *Principles of classroom management: A professional decision-making model* (5th ed). Boston: Pearson Education.

Manning, L. M., & Baruth, L. G. (2009). *Multicultural education of children and adolescents* (5th ed.). New York: Pearson Education.

Manning, L. M., & Bucher, K. T. (2007). *Classroom management: Models, applications, and cases* (2nd ed.). Columbus, OH: Merrill.

Maslow, A. (1954). *Motivation and personality.* New York: Harper and Row.

McNamara, B. E. (2007). *Learning disabilities: Bridging the gap between research and classroom practice.* Upper Saddle River, NJ: Pearson Education.

Mercer, C. D., & Pullen, P.C. (2005). *Students with learning disabilities* (6th ed.). Upper Saddle River, NJ: Merrill/Prentice Hall.

Moir, E. (2007). *Phases of first-year teaching.* Santa Cruz, CA: California New Teacher Project.

National Center for Education Statistics (2003–2004).*Schools and staffing survey.* Washington, DC: Author.

National Center for Education Statistics (2007). Status *and trends in the education of racial and ethnic minorities.* Retrieved from http://nces.ed.gov/pubs2007/minoritytrends/

National Center for Education Statistics (2010). *Teacher attrition and mobility: Results from the 2008-09 teacher follow-up survey.* Washington, DC: Author.

National Commission on Teaching and America's Future. (2003–2004). *Policy brief: The high cost of teacher turnover.* Washington, DC: Author.

National Education Association. (1975). *Code of ethics.* Retrieved from http://www.nea.org/home/30442.htm

National Education Association. (2010). *Status of the American public school teacher, 2005–2006.* Washington, DC: Author.

Nissman, B. S. (2006). *Teacher-tested classroom management strategies.* Upper Saddle River, NJ: Pearson Education.

Olson, L. (2000). Finding and keeping competent teachers. *Education Week, 19*(18), 12–17.

Ornstein, A. C., & Levine, D. U. (2006). *Foundation of education* (9th ed.). Boston: Houghton Mifflin.

Ovando, C. J., Combs, M. C., & Collier, V. P. (2006). *Bilingual and ESL classrooms: Teaching in multicultural contexts* (4th ed.). New York: McGraw-Hill.

Piaget, J. (1952). *The child's conception of number.* London: Routledge & Kegan Paul.

Poor students, green teachers. (2005, December 8). *Sacramento Bee.*

Posner, G. J. (1995). *Analyzing the curriculum.* New York: McGraw-Hill.

Redl, F., & Wineman, D. (1957). *The aggressive child.* New York: Free Press.

Rogers, C. (1967). Learning to be free. In C. Rogers & B. Stevens (Eds.), *The problem of being human.* Lafayette, CA: Real Property Press.

Ryan, K., & Cooper, J. M. (2001). *Those who can, teach* (9th ed.). New York: Houghton Mifflin.

Skinner, B. F. (1974). *About behaviorism.* New York: Knopf.

Snyder, T. D., & Dillow, S. A. (2010). *Digest of education statistics, 2009* (NCES publication 2010–2013). Washington, DC: U.S. Department of Education.

U.S. Census Bureau. (n.d.). *Census 2000 Demographic profile highlights.* Retrieved from http://factfinder.census.gov/servlet/SAFFFacts?_event=&geo_id=01000US&_geoContext=01000US&_street=&_county=&_cityTown=&_state=&_zip=&_lang=en&_sse=on&ActiveGeoDiv=&_useEV=&pctxt=fph&pgsl=010&_submenuId=factsheet_1&ds_name=ACS_2009_5YR_SAFF&_ci_nbr=null&qr_name=null&reg=null%3Anull&_keyword=&_industry=

U.S. Department of Education. (2003). **Guidance on constitutionally protected prayer in public elementary and secondary schools. Retrieved from http://www2.ed.gov/policy/gen/guid/ religionandschools/prayer_guidance.html**

Valance, E. (1995). The public curriculum of orderly images. *Educational Researcher, 24,* 4–13.

Vang, C. T. (2010). *An educational psychology of methods in multicultural education.* New York: Peter Lang Publishing.

Vosniadou, S. (2001). *How children learn* (Educational Practice Series 7). Brussels, Belgium: International Academy of Education.

Vygotsky, L. S. (1978). *Mind in society. The development of higher psychological processes.* Cambridge, MA: Harvard University Press.

Wadsworth, D. (2001). Why new teachers chose to teach. *Educational Leadership, 58*(8), 24–28.

Wayne, A., & Youngs, P. (2003). Teacher characteristics and student achievement gains: A review. *Review of Educational Research, 73*, 89–122. doi: 10.3102/00346543073001089

Weinstein, C. S. (2003). *Secondary classroom management: Lessons from research and practice* (2nd ed.). New York: McGraw-Hill.

Weinstein, C. S., Romano, M. E., & Mignano, A. J, Jr. (2011). *Elementary classroom management: Lessons from research and practice* (5th ed.). New York: McGraw-Hill.

Wood, C. (1999). *Time to time, time to learn: Changing the pace of school.* Greenfield, MA: Northeast Foundation for Children.

Zuker, E. (1983). *Mastering assertive skills: Power and positive influence at work.* New York: AMACON.

INDEX

A

Academic domain, 153, 154
Academic records, 136
Academic standards, 202
Accommodations, 203, 204
Adaptations, 203, 204
ADD, 6
ADHD, 6
Affective domain, 152, 153
API, 5
Approaches, 206
Arbitrary consequences, 81
Area of concern, 220, 221, 222, 223, 224, 225
Areas needing procedures, 181
Assessment, 210, 211, 212
Authoritarian leadership, 237
Authoritative leadership, 237

B

Balanced management and discipline, 236, 237
Basic procedures, 115, 116
BCLAD, 56
Best Professional Practices, 196, 197
Bilingual Education Programs, 56
Bloom's taxonomy, 263, 264
BTSA, 9
Bureaucratic authority, 237

C

CBEST, 9
CCTC, 9
CD, 6
Character education, 261
Charismatic authority, 237
Checklist, 178
Child abuse laws, 54
CLAD, 56
Classroom design, 73
Classroom management, 64
Classroom norms, 259
Classroom procedures, 75
Classroom rules, 75, 114
Classroom structure, 123, 124
Coaching, 17

Code of Ethics, 100
Cognitive domain, 152
Collaboration, 138
Common behaviors, 173, 174, 175
Confidence, 198
Constructivism, 196
Cooperating teacher's roles, 33, 34
Cooperative groups, 186, 187
Co-teaching models, 190, 191
Creativity, 158
Critical pedagogy, 206
CSET, 9
Cultural diversity, 145, 146
Cultural iceberg, 256
Curricular challenges, 162
Curriculum, 134

D

Daily schedule, 113, 114, 129
Disciplinary practices, 93
Discipline, 81, 82
Disruptions, 84, 85
Do's and Don'ts, 238
Documenting, 96
Domains of student learning, 112

E

E Pluribus Unum, 146
Educational psychological question, 162
ELD, 28
ELM, 9
Engagement level, 68, 210
EPT, 9
Equal opportunity, 150
Ethical standards, 26
Expectations, 97
Expulsion, 133
Extracurricular activities, 139

F

Fieldwork experience, 21
Formative assessment, 33, 34, 35
Foundations of education, 41

G

Gender, 159, 160
Goals of management, 191
Greetings, 127, 128
Guided practices, 246

H

Health and safety, 131
Highly qualified teachers, 242
Home visits, 141
Homework, 137, 138
Human needs, 172
Human relations, 107, 138

I

Incentives, 187
Instructional formats, 185
Instructional models, 245, 246
Instructional practices, 204
Instructional process 125, 244
Instructional strategies, 116, 206
Interns, 16
Interruptions, 84, 85
Interventions, 87, 189, 203, 204
Interview process, 49
Interview questions, 49
Inventory checklist, 215

L

Language minority, 160, 161
Learning disabilities, 158, 159
Learning styles, 154, 155
LEP process, 161, 162
Lesson plan design, 27
Liability, 52
Logical consequences, 81, 115
Low achievers, 150, 151

M

Management strategies, 176
Managing stress, 251
Managing student work, 137
Mentoring, 17
Methodology, 206
Misbehavior, 82, 83
Misperceptions, 149
Modeling techniques, 209
Modern models, 205, 206

Modifications, 203, 204
Monitoring medications, 131
Monitoring strategies, 182
Multicultural educator, 166
Multicultural pedagogy, 206
Multiple intelligence, 110,111, 155, 156

N

Natural consequences, 81

O

Optimistic leadership, 237
Orientation, 128, 129

P

Passion, 5
Pedagogical question, 162
Pedagogical skills, 206
Pedagogy, 206
Permissive authority, 237
Personal management plan, 219
Phases of first-year teaching, 248
Philosophical question, 162
Philosophies, 43, 44, 45
Philosophy of education, 169, 170
Philosophy of management, 170, 171
Physical environment, 105
Pitfalls, 95, 96
Placement, 23
Practica, 23
Prevention, 86
Principles, 44, 45
Proactive approaches, 76, 259
Probationary period, 249
Procedures for room use, 180
Professional authority, 237
Professional educator, 254
Professional goals, 253
Providing assistance, 130
Psychomotor domain, 153
Psychosocial environment, 104
Punishment, 217, 218

R

Rapport, 77
Reflection, 116
Reflective educator, 214
Reinforcement, 93
Religion, 139, 140

Reward systems, 187
RICA, 9
Right-and left-brain learners 157, 158

S

Salad Bowl, 146
SB2042, 9
School administrators, 237, 238
School curriculum, 201, 202
School violence, 142, 143
SDAIE, 28
Seating arrangements, 106
SED, 6
Self-management, 95
Social context, 105, 153
Sound discipline, 260
Stages of personality development, 171, 172
Standard-based-education, 202
Strategy, 206
Student responsibilities, 110
Students' privacy rights, 53
Substitution, 136
Summative assessment, 33, 34, 35
Supervisor's roles, 34, 35
Survival tips, 30
Suspension, 133

T

Task strategies, 208, 209
Teacher authority, 237
Teacher tenure, 51, 52
Teacher turnover, 7
Teaching contract, 49
Teaching methodologies, 206
Teaching strategies, 207, 208
Teaching styles, 67, 109
Theories, 43, 44, 45
Time management, 130
TPA, 9, 204, 205
TPE, 9, 204
Traditional authority, 237
Traditional models, 205, 206
Trends, 12
Types of assessment, 213

V

Violence, 52, 53

W

WIC 300, 54, 55

Critical Pedagogical Perspectives

Greg S. Goodman, *General Editor*

Educational Psychology: Critical Pedagogical Perspectives is a series of relevant and dynamic works by scholars and practitioners of critical pedagogy, critical constructivism, and educational psychology. Reflecting a multitude of social, political, and intellectual developments prompted by the mentor Paulo Freire, books in the series enliven the educator's process with theory and practice that promote personal agency, social justice, and academic achievement. Often countering the dominant discourse with provocative and yet practical alternatives, *Educational Psychology: Critical Pedagogical Perspectives* speaks to educators on the forefront of social change and those who champion social justice.

For further information about the series and submitting manuscripts, please contact:

> Dr. Greg S. Goodman
> Department of Education
> Clarion University
> Clarion, Pennsylvania
> *ggoodman@clarion.edu*

To order other books in this series, please contact our Customer Service Department at:

> (800) 770-LANG (within the U.S.)
> (212) 647-7706 (outside the U.S.)
> (212) 647-7707 FAX

Or browse online by series at:

> www.peterlang.com